"Thus Fell Tecumseh"

"THUS FELL TECUMSEH"

Frank E. Kuron

Edited by Judith Justus

KURON PUBLISHING

*Cover Photo – "Death of Tecumseh"(1813). A portion of the frieze of
American History circling the Rotunda of the United States Capitol.
Filippo Costaggini - Artist. Photo courtesy "Architect of the Capitol."*

For Debra
My friend, inspiration and wife

CONTENTS

ILLUSTRATIONS · PHOTOS · MAPS

Preface

I love history. To me, it is like finding buried treasure. As a child I used to dig in my backyard and pull out stones which were, well, just stones; but in my imagination they were certainly ancient Indian artifacts. Now that I'm older, whenever I dig up the origin of an event, or a cultural practice, or even a cliché phrase, like say, *a flash in the pan*, well; it's like finding an artifact. (When a flintlock musket is fired, a flint stone is triggered to strike a steel lid which is situated just over a little *pan* full of gunpowder. This action produces sparks which ignite the gunpowder, which in turn produces a quick little *poof* of an explosion. This brief yet important *flash in the pan* then ignites the larger load of powder in the musket barrel, which forces the ball out of the gun.) I knew you were curious, so I simply told you! In most books you would have had to have gone to a footnote or endnote or appendix to learn this little nugget of knowledge. But look, you already know it and you are still reading along. If that feels comfortable, you may just enjoy this book.

When I read histories or biographies, I love to study the actual words of the person doing the telling. In most books, however, the reader only gets a brief excerpt, or an author's paraphrase of the quote. There are many valid reasons to constrain the use of citations, and often this is made up for by providing a fuller quote or explanation in a footnote. I may be alone, but I still feel a little cheated by this practice and find it more disruptive to the read when I have to turn somewhere else for an additional explanation. Furthermore, upon completion of a book, I often discover that I have learned more from the footnotes than from the story itself. And I yearn for even fuller notes. A complete quote, in context, often can shed light on the little details of the person's life, era, circumstances, and provide a glimpse of their personality. For me, that is the treasure unwrapped from the past.

My whole life has been spent in Toledo, Ohio, a location in the heart of what was called the Northwest Territory in 1813. As I walk through areas like *Side Cut Metropark* in Maumee, Ohio, which lies along the banks of the Maumee River just across from the reconstructed Fort Meigs; I can't help but imagine what life was like just two hundred years ago on the very same ground. Even the great Shawnee Indian chief, Tecumseh, traversed this area frequently during his life. Over the years, as my imagination has prompted me to read more and more about the War of 1812, I have discovered that Tecumseh was instrumental in many of the events before and during this conflict. When I read of his death, it was full of contradictory claims of how, and by whose hand, he fell. My curiosity was instantly piqued, and I just had to learn more about this controversy. It turns out that the mystery over who killed Tecumseh has been debated regularly since it occurred in 1813 and continued to be a hot topic all throughout the 1800s. It is still the subject of hearty discussion today.

In the course of my research into Tecumseh's death, I have found well over a hundred testimonies regarding this event. A handful of them might be in agreement on a few particular details, but overall; there are very few stories that line up exactly on all points with any other. This is why it was, is, and always will be such a mystery. Nepotism, politics, and pride all played their part in the testimonies recorded. It has become apparent that this is not only an intriguing study of the event itself, but of human behavior as well.

I am an American and proud to be one. However, the intent of this book is to present an un-biased compilation of facts. In spite of the huge number of sources cited, the vast majority are from the Americans, some from the British, and only a very few from the Canadians or Indians. This is simply the nature of the records available. Also, the term *Indian* is used in almost all accounts cited from this period. Therefore, for consistency, I have continued to use this term throughout this book. There is no willful intent to offend anyone who believes the term *Native American* should have been used.

An additional fact surrounding this event has drawn my attention and I am compelled to make note of it to you. The men who ended up at the Thames River on the day Tecumseh was killed, be they American, British, Indian or Canadian, endured tremendous hardships as a result of their willingness to participate in the struggles of securing the Northwest Territory. It may sound trite in the reading, but on top of the obvious possibility of death, these men endured all types of severe weather conditions with inadequate clothing, little or no shelter, spoiled and depleted food supplies, neglected weaponry, rampant diseases, extreme fatigue and inadequate medical care – all in defense of their families, beliefs and respective nations. It has humbled me when I consider how petty my daily complaints of discomfiture are by comparison.

The vast majority of the accounts which are reported in this narrative come from primary sources – that is, from the person who wrote it or said it. Only in a few instances, where the primary source has been lost to history, or was inaccessible to the author, is a secondary source used. Typically these secondary sources are early historian's accounts, given to them by informants who were either unidentified or unknown. Sometimes an original-source document, such as a letter written to an early historian, has been forever lost but its content has been recorded in the historian's book. Every effort has been made to track down all known existing primary accounts pertaining to how Tecumseh was killed. It is possible that a few testimonies have inadvertently been overlooked, or that new ones will come to light in the future.

Many accounts presented have been transcribed by the author from hand-written letters which have been preserved in various universities, libraries and historical societies. Some of the originals have faded with time and/or have been photographed to microfilm in a less than readable condition. If words were in-discernable in the original, an ellipsis (. . .) has been added to the text. Such a use of the ellipsis has additionally been made when a segment of the original quote was omitted at the author's discretion. All accounts are given exactly as they were written with only minor punctuation or reference points added, and then so in brackets, [ ], in order to maintain the flow of thought. Parenthesis, ( ), and underlines, (_) are maintained if they were used in the original document by the original author. Any misspellings, odd capitalizations, abbreviations of words, or terms which have since lost their meaning or been deemed inappropriate by current cultural standards, have been recorded here *as they appeared in the originals.* You will notice for example, that many of the people in the 19th century were never formally introduced to a period, and thus give a whole new meaning to what now is commonly referred to as a run-on sentence.

Large passages of the very letters and articles read by early historians in order to write their narratives are now at your disposal. Appreciate the often quirky writing styles. Strive to discern the character of the writer as it distills through his words. It is time for you, the reader, to become the analyst. You will not find me telling you what to think. This book was not written to preach to you what I presume you should believe about this event. I am presenting the facts. You now have the opportunity to weigh all the evidence and solve the mystery yourself.

It is my sincere hope that, along the way, the you will get a glimpse of the realities of life on the frontier during the War of 1812 era, and that this picture will be authentically painted by the words of the people themselves who kept diaries or wrote to friends, historians or newspapers of the day. By means of these genuine testimonies, you can take up the challenge of answering one of the oldest American questions–*Who killed Tecumseh?*

Acknowledgements

"Any story sounds true until someone sets the record straight." Thus reads the simple wisdom of Solomon as written in his *Proverbs* of the *Holy Bible*. Well, whether this book is successful in clarifying, or merely muddying, the tale of Tecumseh's death is left up to the reader to decide. It has been my privilege, however, to have participated in a six-year adventure of gathering the facts of this event, and I have had a lot of help along the way.

I don't believe in coincidence. Six years ago the idea of writing this book popped into my head. Then, one-by-one, influential people appeared in my life to guide me on this journey. Then, significant information repeatedly dropped into my lap from very unexpected sources. Finally, the proper words themselves formed in my mind and I transferred them to paper. All this was not accidental; it was a gift and a challenge. And so, I sincerely thank God, Jesus Christ, who chose me to take up this effort using His gifts.

It is impossible to fully express the gratitude I feel toward my wife, Debra. She has been my mainstay–that's a nautical term for that strong rope which secures the primary mast of a sailing ship. Well, she has certainly been that–the one to secure the sails of my ship as it has drifted through the seas of unexpected challenges and emotions inherent to writing a book. Two of the research trips we embarked on together were actually referred to, by her, as vacations! What further evidence of her support is needed? And no, the microfilm files and old books we poured over while on these *vacations* were nowhere near a tropical paradise. Her unwavering patience, honest opinions and hands-on assistance are the true reasons this project has come to its fruition.

My children, Sara and Matthew, both wise beyond their years, are rightfully next in line to be recognized. To my chagrin, the *history is cool* gene did not pass into their DNA structure; yet they eagerly reviewed segments of this work. As a result, their often keen observations have made it a much-improved read. Additionally, their constant encouragement, as well as that of my son-in-law, Doug Wegrzyn, has been a much appreciated blessing.

When the idea of this book was still in its infancy, my dear friend, Judy Justus, told me that it needed to be written. She convinced this simple history enthusiast that he was capable of being the one to successfully revive interest in this old mystery. Herself an accomplished historian, speaker and author, she graciously offered to become my editor. It is because of her wealth of historical knowledge surrounding events and personalities of the 1812 era, that I am confident this work is as accurate as possible in its detail. Her enthusiasm for life and history are contagious, and I thank her for sharing it.

Over thirty years ago, the first of innumerable conversations about the wild idea of actually *writing a book* occurred between my best friend, John Curtin, and myself. For years, both of us sensed an internal drive *to write*. Now, with much time having run its course, his talents in this arena have been proven. And his relentless prodding of me to pursue my goal has finally borne fruit in the form of this book. I am forever indebted to him for his example and faith in me.

A further thank you goes to each family member and friend, who ever encouraged me, sometimes just by asking, "How is the book coming along?" They are too numerous to mention by name; except for my dear sister, Rita Skelding, who provided a special critique for me through a teacher's eyes.

Many historians have been contacted for insights and information related to the material in this book. I am forever in their debt. Especially helpful were: Jack Bailey and Joseph McClure, Park Managers of the William Whitley State Historic Site, Stanford, KY; Nicky Hughes, noted historian and current Curator of Historic Sites for the City of Frankfort, KY; Tom Fugate, former Curator of the Kentucky Historical Society, Frankfort, KY; Bill Bright, Curator of the Kentucky Military Museum, Frankfort, KY; Russ Hatter, Asst. Curator of the Capital Museum, Frankfort, KY; James Holmberg, Curator of Special Collections at the Filson Historical Society, Louisville, KY; Tim Crumrin, Senior Historian of Conner Prairie, Fishers, IN; Andrew Green, Director of the Georgetown Museum, Georgetown, KY; and Paul Ambrose, owner of Ambrose Antiques, Trumbull, CT.

For sharing her historical information so freely, a special *thank you* goes to Michelle Metty whose 4th-great grandfather was Moses Hodges;

a private in Captain James Davidson's company which made the first charge against the Indian front lines at the Battle of the Thames.

Further appreciation is directed toward the many anonymous employees of the following institutions who graciously gave of their time and knowledge to assist me in my research efforts. These include: The Kentucky Historical Society, The University of Kentucky, The Filson Historical Society, The Louisville Free Public Library, The William Whitley State Historic Site, The Frankfort Cemetery, The Toledo-Lucas County Public Library, The University of Toledo-Carlson Library, The Bowling Green State University-Jerome Library, The Library of Congress, The Smithsonian Institution, The Ohio Historical Society, Fort Meigs, The Minnesota Historical Society, The Rutherford B. Hayes Presidential Center, The Tennessee State Library and Archives, The Chicago History Museum and Parks Canada-Fort Malden.

Finally, though dramatically different in their approach to writing about history, two contemporary authors have had a profound influence upon me and I am compelled to acknowledge them. The first is Allan Eckert, who taught me that history doesn't have to be dull. And the second is John Sugden, who taught me to seek the truth of our past.

CHAPTER 1

The Death of Tecumseh

*Towards the close of the engagement, he [Tecumseh]
had been personally opposed to Colonel Johnson commanding
the American mounted riflemen; and having severely
wounded that officer with a ball from his rifle;
was in the act of springing upon him with
his tomahawk, when his adversary [Johnson]
drew a pistol from his belt and
shot him dead on the spot.*[1]

How does one aptly describe October in the wilderness of Ontario, Canada? Trees and underbrush are ablaze with transcendental color. Tiny woodland creatures scurry here and there foraging for their winter banquet. Leaves, whose grip has tired, waft to the damp woodland floor while cool breezes rustle-about the remainder. Imagine a slow amble along a well-worn path through this wonderland. As you proceed deeper into the forest your eyes keep returning to the amber, crimson, and coffee colors dangling above. The sunlight paints streaks of yellow here and there. Even the lush underbrush is interlaced with sprawling hues of violet and burgundy. The crisp fresh air seems to permeate your very soul. You feel a brief chill now and then even though you're comfortably snuggled in your hooded sweatshirt. The dry leaves crackle under your comfortable and fashionable walking shoes. Look there! Some gloriously delicious-looking red berries tempt your rumbling stomach. Are they edible? You dare not experiment, besides; you'll soon be enjoying a real meal at a local restaurant. The low rushing sound of the nearby river further soothes your senses. As you meander along you can't help but think how lucky you are to be here, even for just a short walkthrough. It's all just so pleasant.

Two hundred years previous, thousands of men found themselves in this same breath-taking Canadian wilderness. At that time it was even more dense and expansive since the clearing for farmland and homes had not yet occurred. Specifically, these men of history were in the woodlands located on the outskirts of present-day Chatham, Ontario.

The magnificent autumn view was the same; but only as casual relief did any one of them take a moment's note of it. The same rambling river wound itself through the trees and brush. The Indians called it the Eskaynaysepe. In 1793 it was given the name *Thames* by then Lt. Governor John G. Simcoe, as it reminded him of the famous river of that name in his English homeland. It would give its name to history for the battle fought along its banks. The five to six thousand men who found themselves here in 1813 were on opposite sides of an issue and little concerned with the autumn splendor. They were about to take up their arms and risk their lives for their families, their nations . . . their principles.

By definition, every conflict must have antagonists. This day, October 5, 1813, it was the Americans versus the British/Indian/Canadian alliance. Over a year of fighting had already ensued between the two sides, through a war which was to be forever remembered by the year of its origin–1812. Many more battles would be fought after this one, until a resolution would finally be reached in 1815. Today, however, after a lengthy pursuit, the Americans found their prey had finally ceased their retreat and positioned themselves for a fight. It was along the steep winding banks of the Thames River. The land was both wooded and swampy. The air was cool and damp. The forces–they were all tired and hungry. Many were already sick, some dying, from the strain of long forced marches, malnutrition, fatigue, and rampant disease. Those who were still capable of it, fought.

This *Battle of the Thames*, as it would be known hereafter in America (and as the *Battle of Moraviantown* in Britain and Canada), marked a turning point in the war. From its start in June of 1812, and into the spring of 1813, few land victories had gone to the Americans. But in the six months previous to this 5th of October, 1813, a series of successes had finally been realized, culminating with a major triumph here at the Thames River. It came on the heels of their surprising and momentous naval victory on the great lake, just a few miles south of their present location. On September 10, 1813, Commodore Oliver Hazard Perry and the United States Navy defeated Lieutenant Robert H. Barclay and his British fleet on Lake Erie. The success would open the lake to the free transport of American supplies from the east. Conversely, the existing British supply route was now closed. This would bode badly for the British forces presently poised for battle against the Americans at the Thames. Fresh from his naval triumph, Commodore Perry docked his ships in Sandusky Bay (in Ohio on the southern coast of Lake Erie) where they were immediately put back into service, now loaded predominantly with American supplies instead of sailors. They would soon set sail alongside the American troops up the Thames River.

During the week since Perry's victory, the troops on both sides had been doing forced marches of twenty to thirty miles a day. In the American camp were soldiers of the U.S. military and less-trained volunteers of the U.S. militia all under the command of Major-General William Henry Harrison. On the run was the esteemed 41st regiment of the British Army under the authority of Major-General Henry Procter, as well as the frontiersmen of the Canadian militia and the warriors from numerous tribes under the command of Tecumseh. All were in motion at a fast and precarious pace.

As September turned into October, with its days growing shorter and its winds blowing colder, many of the American soldiers were still in their summer uniforms. Very few had been issued winter coats. The militia had brought their hunting shirts with jackets to keep them reasonably comfortable. But after treading through multiple creeks and rivers, and enduring repeated cold rains, the wetness remained and the men were often chilled to the bone. The fledgling U.S. government had limited funds and resources. Supplies, clothing and food were always promised, but the reality was that days turned into weeks and weeks turned into months of expectations unmet during this war.

It wasn't just the Americans who were suffering from insufficient supplies. Major-General Henry Procter, commander of the British force, had been promised by his government that reinforcements of food, clothing, and even more importantly–men, were forthcoming. They didn't arrive. Additionally, because the Indian tribes were allied with the British, it was incumbent on the government of England to provide for their partners. And it wasn't just provisions for the warriors that were required; it was for their wives and children as well who were following alongside a few miles distant, away from any potential dangerous encounters.

Considering the amount of men involved in this event, the number of deaths incurred during the fight was low in both camps. Many more died of disease and exhaustion before the battle even began. On the American side, one of the more notable deaths was that of an old, colorful frontiersman and celebrated Indian fighter named William Whitley. A peer of Daniel Boone, William was of the same ilk–daring, brave and intensely patriotic. History, however, never gave him the comparable attention of which he was certainly most deserving.

The British death numbers were also light, most of their soldiers having been taken prisoners instead of being killed. Although shame was here-to-fore foreign to a soldier of the proud 41st British regiment, it fell heavy upon them when their commander, Henry Procter, had galloped off deserting his troops within the first few minutes of this fight. Later, Procter would face a British court martial and be ostracized for his behavior. Though desertion in any form is intolerable, history tends to turn its head away from some of the very real obstacles faced by Procter prompting his behavior. Never-the-less the immediate abandonment of his men at the Thames was, well, remarkable, to say the least.

Perhaps the most significant consequence of this battle was the emotional one felt by the Indian people. Whether allied into his confederation of tribes or not, almost all Indians had revered Tecumseh for his leadership, integrity and fairness. Today Tecumseh was killed in the action. With his death died the dream of a united Indian nation. Never again has there been a substantial attempt to bring together the many individual Indian tribes into one confederacy.

If you research the accounts of the death of Tecumseh at the Battle of the Thames in typical history books, you will most often read that it happened pretty much the way Major John Richardson, a young Canadian who was in the battle, has related it in the introductory quote– Running with tomahawk raised and within only a few feet of a seriously wounded Colonel Richard M. Johnson, Tecumseh was suddenly shot by Johnson who had managed to grasp his pistol and fire at the decisive moment.

Following is a more detailed, though still simplified, overview of how the troops arrived at the scene, the conditions they encountered, the positions they took up and the battle as they fought it.

After days of following the Thames River northeast through Canada, the British and Indians finally ceased their retreat and turned to face the Americans who had been trailing them. The flight was triggered by

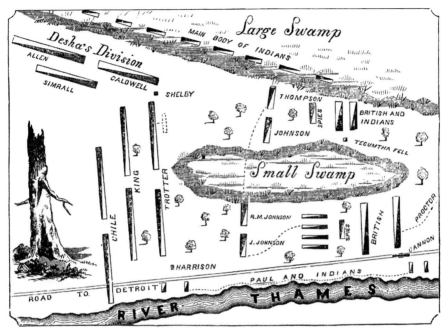

*Map of the Battle of the Thames. Illustrated by Benson J. Lossing
and shown here as it appeared in his Pictorial Fieldbook of the War of 1812
which was originally published in 1868.*

the American forces crossing Lake Erie toward Amherstburg, Ontario, where a British naval yard and fortress lay on the northwest shores of the lake. Rather than remain and fight at this stronghold, as Tecumseh had desired, Procter decided to abandon the location, torch the fort and attempt to out run the Americans. He may have been stalling in hope of receiving promised re-enforcements, or he may have been hoping to reach Burlington, another British post on the opposite end of Lake Erie. Whatever his strategy, after several days of running the Americans caught up to them and the two forces had their showdown.

The geography of the battleground was diverse. The flowing Thames River provided a natural barrier on one side. Inward from it was a narrow dirt trail known as the *Detroit Road*. From there the land was covered by tall woods; some areas sparse others thick. Further left, a few hundred yards from the river, was a small swamp, then a break of dry ground followed by a larger swamp which stretched before a dense forest.

From the Americans' point of view, the river was on their far right. Their forces lined up to counter each of the enemies formations extending from the river to their left. Colonel Paull with a small group of Delaware Indians who were fighting in support of the Americans, took their position between the river and the road in order to attack a British company who had set up before them with only one lone cannon. Colonel James Johnson, Richard's brother, set up on the other side of the road and would lead his mounted militiamen against the majority of the British troops who had positioned themselves in columns in a thinly wooded area left of the road. Still further to the left of Colonel James Johnson, Colonel Richard M. Johnson led his mounted regiment against the Indian contingent which was secreted amidst the underbrush and mud of a large swampy area.

Col. Richard Johnson had asked for twenty volunteers to ride beside him as he led the initial charge against the Indian forces. These brave men knew they were setting themselves up for certain death. The term *Forlorn Hope* was their moniker—an expression used in military circles for years and one as ominous as it sounds. This group is typically sent ahead in order to draw the first fire of the enemy, thus allowing the second wave of attackers to swoop in while the foe is occupied re-loading their weapons. Usually, an officer of lower rank would volunteer for such a treacherous duty, in the hope of surviving and gaining a promotion for his bravery. At the Thames, however, Richard M. Johnson, already a high ranking officer, was the volunteer to lead this small band of brave men. Further to his credit, he had left his comfortable leather seat in the U.S. House of Representatives to put himself into, arguably, the most dangerous position on the field of battle.

At the sound of an American bugle, the battle commenced. Col. James Johnson and Col. Paull led the charge against the British regulars on the right. Simultaneously, Col. Richard Johnson, with his twenty volunteers at the head, led his full regiment in the attack against the Indians on the left. In a hail of gunfire, the *Forlorn Hope* almost immediately lost fifteen of their twenty members to death or wounds. Col. Johnson suffered four severe wounds; his horse likewise was riddled with bullets. Tecumseh saw the American colonel astride his horse and in much agony. He was an easy target, being the lone American in the area still on horseback. Johnson had ordered the others to dismount due to the difficulty of maneuvering the horses through the brushwood and mud of the swamp. Tecumseh took aim and fired his rifle. His shot passed through the knuckles of the colonel's left hand, shredding them as it flew. Growing faint from his wounds, and his horse likewise severely distressed, both rider and mare fell to the ground near a large uprooted tree. Trapped under his steed and critically wounded, Johnson was now easy prey for Tecumseh. Like a panther yearning for the kill, he bounded forward with tomahawk raised. He was within but a few yards, perhaps one more stride of striking the fatal blow, when the unexpected happened. Somehow, the disabled colonel gathered his wits and his strength and found his sidearm pistol. In a swift and pointed move he raised it in his right arm and fired. Tecumseh fell dead next to him, still clutching his tomahawk. Johnson, near death, was promptly removed from the field of battle. Tecumseh's body remained. After the battle, vengeful men of the Kentucky militia, recalling the horrific treatment their fellows received just a few months earlier at the hands of the Indians at the battle of Raisin River, took out their frustrations on the body. They skinned it in strips approximately an inch wide and six inches long, which when later stretched and dried could be used as a razor strop, or just kept as a memento of their famous nemesis.

And so the story goes. What a compelling scenario! Could Hollywood write a more intriguing script? Since the time of the battle, several paintings have been done portraying the event. All depict, in some fashion, an apparent high-ranking American officer squaring off with an Indian who has a tomahawk in hand. In all cases the implication is that it is Colonel Richard M. Johnson killing Tecumseh.

In 1833, William Emmons registered a print created by John Dorival titled *The Battle of the Thames* in which the focus of attention is on a mounted American officer shooting at an Indian with a tomahawk in hand. Another print, also registered by Emmons and probably created by him in 1833, again depicts Johnson on horseback shooting Tecumseh. There are two prints done in the 1840s by Nathaniel Currier, of Currier & Ives fame, both titled *Death of Tecumseh* which still show Johnson on his steed shooting and killing Tecumseh. Numerous other paintings and engravings all portray the same story. Even the frieze circling the rotunda in the U.S. Capitol building, which depicts only the

Battle of the Thames and the Death of Tecumseh by the Kentucky mounted Volunteers led by Colonel Richard M. Johnson. 1833. Registered and likely created by William Emmons. Includes a key to participants in the battle below the print.

Photo courtesy of U.S. Library of Congress.

most notable moments in our history, adds this event as just described (see book cover image).

So what is there to question? Why would anyone doubt that Colonel Richard Mentor Johnson was the American who fired the shot that slew Tecumseh? Why else would all the paintings of the era more-or-less depict the same scene: Johnson either astride or under his horse, discharging his pistol at the approaching Tecumseh; who was but a step or two away with his tomahawk in hand when he was fatally shot? Everyone seems to agree. After all, beyond all this circumstantial evidence, at least thirty-five individuals have testified over the years that, indeed, it was Col. Johnson who killed Tecumseh in just the manner portrayed in these historical paintings. You can't make this stuff up! Or can you?

The problem with this rendition of the events of October 5, 1813 is that there are a significant number of contrary opinions. Yes, if only those people would have kept quiet and gone along with the established story,

Battle of the Thames, Respectfully dedicated to Andrew Jackson, Esq. President of the United States. 1833. John Dorival-Lithographer. This print, registered by William Emmons is very similar to his own print of the same year, (at left) including the use of a key to the participants below the print.

well . . . there would never have been any controversy. But no–little publicized, sometimes acknowledged, and only rarely endorsed; these other testimonies do indeed raise suspicion on the claim that Johnson had killed Tecumseh. There are at least twenty testimonies saying that William Whitley, that old hero of the frontier, had killed Tecumseh. Another fourteen people have said that a young private named David King was the one who did it, or at least might have. And twelve individuals claim credit for themselves as having dealt the fatal blow. As Tecumseh's life slowly ebbed away, the wave of incredulous stories over who took it, rolled in!

So who is telling the truth? It won't be easy to determine, but that is exactly the question we are going to try and resolve. First, let's find out a little about the life of this individual who was so renowned that the manner of his death would cause so many people to comment upon it–Tecumseh.

CHAPTER 2

The Life of Tecumseh

So live your life that the fear of death can never enter your heart.
Trouble no one about their religion; respect others in their view,
and demand that they respect yours.
Love your life, perfect your life, beautify all things in your life.
Seek to make your life long and its purpose in the
service of your people.
Prepare a noble death song for the day when you go over
the great divide. Always give a word or a sign of salute when meeting
or passing a friend, even a stranger, when in a lonely place.
Show respect to all people and grovel to none.
When you arise in the morning give thanks for the food
and for the joy of living. If you see no reason for giving thanks,
the fault lies only in yourself.
Abuse no one and no thing, for abuse turns the wise ones
to fools and robs the spirit of its vision.
When it comes your time to die, be not like those whose hearts
are filled with the fear of death, so that when
their time comes they weep and pray for a little more time
to live their lives over again in a different way.
Sing your death song and
die like a hero going home.[1]

How is one man to make an evaluation of another man's life? Is it by what he has said; by what he has done? Is it by what his friends and family have shared about him? Is it by his enemies—would anything they have to say matter? Most would agree it's all of the above, albeit with an ever wary eye out for hints of bias or embellishment of the truth. So when it comes to a personality as renowned as Tecumseh, wouldn't you like to come to your own conclusion by hearing from people who knew him? Wouldn't you prefer to examine his words, yourself? Wouldn't you factor into your evaluation of the man, the eye-witness stories that have been recorded during his lifetime, or very shortly thereafter, rather than the interpretations of those stories made by historians over the next two centuries?

Tecumseh's personality and accomplishments are attested to in numerous documents. To select only a few is extremely difficult and dangerous without showing prejudice to what one wants the reader to believe. But if we view testimonies from the people who were his contemporaries, not those of later generations who may have wanted to deify or diminish him, we should emerge with a clear picture of the man. Following a brief overview of his lineage, you will have the opportunity to read what some of his friends, enemies, acquaintances, and he himself, had to say.

In what is today southwestern Ohio, on a clear spring evening in 1768, the sky suddenly lit up over a small Shawnee village. The illumination marked the birth of a third son to Chief Pukeshinwa and his wife Methoataske. The story goes that a meteor, or maybe a comet, streaked across the night sky over the place of the birth, on the night of the birth, near the moment of the birth of this newest Shawnee Indian. Whatever the scientific definition of the lights, it was significant enough to draw the attention of many in the vicinity.

According to Shawnee custom, a formal naming ceremony is to be held a short time after the birth of a child. The heavenly light that had shown itself at this birth had made such an impression that it was incorporated into the newborn's name. In English, there are endless translations of it: *Panther Shooting Across the Sky, Panther Across the Sky, Panther in the Sky, Panther Passing Across, Panther Passing, Panther Leaping at Prey, Crouching Panther, Tiger Crouching for its Prey, Shooting Star, Blazing Comet, I Cross the Way...* you get the idea. The Indian spellings are just as numerous: *Tekoomse, Tecompse, Teekumthie, Tecumtha, Tekamthi, Tecumthe, Tecumtheth, and Tecumseh,* to mention just a few. The spelling, *Tecumseh,* is the generally accepted version used in most of American history. At the time of his birth, Shawnee tribes were divided into clans. The clan Tecumseh was born into was named the Panther, hence the attribution in his name. The comet and sky reference, obviously, marked the celestial event at his birth. The name proved to be prophetic, as the boy sprang into life with boundless energy, and his story is still blazing across the pages of history generations after his death.

Unfortunately, when it comes to verifying births, deaths, marriages and children among the Shawnee, especially from a time so distant, there is considerable room for error. Much of what we know, or think we know, is from oral tradition passed down over many years. We

Portrait of Tecumseh. Illustrated by Benson J. Lossing and shown here as it appeared
in his Pictorial Fieldbook of the War of 1812 which was originally published in 1868.
This is the image most frequently cited to be the most accurate depiction of Tecumseh.
However, it was created some fifty years after his death and admitted by Lossing to
be somewhat speculative - based on two purported sketches he had viewed.

would love to think that this is reliable information, but often it cannot
be documented in writing and therefore by its nature alone becomes
suspicious; in the least it is not provable. The few Indian records we
have, including those of the Shawnee, were finally written down well
after the events occurred. There are letters from which we can deduce
some names, places and dates. Interviews were sometimes given to
historians of the day, such as Lyman Draper, or the editors of newspapers. But generally, if no one asked, no one necessarily recorded the
information. It was only after the *Trail of Tears* in 1831, the removal of
Indians from the east to the west of the Mississippi River, that written
documentation began in more earnest. Even so, the tangible records in
existence are often incomplete, imprecise, contradictory and tainted by
personal motives. With this in mind, one can see how in the case of
someone as celebrated as Tecumseh, rumors of illicit affairs, additional
marriages and legitimate or illegitimate children took root. With so
many discrepancies in the stories, it is no wonder historians have come
to varied conclusions.

The immediate family of Tecumseh, which can be agreed to by most historians, consisted of five brothers and one sister. The older brothers were named Cheeseekau and Sauawaseekou. Nehaaseemoo was born after Tecumseh, and he was followed by the birth of triplets. One of the three boys, whose name is unknown, died shortly after his birth. The other two were named Kumskaukua and Laulewasika. His older sister was named Tecumapease. (As with Tecumseh's, the spellings of most of these Indian names varies from source to source.) In order to frame Tecumseh's experience, a brief overview of the most influential family members is required. Tecumseh's notoriety certainly overshadowed all of his siblings, but some of them played a key role in his life and drew some historical attention of their own.

Tecumseh's father, Pukeshinwa, was the War Chief of his tribe but was killed along the banks of the Ohio River in the Battle of Point Pleasant on October 10, 1774, where the noted Shawnee Chief Cornstalk tried but failed to rebuff the Virginia militia from advancing into Ohio lands. Tecumseh was only six years old at the time. Cheeseekau, his eldest brother, stepped in and became probably the most influential person in his life. In the memoirs of John Johnston, an Indian agent who was in regular contact with the Shawnee, is written,

> Although he [Tecumseh] was unquestionably a true patriot, and brave man, it is nevertheless a fact that in the first fight, he was engaged in with the Kentuckians, on the Mad river, he ran away, leaving his brother, wounded, to take care of himself; but he was never to flinch afterwards.[2]

Rather than take Tecumseh's desertion as an affront, Cheeseekau took him under his wing, and with his direction Tecumseh learned how to become a warrior. Throughout his teens and twenties, Tecumseh fought and trained side-by-side with Cheeseekau. His brother introduced him to other tribes and their traditions; that was until one day when he had a premonition of his own death. Sadly, the portent played out. In a battle near present-day Nashville, Tennessee, at a site known as Buchannan's Station, Cheeseekau was killed trying to prevent white men from further encroaching into Indian lands. From that pivotal point on, Tecumseh took what his best friend and brother had taught him and grew to become arguably the most dynamic and influential leader the Indians of North America have ever known.

It is presumed that Sauawaseekau, who was just a couple years older than Tecumseh, died at the Battle of Fallen Timbers in present-day Maumee, Ohio. Of Nehaaseemoo, the first younger brother, little is known. Kumskaukua, one of the triplets, survived the Thames battle and passed away in the early 1820's. The youngest brother, originally named Laloeshiga, but soon morphed into Lalawethika, would gain notoriety alongside Tecumseh, though not of a nature as flattering or influential.[3]

Lalawethika was very different from his increasingly popular brother. Keeping in mind how events surrounding the birth of a Shawnee can influence the name he receives, Lalawethika was quite possibly a handful as an infant. His name in English translates to *The Rattle*, or, *He Makes a Loud Noise*. He never became skilled in the manly arts of the Indians, never acquired good social skills and was, well, less then handsome. One day in his youth, his inept warrior skills ended up compounding his appearance problems. Legend holds that on a certain occasion he misfired an arrow; resulting in the permanent disfigurement of his eye. Add to all of this, the fact that everyone revered his brother, Tecumseh; it was not surprising that Lalawethika turned to alcohol for comfort. But this only caused him further embarrassment, and drew more ridicule from his fellow Indians, at least for a time.

One day in 1805, at the age of thirty, he fell into a long and deep trance from which he awoke proclaiming that he had received a vision from the Great Spirit. He declared his name changed to Tenskwatawa (or Elkswatana), translated as *The Open Door* in English. In spite of this name alteration, he would henceforth become generally known as *The Prophet*, due to his spiritually-inspired predictions and preachings. He became intimately involved in Tecumseh's efforts to solidify the Indians into a confederation and earned fame in his own right. For a time, he successfully helped to unite the tribes whom Tecumseh had solicited, particularly on a spiritual footing. Because of him, many Indians gave up the use of alcohol. Some relinquished the use of other white man's ways which they had begun to readily adopt. The Prophet's esteem, however, faltered after a few too many blunders and prophesies that were not fulfilled. Perhaps the greatest of these occurred in 1811, when he convinced his warriors living along the Tippecanoe River that American bullets could not harm them. A battle, which we'll soon review further, was fought with the nearby American force. As a result the entire Indian village was destroyed. Any influence and popularity the Prophet had acquired, waned after a few years; and with Tecumseh's death, he slowly faded into obscurity.

The marriage or marriages of Tecumseh are the subject of the same type of debate that surrounds his immediate family members. Therefore we can address only one marriage with certainty. This was to a mixed blood (White and Shawnee) woman named Mamate; who bore his only verifiable son, Paukeesaa. There is good evidence that he may have also fathered a daughter with a Cherokee woman. The names of the woman and daughter, however; are not certain.[4] There is plenty of speculation about other wives and children, as well, but none are provable.

Tecumapease had a close relationship with her brother. It is certain that she took in and helped raise Tecumseh's son, Paukeesaa, for an extended period of time. Sadly, Tecumapease would lose both her husband, Stand Firm, and her brother at the Battle of the Thames.

Photo courtesy of Judith Justus.

The refurbished Galloway home in Xenia, Ohio, circa 1990s.

Tecumseh did not remain in any one locale for more than a few years at a time. He lived in numerous villages across what became the states of Ohio and Indiana. Henry Howe was an early resident of Greene County, Ohio, an area Tecumseh called home for a good stretch of time. He provides one of the accounts which have helped to fuel an ongoing rumor of a romance Tecumseh may have had with a white woman named Rebecca Galloway. Writing in the late 1800s, Howe relates an interview he had with Mr. Galloway who was Rebecca's nephew. His story reads:

> Tecumseh . . . was a young man of about thirty years when my grandfather first moved into Greene County. He lived some fifteen or twenty miles away. They became great friends, Tecumseh being a frequent visitor. Whether the chief was attracted by friendship for grandfather or his fancy for his daughter, my aunt Rebecca, was at first a matter of conjecture; it was soon evident however, that he was smitten with the "white girl" but according to the Indian custom he made his advances to the father, who referred him to his daughter.

> Although Tecumseh was brave in battle he was timid in love, and it was a long time before he could get his courage up to the sticking-point, which he did finally, and proposed, offering her fifty broaches of silver. She declined, telling him she did not wish to be a wild woman and work like an Indian squaw. He replied that she need not work, as he would make her a "great squaw." Notwithstanding his rejection, he ever remained friendly with the family.[5]

Other accounts, most being unverifiable or fictionalized in literature, have since embellished and promulgated this story of romance. There are rumors that Rebecca used her father's library of books to teach Tecumseh on various subjects. It's even plausible that he had learned some English from her, but it seems unlikely that Tecumseh spoke English when dealing with white men. Historians most often cite interpreters present at the treaty talks he was involved in.

In 1807, with tensions high along the frontier, Tecumseh spoke to a mass gathering of American leaders and citizens in Chillicothe, Ohio. His speech was so eloquent and sincere that he put to rest any fears that the Indians were preparing for war during their recent assembly at nearby Greenville, Ohio. With tensions eased, a gesture of friendship was offered by the esteemed American Senator, Thomas Worthington. At his self-named estate, Adena (a variation of Eden),

Worthington's newly built mansion was the site of a lavish banquet in honor of Tecumseh and his entourage of Indian chiefs. Worthington himself was highly influential in the process of Ohio becoming a state, and would later serve as its sixth governor. His family members mentioned that they heard scant use of English by Tecumseh when he was at their home.[6] So whether Tecumseh indeed knew English and simply favored his own language has to be left to speculation. Perhaps during negotiations with the white men, it was simply a matter of cultural pride and preference that his fellow Indians could directly understand what was being said by him.

A white man named William Conner lived among the Delaware Indians in the White River area of southern Indiana. He was a neighbor to Tecumseh in the early 1800s. Acting as an interpreter and spy for the Americans in the War of 1812, he led the Delawares, who were allied with the Americans, into the Battle of the Thames. A letter from William's son, A. J. Conner, to the historian Lyman Draper explains a bit of Tecumseh's attitude toward the expansion of the white men.

> My father knew Tecumsthe and the Prophet quite intimately. The Prophet had often befriended him, and had been found in every way truthful and sociable. My father always spoke well of these great Indians . . . in regard to his attitude towards the United States, and of the Indian tribes under his control and direction, Tecumsthe fully gave his reasons for his adherence to the British cause, and his cooperation with that country in the war that followed.
>
> He felt there was no security for the Indians under the management and agreements of the United States; and clearly foresaw that the time was not distant when the Indians would [neither] possess nor control any part of the domain he had inherited from his fathers . . . . He seemed to be fully aware, that step by step the tribes would be pushed further west or exterminated through the bitterness and hate of the white man . . . With a power, warlike and aggressive, as Great Britain to ally the Indians, he hoped to put off the final day, and possibly save a remnant of his people from total annihilation.[7]

To this end, Tecumseh relentlessly tried to unite as many tribes as possible into a single confederacy. He held firm to the belief that land was not something owned by one particular tribe. It belonged to all tribes to share.

Adena Mansion circa 1990s. Home of Thomas Worthington (1773-1827). Designed by Benjamin Henry Latrobe, who was the esteemed architect of the U.S. Capitol and White House. Here Tecumseh, the Prophet and other Indian and American dignitaries celebrated mutual promises of peace in 1807.

A ceremonial tomahawk presented to Worthington by Tecumseh on the occasion of his 1807 visit.

In late summer of 1810, William Henry Harrison and Tecumseh met for the first time as heads of their respective constituencies. The two had known of each other for years, but were only in each others' presence a few times before. One occasion was in 1794 when a young Harrison was fighting in the shadow of General Anthony Wayne at the Battle of Fallen Timbers against a multitude of Indians, of which Tecumseh was one. A year later in 1795, they were both present at the signing of the Treaty of Greenville. Harrison made his mark on the document as an aide-de-camp to Anthony Wayne. Tecumseh refused to sign. This day, some fifteen years later, Harrison was not only governor of the Indiana Territory, but commander of the United States forces in the Northwest. Tecumseh was a war chief of his Shawnee tribe and leader of the growing Indian coalition.

The subject of this discussion was a treaty previously signed at Fort Wayne in 1809 by the Miami and a few other tribes. Said treaty resulted in the sale of more tracts of Indian land to the United States. Tecumseh was not involved in this pact, and was vehemently opposed to it. Harrison knew of both the Prophet's and Tecumseh's opposition.

Before this meeting occurred, in an attempt to dissuade the Prophet from acting on his threats to attack the United States, Harrison extended him an invitation to meet with President Madison and discuss the treaty. As he waited for a response from the Prophet, Harrison learned from a messenger that "it [an answer] is to be brought by the brother of the Prophet who will be here in a few days." Harrison further noted in a letter to the Secretary of War that "this brother [Tecumseh] is really the efficient man—the Moses of the family. I have not seen him since the treaty of Greenville and should not know him. He is however described by all as a bold, active, sensible man daring in the extreme and capable of any undertaking."[8]

The meeting took place on the grounds of Harrison's home and office as governor of the Indiana Territory at Vincennes. Tecumseh and his entourage of several hundred Indians made a camp near the estate. Harrison had plenty of military personnel present to deter any potential violence. Delegates of the two groups formed in an open grassy area across from each other and there began to deliberate. Harrison listened to Tecumseh explain his views on land ownership. When Harrison spoke in turn, he ended his words to Tecumseh by explaining that

> the lands had been purchased from the Miamis, who were the true and original owners of it . . . it was ridiculous to assert that all Indians were one nation; for if such had been the intention of the Great Spirit, he would not have put six different tongues into their heads . . . and the Shawanese had no right to come from a distant country and control the Miamis in the disposal of their own property.

As the interpreter finished repeating Harrison's words, Tecumseh exclaimed, "It is all false!" The entourage of Indians all rose with war clubs at the ready. Harrison stood and drew his sword. An engagement seemed imminent. After Harrison learned what Tecumseh had said, he told him, "He was a bad man—that he would have no further talk with him—that he must return to his camp, and set out for his home immediately."

The next morning, Tecumseh reflected on his outburst and requested a second meeting with Harrison. The disagreement was still not resolved, but according to Harrison, "The behavior of Tecumseh at this interview was very different from what it was the day before. His deportment was dignified and collected, and he showed not the least disposition to be insolent." Nonetheless, Tecumseh was determined to adhere to the old, pre-treaty boundaries.

Harrison thought a third meeting, in private, might resolve the standoff; and so he visited Tecumseh's camp the next day. The two talked for some time. But Tecumseh did not waiver from his original request.

> It was with great reluctance, he [Tecumseh] would make war with the United States – against whom he had no other complaint, but their purchasing the Indian's land; that he was very anxious to be their friend, and if he [the governor], would prevail upon the President to give up the lands lately purchased, and agree never to make another treaty, without the consent of *all* the tribes, he would be a faithful ally, and assist them in all their wars with the English.

Further, Tecumseh explained:

> I hope the Great Spirit will put sense enough in his head [President Madison], to induce him to direct you to give up this land. It is true, he is so far off; he will not be injured by the war. He may sit still in his town, and drink his wine, whilst you and I will have to fight it out . . . . It is my determination; nor will I give rest to my feet, until I have united all the red men in the like revolution.[9]

There is some disagreement whether it was at this same meeting, or another that Tecumseh's tenacity was curiously on display. It seems that after Tecumseh had finished a speech, he went to sit in a chair that was inadvertently not provided for him! Harrison, embarrassed, immediately ordered that one be brought for the chief. Tecumseh, when told, "Your father requests that you take a chair" responded, "My father? The sun is my father, and the earth is my mother; and on her bosom I will repose."[10] He then proceeded to sit cross-legged, in the manner generally referred to as Indian-style, upon the grass.

Tecumseh travelled far and wide for years soliciting tribes to sign-on with him in union against the white men. On one such call, Tecumseh's shrewd art of persuasion, and eerie clairvoyance, is evidenced. He gave a dire warning to an Indian chief named Big Warrior who refused to join the confederation. It was late in 1811, in an old Creek village named Tuckhabatchee near present-day Montgomery, Alabama. Tecumseh had just spent a great deal of time trying to persuade the chief to change his mind. He had even showered him with gifts, but to

no avail. Frustrated, Tecumseh finally answered Big Warrior's rebuff
with distinct anger.

> Tecumthe, reading the spirit and intentions of the Big Warrior, looked
> him in the eye, and pointing his finger towards [his] face, said, "Your
> blood is white. You have taken my talk, and the sticks, and the wampum,
> and the hatchet, but you do not mean to fight. I know the reason. You do
> not believe the Great Spirit has sent me. You shall know. I leave Tuck-
> habatchee directly and shall go straight to Detroit. When I arrive there, I
> will stamp on the ground with my foot, and shake down every house in
> Tuckhabatchee."[11]

And so he left. A short time later, whether Tecumseh was actually at
Detroit or not cannot be determined, but the earth indeed shook—vio-
lently. Big Warrior's village was leveled. The Mississippi River was so
disrupted that it flowed backwards for a short time. A very broad area
of the Mississippi valley and beyond felt the tremors of what would become known as *The New Madrid Earthquakes.* They are, to date, the
strongest series of quakes to hit the middle of the country. The first occurred on December 17, 1811 and several more would occur in January
and February of 1812. Five of them are estimated by scientists today to
have been 8.0 or higher magnitude on the Richter scale. With this event,
Chief Big Warrior quickly came around to Tecumseh's perspective on
a coalition of Indian tribes. Some historians speculate that scientists
from the East, who came to the frontier in anticipation of this upcoming
event, may have shared their theory of it with Tecumseh through casual
contact at trading posts along the frontier. Still, the occurrence of this
event in the timeline of Tecumseh's prediction remains uncanny.

Upon his return from this trip to the South, Tecumseh was furious
to learn that his brother, the Prophet, and Gen. Harrison, had engaged
each other in battle. The Prophet had been warned by Tecumseh not
to antagonize the enemy while he was away. Yet on November 7, 1811
he attacked the American force outside his village of Prophetstown,
located along the Tippecanoe River in northern Indiana. Perhaps the
best synopsis of what happened on this day comes from Colonel R. T.
Durrett via his Introduction to a book titled *The Battle of Tippecanoe*
(written by Alfred Pirtle). Durrett explains:

> The Battle of Tippecanoe has been supposed to have been the result of

the ambition of General Harrison for military glory. Others thought that it was caused by the depredations of Indians upon the life and property of the white settlers in the Indiana Territory. Yet others have believed that it was nothing more nor less than the traditional and the inevitable result of the contact of civilization with barbarism. While all of these as well as other causes may have their share in this battle, there was one supreme and controlling cause which brought the white man and the red man together in mortal conflict on the banks of the Tippecanoe. That cause was a struggle for the land on which the battle was fought, and for the adjacent and the far-away lands of the Indians.[12]

For all these reasons, Harrison was found camped outside the village of Prophetstown on the night of November 6, 1811. He was expecting to meet with the Prophet in the morning for talks, but was suspicious of an attack by him in the night. His hunch was right. The Indians attacked Harrison's camp in the darkness. Only Harrison's foresight to position his alert and wary troops in a square formation of defense allowed him to win the day, or should we say the night. Harrison proceeded to totally destroy the Shawnee town. The event was a huge boom for American morale at the time, as well as for Harrison's notoriety. Years later, he would use his fame from this confrontation and take the river's name as a political nickname of sorts – *Ol' Tippecanoe*. Still later, on his way to the White House in 1840, *Tippecanoe and Tyler Too* became John Tyler's and his campaign slogan. It was this battle and the devastation Harrison wreaked on Prophetstown that fueled the animosity between Tecumseh and Harrison.

Back in his childhood, Tecumseh had a dear friend named Stephen Ruddell. Stephen was abducted by British soldiers and given to the Shawnee Indians when he was but a young boy of seven years. He grew up as an adopted brother to Tecumseh for some twelve years. When he became a young adult, he chose to return to the white man's way of life, but his friendship and admiration of Tecumseh never waned. Of Tecumseh, Ruddell says:

There was a certain something in his countenance and manner that always commanded respect and at the same time made those about him love him . . . he was a great hunter . . . he was free hearted and generous to excess – always ready to relieve the wants of others . . . he rarely ever drank ardent spirits to excess . . . he was by no means savage in his nature–always expressed the greatest abhorrence when he heard of, or saw acts of cruelty or barbarity practiced . . . from his earliest days, he was remarkably easily awoke out of sleep–he was always on the alert, and it was impossible to take him by surprise . . . when prisoners fell into his hands, he always treated them with much humanity as if they had been in the hands of civilized people. No burning. No torturing . . . He was a man of great courage and conduct–perfectly fearless of danger. He always inspired his companions with confidence and valor . . . He never evinced any great regard for the female sex–it was a custom among the Shawnee to marry as many wives as they pleased and to keep them as long as they pleased. Tecumtheth had at different times a wife whom he did not keep very long before he parted from her . . . He was a very jovial companion–fond of cracking his jokes; but his wit was never aimed to wound the feelings of his comrades . . . . He was naturally eloquent–very fluent–graceful in his gesticulation but not in the habit of using many gestures. There was no violence–no vehemence in his mode of delivering his speeches. He always made a great impression on his audience. He was about five feet ten inches high, very well made, full of maturity and possessed of great strength . . . His talents, rectitude of deportment, and friendly disposition commanded the respect and regard of all about him. In short, I consider him a very great, as well as a very good, man who if he had enjoyed the advantage of a liberal education, would have done honor to any age or any nation. [13]

Just days before the Battle of the Thames occurred Tecumseh was camped around Amherstburg, Ontario. He was at this British post on the northwestern coast of Lake Erie in anticipation of a battle there against the on-coming Americans. A ten year old boy who was living near the fort witnessed Tecumseh about the area. Many years later, the grown-up John Bertrand related to his friend Alex Halls the childhood recollections he had, or had heard, of Tecumseh. He explains:

He [Tecumseh] was about 5 feet 9 inches–a great, stout, broad-shouldered man. Heard him call Gen. Proctor a coward, Sept. 10th 1813; the day of the battle with Barclay and Perry. At the Battle of Monroe [Frenchtown], Jan. 21, 1813, Tecumseh saved about 600 American prisoners . . . Tecumseh when about Amherstburg used to stop at Colonel Elliot's [a British officer]; he would eat with the family; but he would never go to a bed. He kept in a loft over the granary. He would not go to [a] bed, and leave his warriors camping out.

Another young man, a teenager named Abraham Holmes, was a witness to the charity of Tecumseh. It was on the very day of the battle in which Tecumseh would die. Abraham was living in a small Canadian village located very near what was to become the Thames battleground. Only hours before the conflict occurred, he happened to see Tecumseh lingering at Arnold's Mill, the storehouse of grain for the locals. In a letter written years later by Abraham's son, we see how Tecumseh risked his own safety for these innocent white men living in the area. The Americans were approaching fast, only a mile or two away. He knew that his fellow warriors' blood was boiling in anticipation of the imminent fight, and that they were capable of recklessly destroying anything in site.

> My father [Abraham] says he knows very little of Tecumseh, but it might be interesting . . . to know that in his retreat, he manifested a principle worthy of an enlightened and philanthropic general in successfully preventing his men [fellow Indians] from burning, what was known as Arnold's Mill, near my father's home. He [Tecumseh] remained at the mill until the last Indian had gone, lest some stragglers might set it on fire, a calamity that would have been almost irreparable to the early settlers in the vicinity. My father was sixteen years old in 1813, and remembered Tecumseh as a handsome strongly built man of medium height and broad chest and shoulders.[15]

Abraham was so impressed by this man, and his benevolent action that day, that he named his son, the author of this letter, after him–Tecumseh K. Holmes.

Yet another story to shine a light on Tecumseh's sense of fairness and compassion comes to us via Captain James Knaggs, an American officer who fought at the Battle of the Thames. The Knaggs family lived for years in the Detroit area, not far from the Raisin River. James knew many Indians of the area personally. It seems Tecumseh was in the vicinity at a time when the British, whom he was allied with, had command of it. He was in need of food for his desperately hungry warriors. There was little to be had since the local people had already been stripped of whatever foodstuffs they may have possessed. Knaggs' account reads:

> A man named Rivard lived in the area. He was both elderly and lame, thus unable to provide for his family through regular means. He only had

a pair of oxen, with which his son managed to secure a meager income for the family. He knew of the British and Indian need for food and so tried to hide his meager assets from them. One day, however, while his son was walking the oxen in the road, Tecumseh happened to approach. He said, "My friend, I must have those oxen. My young men are very hungry; they have nothing to eat. We must have the oxen."

Rivard's son responded that his father would starve if he were to give up the two oxen.

Tecumseh retorted a bit pompously, "Well, we are the conquerors, and everything we want is ours. I must have the oxen; my people must not starve." Then he continued in a spirit of good faith. "But, I will not be so mean as to rob you of them. I will pay you one hundred dollars for them, and that is far more than they are worth; but we must have them."

The British Indian Agent was Col. Elliot [the same colonel with whom Tecumseh frequently dined]. He was further down river at this time. Tecumseh found a white man to write up an order stating that the British would cover the cost. [The British were expected to provide for their allies]. The young warriors feasted on the oxen as the young Rivard boy headed off to meet Col. Elliot for payment, which was promptly refused. "We are entitled to our support from the country we have conquered. I will not pay it." said Elliot. With much chagrin, the boy told Tecumseh of his encounter.

"He won't pay it, will he? Stay all night, and tomorrow we will see," Tecumseh told him. In the morning the two of them went downriver to meet with Col. Elliot.

"Do you refuse to pay for the oxen I bought?" Tecumseh incredulously asked.

"Yes," the colonel replied, reiterating his opinion that this was conquered land . . .

"I bought them, for my young men were very hungry," exclaimed Tecumseh, "I promised to pay for them, and they shall be paid for. I have always heard that white men went to war with each other, and not with peaceful individuals; that they did not rob and plunder poor people. I will not."

"Well, I will not pay for them," responded the colonel.

"You can do as you please," Tecumseh warned, "but before Tecumseh and his warriors came to fight the battles of the great King, they had enough to eat, for which they had only to thank the Master of Life and their good rifles. Their hunting grounds supplied them food enough; to them they can return."

*Portrait of John Johnston, American Agent for Indian Affairs in the Northwest
for thirty-one years. From a plate published in Moore's Masonic Review.
Shown here as it appeared in Benson J. Lossing's Pictorial Fieldbook of the
War of 1812 which was originally published in 1868.*

The threat of Tecumseh and all of his warriors abandoning the British
over such a small issue, took the colonel aback. He well knew the importance of the Indian alliance. "Well, if I must pay, I will," the colonel
lamented.

"Give me hard money, not rag money (Army bills)," Tecumseh demanded.

Tecumseh and the Rivard boy watched as the Colonel counted out one
hundred dollars in coin. Tecumseh passed on the sum to the boy after
receiving it.

Then Tecumseh said to Col. Elliot, "Give me one dollar more."

The colonel obliged and Tecumseh passed the extra dollar to young
Revard, saying, "take that; it will pay for the time you have lost in getting
your money."[16]

The American counterpart to the British Indian agent Colonel Matthew Elliott was John Johnston. Well-acquainted with the Shawnee Indians of his jurisdiction, Johnston in his memoirs writes:

He [Tecumseh] was undoubtedly a great man of his race, and aimed
at the independence of his people by a union of all the Indians, North
and South, against the encroachments of the whites. Had he appeared
fifty years sooner he might have set bounds to the Anglo-Saxon race in
the West; but he came upon the stage of action too late, when the power

and resources of the Indians were so much impaired and weakened as to render them unable to effect anything against their powerful neighbors ... This celebrated man was about five feet ten inches in height, square, well-built form for strength and agility; about forty-eight or fifty years old when he fell at the battle of the Thames, during the last war.[17]

Johnston's wife was also impressed by Tecumseh. Their son Stephen recollects in a letter to the historian Lyman Draper his mother's thoughts of the chieftain.

My mother had frequent talks with us in relation to this man Tecumseh. The Kentuckians at the battle of the Thames claimed to have gotten possession of the body of Tecumseh, and he was described as a large man. My mother always said to me that this was a mistake. Tecumseh was not a large man, but medium in size. She, furthermore, said that his "manner was always dignified and polite. His person compact and erect," and to use her words, she said he was the "proudest man" she had ever seen; that in his walk, he "seemed to disdain the ground he walked upon."[18]

Shortly before his death, Tecumseh delivered one of his most famous speeches to a fully attended council of British and Indians. They were at Fort Malden in Amherstburg, the British fortress and naval shipyard on the northwestern corner of Lake Erie. In this oration, we hear Tecumseh's firm determination and readiness to fight for his cause. A week earlier, the Americans under Commodore Oliver H. Perry had defeated Commander Robert H. Barclay and the British fleet on Lake Erie. It was a major setback for the British. Tecumseh and his band of Indians as well as General Procter and the British forces heard the cannon blasts echoing through the woods from offshore. Procter had become apprised of the negative outcome from the British perspective, but had avoided telling Tecumseh of the result, fearing the news would cause the loss of his support. Tecumseh sensed that something was awry. Procter had ordered his troops to begin dismantling the fortress and seemed to be preparing to retreat further into Canada rather than remain and fight the approaching Americans. Tecumseh, concerned and agitated, spoke loud and clear in the council and squarely at Procter:

Father, listen! Our fleet has gone out; we know they have fought; we have heard the great guns; but we know nothing of what has happened to our father with that arm [Barclay]. Our ships have gone one way, and we are much astonished to see our father tying up every thing and preparing to run away the other, without letting his red children know what his intentions are. You always told us to remain here and take care of our lands; it made our hearts glad to hear that was your wish. Our great father, the King, is the head, and you represent him. You always told us that you would never draw your foot off British ground; but now, father, we see you are drawing back, and we are sorry to see our father doing so without seeing the enemy. We must compare our father's conduct to a fat dog, that carries its tail upon its back, but when affrighted, it drops it between its legs and runs off.

Father Listen! The Americans have not defeated us by land; neither are we sure they have done so by water; we, therefore, wish to remain here and fight our enemy, should they make their appearance. If they defeat us, we will then retreat with our father.

At the battle of the Rapids, last year, the Americans certainly defeated us, and when we retreated to our father's fort at that place, the gates were shut against us. We were afraid that it would now be the case; but, instead of that, we now see our British father preparing to march out of his garrison.

Father! You have got arms and ammunition which our great father sent for his red children. If you have an idea of going away, give them to us, and you may go, and welcome for us. Our lives are in the hands of the Great Spirit. We are determined to defend our lands and if it be His will, we wish to leave our bones upon them.[19]

What a display of forthright courage. Not only did Tecumseh boldly declare his readiness to face down the enemy, but he unflinchingly confronted his own ally. On occasion this blunt leadership was even directed at his own warriors. Tecumseh was adamant that any white prisoners taken by the Indians would be treated in a humane fashion. Evidence of the seriousness of this conviction is attested to by the early nineteenth century historian Samuel Drake. "Although Tecumseh was not himself in that battle [River Raisin], yet he arrived after the massacre commenced, and actually put to death with his own hand a chief who would not desist from murdering the American soldiers."[20]

When it came to torture at the hands of Indians, Simon Kenton had seen and felt his share. Kenton was one of America's earliest and most legendary pioneers, having survived many Indian conflicts, personal beatings and capture. He had fought against Tecumseh in several battles, had been in councils with him, and even had private negotiations with him regarding Ohio land treaties. One council attended by both men occurred in 1807 in the Mad River valley of Ohio and gives us a glimpse of Tecumseh's stubborn streak as well as his reaction to a perceived effrontery.

The council was called in an attempt to quell the rising tensions between the Whites and the Indians. The murder of a man named Bowyer was one key issue. Tecumseh arrived angry that his group of Shawnees had been blamed for this murder, when he knew it was another Shawnee chief named Black Hoof who committed it. As it was, Black Hoof and Tecumseh rarely saw eye-to-eye. A segment of the Shawnee tribe, led by Black Hoof, refused to join Tecumseh's confederation and supported the Americans through the War of 1812.

On the way to the council most of the Indians and white men actually paraded side-by-side through the town of Urbana, Ohio and all were laden with weapons. It was agreed that all parties would leave their arms at a home along the way. Tecumseh had heard of this plan, and so avoided the parade by bringing his tribe in by a different route. When he arrived at the appointed council site, however, his Indians were required to surrender their weapons. All did except Tecumseh. As the negotiators proceeded into the open area agreed upon for the dialogue, Tecumseh came forward bearing his combination tomahawk/pipe and explained that he must smoke his pipe through the discussions and so would retain it. Tension filled the air for a brief time, but finally Tecumseh passed his pipe to one of his Indians who took it away. Kenton, who trusted Tecumseh, explains, "Tecumseh wanted his pipe to smoke. Pinchard [an American present] made him a corn cob [pipe] and presented it [to Tecumseh] – [Tecumseh] gave Pinchard a look and tossed the pipe over his head, and did not afterwards deign to see him."[21]

As time went on the stories about Tecumseh began to take on a more fantastic nature in order to further embellish the legend. One such account came from an elderly Ho-Chunk Indian chief named Spoon Decorah. He spoke with Reuben Thwaites in an 1887 interview. Thwaites was the well-respected editor of the *Wisconsin State Journal* and the *Wisconsin Historical Collections*. Decorah's story, provides a perfect example of how fiction can overwhelm fact.

Our old people talk much about Tecumseh. Some Winnebagoes once fought under him, but none of my relations ever did. Tecumseh's skin was bullet-proof. When he went into battle, he always wore a white deerskin hunting shirt, around which was girt a strap. The bullets shot at him would go through his shirt, and fall harmless inside. When the weight of the bullets inside the shirt became too great, he would unstrap his belt and let them fall through to the ground. He was a brave man, as a man whom bullets could not wound would of course be; he never used a gun in battle, only a hatchet. Tecumseh had but one son. One day, when the great warrior had grown old and feeble, he called his son to him and said: "I am getting old. I want to leave you what has made me proof against bullets." Thereupon Tecumseh commenced to retch, and try to vomit. He repeated this several times and finally threw up a smooth, black stone, about three inches long. That stone was Tecumseh's soul. Handing it to his son, he said: "I could not be killed by a bullet, but will die only of old age. This is to be your charm against bullets also." And so his son swallowed it, that he, likewise, might never be killed by a bullet. And he never was.[22]

Wow! We do see from stories such as these, the awe with which Tecumseh was viewed, and the lengths to which some would go to advance his stature.

Likewise, the literature venue was no small player in the promulgation of the Tecumseh mystique. One early American author named Julia L. Dumont intently fostered the legend of Tecumseh. She was an exceptional fiction writer of the early and mid 1800s. She sympathized with the Indian plight and held Tecumseh in very high esteem. A taste of her interpretation of Tecumseh's youth follows:

Tecumseh became immoderately fond of hunting in his earliest childhood. Disdaining every kind of hardship, he soon inured himself to hunger and thirst; to the damps of midnight, and the fervors of meridian day. His body seemed to acquire a kind of supernatural invulnerability. Fatigue had no power over him, and he laughed scornfully in the face of danger. Nothing could elude his vigilance, exhaust his perseverance, or thwart his determination. The deer could not out speed him, and he swam the proud waters with the skill of their native tenants. Ere he was ten years of age, his mother's lodge was decorated with the richest spoils of the chase; and the tribe to which he belonged, already looked upon him as their future chief. The old men admitted him to their councils, and the youth emulated his example.[23]

Another author, the Canadian John Richardson, knew Tecumseh from his youth and his admiration of him ran deep. At the tender age of seventeen Richardson was a member of the British ranks and fought alongside his idol at the Thames. He saw this remarkable chieftain in the same way many others had viewed him, as a superior man of honor and wisdom who would have reached historical heights as a renowned statesman in any other culture.

Richardson gained some acclaim, but only after his death, as Canada's first man of literature. His initial writing venture of any significance, an epic style poem simply titled *Tecumseh*, evinced his fascination with the man. Few read it in Britain, most likely because Richardson's generation was by-and-large not interested in old military affairs in far off Canada. Further, they didn't understand nor care to learn much about the Indians of whom he wrote. His Canadian audience was small and had little leisure time for reading. Still, this work, written in a classic heroic style, gives evidence to the great esteem that the name Tecumseh evoked. A segment of this poem portrays the historical scene whence Colonel Johnson slays Tecumseh. It reads:

> Like the quick bolt which follows on the flash
> Which rends the mountain oak in fearful twain,
> So sprang the Warrior with impetuous dash,
>
> Upon the Christian writhing in his pain.
> High gleam'd his hatchet, ready now to crash,
> Along the fibres of his swimming brain,
> When from the adverse arm a bullet flew
> With force resistless, and with aim too true.
>
> The baffled Chieftain tottered, sank and fell—
> Rage in his heart, and vengeance in his glance:
> His features ghastly pale – his breast was hell—
> One bound he made to seize his fallen lance,
> But quick the death-shades o'er his vision swell,
>
> His arm drops nerveless—straining to advance—
> One look of hatred, and the last he gave,
> Then sank and slumbered with the fallen brave.[24]

One of the few opinions in the annals of Tecumseh's life which somewhat diminishes his stature comes from Caleb Atwater. In his *History of the State of Ohio*, Atwater explains that he was frequently with the Prophet and Tecumseh. He made a tour of the six nations of New York with the two brothers in 1809, acting as their interpreter. Through the 1820s, Atwater continued relations with many tribes as the U. S. Commissioner of Indian Affairs. His opinion of Tecumseh reads:

> By those who neither knew him, nor any other wild Indians, he is often represented as being something very uncommon; whereas all his movements originated with the Canadian Indian department. In obedience to their orders, he visited nearly all the Indian nations of North America, stirring them all up, against the Americans. He told the Onondigoes, through (myself), as his interpreter, "that he had visited the Florida Indians, and even the Indians so far to the north that the snow covered the ground in midsummer." He was a warrior, and Elsquataway acted as a prophet, dissuading the Indians from drinking ardent spirits. As to real talent, he possessed no more of it than any one of thousands of his people, in the northwest. Being much with the British officers, he had enlarged his ideas very much.[25]

A final story, which suggests that Tecumseh was human after all, is offered up by the same Mr. Galloway cited earlier. Tecumseh is known to have been extremely temperate in his use of alcohol throughout most of his adult life. He had witnessed the frenzied behavior it fostered in his fellow Indians. As their chieftain he strove to curb their use of it, and for awhile with his brother's, the Prophet's, help he was successful. If Mr. Galloway's account is to be believed, however; Tecumseh learned first-hand at an early age the evil effects that can result from over-indulgence in the spirits. Perhaps it was episodes like this that convinced Tecumseh to steer clear of intoxicants as he matured. Mr. Galloway relates:

> The books speak of Tecumseh having been a large man; but this, I can assure you was not so; he was but a moderate-sized Indian. He was fond of "fire-water," and would go on a spree sometimes, when he would become very troublesome and provoking. On one occasion, when at the shop of "Blacksmith" James Galloway (a cousin of my grandfather's who lived on the banks of Mad River), Tecumseh, being on one of his big "drunks," became very insulting and annoying. Galloway grew angry, and being a very powerful man took him, much to his disgust, and tied him up to a tree until he became more sober and quiet.[26]

Where do we cease detailing the stories and opinions which are on record regarding Tecumseh? The only sure place is where fact and fancy meet. As the years accumulated after his death the significance of this man became more and more apparent on its own accord. No further embellishment was really necessary. Exaggeration of the truth is probably natural to anyone of celebrity, especially after they have passed on, but in Tecumseh's case, the true verifiable events of his life are beyond a doubt sufficient to know him. From these few accounts, and Tecumseh's own words, it is easy to see how he came to be held in such esteem and how he became the primary subject of literature and poetry for generations. Hopefully, we now have an inkling as to why so much attention has been given to how, and by whose hand, he died.

CHAPTER 3

Independence Challenged

By the President of the United States
A PROCLAMATION

Whereas the Congress of the United States, by virtue of the
Constituted Authority vested in them, have declared by their act,
bearing date the eighteenth day of the present month, that War exists
between the United Kingdom of Great Britain and Ireland, and the
Dependencies thereof, and the United States of America and their
territories; Now therefore I, JAMES MADISON; President of the United
States of America, do hereby proclaim the same to all whom it may
concern: And I do specially enjoin on all persons holding offices,
civil or military, under the authority of the United States, that they be
vigilant and zealous, in discharging the duties respectively incident
thereto: And I do moreover exhort all the good people of the United
States, as they love their country; as they value the precious heritage
derived from the virtue and valor of their fathers: As they feel the
wrongs which have forced on them the last resort of injured nations;
and as they consult the best means under the blessing of Divine
Providence, of abridging its calamities; that they exert themselves in
preserving order, in promoting concord, in maintaining the authority
and the efficacy of the laws, and in supporting and invigorating all the
measures which may be adopted by the Constituted Authorities, for
obtaining a speedy, a just, and an honorable peace.

In testimony whereof I have hereunto set my hand, and caused the seal
of the United States to be affixed these presents.

Done at the city of Washington, the nineteenth day of June,
one thousand eight hundred and twelve; and of the
Independence of the United States
the thirty-sixth.

(Signed) By the President, James Madison
(Signed) James Monroe, Secretary of State [1]

It was late June, 1812 when a copy of the *Georgetown Telegraph*
reached the hands of William Whitley at his home in Crab Orchard,
Kentucky. A stern smile crossed the face of this long-time Kentuckian
as he read the proclamation of war (introductory quote above) issued
by his government against those detestable Tories. The news pumped
new energy into his rugged 64-year-old frame. Certainly, his hope was
rekindled that this action would result in a safer life for his family and

neighbors along the frontier. Just a year later, in the fall of 1813, the still inspired Whitley would be found riding as a volunteer alongside members of Captain James Davidson's company within Colonel Richard M. Johnson's newly formed Mounted Regiment. The Kentucky force was mustered to fight under Major-General William H. Harrison in the struggle for the Northwest Territory. It would be Whitley's last act of service, after a lifetime of such to his country, as his spirit would be released in the muddy swamps along the Thames River.

On the eastern seaboard, however, the mayor of New York, DeWitt Clinton, read the announcement in the *New York Herald* with angst. In his opinion, war was not the right road for this country to follow. More negotiations were necessary before putting American lives, and businesses, on the line. Clinton would use his disdain for this barbarous congressional action to his advantage. His Federalist party, ardent supporters of peace, would back him in an attempt to win Madison's Presidential seat. The lines were clearly drawn. Clinton and his Federalist advocates represented the *end the war now* crowd. The Democrat-Republicans, led by President Madison, had had a stomach full of unsuccessful negotiations and could sit back no longer. The presidential election in November of 1812 would thus determine if the country approved of this war or not. History shows the result–Madison won a second term, but it was close.

Back in June, by means of posting and publishing this proclamation, President Madison announced to this divided American citizenry that their government had made its final decision to officially declare war against another nation. According to the Constitution, *fathered* years earlier by the now *President* James Madison; Congress was the governmental body vested with the authority to declare war. And so, the Constitution was adhered to. The House of Representatives had one hundred and twenty-eight members in 1812. Forty-nine of them, over a third, still said no to war. The Senate had thirty-two members. The vote was even closer, nineteen to thirteen, but still in approval. Both camps were strident in their opinions. The vote was along party lines. Madison and members of his Democrat-Republican political party, with their so-called *War Hawks*, had won the day against the Federalists. It was no secret that Madison was encouraging the affirmative action. Eighteen days earlier he spelled out his reasons for war in a special address to the Congressmen.

An interesting footnote to this historical period comes to light via an article in the *Cincinnati Daily Gazette* of 1873. Referring to the status of arms available for the men who were joining the army in the years just prior to the War of 1812, the author observes:

> A great many of the men were armed with cornstalks and umbrellas, but that imported little; if the government could get able bodied men, it could soon furnish arms, It was just about that time that Mr. Madison made a contract with the celebrated Eli Whitney [inventor of the cotton gin] to furnish so many thousand muskets. Whitney had neither factory nor machinery, but if he could get money his invention would do the rest. So, Mr. Madison advanced him money on the contract, and Whitney built his factory at Mill River, near New Haven [CT], and furnished the government with good arms, and made more profits than he ever did by the cotton gin.[2]

It had been only about thirty years since the British Crown had finally conceded that the United States of America was indeed an independent country. Not enough time, apparently, to legitimatize that fact in many British minds. As well, many of the Indian nations felt that the imposition of the Americans further and further west into their lands had to be stopped. They concluded that an alliance with the British was the best means available to cease the American encroachment.

It could be said that the war had begun much sooner and was merely made official on June 18th of 1812. The antagonism between the primary foes, the British and Americans, finally grew to the extreme of war for many reasons. Chronic trade disputes between three countries; the United States, Britain and France laid the primary foundation for the conflict. In 1812, the Napoleonic War between England and France was still in full swing within the European theatre. It had the complete attention of the British and French. As a side-effect American import and export activity was directly impacted by these two countries. Naval blockades were formed, embargoes were declared, and skirmishes were fought on land and sea as a maturing America became entangled in the battle for free trade. England did not want the U.S. to provide goods of any kind to France, and France obviously felt the same about the British receiving American commodities. After a decade of coping with these obstacles, Americans were left in want of the goods they

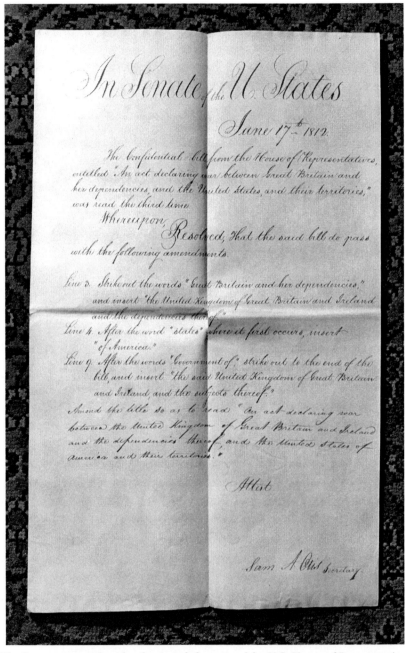

The Senate approval, with a few noted changes, of the U.S. House of Repesentative's "Confidential Bill" to declare war in 1812. Per the Library of Congress records, this document was thought to have been lost in the flames set to the U.S. Capitol building by the British in 1814.

needed to import, and blocked from selling the goods they produced for export.

A second root cause of this war being declared was the refusal of the British to cease their interference in American territories, especially in the Great Lakes area. British posts near the American borders traded with the Indians and indulged and encouraged their resentment toward the Americans. For some time, this was just a nuisance, but it grew into a very real threat. By 1812 the Indians of this Northwest Frontier (present-day Ohio, Michigan, Indiana, Illinois and Wisconsin) were persuaded to ally with the British Crown in order to stop American expansion. The preponderance of the British force, however, was stationed in Europe fighting Napoleon on a much grander scale. Supplemental manpower for the British effort in North America, albeit unmanageable and unpredictable, presented itself right under their noses – these Indian nations. Already incensed against the Americans, they were ripe for coercion into an alliance.

For many years, deadly encounters were had between Indians and isolated settlers as the frontier line moved ever westward. Plenty of atrocities were committed by both parties. Treaties were made and then disputed. Since the Indians held a general belief that the land was not something any person or group, white or Indian, could own; treaties were inherently controversial. Often one tribe would argue that another had no right to even consider selling a piece of land even if they were the ones occupying it at the time. Technically, it still belonged to all tribes. Yet treaties were repeatedly signed due to the lure of gifts and monies.

After the fact, Americans continued to point out to the tribes who argued against the sales that they indeed had, in-hand, signed, binding agreements. Of course the disputes grew more and more heated as the whole of the Indian nation found itself with less and less land to hunt and farm for their survival. There can be no denying that plenty of advantage was taken of these circumstances by the Americans as they continued to expand. All-in-all tensions on both sides grew worse every year. By 1812, instead of random individual confrontations, real military strategies were beginning to be employed in both camps to resolve the disputes.

The third and perhaps last straw prompting a proclamation of war, from the Americans' point of view, was the repeated *impressments* of their sailors by the British fleet. Normal procedure for the Royal Navy at this time was to impress, or draft, their men into service on their ships if they had any seafaring experience whatsoever. The war with France in Europe was in full stride and every possible body was needed in that effort. Since the British authorities still viewed the Americans as little more than traitors to the Crown, when the opportunity presented itself, they would abduct American sailors off of American ships. The British reasoning was that these men were still British. After all, most of these abductees had only recently renounced their English citizenship for the lure of the expanding American trade markets, higher compensation for their services, and of course the freedom the United States offered. The British felt this practice of hauling off sailors against their will was fair game. The Americans held a contrary view.

It wasn't until October 5, 1813, sixteen months into the war, that the Battle of the Thames was fought. For the Americans, it was arguably the most significant land confrontation of the war to date. Many of the men on both sides of this confrontation were already distinguished in the eyes of their fellows; and many more would earn hero status as a result of their bravery on this day. Tragically, it would be the last event in the lives of many. A candid discussion between men from both camps would conclude that, of all those deaths, the most impactful on the future course of events was that of Tecumseh. Before delving into the mystery of who in particular was responsible for delivering the fatal blow to this most-respected Indian leader, let's catch a glimpse of at least some of the major confrontations that had led up to this event. We'll see how the mood of the country, as well as that of the men who fought the battles, ebbed and flowed before the decisive fight along the Thames River took place.

From the United States' perspective, it had all begun quite poorly. A month into the war, in July, 1812, led by General William Hull, the American forces' made their first strategic land offensive. Crossing over the Detroit River into Canada, they marched on toward their goal of attacking the British fort at Amherstburg, situated only twenty miles from Detroit on the northwestern corner of Lake Erie. However, to the surprise of his men, General Hull deemed it necessary to abandon the effort just short of attempting it. While poised for the attack on Amherstburg, he ordered his men to retreat back to the safety of Fort Detroit. One fact driving Hull's decision to withdraw was the news he had just received. It stated that a British unit to the north, with the support of numerous Indians, had captured Fort Mackinac. Located on present-day Mackinac Island, where lower and upper Michigan meet; its loss signaled an immediate threat in Hull's mind. Even though they were almost three hundred miles away from Fort Mackinac, he speculated that this huge force was closing fast upon them. Already short of men and artillery, fear ruled Hull's day.

With the American troops in full retreat, having accomplished nothing more than a long march, the British forces, strengthened by Tecumseh and his Indians, took advantage of Hull's peculiar action. They donned an offensive posture and attacked Fort Detroit. In due course, General Isaac Brock would accept the Americans' surrender of this key outpost. The defeat rattled the American spirit especially on the now vulnerable northwest frontier. Though some legitimate tactical problems influenced Hull's actions, he would never recover his reputation. He was court-martialed and sentenced to death which was stayed only due to his friendship with President Madison, who was considerate of his former honorable service years earlier in the Revolution.

In just a few weeks time, two key American strongholds were now in the possession of the British; Mackinac and Detroit, and Fort Amherstburg as well still proudly flew the Union flag.

The American failures continued to mount. In October of 1812, the American forces under Major General Stephen Van Rensselaer made an attempt to take the British site at Queenstown Heights on the Niagara River. They might have won that day, in fact Van Rensselaer was certain of it, had it not been for an unusual lack of courage, or commitment, displayed by the New York militia at the pivotal moment of the conflict.

As the engagement began, nearly one thousand American men had crossed the river and battled on the Canadian soil. After thirteen long hours, these Americans were on the verge of tasting victory. The only thing lacking was reinforcements. Upwards of five thousand of them, yes five thousand, stood on the American side of the Niagara River in the form of the New York militia. Young and inexperienced in fighting, they refused to cross the river and assist in finishing off the enemy. As a result, reinforcements shortly arrived and saved the day for the British. Americans, now outnumbered, stood no chance of winning and ran for their lives across the Canadian soil. When ordered to at least cross the river to aid the men who were now in retreat, the volunteers on the American shore still refused to board boats and assist in the rescue. They looked on as some of their fellow citizens chose to jump off a cliff over the river rather than die by the hand of the enemy.

After the fact, the militia cited a loophole in their contracts which stated that they were not obligated to fight on foreign soil. This was true enough, but from its onset, the venture inherently included a confrontation on Canadian soil, as the goal was to capture Queenstown Heights—in Upper Canada. How could all these Americans watch their fellows meet their death or capture by the enemy? A little insight may be gained from reading a correspondence made a month earlier by Van Rensselaer to the New York governor. In his letter Van Rensselaer expressed his concerns regarding the disposition of the militia. "Alarm pervades the country, and distrust among the troops. They are incessantly pressing for furloughs under every possible pretence. Many are without shoes, all clamorous for pay; many are sick . . ."[3] Van Rensselaer himself was a Federalist and that added some political uneasiness to the situation as well, since the Federalists were not in favor of this war from the onset. One other widely known, but little admitted to, factor which created much apprehension was the presence of the Mohawk Indians. Their reputation, this day enhanced by their chilling hoots and war yells echoing across the river, had absolutely terrified the young untrained citizens who had volunteered for this militia. Such was the power of intimidation and fear wielded by the Indians.

In spite of the British victory, there was mourning in the British ranks for the death of their heroic leader, General Isaac Brock. While leading a charge of his men this day at Queenstown Heights he was struck down. It was a great loss to both Canadian and British patriots, but it would foster a greater resolve throughout their ranks to fight this war.

In contrast to the land battles, several conflicts were won at sea by the United States. Early on, The USS *Essex* defeated the British *Alert*, and the USS *Constitution* overpowered the British ship *Guerriere*. In late October, 1812, just after the American citizenry learned of their troop's embarrassing loss at Queenstown Heights, the frigate named the *United States* overtook the *Macedonian*. When this British ship was brought into New York harbor as spoils, the spirits of the American spectators swelled. The nation as a whole finally had some of her pride and hope restored in the war effort. Consider that some of the sailors on-board the *Macedonian* when it was conquered were impressed Americans who were used to being whipped into British service. No, not metaphorically whipped up into an enthusiastic frenzy to serve, but physically whipped by the orders of the British Captain James Surman Carden, known as a *lover of whip discipline*. And, consider that many of the British sailors on the *Macedonian* deserted to the United States after its capture. A final slap in the British face came when their own ship's musical band actually led the Americans' victory parade through the streets of New York City![4]

As 1813 dawned, the American land forces continued to meet defeat. On the 23rd day of January, a massacre of American men took place along the Raisin River (present-day Monroe, Michigan). This atrocity, ironically, energized the American spirit. With a surprise attack, a combined force of British and Indians, lead by General Henry Procter defeated the American encampment. Many of the Americans were killed in the battle, but many more were taken prisoner. It can safely be said that Gen. Procter was at best *careless* in his protection of his sick and wounded American prisoners of war. Procter left the area shortly after the battle, and thus abdicated his responsibility of protecting the POWs. His Indian allies, left to their own volition, brutally tortured and killed almost all of the defenseless, wounded men. Most of the victims were young Kentuckians, who because of their bravery and the uncivilized manner in which they were murdered, became immortalized to this day by the motto that inspired the American troops henceforth–*Remember the Raisin!*

As winter turned to spring in 1813, the Americans continued on the offensive. Their first bona-fide land victory finally came on April 27, 1813 at York, present-day Toronto, which was the capital of Upper Canada (Ontario) at that time.

A success at last was indeed sweet, but it was costly in at least two ways. First, one of America's most prominent personalities was lost. Here on the northern shore of Lake Ontario, while personally leading several hundred American soldiers along a dirt road approaching the fort, the American commander seemed certain of an easy victory. His docked ship fired cannon balls over his head at the stronghold ahead. A few more minutes and the day would be won. But very unexpectedly a nearby ammunitions building was purposefully blown up by the enemy. The flying debris was the last thing ever seen by this Brigadier General and several of his men. After trekking across vast stretches of America to find the sources of the Mississippi and Arkansas rivers, and then having a mountain peak named after him, General Zebulon Pike was killed at the age of thirty-four.

Vengeance for the loss of this American icon was inevitable and led to the second major consequence of this victory. History shows some argument over who, if anyone, ordered the burning of the rest of the main government buildings in York by the Americans, but they were burned down. Some Americans, in their anger, also took it upon themselves to loot the abandoned Canadian militiamen's homes. These actions unfortunately laid the groundwork, in the British mind, as justification for similar retaliatory measures when they later successfully attacked Washington City.

By the summer of 1813, the war had expanded from the Northwest and high seas arenas into other regions of the nation. Near present-day Mobile, Alabama, the Creek Indians massacred Americans at Fort Mims. This led to retaliatory actions by the Americans under Andrew Jackson, both there, and later to the south in New Orleans. Other battles were fought in Florida, North Carolina and Virginia. But here in the Northwest Territory a new series of battles which would conclude with Battle of the Thames was begun in early 1813. The majority of the men who would participate in all or most of these successive conflicts in the vicinity of Lake Erie were Kentuckians.

CHAPTER 4

The Call to Kentucky

KENTUCKY PATRIOTISM
A CALL FOR THE MOUNTED REGIMENT–

The Regiment of mounted Volunteers was Organized under the
Authority of the War department to await the Call or to meet any Crisis
which might involve the honor, the right, and the safety of the Country.

That Crisis has arrived! Fort Meigs is attacked–the
North Western army is Surrounded by the enemy, and under the
Command of Gen'l Harrison nobly defending the Sacred Cause of the
Country against a Combined enemy, the British & Indians. They
will maintain the ground until relieved, the intermediate garrisons are
also in imminent danger & may fall a bleeding Sacrifice to
Savage Cruelty, unless timely reinforced, the frontiers may be
deluged in blood, the Mounted Regiment will present a Shield to the
defenceless and United with the forces Marching, and the Ohio
volunteers raising for the same purpose, the enemy will be driven from
our Soil therefore on Thursday the 20th of this month (May)
the regiment will rendezvous at the Great Crossings, Scott County;
except the Companies and fractions of Companies, raised in Henry,
Gallatin, Boone, Campbell, Pendleton, Bracken and Mason will
rendezvous on the 22nd at Newport; at which place the whole Corps
will Draw arms, Rifles and Muskets, ammunition and such Camp
Equipage as may be necessary.

The Staff of the Regt. will be put in immediate requisition,
and from Newport to the Rapids, forage with rations will be provided,
also forage from the Great Crossings to Newport. Each Man
will take 10 or 15 days provisions and go
as lightly burthened as possible.

The fractions of Companies shall be organized at the Great
Crossings and at Newport, at which place Commissions from the
Governor will be given to each officer. Every Arrangement Shall be
made, there shall be no delay–The Soldier's wealth is honor–connected
with his country's cause is its Liberty, independence and glory,
without exertions Rezin's bloody scene may be acted over again and to
permit would stain the national character.

The companies or fractions of companies will therefore be
punctual in their attendance. The officers of every description
belonging to this Corps, upon receipt of this order will
proceed forthwith to aid in its execution.

(Signed) RH. M. JOHNSON,
Col. Rgt. Mt. Vol.[1]

By May of 1813, Colonel Richard Mentor Johnson had had enough of the indecisiveness emanating from Washington City. He had been writing to John Armstrong, the Secretary of War, for months trying to secure permission to move his mounted regiment of Kentucky militiamen to the aid of Major-General William Harrison. No responses came. Finally, he boldly informed Armstrong in a letter dated May 12, 1813. "I enclose you a handbill (introductory quote) which will apprise you of the rendezvous of the Mounted Regiment. It is to be regretted that a state of things should exist which leaves no doubt upon our minds as to the propriety of anticipating your wishes as to our march; at a crisis so momentous to the Western Country . . ."[2] The Kentucky legislature met Johnson's handbill with applause. The heading *Kentucky Patriotism* was enthusiastically added by Richard's proud father Robert Johnson, himself a member of the Kentucky legislature. Robert personally took the lead in circulating his son's call to action across the state.

In the months previous to this valiant move by Johnson, many leading personalities of the day had been shuffled into new roles. Key amongst these was: Isaac Shelby who at age sixty-two was again elected governor of Kentucky; William H. Harrison who was made a major-general and commander of the Northwest Army; Richard M. Johnson himself who was promoted to colonel of the one thousand-strong Kentucky mounted militia regiment; and John Armstrong who was appointed Secretary of War by President Madison.

Miscommunications and disputes over authority between these major players during this period of time seriously disrupted the war effort. John Armstrong seemed to be the flash-point of most controversies. In an exhaustive history written by Henry Adams, John's great-grandson, it is explained:

> Against Harrison, Armstrong from the first entertained a prejudice. Believing him to be weak and pretentious, the Secretary of War showed the opinion by leaving him in nominal command in the northwest, but sending all his troops in different directions, without consulting him even in regard to movements within his own military department.[3]

Adams further relates:

> John Armstrong was an unusual character . . . the faculty of doing a harsh act in a harsh way, and of expressing rough opinions in a caustic

tone, was not what the Virginians most disliked in Armstrong. His chief fault in their eyes, and one which they could not be blamed for resenting, was his avowed want of admiration for the Virginians themselves.[4]

Armstrong was a bit arrogant about his *modern* New York heritage and seemed to talk down to the simpler, *old-fashioned* Virginians who were active in the affairs around Washington.

In spite of Armstrong's services, abilities, and experience, something in his character always created distrust . . . but he suffered from the reputation of indolence and intrigue. So strong was the prejudice against him that he obtained only eighteen votes against fifteen in the Senate on his confirmation [as Secretary of War]; and while the two senators from Virginia did not vote at all, the two from Kentucky voted in the negative.[5]

Even President Madison admitted years later his reluctance to nominate Armstrong to the position saying he did so only because other more capable and less controversial men declined the opportunity.

Isaac Shelby was only a few months into his term as the fifth governor of Kentucky at this time. Twenty years earlier he had been elected as the state's first leader. Now at age sixty-three, beloved and re-elected, he was requested and authorized by his fellow statesmen to form, and personally lead, a new militia force into battle. Shelby was a soldier for much of his life, a heroic fighter in the Revolution and an honorable statesman. He originally had no plans of running for another term as Governor. But, only a month before the election, because of the impending military conflicts (which he personally wanted to direct), and through popular persuasion; he threw his hat back into the political ring and won handily. An illustration of his character can be seen in an event that occurred after the Thames battle had been fought. The U.S. Congress had authorized a commemorative gold coin to be cast for each of two heroes of the Thames, Harrison and Shelby. Due to some public outcry over a few of Harrison's military decisions, the Congress put Harrison's award temporarily on hold. When Shelby was apprised of this decision, besides being personally appalled at the public questioning of Harrison's character; he told his fellow congressmen that he would not accept any medal unless Harrison received his concurrently. In short order, both coins were minted and presented.

Aside from this later probe into some of his military discretions, Harrison was an esteemed political and military personality. With a stellar military career already behind him by 1811, Harrison found himself back in uniform and leading a force of Americans against the hostile Indians. Attacks and threats of attacks had become more frequent in the western country, so when Harrison defeated the Shawnee village belonging to Tecumseh and the Prophet along the Tippecanoe River in Indiana, it vaulted him to a new level of celebrity. By the spring of 1813, he had already served over twelve years as the Governor of the Indiana Territory which included present-day Indiana and much of what would become Illinois, Wisconsin and Michigan. Throughout much of this time period he also served as Superintendent for Indian Affairs in the American Northwest. Harrison had long been recognized by his peers as a savvy politician. He frequently and successfully employed these negotiating skills in his dealings with the Indians, thus securing more of their lands for the United States. The deals struck for the acreage in the Northwest Territory, would fuel the disdain between Harrison and Tecumseh. So we see that Harrison found himself wearing three hats: he acted as Governor, Indian Diplomat, and Military Commander. With the war effort being earnestly pressed in the summer of 1812, his military hat had the best fit.

One of Harrison's first moves as the new head of the Army was to solicit Kentucky in August, 1812 to provide a militia in support of the efforts of General Hull at Detroit. Richard M. Johnson was the man who answered the call. He raised a mounted infantry of five hundred men and in little over a week the force was organized and on its way north. Richard Johnson, a representative of Kentucky in the United States Congress at the time, was no ordinary politician. He was a restless and relentless patriot. A war hawk, to be certain, he verbally fought for the war to be declared and when such took effect he personally fought in it. He saw no honor in directing others to fight while he lounged in his safe, comfortable chair in Washington City (as Washington, D.C. was known at this time). He repeatedly took the initiative to organize and personally lead whoever he could to seek out the enemy and engage them.

So it was on August 31, 1812, from Georgetown, Kentucky, that Johnson moved out his hastily formed mounted militia toward Detroit. They were dispatched as aid to General Hull who, as we already reviewed, would have a quite unsuccessful campaign. At their first stop

heading north, Newport, Kentucky, the men learned of Hull's surrender. Shaken by the news, they awaited word from Harrison as to their
next move. It was feared that further trouble would erupt at Fort Wayne
as a result of this loss of Detroit, and so Harrison ordered Johnson and
his cavalry to continue northward and to destroy the troublesome Potawatomie village in the Fort Wayne vicinity. Johnson's militia handled
their task. Less than two months after their call-up, with tensions eased
for the moment, Harrison honorably discharged Johnson's regiment in
October 1812, stating, "These men have rendered the most essential
service to their country . . . The General feels particular obligation to
Col. R. M. Johnson, for his zeal and ability."[6] Zeal indeed–that may
be the most apt word to define Richard Mentor Johnson as we will
further witness.

Johnson left the battlefield and took a brief respite from military
action. On November 4, 1812 he returned to his seat in Washington
City. He was just in time to hear the reading of Madison's annual
message to Congress (what would later become known as the State
of the Union address). In it the president encouraged his citizenry by
expressing his confidence in the new commander of the Northwest,
William H. Harrison, and by praising his first prompt success, the for-
tifying of Fort Wayne.

Six days later, a restless Johnson presented to Congress a resolution to take a mounted force once again on the offensive. This time,
he wanted to immediately take out the hostile Indians on the frontier.
He reasoned that right now, this winter, was the time to strike since
the ground of the *Black Swamp*, which covered much of northwest
Ohio, was still frozen. Though endorsed by Congress, when his plan
was sent to Harrison for final approval it was dismissed. Harrison laid
out very valid and practical reasons for rejecting the plan based on the
knowledge he had of the traditional behavior of the Indians during
winter. Frustrated, but understanding, this decision would not in the
least diminish Johnson's fervor to engage the enemy.

On February 2, 1813, news of the revolting murder of young wounded Kentucky POWs at the Raisin River had reached the boys' home
state. While Isaac Shelby and many of the inhabitants of Frankfort,
Kentucky were enjoying a performance, Colonel Samuel Wells arrived at the local theatre and pulled the governor aside for a word.

Wells gave Shelby a note from Harrison which explained the trag-
edy suffered upon the sons and relatives of many of those who were
present with him at that moment. The news was passed along rapidly
through the playhouse and by the end of the show most of the audience was absent. A reporter from the *Niles Weekly Register* describes
the scene that night:

> You see fathers going about half distracted, while mothers, wives, and
> sisters are weeping at home. The voice of lamentation is loud; the dis-
> tress is deep; yet neither public nor private distress can damp the ardor
> of the people. Already they propose raising a new army to revenge the
> loss of their brave countrymen.[7]

Not only did these relatives have to cope with the loss of their loved
ones, but what so stirred their blood can be glimpsed in the narrative
of Mr. Mallary who was an eyewitness American participant in the
battle. Having been assigned to care for the wounded POWs, Mallary
explains that Procter, who left the prisoners behind and headed back
to Fort Amherstburg, had promised to send additional sleighs very
soon to carry the injured Americans up to the Canadian fortress. The
sleighs never arrived. Procter had left only a few British interpreters
as guards over the American prisoners. Soon these guards abandoned
their watch, leaving the wounded captives to the whims of the Indians.
Defenseless, and seeing that the Indians were already ransacking the
store houses, the Americans suffered and prayed that their worst fears
would not be realized. Mallory relates:

> But, alas! Instead of the sleighs, about an hour by sun, a great number
> of savages, painted with various colours, came yelling in the most hid-
> eous manner! These blood-thirsty, terrific savages, (sent here by their
> more cruel and perfidious allies, the British,) rushed into houses, where
> the desponding wounded lay, and insolently stripped them of their blan-
> kets, and all their best clothes, and ordered them out of the house! . . .
> My feeble powers cannot describe the dismal scenes here exhibited. I
> saw my fellow soldiers naked and wounded, crawling out of the houses
> to avoid being consumed in the flames. Some that had not been able to
> turn themselves on their beds for four days, through fear of being burned
> to death, arose and walked out and about through the yard. Some cried
> for help, but there was none to help them . . . The savages rushed on the
> wounded, and, in their barbarous manner, shot and tomahawked, and
> scalped them; and cruelly mangled their naked bodies while they lay

agonizing and weltering in their blood. A number were taken towards Malden (Fort Amherstburg), but being unable to march with speed, were inhumanely massacred. The road was, for miles, strewed with the mangled bodies, and all of them were left like those slain in battle on the 22d, for birds and beasts to tear into pieces and devour.[8]

Harrison was several miles south of the River Raisin when a few American survivors of this attack ran into his troops. They told him of the surprise British assault. With horrific detail, they described the battle and the subsequent massacre of the American prisoners. Since the size of Colonel Henry Procter's force was believed to be extremely large, and presumed to be in hot pursuit of him, Harrison had no choice but to order a retreat. Only later was it learned that Procter had himself retreated back to Malden in Upper Canada, in fear of Harrison's large approaching force. Like repelling magnets, the two armies were now headed in opposite directions. The only good to come of this was a little time for Harrison to strategize his next move.

Any further loss of territory in Ohio had to be avoided. For this and other reasons, not the least of which was the fact that Lake Erie had not completely frozen over, the original drive into Upper Canada was delayed. Harrison decided to establish two new posts in northwestern Ohio. One was built on a bluff along the rapids of the Maumee River (present-day Perrysburg, Ohio, ten miles south of Toledo) and was named in honor of the then Governor of Ohio, Return Jonathon Meigs, Jr. It was constructed under the discerning engineering eye of Captain Eleazar Wood. (The county, in which this fort still stands, bears his name.) It would be attacked within months of its completion by the joint forces of Procter and Tecumseh–twice. The first assault began on April 28th and ended on May 9th of 1813. The second attack lasted from July 21st through the 28th. The other stronghold built at about the same time was at Lower Sandusky (present-day Fremont, Ohio) and was named Fort Stephenson after its builder Colonel Mills Stephenson. In August of 1813, it too would be the site of an attack from the same forces that had besieged Fort Meigs earlier. This fight would go down in history as one of the greatest victories of *the few over the many* ever to be recorded. But all of this was yet to occur.

As February of 1813 unfolded, what with Hull's defeat at Detroit, the loss of Mackinac, and now this massacre at the Raisin River, it's obvious to see how tempers and patriotism rose to a fever pitch across the country, particularly in Kentucky. The idea of waiting weeks for communications to be sent back and forth between Washington City and Kentucky in order to determine the next course of action was just not acceptable. Kentucky quickly took matters into its own hands and that was ultimately fortunate for the country.

The Kentucky legislature authorized three thousand troops to be raised immediately and to be lead by the new Governor himself, Isaac Shelby. At this time, Johnson proposed to the new Secretary of War, John Armstrong, that a mounted militia regiment be raised yet again, as a part of these troops being recruited in Kentucky. He suggested that this mounted regiment of volunteers be trained and held in reserve for duty. Because it was militia, not regular army, the idea was a bit novel – a trained and armed force of locals that could be formed-up and moving within days of a call to action. Johnson wrote, "I will take any place or situation that the men may give me – I want nothing for my trouble or services – If any opportunity of service offers, I do not wish to be idle during the recess of Congress . . ."[9] Surprisingly, only a few days later Armstrong responded, "You are hereby authorized to organize and hold in readiness, a regiment of mounted Volunteers."[10] Said regiment was immediately recruited, trained and standing by. As the saying goes, *all dressed up and nowhere to go*, was now ringing true. Johnson and the men knew there was indeed a place to go; it was north to the aid of Harrison who was at this time under siege at Fort Meigs. But Johnson needed federal authority from John Armstrong to put the men in motion. The repeated snub of his letters by Armstrong enraged Johnson. As explained in his final letter to the Secretary of War on May 12th, Johnson's men gathered as requested by his handbill (the introductory quote), at the Great Crossings on May 20, 1813.

Back in March, before Johnson's regiment was formed, Isaac Shelby had already dispatched General Green Clay to the aid of Harrison. Clay and his twelve-hundred Kentuckians were deliberate in their effort to reach Fort Meigs, but the swollen waterways and the muck of the *Black Swamp* in the spring delayed their arrival time by weeks. They finally landed on the shores of the Maumee River in May, a few days into the on-going siege by Procter and Tecumseh upon the fort. Their appearance turned the day to the favor of the Americans and played a significant part in shortening the ultimately unsuccessful attack upon the fortress.

In spite of the continuous battles in the area, there was a slow swelling of confidence in the American effort through the winter and spring of 1813. Israel Harrington, a life-long resident along the southern shores of Lake Erie explains, "permit me to observe, that when it was known that Gen. Harrison was appointed to the command of the army, that it gave universal satisfaction throughout the country, and as soon as the army moved on to Fort Meigs, [February, 1813] the former inhabitants returned to their homes as far north and west as Lower Sandusky."[11] With good reason, many of the settlers in northern Ohio, and what would become southern Michigan, had fled their homes when the war had begun in June of 1812. Some had left even sooner due to the random persistent attacks by the Indians against their homesteads. Curiously, Fort Meigs itself was built on property owned by Major Amos Spafford and his family. Spafford, the first settler in what would become Perrysburg, Ohio, gave up a large portion of his acreage to the government for construction of the fortress. With battles imminent he left the area, just as many other residents had, returning only when the fighting had ended. (A few years later, in 1816 Spafford would name his growing river town to the honor of Commodore Oliver H. Perry in lieu of his recent naval victory over the British fleet). We can see that by April, 1813 the new Fort Meigs and Fort Stephenson provided the citizenry with a certain level of optimism. Harrison had established his presence and continuously worked on his plans to drive into Canada. The Americans' situation seemed on the brink of a positive turnaround prompted even more so by Johnson's mounted regiment soon to be heading north to reinforce the effort.

As requested in Johnson's handbill, on Thursday, the 20th of May, over a thousand men assembled, knowing they might not return to their families. These men, who would serve together for five months, march some four hundred miles away from their homes, and fight side-by-side along a river they had never before heard of in Upper Canada, had immediately jelled into a regiment. Richard Johnson oversaw the proceedings that day at what was known as the Great Crossings, very near Georgetown, Kentucky. Great Crossings was an obvious choice for Johnson as that was his childhood hometown. Even more men

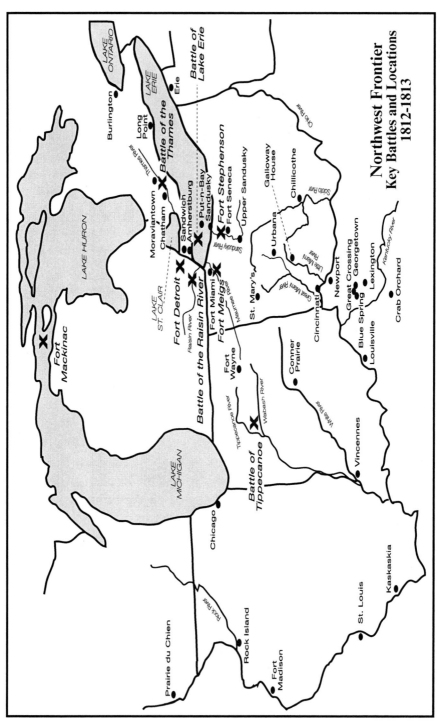

Northwest Frontier
Key Battles and Locations
1812-1813

Map created by Author.

Portrait of William Henry Harrison
drawn on stone by Chas. Fenderich from a painting by Mr. Franquinet.

Portrait of Henry Procter by J.C.H. Forster.

gathered at Newport, KY and would be met soon by Johnson and this group.

From counties all across the state, men arrived singly and in groups. One of them was a young man, who that day was only eighteen years old. He rode into town with a few of his buddies and relatives from the heart of Kentucky–Lincoln County. His name was David King.

King had to be proud to see such a good showing of volunteers from his neighborhood. George Davidson, his cousin, enlisted as a private just as he had. His friend Thomas Clark was made a 4th Corporal right off. His uncles, Mike and James Davidson, enlisted. In fact, James would be made a Captain and assigned command of the very company that David and many of his friends would serve in. A neighbor of David's, an old man with more energy than many of the youth who had volunteered, rode into town with distinct purpose. His name was William Whitley.

Already a renowned personality throughout Kentucky, Whitley wanted nothing but the opportunity to serve his country again. He was one of the early American pioneers who spent his whole life trying to make Kentucky and the nation safe from Indian attacks and free from British control. He could have rightfully been made a general in this expedition, but signed the roster as a private in Captain Davidson's company. Serving *on his own hook*, as it was referred to, he participated with no expectation of pay. Before, throughout and since the Revolution, Whitley had repeatedly proven his patriotism and fighting skills.

Many other men arrived who would later be noted as major players in the events yet to unfold. One of them was Robert McAfee, a law graduate from Transylvania University in Lexington, KY. As well as being a seasoned military man, McAfee served in the Kentucky Congress both before and after this military march. His highest political office would be attained in 1824 when he became Lieutenant Governor of the state. It is believed McAfee came to befriend Johnson as they studied law together. When he met his fellow volunteers this day, he was awarded a Captain's commission from Governor Shelby. The journal he kept of the adventures of his one hundred and forty-man company in Johnson's regiment is a national treasure, shining light on the events and conditions endured. Later, McAfee would write a full narrative of the war titled *The History of the Late War in the Western Country.*

Another man of note who arrived at Great Crossings was Major David Thompson. At the Thames, Thompson was second in command under Johnson, and would end up taking full command of the front lines against the Indians after Johnson was wounded and carried off. Thompson also was a lawyer schooled at Transylvania University and was a senator in the Kentucky legislature before and after his service at the Thames.

Of course James Johnson, Richard's brother was there too. He would lead half of the mounted regiment against the British lines as they engaged Procter at the Thames. He had served in Kentucky's legislature before the war and years later would be elected to the U. S. Congress.

It is an intriguing fact that so many state and federal politicians, most of whom were sitting, elected officials volunteered to risk their lives by joining either Johnson's mounted regiment or Shelby's infantry. After the Thames battle, even more of these participants would reach political office on the basis of their heroic efforts there. For instance, Captain James Davidson would go on to become a state senator and treasurer; C. S. Todd, who came from a distinguished family of lawyers, and was commissioned as a captain and personal aid to Harrison, would later serve in several political offices including Secretary of State in Kentucky. He organized the volunteers gathering at Newport for the march to Fort Meigs. Joseph Desha was there with Todd, having just left his congressional seat in Washington to become the leader of a full division of men at the Thames. Years later Desha would be elected Governor of Kentucky.

The list of men who were or would become political figures and risked everything at the Thames is staggering. It seems that in 1813 any idea of using one's position as an elected official as an inherent excuse to not participate in actual battle was unheard of, especially in Kentucky. These men, who were in powerful political positions, relished rather than relinquished the opportunity to serve their country on the battlefield—more than willing to put their life on the line for their beliefs, their families, and their country.

CHAPTER 5

North to Lake Erie

The Mounted Regiment shall march in five lines . . .
Each flank shall furnish videts [advance guards] to their respective lines.
The different lines will keep the distance of two hundred yards
from each other when the wood will admit. A Spy department
shall be organized, which shall furnish a front and rear guard
to the regiment spies for the purpose of giving information
as to the enemy. This department shall keep spies
a mile or further in advance
of the advance guard . . . [1]

When dawn broke on the 21st day of May, 1813, the men who had camped overnight about the Great Crossings area gathered up their belongings and readied their horses for a long march. Imagine being an onlooker that day as one of your loved ones sought out his proper place in the formation. What a spectacle of men and beasts, weapons and supplies, all being transformed from random anticipation into orderly motion. Can you hear the officers barking out orders, the clanks and clunks of supply wagons juggling their loads on cobblestone streets, and the anxious chatter of the men? Can you hear the horses' hooves clattering against the road as they are led slowly here, and ridden briskly there? What a pounding must have thumped the bodies present as more than a thousand horsemen finally formed into columns within their companies. After a brief attentive silence, the order to move out echoes from one officer to the next and the knock of iron against the earth swells to a deafening roar only to soon fade slowly into the countryside. For these brave frontiersmen it was on to Newport a mere seventy miles due north at the Ohio River, just opposite Cincinnati. They would there unite with even more volunteers from the north-eastern counties of Kentucky, to be supplied with food and arms.

Only twelve miles into their journey, however, confusion would strike as a lone soldier approached them on horseback. Ironically, it was in this very same vicinity of Kentucky only eight months earlier that Johnson's first regiment was bewildered to learn of Hull's surrender. That news had redirected their initial effort then, the message of this rider threatened to do the same now.

The front company halted as the distressed horseman rode up to them. He was escorted back to the commanding officers to deliver his message. Immediately, Richard and James recognized their kid brother, John Johnson. Wounded and with fever, he had been riding for days from Fort Meigs where he had been doing his part to repulse the seige of Proctor and Tecumseh. His message was from Harrison himself, it stated that the General was now *not* authorized to receive their unit. The siege of the fort had ceased, and Johnson's men were no longer needed. Perplexed and incredulous that yet again he was stymied, after all his effort to raise this regiment, Johnson considered his next move. It didn't take long. Richard over-ruled Harrison's message, at least for the moment, and ordered the men to resume their course toward Newport. With eagerness, tempered by puzzlement, the men turned north again.

The regiment soon camped for the night and rode again all the next day. They stopped the following night along a ridge near the residence of Samuel Theobold. A studied physician and lawyer, and another alumnus of Transylvania University, Theobold would join the regiment here and be assigned as a personal advocate to Colonel Richard Johnson. Later, just before the start of the battle of the Thames, he would be one of only twenty men to volunteer as a frontline attacker in a group referred to as the *Forlorn Hope*. This station allowed him to provide first-hand testimony of the fight which would become one of the primary accounts used by early historians to document the events of that day, especially the movements of Col. Richard Johnson.

On the following morning, the 23rd, Johnson and some of his officers rode ahead to Cincinnati, where Harrison happened to be making a quick visit to his family. Harrison received them cordially and explained the regrets he had, but confirmed that he was not able to accept their services. Johnson, not to be dismissed so easily, promptly wrote a letter. He addressed it to Harrison, delivered it to him later that day, and certainly believed it would find its way to John Armstrong, which it did. Johnson wrote:

> The attack upon Fort Meigs, the small force which you were known to have to defend that important post . . . Induced me to anticipate the wishes of the President and Secretary of War in marching the Regt. of Mounted Volunteers to your command with every practicable dispatch

. . . After having fixed the day of Rendezvous I was happy to receive a letter from the Secretary of War in which he intimated that you were authorized to call the Regt . . . I considered it my indispensible duty to march the Regt. to the Ohio River and prepare for actual service. I am well convinced that if the Regt. should now be dismissed, it cannot easily be collected . . . I am now anxiously awaiting to know what is your determination and whether you consider the service of the Regt. at this time important and necessary . . . I am convinced that whatever course you may pursue, it will meet the entire approbation of the President of the U. States and Secretary of War.[2]

Gen. Harrison took Johnson's reasoning to heart and wrote to Armstrong that very day, attaching Johnson's letter, and explaining that he was going to use Johnson's men after all. For the moment they would be sent in the defense of Fort Winchester (near present-day Defiance, Ohio and approximately fifty miles southwest of Fort Meigs). Of course the spirits of the men rose once again with this news, and Johnson led his contingent toward their first extended stop, St. Mary's, Ohio, a supply depot midway between Dayton and Fort Winchester.

It was here at St. Mary's that it became necessary to establish an impromptu gunsmith shop. Johnson directed the captains of each company to be earnest in overseeing that each man's weapon was in proper working order. Target practice was encouraged, with supervision of course, so that every volunteer was certain of their weapon's ability, as well as their personal aim. About a month later, having endured these extra measures, Johnson couldn't resist taking a bit of a jab at Armstrong for providing his men with such shoddy armaments. In a letter to the Secretary he pointed out that most of the government issued weapons were "without sights, without main springs, without screws &c.,"[3] and that if he hadn't taken the initiative to bring along a number of experienced gunsmiths, his men would have been seriously handicapped.

As the men journeyed further north, spring unfolded into summer but the travel became more and more difficult. This part of the country was far from ordinary. Most of the northwestern quarter of the new state of Ohio was so treacherous and foreboding that it was appropriately dubbed The *Black Swamp*. In fact it was a giant quagmire, correct by both definitions of that word – a marshland and a predicament (at least for anyone attempting to tread across it). Damp heavy air permeated this bug-infested region in summer. Stagnant ponds fostered the growth of disease-laden micro-organisms and malaria-carrying mosquitoes that lay in wait for a suitable victim. Stretches of dense forest blocked the sun's rays, making one's travel through it feel all the more dismal. Occasional clearings would delight the traveler's soul with their acres of wild flowers and tall grasses, but lurking here and there below these beautiful canopies were pockets of murky waters teeming with snakes and multiple unknown hazards.

If we momentarily step back in time just a few months, the struggles faced by the militia of Petersburg, Virginia will highlight the dangers of the *Black Swamp* in winter. While Johnson's regiment had been making their way northward from Kentucky during the warming months of spring on a path just a few miles inside and along the western border of Ohio; these Virginians had trekked during the cold of the previous winter westward across the middle and northern area of the state from its eastern edge. The Virginians' purpose was the construction of the fortress Johnson would eventually be heading toward – Fort Meigs.

A Methodist minister, Rev. Alfred M. Lorraine, a member of this group of Petersburg volunteers, gives an eyewitness perspective on some of the winter hardships endured as he and his fellow Americans traversed the bog on their way to the Maumee River. Rev. Lorraine explains that his contingent of men had to march through what the frontiersmen referred to as the swales or stagnant ponds of the swamp.

> Those swales were often a quarter of a mile long. They were, moreover, very unequal in their soundings. In common, they were not more than half-leg deep; but sometimes, at a moment when we were not expecting it, we suddenly sank down to our cartridge-boxes. While fording such places our feet would get so be-numbed that we seemed to be walking on rags . . .
>
> Occasionally a poor packhorse would fall down in its track – if tracks they were – to rise no more, forever. It was heart-rending to see them roll their flashing eyes indignantly on the passing soldiers, as though to rebuke the madness of the people in driving to such an extremity of suffering. Droves of hogs, which had been abandoned to the wilds, grim, gaunt, and hungry as the grave, were squealing through the woods, and rooting up the snow; and under the relentless scourge of war the whole creation seemed to groan in pain . . . Some may think that we are exaggerating, but several of our young men fell victims to diseases which were engendered by the march through the *Black Swamp*.[4]

Rev. Lorraine further points out that beyond the environmental hazards, hunger plagued the men. Little more was available than flour for biscuits, and occasionally some pork. More often than not, there was no time to eat, what with the incessant marching. One such day, Lorraine and his company of malnourished men came upon a large field of corn.

> As soon as we entered this inviting field, the army broke in every direction, like a drove of frightened cattle. Deaf to the commands of our officers, and regardless of all military order, we tore down the precious ears, and filled our pockets and our bosoms until we were richly laden with the spoils of the field. With musket in one hand, and an ear of corn in the other, we marched on, greedily devouring the unstinted supply of a merciful Providence. No pound cake ever tasted half as delicious, until the wire-edge of our starvation was worn off. We were amazed that we had lived so long in the world, and had never discovered before the transcendent luxury of raw corn.[5]

With clothing and footwear ashamedly insufficient for the challenging conditions, they marched on until they arrived at the bluff over the Maumee River. The trek through the swamp was over, but their work was just about to begin. Trees needed to be felled, hauled, cut and posted into troughs as walls of protection. Pick axes and shovels ricocheted off the frozen ground in their attempt to dig trenches. Snow piled up, often upon their very selves as they slept many a night without a tent to cover them. Blustery winds had nothing to block their bite. Yet, through it all, the men of the Petersburg, Virginia militia had turned a barren rise of land over a northern Ohio River into a fortress.

Naturally, some of the miserable conditions improved with the completion of the stronghold, but many remained and new threats would blossom.

> The winter was unusually severe, even on the frontiers. One unfortunate sentinel froze at his post in less than two hours . . . Numbers were swept off by the mumps, measles, whooping cough, and other distempers, which came upon them at this unpropitious time and place, where there was little remedy and less medical skill, and where the soft hand of the warm-hearted mother . . . could not reach them. They died daily . . . the sharp rifle cracks of the platoon told how many were borne to their long home. A deadly homesickness overwhelmed our troops, and we believe a repentance of war was kindled in every bosom, from the highest to the lowest.[6]

It is a sad historical fact that so many men were taken ill or dying from circumstances other than combat. The records of troops listed as participating in many of the battles of this era, especially in the North-west Territory conflicts, were very misleading. Often, upwards of a full third of the men listed as present, were in fact too sick or wounded to actually fight. Still others died from disease, hunger and extreme fatigue on the way to battle. This explains some of the discrepancies in the accounts of historians as to the actual size of the forces squaring off in various confrontations. But let's not forget, as well, the prejudices which sometimes inflated or deflated the numbers as deemed neces-sary to either excuse a defeat or to enhance a victory.

There was a very intriguing event which took place one day while the Petersburg militia was still constructing Fort Meigs.

> One afternoon, as numbers were gathered together on the "parade," two strangers, finely mounted, appeared on the western bank of the river [the opposite shore], and seemed to be taking a very calm and deliberate survey of our works. It was a strange thing to see travelers in that wild country, and we commonly held such to be enemies, until they proved themselves to be friends. So one of our batteries was cleared forthwith, and the gentlemen were saluted with a shot that tore up the earth about them, and put them to a hasty flight. If that ball had struck its mark much bloodshed might have been prevented; for we learned subsequently that our illustrious visitors were Proctor and Tecumseh.[7]

The first siege against Fort Meigs had begun three weeks before Johnson's regiment had even moved out of Great Crossings. The com-bined forces of General Henry Procter's Englishmen and Tecumseh's confederation of Indians attacked the fortress for the first eight days of May. Because of extensive traverses created inside the fort by the inhabitant's, the cannon balls and mortars of the enemy had only a minor effect. Long trenches, several feet deep and running parallel to the river, with the dirt mounded up many more feet in front of them; provided a perfect defense to the in-coming cannon balls. The men who were not on-duty simply huddled safely in the protective fur-rows. A frustrated Tecumseh was quoted in a speech to Col. Procter as saying, "It is hard to fight people who live like ground hogs."[8]

The battle ended in a stalemate of sorts as the enemy eventually re-treated. The regiment sent earlier by Governor Shelby, led by Green Clay, was instrumental in the victorious stance. The American's would have sustained only a few casualties, except for what became known as *Dudley's Defeat*. Col. William Dudley had led an attack on the British position across the river. After successfully spiking the enemy cannons, the men were enticed to pursue the Indians deeper into the woods away from the river. This was a cunning trap set by the Indians and by chasing them the men were disobeying a direct order of Harrison to return to the fort upon completion of their mission. Ending up right where the Indians wanted them, hundreds of men were soon surrounded and slaughtered, Dudley included.

The American survivors of this massacre were rounded up as prisoners and led to the British Fort Miami a mile away. Leslie Combs was one of their number. Many years later Combs explained:

> I never saw Tecumseh but once. The afternoon of the 5th of May, 1813 when Col. Dudley was defeated & killed on the north side of the Maumee river opposite Fort Meigs, on which occasion, then a beardless boy of 19, I was Capt. of a spy company of picked Kentucky riflemen. I commanded the vanguard – was severely wounded, taken prisoner and forced to run the gauntlet. In doing this I was not touched, although the man ahead of me was shot down and fell across my way. I did not stop . . . but leaped over his body & went through "double-quick." I was near Tecumseh when he made his speech, reported in history, whereby the lives of hundreds of prisoners were saved – of whom I was one . . . he was a truly great man and gallant warrior.[9]

Another person whose life was spared that day due to Tecumseh's timely arrival was Samuel Hatter. Alive and well, and somewhat ironically working at a historical museum (the Capital City Museum in Frankfort, KY), is one Russ Hatter. Russ says, "Our family has a special fondness for Tecumseh." One would bet such is the case since Russ would never have been born had not Tecumseh shown his character just before his great-great-great-grandfather Samuel had finished running the gauntlet that day in 1813![10]

It was at this event inside Fort Miami, to which Tecumseh arrived while the slaughter was already in progress, that he not only demonstrated his integrity but delivered one of his most colorful insults to Procter. After severely rebuking his own warriors, Tecumseh turned

> to Gen. Proctor, he demanded why such butchery had been permitted by him. The General replied that he could not restrain the savages. With a look

of withering scorn and contempt Tecumseh told Proctor that he was not fit to command men and that he ought, "to go home, and put on petticoats."[11]

Just as the men of Kentucky and Virginia were stirred to take up arms and leave their loved ones behind for the greater good, so too did men respond from other parts of the country. One such man was Alfred Brunson, originally of New York but now living near the southeastern shores of Lake Erie. He explains that with Hull's surrender, people as far west as where he had settled (close to the Pennsylvania border of northern Ohio) were terrified of the potential attacks forthcoming from both the British and Indians. In Alfred's words, "I concluded, with many others, that it was better to meet the foe by the side of companions in arms, and led by skillful officers, than to meet him at my own door, single-handed, and that perhaps, in the night."[12]

At this time Mr. Brunson was still a young man who was somewhat stymied in his bent toward a career of service to God as a Methodist minister. He felt that a brief diversion into the military might help him mature. He was moved by the recent loss of Benjamin Pierce (a revolutionary war hero and father of the future president Franklin Pierce) in the battle of Sandy Hook which occurred near his home. And so he explains that later

> when our ship, the *Chesapeake*, was fired into by the *Leopard*, and five of my wife's brothers had been impressed into the British Navy, and never again got home, my patriotic blood was up to fighting heat. And I enlisted for a year in the Twenty-Seventh Regiment, United States Infantry ... The company was recruited in Warren, Trumbull County, Ohio; and was marched to Cleveland, where it was organized, and I was appointed Orderly Sergeant. From Cleveland we went in open Mackinaw boats [flat-bottomed, canoe-shaped vessels usually about twenty feet long with a sail] loaded with corn, to Lower Sandusky, or Fort Stephenson.[13]

At the Sandusky Bay, he and his small group of fellow soldiers made do as best they could to cook a meal.

> We drew pork and flour, but we had no camp equipage, not yet having reached our regiment. We kindled fires of driftwood found on the beach. We took the flour, some pieces of bark, and some in dirty pocket handkerchiefs. If we had cups, we ladled the water from the bay into the flour, and those who had no cups lifted the water with their two hands so arranged as to form a cup. The flour was wet, without salt, yeast, or shortening; was

Image courtesy of The Minnesota Historical Society.

Portrait of Rev. Alfred Brunson. Artist Unknown.

baked, some on pieces of bark before the fire, hoe-cake or Johnny-cake fashion; and some removed the fire and put the dough into the hot sand, wrapped in leaves or paper. Our pork we cooked in the blaze of the fire, on points of sticks. Having a good appetite, I thought the bread baked in the hot sand was very sweet, and the pork very palatable.[14]

About the time Brunson was at the Sandusky Bay, Johnson's mounted regiment was still moving northward through Ohio, and in Kentucky even more volunteers were being molded into military companies in numerous cities as part of Shelby's overall recruitment efforts.

One rather flamboyant member of the 28th regiment, which formed at Lexington, relates some of his experiences during his march to Harrison's aid. He was known by the name of Terrence Kirby. During his first tour of duty, as a mere boy of sixteen, he fought with Harrison at Tippecanoe and the experience left an indelible mark on his spirit. "In our march, many times we found men, women and children slain and scalped; the children's brains on the walls of the house, where they had been dashed by the ruthless savages."[15]

His first tour of duty having been served, Kirby returned home to his loving mother in early 1813. But it was only a short time before word of the Raisin River massacre reached him.

> I volunteered at the first tap of the drum, to avenge their blood; and then marched to Lexington to organize a regiment of light dragoons . . . instead of dragoons, we were turned into United States Infantry; many were so displeased with the arrangement that they said they would not go; many employed legal counsel, to get clear, but failed; they had taken the bounty, and had to serve.[16]

Kirby's sentiments draw attention to a major military consideration of the time – *horses*. Governor Shelby knew the importance of men on horseback. In a letter to Harrison during the recruiting process, he highlighted the danger of confrontations with the Indians without them. "I am thoroughly convinced of the absolute necessity of a considerable force of cavalry or mounted Infantry in the advance, without it you will be perpetually harassed by small parties of Indians who will defy the pursuit of footmen . . ."[17] Indians on horseback would make easy game of tracking and killing men who were depending on their power of foot alone. Even General Procter observed the intimidation effect of Americans on horseback. "The Indians have always had a dread of cavalry of which the enemy have a considerable number."[18] The men instinctively understood this, and additionally, it was obvious that the trek of hundreds of miles, which was now upon them, would be much less burdensome on horseback.

But practical concerns had to balance with the obvious advantages of taking large numbers of horses on such a long march, especially through the *Black Swamp*. There was the mud that hindered the beasts who not only carried men on their backs, but also pulled cannons and wagons loaded with supplies. The animals also needed to eat. Enough forage to feed thousands of animals had to be anticipated the same way the food for the men was planned for and stocked at depots throughout the countryside. As Shelby readied his volunteers into service he pointed out to Harrison no less than five times, in letters sent over a two month period, the extreme need to secure provisions ahead of time.

> I need not observe to you how important it will be to have rations and forage laid in on the way, it will be impossible to move on without the latter . . . I beg you to attend to this subject and let me know what is to

be expected, seeing that you cannot be reinforced in any other way, the government must not stickle at the trifling expense of a little forage to obtain a sufficient force for the main objects of the campaign.[19]

From this last note of the Governor, we glimpse yet another current of trouble running through this river of war—*money*. In Shelby's eyes, the importance of payment for services rendered was second only to the need for food and forage; and was followed thirdly by the necessity of a massive overall military presence against the enemy, which he was recruiting. As early as March of 1813, Shelby expressed some alarm to Harrison regarding the payment that had been agreed upon for the volunteers.

> I have with considerable concern learned that the Militia who served under you [previous], have not received their pay. I do not know where the fault lies, nor that it will be in your power to remedy it; should it be, I know you will interpose with cheerfulness.[20]

As the troops had begun reporting for duty in Kentucky, they had heard rumors that only up to two thousand of the men would be paid for their service. Shelby himself asked Harrison, fearing such was the case, how he would possibly distinguish which two thousand of the probable four thousand volunteers were to receive the money? Reflecting on how this wore on the men, he further told Harrison that

> their ardor has greatly subsided & inquiry from all points is, "what pay are we to receive, shall we get paid for our lost horses and is forage laid on the way for them etc." I am greatly mortified at the present prospect, but shall continue to exert every power to get out as large a force as possible.[21]

So it was that besides the lack of proper provisions of clothing, food and medical personnel for the war effort at hand, so too the payment promised for risking one's life was in question. Don't be misled however. The fury of these Americans, especially of these frontiersmen, trumped all the short-comings of serving in this fight. Their rage over the murder of innocence, as well as the depravity shown by the enemy in the affairs of this war, prompted most to serve for the cause regardless of compensation. As well, many lived on these front lines and they would do anything to protect their families and their homesteads. But as human nature is prone to exhibit itself after the fact, what was promised was expected. At this point, and for some time to come, the United States government was ill-prepared to deliver on its financial pledge.

Image courtesy of U.S. Library of Congress.

Portrait of Isaac Shelby by Matthew H. Jouett.

Between March and September of 1813 company after company were arriving in northwest Ohio from the east coast as well as from the southern states. Each was moving into strategic positions in this Northwest Territory. Eventually, most of these infantry and militia units would unite as one massive force readied for the push into Canada.

Let's pickup the movements of the companies we've been following as of June, 1813.

The first seige of Fort Meigs has ended with the Americans still holding the fortress. Richard Johnson's regiment moved out of St. Mary's, with cleaned and retooled rifles and muskets during the first week of June, and headed to Fort Wayne. They combed the area around the fort for a week, as far north as the southern shores of Lake Michigan. Their mission was to confront and take out any pockets of hostile Indians. This mission completed, they moved on to Fort Winchester. It was a brief stop. All being in order, they continued on to Fort Meigs, arriving on June 22nd. A few days after their arrival, Harrison ordered Johnson to take a contingent force to the Raisin River for the purpose of scouting the enemy and to bury the corpses of the men whose bodies had been lying unburied for over five months.

About this time, Terrence Kirby had completed his march from Lexington, across the Ohio River, through Franklin, Ohio, on to Upper Sandusky, and finally arriving at Fort Seneca which was just 9 miles south of Fort Stephenson. While here, Harrison called for more volunteers to join Col. Johnson on his mission to the Raisin River. Kirby enthusiastically answered the call.

> I was the first boy that shouldered my musket, to make a forced march on the Indian trail, to meet their bloody tomahawks, scalping knives, war clubs and deadly rifles – Indians swearing in Indian language, like ten thousand wild panthers, in the wood, around my ears in the Black Swamp, they would have my hair or scalp before day, or make their hatchets or tomahawks drunk in my blood; but we got safe to Fort Meigs; then we marched down the river rapids. The second day we crossed the rapids at Fort Defiance; the third day we landed on the battlefield; the fourth day we took the town, ran the Indians off. There we commenced digging pits to bury the slain; with mournful beating hearts we threw them in . . .[22]

This was a second burial of what would be many burials of these beleaguered bones. Johnson again would be back to re-bury the same bones on his way to the Thames just two months later, which had been un-interred again by the Indians. The history of the mistreatment of these men's remains is amazing as they were unearthed yet again and finally re-buried by Shelby's men on their way home a week after the Thames victory. Sadly, the remains of these Kentuckians would continue to have a storied fate of repeated re-internment for years to come.

Shelby's infantry, numbering a few thousand, was organized in late August and headed into Ohio during the first week of September. On the ninth of the month, Shelby stopped in Urbana, Ohio and looked up his old buddy Simon Kenton. According to a friend of Kenton:

> The old governor insisted on Kenton going with him, not as a common soldier but as a counselor. He consented, and when they landed in Canada, Proctor, the British commander, had fled from Fort Malden, and then came a forced march to overtake him if possible. All were on foot except Col. R. M. Johnson's regiment. History tells the result of the campaign! After the army returned, Kenton was asked how he stood the forced march, [he] answered, very well, and could have marched as much farther at night (their march was 30 miles a day). This campaign was the last of his military services; for he was a little over sixty years of age.[23]

Simon Kenton was yet another legend in the annals of the early frontier life in America. He fought many a battle against the Indians. He encountered Tecumseh several times. Now, like William Whitley and Governor Shelby who were also in their sixties, he was willing and eager to fight for his country once more.

About this time a number of Indians who found it in their best interest to side with the Americans did so. Although Harrison was hesitant to trust any Indian tribes, he employed a number of the Delaware, Wyandot, Seneca and Mingo. William Conner was a trader among the Delawares in southern Indiana. Because of his close relationship with this friendly tribe, he was called upon by Harrison to serve as an interpreter during the Americans' trek north. Mr. Conner agreed and up to and through the Battle of the Thames he functioned as both interpreter and soldier. He would inadvertently have a key role in the battles to come, especially the attack upon Fort Stephenson.

On July 21st, Henry Procter returned to Fort Meigs to lay his second siege upon the structure. His men now addressed him by the same military title as his American nemesis William H. Harrison – that of *Major-General*. This higher rank was conferred upon him in recognition of his success at the Raisin River. Here at Fort Meigs Procter found himself trying to appease a large restless band of Indians who wanted to fight. They had already been growing impatient with his previous lack of action. The real threat at hand for Procter was that the Indians would grow so disgruntled they would abandon the British effort altogether; or worse, turn against them. Therefore he appeased them by approving a second attack on this fortress which loomed over the Maumee River, but he was neither confident nor earnest in the attempt.

This second assault was highlighted only by a ruse that the Indians tried to create under Tecumseh's direction. On the south-eastern side of the fort a large group of Indians pretended to be attacking an incoming band of American reinforcements. The strategy was for the inhabitants of the fort to witness their men in the field being attacked, thus enticing them to leave the fort and to come to their aid. Once out from behind the walls, the Indians would have the hand-to-hand fight they always preferred. The plan might have worked, except General Green Clay, in command of the fort at this point in time, knew that no reinforcements were expected. He further knew that more forces were gathering, and remaining, at Fort Seneca to which General Harrison had just retired.

With this second failure to capture Fort Meigs, Procter and Tecumseh decided to move eastward and do away with an easier target, Fort Stephenson; a much smaller fortress located at Lower Sandusky. This stronghold was the first line of defense for an American supply depot at Fort Seneca, situated just a few miles south of it. On the surface, it should have been an easy British/Indian victory, but the task would prove to be far from the simple affair they had expected.

Again, bands of men were in motion all across the state. Harrison had already moved a part of his force from Fort Meigs to the Fort Seneca supply depot (near present-day Tiffin, Ohio). Because he expected Procter and the Indians to attack the area with an overwhelming force, Harrison remained with his men at Fort Seneca to protect the massive store of munitions, food and other supplies. As the American spies had warned, Procter and the Indians under Tecumseh arrived in the area at the end of July. Fort Stephenson was under the command of a young Major named George Croghan who was all of twenty-one years old. With him were less than two hundred men and one lone six-pound cannon nicknamed *Old Betsy.*

Alfred Brunson and his company were heading south from the shores of Lake Erie toward Fort Seneca at this time and he explains:

> We were ordered into the line of march with several other companies for Seneca, ten miles up the Sandusky River. Here for the first time I saw General Harrison, then the lion of the North-West, who marched with us to Seneca. He expected an attack on the way, and gave the necessary orders; but we escaped again. At Seneca we met our regiment, which had come in through the wilderness, and we soon got our clothing, tents, and camp cooking apparatus. Our guns and a stock of ammunition we received at Cleveland. Our camp at Seneca was on the site of an old Indian village. In it were the Twenty-Seventh, Twenty-Eighth, and Seventeenth Regiments; also a squadron of dragoons, in all about two thousand five hundred men . . . We lay on our arms for ten nights previous to the battle at Fort Stevenson, and had more or less alarms every night, and some in the day-time. Men passing to and from our camp to others were frequently killed or wounded by prowling Indians. [24]

Of course nerves were raw in such an apprehensive atmosphere. At times, however, the anxiety literally triggered a few men to shoot before being certain of their target, especially in shadows of the evening. Should any sentinel fire, all men rose from their positions expecting a full engagement with the enemy. More often than not, such a shot fired turned out to have been at nothing more than a passing deer or raccoon casually roaming the premises. Brunson tells of one amusing event of this nature that occurred at Seneca.

> The sentinel fired without hailing. It was supposed the enemy must surely be in sight, and every man was instantly at his post. The drum beat to arms, and all was excitement, expecting now a fight in good earnest. But soon the word "dismiss" came round; and when the officer of the day and the General [Harrison] himself reached the spot, the sentinel said that he saw something black moving through and under some brush, which he thought was an Indian trying to get a shot at him, and he thought it best and safest to take the first chance himself, and so blazed away. [Whereupon] the Sergeant of the guard, going to the place pointed out, he found a large turkey; and wild turkeys being nearly black, the General commended the sentinel for his caution, and said he should have the turkey for his dinner. Some of the boys thought it more likely that the sentinel could distinguish between a turkey and an Indian in broad daylight, but coveting a good dinner, took that method to obtain it, trusting to stratagem for an excuse, in which he succeeded. [25]

Another volunteer, a drummer boy and soon-to-be Ordinance Sergeant, William Gaines, had come up from Tennessee with the 24th regiment of the US infantry. He was at Fort Meigs during the May siege, and later was one of the chosen from this locale to fortify Fort Stephenson. As he explains it, "a detail was made from the different companies [at Fort Meigs] to relieve Fort Stephenson; and that was done that each company should have equal chance in the glory." Gaines says, "[I] exchanged my drum for a musket," [26] and he proceeded to Lower Sandusky. He was a mere thirteen-year-old boy at the time. A full lifetime later, in his nineties, Gaines was invited to the White House by then President Rutherford B. Hayes in honor of his being the last surviving American participant in the battle at Fort Stephenson. Elderly, yet still very astute, Gaines was to have his picture taken with the president. When presented with a full-dress uniform to wear for the event, Gaines, a proud and meticulous man, realized that the stripes of his rank were not attached. This broke protocol and unnerved him. To his surprise the president's wife, who had come to greet him, upon

Arial view of the reconstructed Fort Meigs in Perrysburg, Ohio. Note the numerous ridges in the fort which were the traverses often referred to in historical accounts.

Photo courtesy of Elizabeth Raymond–Boundless Beauty Studio–2009.

learning of the old soldier's dilemma, asked for needle and thread, sat on the floor and stitched the insignias on his uniform for him.

By the 29th of July, the bulk of the troops had coalesced within a ten mile circle enveloping both Fort Seneca and Fort Stephenson. Harrison was at Fort Seneca with a very large force, by most accounts well over two thousand men. Fort Stephenson, a few miles downriver to the north was manned by less than two hundred men. Fort Meigs, forty miles west, was manned by just enough men to put up a good fight, but not armed to capacity. And at this time Shelby's troops were still being solicited in Kentucky and would increase the size of the force when they arrived in another month.

The spies of Major Croghan at Fort Stephenson speculated that Procter's approaching force was minimal and that many of Tecumseh's Indians had abandoned the effort and returned to their villages. Harrison's spies had a different view. They anticipated a much larger body of Indians along with Procter's 41st regiment to attack; and more importantly, they believed they may strike Fort Seneca directly. Harrison was conflicted. He couldn't risk the loss of his supply depot at Fort Seneca, as that would certainly squelch his move into Canada. He also couldn't leave Major Croghan to defend Fort Stephenson with just a handful of men. Harrison considered abandoning both locations and retreating even farther south to Upper Sandusky in wait of several thousands of troops coming north with Ohio's Governor Jonathon Meigs, Jr. A conference was held amongst the staff officers. General Lewis Cass, head of the brigade and soon-to-be governor of the Michigan Territory, was the key strategist. It was decided to abandon Fort Stephenson immediately. As for seeking refuge by moving the troops south to Upper Sandusky, Harrison asked Cass for his perspective.

"General [Harrison], you are in command; you must do as you think best."

"But," said Harrison, "two heads are better than one, and I want your opinion."

"Well, it is my opinion, then, that we would better not to retreat till we see something to retreat from." This settled the question; and every man was set to work to strengthen our defense, and prepare for the worst.[27]

And so, at ten o'clock on the evening of the 29th of July a chaotic series of events began. William Conner, the interpreter Harrison brought along with the Delawares, was sent to Fort Stephenson with two Indians. Under cover of darkness, Conner carried a written order from Harrison to Major Croghan. It read:

Sir, Immediately on receiving this letter, you will abandon fort Stephenson, set fire to it, and repair with your command this night to head quarters. Cross the river and come up on the opposite side. If you should deem and find it impracticable to make good your march to this place, take the road to Huron and pursue it with the utmost circumspection and dispatch.[28]

The message should have reached Croghan within a few hours since Conner had only a nine or ten mile hike. However, he didn't arrive until ten o'clock the next morning. Purposefully not following a set path in order to avoid capture, he and his Indian partners became lost in the darkness of the woods! Twelve hours later, upon receiving the order, Croghan perceived more danger in leaving the post than in remaining, and sent a message saying as much back with William Conner to Harrison.

Sir, just received yours of yesterday, 10 o'clock P.M. ordering me to destroy this place and make good my retreat, which was received too late to be carried into execution. We have determined to maintain this place, and by heavens we can.[29]

Harrison didn't take kindly to this insubordination, especially from someone he had mentored in military affairs. Colonel Samuel Wells, the same person who delivered the sad news of the Raisin River massacre to Governor Shelby at the Frankfort theatre six months earlier, was sent to relieve Croghan. The Major returned to Harrison under arrest and explained his reasoning. If the order had been received the night before he would have followed it; but by morning his spies had reported an attack was imminent. Harrison was finally satisfied with the thought process and Croghan was released and sent back to his command.

On August 1, the British vessels rowed up the Sandusky River toward Fort Stephenson. Harrison's spies watched them arrive from a distance but they had a difficult time of providing details of numbers and cargo because they incredibly had no spy glasses! Harrison had to write to John Armstrong pleading with him to provide such fundamentals which should have already been available.

One of these approaching gunboats carried John Richardson, a very proud Canadian boy. Over the years of his military service, John rubbed shoulders with many of the personalities later to become the subject of American, British, Canadian and Indian folklore. He served in all the actions of the British 41st regiment during this chapter of the war, up to and through the Battle of the Thames. One of the first and fondest thrills of his life occurred just a year previous when he was a mere boy of sixteen years. Having helped in the defeat of the Americans under General Hull at Fort Detroit, young John was selected to raise the British colors to the top of the fortress's flag pole, thus marking their victory. This privilege, at such a young age, ignited his patriotism.

Already a veteran of the battles at Detroit, the Raisin River, and Fort Meigs, Richardson now found himself engaged against the soldiers of Fort Stephenson. On the night of the attack, he had a close brush with death. Somehow he became isolated on the far left of his regiment's full position. He lay motionless in a cold muddy ravine near the fort for some time. Finally, he discerned from indistinct and distant voices that the rest of his troops had withdrawn. He decided to rise and make his retreat alone from

immediately in front of the fortress; but not withstanding all my caution, I had not advanced many paces, when I stumbled over the dead body of a soldier, who, after having received a mortal wound had evidently crawled on his hands and knees to rest his bleeding form against a clump of bushes, and had died in that singular position. The noise occasioned by my fall put the enemy once more on alert; and as the moonbeams reflected on my arms and regimentals, I had no sooner ascended the opposite side of the ravine, than the whole front of the fort was lighted up with their fire. Not an individual, save myself, was exposed to their aim, and the distance did not exceed fifty paces; yet, although the balls whistled round my ears in every direction, and hissed through the long grass with which the plain was covered, I did not sustain the slightest injury, even though a second volley was fired after the interval of half a minute. On reaching the spot where the columns had been originally formed for the assault, I found that my retreat had been well-timed, for the troops were already in motion toward the boats. . . .

He further relates the delightful discovery he made as he collapsed into his retreating boat, "a luxury that I would not at the moment have exchanged for a throne." It was a bottle of port wine which he states had given him, "the most delicious moments of repose I recollect ever having experienced."[30]

Richardson's idol, Tecumseh, was not the only prestigious warrior on the scene of this battle. The Sioux Indian Chief, Little Crow, was only eighteen years old when he fought here. He explains that:

Dixon [Robert Dickson], the British trader and agent, on the west of Lake Michigan, went among the Sioux and raised one hundred and fifty men; among the Winnebagos, one hundred and fifty; and among the Sacs and Foxes, three hundred . . . Dixon told these Indians that the Yankees were great cowards, but rich in spoils; that one Indian could whip five Yankees, and that they would be loaded with money and goods.

When one hundred fellow Indians lay dead after this battle, which should have been easily won, Little Crow explains, "the Indians became disheartened and disgusted with the deceptions that had been played on them . . . they left the British . . . This was the first and last time the Sioux of the River ever lifted the tomahawk against the whites."[31]

Black Hawk was also present as the head of the Sacs and the Foxes. In his autobiography he states:

The British advanced and commenced the attack, fighting like true braves, but were defeated by the braves in the fort, and a great number of our men were killed. The British army was making preparations to retreat. I was now tired of being with them, our success being bad, and having got no plunder. I determined on leaving them and returning to Rock River, to see what had become of my wife and children, as I had not heard from them since I left home. That night I took twenty of my braves, and left the British camp for home.[32]

We will soon see that this testimony of Chief Black Hawk is a controversial one as he later claimed to be at Tecumseh's side at the Thames battle which occurred just two months later and five hundred miles from his home at Rock River (present-day Rock Island, Illinois).

Just two days after the battle Harrison reported to John Armstrong, the Secretary of War:

I was informed by the [British] prisoners that the enemy's forces consisted of 490 regular troops, and 500 [of] Dixon's Indians, commanded by general [Henry] Proctor in person, and that Tecumseh, with about 2000 warriors, was somewhere in the swamps, between this [fort] and Fort Meigs, expecting my advancing, or that of a convoy of provisions.[33]

Major Croghan and his small band of soldiers with their lone cannon indeed won the day; and it would mark one of the more incredible lopsided victories in history. Alfred Brunson expresses the emotions of the 27th regiment during the night of the attack.

While the battle was raging at Fort Stevenson, the booming of the cannon reached our ears at Seneca, and our men showed unmistakable signs of uneasiness and discontent at the thought of so many of us having no part in the fray. Some murmurings would break out, because they were not lead to the scene of the action, and some fears were expressed as to the fate of that little band of brave men. It was but a few hours, however, until suspense was at an end, for a foaming steed came into camp, and the rider handed a letter to the General, giving a brief statement of the affair, and then followed a deafening roar of shouts and rejoicing.[34]

Terrence Kirby, with the 28th regiment concurred.

Our Indians [Delawares and Senecas] . . . would dance and sing, being very anxious to be permitted to go [to the defense of Fort Stephenson], but Gen. Harrison steadily refused, though the earth upon which we stood was made to tremble, from the artillery belching forth its iron missiles of death only nine miles from us. I take no pleasure in making this statement, Gen. Harrison being dead; but I know I have to die, and come to judgment, therefore I can not but tell the truth, offend or please who it may. I make no charge of cowardice against Gen. Harrison; I believe he was a good man, but had too much feeling for the safety of the men under his command.[35]

This decision of Harrison's, to keep the main body of troops at Seneca and not aid the meagerly staffed fort at Lower Sandusky, was one of the questionable judgment calls that lingered in the minds of the public for years to come, especially when accolades were proposed for him as a hero of the war. It was one of the major obstacles that had delayed the medal presentation from Congress to him and Governor Shelby.

After the defeat at Fort Stephenson, Major General Henry Procter wrote to his commander, Sir George Prevost, an account of how and why he was thus humiliated. He explained that the Indians were restless and hard to control, except for those who came under Robert Dickson's leadership. He reiterated how the Indians wanted a fight and how he was coerced by them to try and draw out the men at Fort Meigs in the ruse attack which failed; after which many Indians deserted the effort. He decided to move on to Fort Stephenson but with only hundreds of Indians instead of the thousands he had anticipated. We glimpse that Procter was beginning to lose some of his control over the Indians as well as his own troops by the time they had arrived at Fort Stephenson. He wrote Prevost:

> The fort at Sandusky . . . is calculated for a garrison of five or six hundred men. I formed an opinion entirely different from any person under my command. The general idea being that the garrison did not exceed fifty men, and that the fort could easily be carried by assault. On the morning of the 2nd, the gentlemen of the Indian department, who had the direction of it, declared formally their decided opinion that unless the fort was stormed we should never be able to bring an Indian warrior into the field with us, and that they proposed and were ready to storm one fan of the fort if we would attempt another. I have also to observe that in this instance my judgment had not that weight with the troops I hope I might reasonably have expected. If I had withdrawn without having permitted the assault, as my judgment certainly dictated, much satisfaction would have followed me and I could scarcely have reconciled to myself to have continued to direct their movements. I thus with all the responsibility resting on me was obliged to yield to circumstances I could not possibly have prevented.[36]

Procter continued to point out to his superior that the reason for their defeat was the insufficient amount of troops he had.

Whatever may happen to be regretted, may be fairly attributed to the delays in sending here the force your Excellency directed should be sent. Had it been sent at once, it could have been used to the greatest advantage, but it arrived in such small portions and with such delays that the opportunities have been lost . . . I must entreat your Excellency to send me more troops, even the 2nd battalion of the 41st Regiment, though weak, would be extremely acceptable. If the enemy should be able to establish themselves in the Territory it will operate strongly against us with our Indian allies. Your Excellency may rely on my best endeavors, but I rely on troops alone, and they are but few and I am necessitated to man the vessels with them. I have never desponded, nor do I now, but I conceive it my duty to state to your Excellency the inadequateness of my force.[37]

So it was that Procter legitimately was under-manned from what was promised to him by Prevost. He also had valid apprehensions over controlling and keeping the Indians as allies. That having been said he did have a force in the neighborhood of five hundred troops and at least five hundred Indians under Dickson as he attacked Fort Stephenson. And Tecumseh, although half of his four thousand warriors may have abandoned this effort, was in the general vicinity ready to fight should Harrison have moved from Fort Seneca. Croghan, with a mere one hundred and sixty men and a single cannon in his fortress still won the day.

A footnote to this battle comes via William James, a British historian and genuine patriot of his country, who seemed to disagree with the Indians' testimony of the day's events. Whereas the Indians claimed to have lost at least a hundred warriors in the battle, James contends, in quoting a Mr. O'Conner that, "not one Indian was found among the dead, although it was known that three to four hundred were present."[38] James was a contrarian to many of the Americans' views on the events of this war. We will later see how he embittered Harrison and many others with his opinions surrounding the battle at the Thames. Besides, it is pure speculation but plausible that the Indians had already pulled their dead from the field, as they were known to do, before Mr. O'Conner took his supposed inventory.

With this defeat at Fort Stephenson, Procter and Tecumseh retreated to Amherstburg, the British stronghold on the northwest corner of Lake Erie. They hoped to regroup and make a defensive stand against the emergent American force which they expected to pursue them. As the enemy fled to Canada, multiple American volunteer and infantry units

Photo courtesy of Judith Justus.

Old Betsy–The lone, 6-pounder cannon as displayed on the grounds of its use, the former Fort Stephenson, in Fremont, Ohio, 2010.

moved across this area of Ohio toward the shores of Lake Erie, specifically to Sandusky Bay (present-day Port Clinton, Ohio). From here the mass of troops would soon traverse the lake expecting to do battle at Fort Amherstburg.

Let's briefly step back once again to a month before this battle occurred so we can retrace the movements of Colonel Richard Johnson's mounted regiment. Recall that they had arrived at Fort Meigs in late June. From this fort, units of men were dispersed in different directions with particular missions to accomplish. Richard and James Johnson, as we've seen, took a group to the Raisin River. With one hundred men, Robert McAfee escorted General Harrison to Fort Stephenson on July 1st. Over the next few days, Harrison moved on to Cleveland where he remained for a brief time before heading back down to Fort Seneca. Much of the remainder of the mounted regiment came down from Fort Meigs and the whole camped outside of Fort Stephenson. There they spent the 4th of July in celebration.

> Col. Johnson delivered an Address to his men and a number of toasts which we had written were drank with great applause, decency, good order; & hilarity prevailed amongst all and the day was passed off without

any event to damp the spirits of the men.[39]

A few days later the regiment moved toward Cleveland anticipating the push into Canada to be imminent. However, disappointment loomed once again over the men of Johnson's mounted regiment.

On July 9th, Johnson showed McAfee the letter he had just received from Harrison. In it was an order, a directive from John Armstrong the Secretary of War, for the regiment to immediately set out for Kaskaskia, just south of St. Louis! McAfee notes that the order was "wild in the extreme because it would be a month before we could get there and then our time would nearly be out."[40] Johnson was incredulous and communicated yet again to Harrison that this would destroy the spirit of the men so eager to make their presence felt in the upcoming attack on Fort Malden at Amherstburg. He further stressed to Harrison that he did not believe there was a threat from Indians at Kaskaskia, and that he was ready to accept full blame if Harrison could delay the execution of the order and retain the regiment in place. It was a gallant effort, as they say, but on the 13th of July the regiment began heading south.

With the men dispirited and their horses exhausted, Robert McAfee himself wrote up a request, which was granted by Johnson, to change the route of the march to Kaskaskia. Since the course took them close to the northern border of Kentucky, he asked that the men be allowed to return to their homes in that state and refresh or exchange their horses. The men eagerly marched to their homes for a brief reprieve. They were ordered to reassemble in certain cities in late August in order to continue their movement toward the soon-to-be first capital city of the state of Illinois.

On July 26th, McAfee arrived at his home. The respite was short, however, for only five days later an exciting notice came from Col. Johnson. "The march of the Mounted Regt. is changed and again attached to the North Western Army under the command of Gen'l Harrison."[41] And so the men regrouped a little sooner than expected. They gathered at Great Crossings on the 15th and at Newport on the 17th of August and then retraced the three hundred plus miles northward again to Fort Meigs.

Interesting enough, McAfee's brief return home came at an opportune time for him. A state election was held on August 3rd. On this same day, while the men of Fort Stephenson hundreds of miles away celebrated their victory, McAfee was likewise victorious in winning a seat in the Kentucky House of Representatives.

By September 3rd the mounted regiment was at Fort Amanda (near present-day Lima, Ohio). Johnson ordered spy companies to be sent out ahead of the regular units from this point on. Anthony Shane was directed to proceed with Major Thompson in this effort.

Shane was born of a French father and Ottawa Indian mother. He had spent his youth amongst the Shawnee and he knew Tecumseh. When the War of 1812 began, his knowledge of at least five Indian dialects provided him a career as an interpreter between the whites and the Indians. He chose to serve the Americans effort during the war as early on as the time of Hull's disaster in 1812. He was with Johnson when he secured the Fort Wayne area and was nearly scalped during the first attack on Fort Meigs. Now he served as a spy and interpreter as the regiment headed back to Fort Meigs for further orders.

All American troop movement was now toward the mouth of the Portage, or Carrying River near the Sandusky Bay. From here some of the men would board boats to cross to the islands of the Lake and then on to Fort Amherstburg. Others would proceed to the fortress on foot or horseback around the southwestern end of the lake to Detroit and then across the Detroit River. But before these men would be set in motion again, another battle would be fought, this time on water. Another young American leader, Commodore Oliver Hazard Perry would heroically step up and challenge Lieutenant Robert Barclay and the British fleet.

CHAPTER 6

By Land and By Sea

Dear General: We have met the enemy and they are ours.
Two ships, two brigs, one schooner and one sloop.
Yours with great respect
and esteem–O.H. Perry [1]

In the midst of his debris-ridden ship the *Niagara*, just moments after engaging the British fleet, Commodore Perry managed to scribble the famous lines (introductory quote above) of his success on the back of an old envelope. Peter Navarre, an American spy who was held in high-esteem by Harrison delivered the note to the general and it was received with unbounded joy, and relief. The final barrier to the pursuit of the enemy into Canada had just been vanquished. A New York newspaper of the day, *The War*, may be one of the first public venues to publicize and elevate Perry's succinct words. Ironically published on the very day that the Thames battle was being played out, it printed:

> Cesarean brevity. The first of the following letters from Commodore Perry to General Harrison is more laconic than any of Bonaparte's dispatches, and resembles the veni, vidi, vici, of the immortal Julius more than any thing we have before seen.[2]

The preparations for this stellar naval victory began many months earlier. It was always imminent. The British had a well-established shipbuilding yard at Amherstburg on the northwest corner of Lake Erie where crafts were continuously in construction or repair. The Royal Navy was world-renowned and feared, but to the Americans' advantage the fleet they dispatched to manage the lakes was minimal in comparison to the whole. At that time most British ships were busy defending their homeland from Napoleon Bonaparte. Still, control of the waters of Lake Erie was in the hands of the British allowing them to transport supplies and men at will. For the Americans to invade Canada without control of this water was potentially disastrous. To that end, early in 1813, at the opposite end of the lake in the then desolate little settlement of Erie, Pennsylvania, they established their own shipbuilding yard. The existing American fleet of moderate sized gunboats was soon deemed inadequate and so several larger ships were ordered to be constructed and were amazingly finished in less than eight months time.

By late August, the ships were declared seaworthy and sailed westward across the southern shores of the lake. On the 22nd of August, while he was at Seneca, Harrison wrote to John Armstrong, the Secretary of War, of Perry's and his own situation.

> I returned this day from a visit to Commodore Perry, who is now with his fleet (10 sails) off the mouth of the Sandusky bay. He received an accession of officers and seamen before he left Erie, but he is still very deficient in both in the number and quality of the latter. To remedy this defect as far as possible, I have furnished him with one hundred of my best men, including all seamen that could be found in the companies here. An order has also been forwarded to Fort Meigs to select all of the latter that are there . . .[3]

Terrence Kirby was still at Seneca the day after the Battle of Fort Stephenson when word came down that Commodore Perry was shorthanded and in need of volunteers to engage the enemy on the water. Kirby's excitement over this solicitation is hard to diminish.

> To go on Lake Erie, on his large vessel, the *Niagara*; he wanted two hundred brave young men, that were not afraid of death, to carry balls from the hold to the deck, to fight Com. Barclay, on the 10th of September. When the call was made, I was the first boy that responded to it, and old Col. Owens ordered me back into the ranks. I told him I came to fight the battles of our country, and my blood and life was no more than others, who might go. He said he could not spare me . . . I shed tears when he ordered me into the ranks. Gen. Cass turned round to Col. Owens and told him such a boy as that was worth a dozen, who had to be forced at the point of a bayonet.[4]

Alfred Brunson, also at Seneca, had similar ambition but was likewise thwarted. Brunson says, "I tried to be one of them, but my colonel refused to let me go, saying he could not spare me."[5]

Harrison further explained to Armstrong his next move. "The Commodore and myself have agreed upon the propriety of his proceeding immediately off Malden to brave the enemies' fleet, and if possible bring them to action before he shall be encumbered with our troops."[6] With all preparations being made for the sea battle, Perry set sail for the islands of the lake. Samuel Brown, who was a witness to the battle from the shores of Put-in-Bay Island, relates that a few days before the encounter:

> Com. Perry appeared before Malden, offered battle, reconnoitered the enemy and retired to Put-in-Bay, thirty-five miles distant from his antagonist. Both parties remained a few days inactive; but their repose was that of the lion.[7]

Much like Perry's dilemma of being understaffed, the British Commander Robert H. Barclay was also found in want of seasoned sailors. He had plenty of ships, but not enough mariners to sail them all. Promises of Sir George Prevost, the commander-in-chief of the British forces in North America, to send more men never materialized. As a result, Major-General Procter had to give up over a hundred soldiers of his 41st regiment to Barclay. Incredible as it seems, both fleets were staffed with a significant number of men who knew not the difference between port and starboard!

While he recovered from very serious wounds at Put-in-Bay after the battle, Barclay wrote a letter to Prevost detailing the battle as well as his reasons for provoking it.

> I [previously] informed you, that unless certain intimation was received of more seamen on their way to Amherstburg, I should be obliged to sail with the squadron, deplorably manned as it was, to fight the enemy [who blockaded the harbor], to enable us to get supplies of provisions and stores of every description; so perfectly destitute of provisions was the port, that there was not a day's flour in the store, and the squadron under my command were on half allowances of many things, and when that was done, there was no more. Such were the motives which induced Major-general Proctor . . . to concur in the necessity of a battle being risked under the many disadvantages which I labored. . . .[8]

Samuel Brown shares details of the actions and emotions of the American sailors.

> On the morning of the 10th of September, at sunrise, the enemy were discovered bearing down from Malden for the evident purpose of attacking our squadron, then at anchor in Put-n-Bay. Not a moment was to be lost. Our squadron immediately got under way and stood out to meet the British fleet, which at this time had the weather gauge. At 10 A.M. the wind shifted from S.W. to S.E. which brought our squadron to windward.

The wind was light, the day beautiful – not a cloud obscured the horizon. The line was formed at 11. And com. Perry caused an elegant flag, which he had privately prepared, to be hoisted at the mast head of the Lawrence; on this flag was painted in characters, legible to the whole fleet, the dying words of the immortal LAWRENCE:–'DON'T GIVE UP THE SHIP.' Its effect is not to be described – every heart was electrified.[9]

History bears Brown's conclusion out. Captain James Lawrence's words remain an iconic battle call of American history. On June 1, 1813, Lawrence was commanding the USS *Chesapeake* when he was seriously wounded by fire from the British HMS *Shannon*. Lying wounded on deck he ordered his men, "Don't give up the ship. Fight her til she sinks!" The ship was still captured, and Lawrence died of his wounds a few days later. So moved by this event was his dear friend Oliver Perry, that he had Lawrence's words stitched into a flag. Perry christened his new ship the *Lawrence* and rallied his own men aboard it by raising his friend's words to the top of the mast.

The commanders strategized their optimum positions for battle and navigated their ships accordingly. The shifting winds played to the advantage of the Americans. In due time, the British ship *Detroit* fired the first shot upon the Americans' *Lawrence*. Brown continues:

The firing was incessant for the space of three hours, and continued at short intervals forty-five minutes longer. In less than one hour after the battle began, most of the vessels of both fleets were enveloped in a cloud of smoak, which rendered the issue of the action uncertain, till the next morning, when we visited the fleet in the harbor on the opposite side of the island.[10]

Brown observed the men and the ships upon their return to Put-in-Bay. Of the captured British ships he states:

The carnage on board the prizes was prodigious – they must have lost 200 in killed besides wounded. The sides of the Detroit and Queen Charlotte were shattered from bow to stern; there was scarcely room to place one's hand on their larboard sides without touching the impression of a shot – a great many balls, canister and grape, were found lodged in their bulwarks, which were too thick to be penetrated by our carronades, unless within pistol shot distance. Their masts were so much shattered that they fell overboard soon after they got into the bay.[11]

William Coffin, an early Canadian historian, further comments on

Photo courtesy of U.S. Library of Congress.

The Niagara, Oliver H. Perry's flagship with two other ships in the Put-in-Bay harbor, Lake Erie. Photographed on July 23, 1913 a hundred years after the original battle of September 10, 1813.

how the discrepancy in size of cannon balls affected the outcome. "The men told me that when engaged with the American schooners, their 32s crashed through her; while, in return, our balls stuck in the side of the American[s'], like currants in a pudding."[12]

Commander Barclay personally suffered a dismal fate as a result of this conflict. Once again Brown explains that

> to the loss of the day was superadded grievous and dangerous wounds; he had before lost an arm; it was now his hard fortune to lose the use of the other, by a shot that carried away the blade of the right shoulder; a canister shot made a violent contusion in his hip: his wounds were for some days considered mortal.[13]

Barclay's physical and emotional condition would be forever altered. He survived, but presented a pitiful sight: one arm missing, another deformed and of little use, and a portion of one thigh blown away causing him walk with much struggle. But for his fiancée, refusing his forlorn request to abandon their marriage plans due to his pathetic state, he might have sunk irrevocably into the depths of depression. To their credit, and Barclay's admiration, both Perry and Harrison showed him all the respect he deserved as a valiant combatant.

> Every possible attention was paid to his situation – When com. Perry sailed for Buffalo, he was so far recovered that he took passage on board

our fleet. The fleet touched at Erie. The citizens saw the affecting spectacle of Harrison and Perry supporting the wounded British hero, still unable to walk without help, from the beach to their lodgings.[14]

Although the victory went to the Americans, the final analysis of their situation is likewise startling and horrific.

The loss of the Americans was severe, particularly on board the Lawrence. When her flag was struck she had but nine men fit for duty remaining on deck. Her sides were completely riddled by the shot from the long guns of the British ships. Her deck, the morning after the conflict, when I first went on board, exhibited a scene that defies description – for it was literally covered with blood, which still adhered to the plank . . . brains, hair, and fragments of bones were still sticking to the rigging and sides. The surgeons were still busy with the wounded – enough horror appalled my senses . . . The killed of both fleets were thrown overboard as fast as they fell. Several were washed ashore upon the island and the main [land] during the gales that succeeded the action.[15]

Command of the lake was now in the hands of the Americans. From this point on, the movement of Harrison's troops was rapid and determined. The forces were to be concentrated at Sandusky Bay. The bulk of the troops had already mustered twenty miles up the Sandusky River at Seneca. They consisted of Kentuckians, Virginians and Pennsylvanians; many who had been there since the battle of Fort Stephenson a month earlier. Now they were set into motion toward the bay, led by General Cass.

The Ohio militia had also made its way up to Seneca by this time. The dramatic response from Ohioans rivaled that of the Kentuckians. General Duncan McArthur was instrumental in recruiting men from his state to form this militia, which for all intents had congealed on a moment's notice. Once Governor Meigs had heard of General McArthur's call to arms, he stepped up and assumed command of the swelling militia. It all mirrored the call to Kentucky and Johnson's and Shelby's comparable actions.

Governor Meigs vast force waited at Seneca for Harrison's next order. These Ohio volunteers came from all walks of life.

Among these eight thousand militia; were found in the ranks as private soldiers: judges, merchants, lawyers, preachers, doctors, mechanics, farmers, and laborers of every description; all anxious to repulse the ruthless invaders of our soil.[16]

Obviously, the citizens of Ohio were just as eager and earnest in their desire to protect the Northwest Territory as were their fellow countrymen from Kentucky. Yet, when Harrison gave his next order it was shocking. Three-quarters of this massive Ohio militia were dismissed as suddenly as they were called into service! Whereas Harrison, just weeks earlier, was on verge of relying on them for support as the attack on Fort Stephenson unfolded; he now executed an order to have most of them dispersed. "General Harrison directed Governor Meigs to discharge all his men but two thousand."[17] Of course the Ohio volunteers took offense to such an order. Surely Meigs could have empathized with Johnson's similar rebuff a few months earlier from Harrison as he had anxiously brought his Kentucky volunteers north. These Ohioans had the same fervor to fight as had anyone else now engaged, especially the Kentuckians. But Harrison knew that Shelby was soon to arrive with four thousand troops. Governor Meigs and the Ohio troops recognized Harrison's bias toward the Kentuckians, but there was no recourse. Perhaps it was Harrison's long friendship with Shelby that prompted favor in his direction. Still, it is interesting to note how, though united against a common enemy, the zest to boldly defend liberty birthed inter-state rivalries between the men. General McArthur relays an example of the nineteenth century *smack-talk* thrown by the Ohioans towards Kentuckians, He says, "They blamed General Harrison for partiality in favor of the land that breeds 'half-horse, half-alligator, tipped off with the snapping turtle."[18] Obviously, the Kentuckians were a rather tough bunch.

By the 13th of September, Harrison arrived at Sandusky Bay as the troops continued to flow in. For several days they would keep coming. "On the 17th, gov. Shelby with 4000 volunteers, arrived at head quarters. This formidable corps were all mounted; but it was deemed best for them to act as infantry, and leave their horses on the peninsula."[19] Five days before Governor Shelby reached the lake, Governor Harrison alerted him by letter that his chronic admonitions over fodder for the horses had been heeded.

> With respect to a station for your horses, there is the best in the world immediately at the place of embarkation. The Sandusky bay, lake Erie,

and Portage river form between them a peninsula, the isthmus of which is only one mile and a half across. A fence of that length, and a sufficient guard left there, would make all the horses of the army safe. It would enclose fifty or sixty thousand acres, in which are cultivated fields, which having been abandoned, are now grown up with the finest grass. Your sick had better be left at Upper Sandusky or here.[20]

General MacArthur, who was now commanding Fort Meigs, led his men eastward to the bay in what was a fatiguing march of three days along the northern edge of the lake.

The guides often lost the point of direction as they were struggling with the thick and lofty grass that impeded their progress. Frequently it became necessary, to hoist a soldier until his feet rested upon the shoulders of another, before he could get a view above the top of the grass to ascertain their course.

In short about 7000 men were in motion for the long-delayed invasion of Canada. The greatest activity was visible in camp [at the mouth of the Portage]. Boats were collected; beef jerked; bread baked, and the superfluous baggage secured in block houses.[21]

For several days the men boarded either small boats or Perry's large ships and sailed to the islands of the lake. That crossing was not always as leisurely a sail as one might expect. Alfred Brunson acquaints us with the treacherous and sudden winds and waves of Lake Erie.

The boat I went in was an old Mackinaw trading-boat . . . twenty-seven of us got into it and started. The wind soon rose to a gale, dead ahead. The sail vessels, which were full of men, were obliged to come to anchor, and all open boats, except ours, turned back. Ours was so heavily loaded, that to turn in the troughs of the seas would have been to flounder, when most likely all would have been drowned.

I sat at the helm, and apprised the officer in command of the danger we were in, and that our only safety was in keeping the boat in the wind's eye, and to double-man the oars, keeping one or two to bail out the water that dashed over the sides. The top of the boat was no more than one foot above the water when in calm, and of course most of the swells would throw the spray over her sides. I sat at the helm for eleven hours without any change, to go about twelve miles . . . as we came under the lee of the island the wind had less effect, the water became smoother, and finally, when close in shore, a calm.[22]

While the Americans were thus sailing to the islands and making preparations for their attack, across the water at Amherstburg, Tecumseh grew ever anxious and incensed with his British ally, Major-General Henry Procter. Lieutenant-Colonel Matthew Elliott, Indian agent and key officer in Procter's campaign, explains that:

A few days after that event [the defeat of the British fleet] Major-General Proctor gave orders to remove the stores and dismantle the fort preparative to the retreat of the troops. This being done without the Indians being consulted caused a very great jealousy, from the supposition that their father was about to desert them. This was heightened by the uncertainty they labored under with respect to the fate of the fleet. To obtain an explanation Tecumtha and the other chiefs requested General Proctor and myself to meet them in council.[23]

In that council meeting the great chief perched himself on a large boulder in the center of the lodge and let his sentiments be known in a clear, succinct and eloquent fashion.

Listen! When war was declared, our father stood up and gave us the tomahawk, and told us that he was then ready to strike the Americans; that he wanted our assistance and that he would certainly get us our lands back, which the Americans had taken from us . . . Listen! You told us at that time, to bring forward our families to this place; and we did so; and you promised to take care of them . . . while the men go and fight the enemy . . . You also told your red children, that you would take care of your garrison here, which made our hearts glad . . . Father Listen! Our fleet has gone out; we know they have fought; we have heard the great guns; but know nothing of what has happened to our father with one arm [Barclay]. Our ships have gone one way, and we are much astonished to see our father tying everything up and preparing to run away the other, without letting his red children know what his intentions are . . . We must compare our father's conduct to a fat animal, that carries its tail upon its back, but when affrighted, he drops it between his legs and runs off. . . .[24]

John Richardson tells us further that:

No sooner had the last words of this startling speech died away upon his lips, than the various chieftains started up to a man, and brandishing their tomahawks in the most menacing manner, vociferated their approbation of his sentiments. The scene altogether was of the most imposing character. The council room was a large, lofty building, the vaulted roof of which echoed back the wild yell of the Indians; while the threatening attitude and diversified costume of these later formed a striking contrast with the calm demeanor and military garb of the officers grouped around the walls. The most prominent feature in the picture, however, was Tecumseh. Habited in a close leather dress, his athletic proportions were admirably delineated, while a large plume of white ostrich feathers, by which he was generally distinguished, overshadowing his brow, and contrasting with the darkness of his complexion and the brilliancy of his black and piercing eye, gave a singularly wild and terrific expression of his features. It was evident that he could be terrible.[25]

Procter was on the ropes with Tecumseh. If he had received the reinforcements, food and supplies he had requested from Prevost earlier, he could have met the enemy at Malden. But now, after having to give up too much of the little he had to help Barclay, his needs could only be met at Burlington–two hundred miles due east. Tecumseh would have no part of such a plan. Procter desperately needed the Indian warriors, so he was forced to walk an extremely thin line of appeasement with Tecumseh. He also knew the Indians could turn on him and his men if they sensed betrayal and cowardice. He made a second proposal. This plan would take the forces approximately half the distance to Procter's preferred destination. They would stop and form for battle near Moraviantown, the home of the Delaware Indians. Procter explained to Tecumseh that once there, they would be out of reach of the American ships from the lake and that the area would be militarily suited to their advantage. As well, the Thames River narrowed further inland and would only allow small ships any further progress. Tecumseh reluctantly agreed, and so the dismantling of the fortifications at Malden was resumed in earnest.

The work of demolition having been completed and the baggage wagons and boats sent on in advance, the troops commenced their march; and never was a march set out on, under more dispiriting circumstances. The situation of the men was deplorable in the extreme; they had been for some time on short allowance; and even their pay had not been regularly received. Arrears were due, to some for six, and to others for nine months. A Canadian winter was fast approaching, and few troops had blankets; to all greatcoats were a luxury quite unknown . . .[26]

And so, having torched the fort and many other buildings so the Americans could not gain from their loss, the Indians and British loaded what arms and food they could into wagons and ships and headed east.

Likewise at Detroit, all was panic when word of Barclay's defeat arrived. Aura Stewart, an early settler of the Detroit area, relates her father's narrative of the alarm on those days. "The British while holding Detroit, to prevent Gen. Harrison from gaining information of their strength and operations, kept a strict guard over their [American] citizen prisoners. Allowing none to leave town . . ." He explains how a lone merchant was granted permission to go to Malden to settle a business issue. This gentleman happened to be at Malden as the ships were battling on the lake. He found a ladder and a telescope and discerned that the Americans had won the day. Upon his return home the merchant relayed the news of Perry's victory. Stewart continues:

> Now followed great confusion at the fort and in the town; the British were in a hurry to evacuate the town, and seized every boat and canoe to convey them and their baggage across the Detroit river. Amid this confusion and hurry of the British, the Americans collected and held a secret consultation; they knew that the British soldiers would leave Detroit that night; but they had greater anxiety about those six hundred wild Indians lying at the river Ecorse; fearing they would rush into town and rob, and perhaps murder the citizens, it was thought a messenger should be sent to Commodore Perry requesting him to send them succor as soon as possible.

Among the eight persons selected to solicit Perry was James Knaggs. It's speculation, but likely, that Knaggs' kinsman, Medard Labadie was also in this group.

> Our messengers, each paddle in hand, jumped into their canoe, and propelled it down the Detroit river, exerting themselves to deliver the message to Commodore Perry as soon as possible. The night was dark, and on arriving at the mouth of the Detroit river, no shipping could be seen; but they heard the sound of oars, and judging from the peculiar sound of the oars that it must be a ship's boat, they hailed, "Boat, Ahoy!" the answer was, "Ariel"; the boat hailed in turn; the answer was, "A canoe from Detroit with a message for the Commodore!" The officer in charge of the boat, took the canoe in tow, and brought the messengers to the Commodore's ship, where they remained that night; the Commodore assuring the messengers that if the "Lord, would permit, he would relieve their anxiety by bringing his ships before their town by nine o'clock

the next morning." The Commodore asked the messengers many questions, and, on hearing that they were all well acquainted with the sections of country through which General Harrison would have to pass in his pursuit of the British troops, he gave them his letter of introduction to General Harrison, who, on a further examination, employed the whole eight persons as guides of his army up the river Thames.[27]

Knaggs and Labadie did serve as guides/spies for the troops making their way along the Thames, and would later have something to say about the death of Tecumseh.

By September 22nd the vast majority of the Northwestern Army was blanketing the island of Put-in-Bay in anticipation of the imminent move upon Malden. Aside from a handful of men assigned to stay in defense of Fort Meigs and the Upper Sandusky area, only one force of substance was still on the mainland - Colonel Johnson's mounted regiment. They had arrived at Fort Meigs about a week previous and helped to unload supplies from the fort and move them to an island downriver, where they were then reloaded onto ships for the trip into Canada. The militia also moved their horses from the fort to one of the river islands so they could feast on its luxurious blue grass. The fortress was reduced in size from seven to about half an acre. Day after day these Kentuckians waited for orders to move out. Robert McAfee wrote in his diary three days earlier that

> in the evening an express arrived from Gen'l Harrison informing us that he would call us in a few days to Detroit and to hold ourselves in readiness at a moment's warning, this infused new life into every man of the Regt. who felt the Interest of his country at heart.[28]

CHAPTER 7

Into Canada

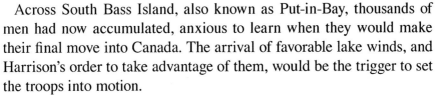

*It is the intention of the Gen'l to land the army
upon the enemys Shore[1]*

Across South Bass Island, also known as Put-in-Bay, thousands of men had now accumulated, anxious to learn when they would make their final move into Canada. The arrival of favorable lake winds, and Harrison's order to take advantage of them, would be the trigger to set the troops into motion.

Put-in-Bay Island to the present day is the site of an ancient cavern, now appropriately named Perry's Cave. Discovered by an adventurous member of these troops, its fresh water not only kept the men hydrated but also nurtured the sick among them. Alfred Brunson relates his escapade into this island fissure.

> While on this island, the water of the lake being rather too warm to be palatable for drinking, and hearing of a cave somewhere on the island in which cool water could be obtained, I went for it, and soon found a large string of men going to and returning from it with canteens and camp-kettles. The mouth of the cave was rather low, so that we had to crawl in and out, and so much water had been spilled there, it was quite muddy and slippery. We had to use candles or torches. There was, inside, a large room, the arch overhead being perhaps ten feet high. The water was on one side of it; and the motion of the water, and the presence of fish, proved there was a communication with the lake. The water was evidently lake water, but was cooler than that which was daily under the influence of the sun and the warm air. But the atmosphere in the cave was oppressive, probably more so than common, from the great number of heated human bodies, and their breath, that were constantly going in and out. I soon grew tired of this subterranean abode, and got out as soon as possible, with no desire to visit caves any more, at least such ones.[2]

Though the troops were on this island but a few days, many of them were witnesses to a rare military event that happened to occur during their stay – the execution of a deserter. The man about to meet his

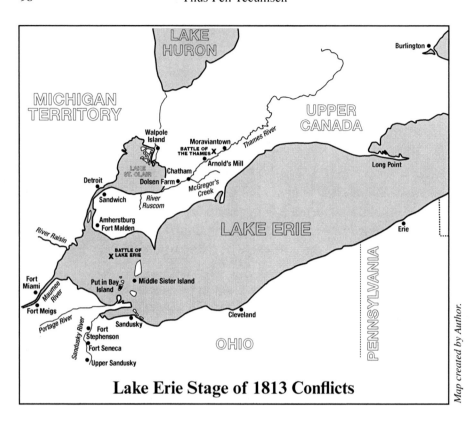

Lake Erie Stage of 1813 Conflicts

Map created by Author.

maker had been tried and condemned for a fourth attempt at escape. Brunson, again, is the one to tell us how the incident played out.

> This thing of shooting men judicially is very serious business. The army is formed into a hollow square on the ground rising from the center each way, if to be had, so that all can see to advantage. The condemned man is placed on his knees in the center, and twelve men are detailed to do the work of death. Their guns are loaded by the officers, one of which is left without a ball, but the men know not which it is, so that each one hopes it is his. The prisoner is blindfolded and shot at the word of command, "ready, aim, fire." If he is not killed at the first shot, the guns are reloaded and the firing repeated as soon as possible. No one feels like deserting after such a sight.[3]

Desertion was very infrequent in the army of the Northwest. Only two soldiers were ever executed in this manner. One soldier who fell asleep at his post a month earlier at Fort Seneca was condemned to be put to death, but received a very personal pardon at the very last instant. On his knees with twelve rifles from every direction pointed at him, he heard the call "ready". But instead of it being followed by the expected "aim," the words "as you were!" echoed loudly from the lips of General Harrison himself. After a lecture to the whole army present on how the lives of all were dependent on the guards staying awake, his pardon was officially granted.

Major Eleazar Wood, commanding the army's detachment of artillery in this pursuit, writes in his journal on the 25th of September:

> To-day the army left Put-in-Bay and went to the Middle Sister, a small island situated in the Lake, and about 18 miles from Malden. That night, after we arrived on the island, General Harrison, Commodore Perry, the General Staff and myself went on board a pilot boat, for the purpose of going on a reconnoitering trip to Malden. The wind being fair, at break of day we got under way, and run up to Malden – or within a very short distance of Amherstburg, took soundings and examined the coast for three or four miles below the town. We discovered that Malden and all the public buildings had been burnt. Its ruins were yet smoking.[4]

By this statement we can ascertain that at least the officers in command knew beforehand that the fort and other buildings at Amherstburg had been set on fire; but they also knew it didn't necessarily mean that the enemy had departed.

The stay at Middle (or Eastern) Sister Island was brief and congested. On this nine acre space had landed nearly seven thousand men! General McArthur with his troops from Fort Meigs had skipped the interim trip to Put-in-Bay and met the rest of the forces here, swelling their number even further. There were a few peculiarities to this tiny island. One was the crunching sound made by the men as they stepped almost anywhere, for virtually the whole island was covered in snails! The other was an unusual vegetable found growing abundantly across the island. Brunson tells us that this special treat was

> leeks, a kind of wild onion; and we having been so long without any vegetable of the root kind, were all eager for something besides bread and meat. As soon as the discovery was made, the news of it spread like wildfire, and every man that could was scratching and digging with his fingers, scalping knife, or a stick, and probably in fifteen or twenty minutes the whole island was dug over. I got half a dozen, which I relished with a zest.[5]

Back on the mainland, a few days earlier Colonel Richard Johnson gave orders to his men detailing the proper formation that they were to assemble into when the anticipated call to move out finally arrived. It was a short wait. That evening, the 25th of September, McAfee explains that:

> An express arrived from Gen'l Harrison with orders to march our regiment on to the River Rezin, which infused life & animation into every part of our preparatory measures & we immediately commenced drawing ten days Rations, but owing to the pickled beef being so bad we only got five days of beef & many of the messes scarcely took any part of it.[6]

It's evident that the quartermaster's job was not always an easy one, being challenged to keep the meats fresh and other foodstuffs dry as the men travelled by land and sea and in all types of weather.

Johnson's regiment spent the next day marching toward the Raisin River, stopping for the night a few miles short of the site. The following morning of the 27th was crisp and beautiful, and they resumed their advance. But as they drew into the Raisin area, the same sunlight that had splendidly shone upon the nature about them, now spotlighted both the baked-white and still charred bones of these men's fellow Kentuckians. Un-interred again by the Indians, just since last June when Johnson had buried them, the Indians had strewn them across a three mile area. Some of the men present would re-bury them yet again on their return home after the battle at the Thames.

Out on the lake, the 26th was another day of waiting as the winds displayed their fickleness. In fact while the sun set that evening officers were calmly finishing the numbering and arrangement of vessels in the fleet when suddenly the winds began to intensify. The raising swells of lake water were so violent that they struck fear into many of the men that the tiny Middle Sister Island might be totally washed over by the morning. Luckily, as suddenly as the weather kicked up it died away, leaving both boats and men intact to greet the same beautiful sunrise the next morning that had awakened Col. Johnson's men near the Raisin.

While on Middle Sister Island Samuel Brown painted a picture of that day:

> On the 27th, at nine in the morning, the army made its final embarkation. The day was fine, and a propitious breeze made our passage a pleasing pastime. It was a sublime and delightful spectacle to behold sixteen

ships of war and one hundred boats filled with men, borne rapidly and majestically to the long-sought shores of the enemy. The recollections of this day can never be effaced from my memory. There was something truly grand and animating in the looks of the men. There was an air of confidence in every countenance. The troops panted for an opportunity to rival their naval brethren in feats of courage and skill, they seemed to envy the good fortune of our brave tars . . . the belief was current among the troops that the enemy were in great force; for it was believed that Dixon's Indians as well as Tecumseh's were at Malden.[7]

Although the smoke seen previously led Harrison to believe that the fort was destroyed, there was no reason to believe all the Indians and Procter had abandoned the area. The Americans could not be sure of exactly where they might be ambushed as they moved inland, but they certainly did expect a fight.

Alfred Lorraine was aboard the *Ariel* with his fellows from Petersburg, Virginia, and thus had the opportunity to rub shoulders with General Harrison and Commodore Perry. He observes how the men's pride and patriotism bloomed on this day:

The morning was beautiful beyond description. The sun shone with refulgent splendor on our polished arms. The martial waving of the snow-white plumes of the officers, the various uniforms of the regulars and volunteers, the solemn silence, interrupted only by the regular movement of springing oars, altogether formed a scene awfully grand. But the scene became even more imposing, when, arriving within a few rods of the shore, every soldier expecting to breast the fury of an ambushed foe, all at once the flapping banner of our host was unfurled to the whistling wind, the concentrated music of the whole army burst, in a national air, on the ears of a feeling soldiery, and the whole atmosphere around us was filled with the shouts of freemen.[8]

Additionally, Alfred Brunson explains the orderliness of the debarkation:

The boats moved abreast, about as far apart as the men on board, when in line, two deep, would fill the space. The line, when landed, stretched about a mile and a half. The place of landing was on the beach of the lake, three miles below Malden. In two minutes from the time the first boot struck the beach, the whole line was formed, ready for action. Before reaching the shore I saw the inhabitants about the house in front of us, and said there was no fighting to be done there, for the enemy would not leave their own people between us and them; and so it proved. Every drum and fife was playing "Yankee Doodle" till we struck the beach, and then all was silent. I sprang from the boat to the beach at the same moment General Harrison did, and within six or eight rods of him, and had my company in line as soon as any other.[9]

Later that day, Harrison gave an official report of the event via a letter to John Armstrong.

I have the honor to inform you that I landed the army under my command about 3 miles below this place [Amherstburg] at 3 o'clock this evening without opposition and took possession of the Town in an hour after. Genl. [Henry] Proctor has retreated to Sandwich . . . I will pursue the enemy tomorrow although there is no probability of overtaking him as he has upwards of 1000 horses and we have not one in the army.[10]

On this same day of landing Harrison wrote to Governor Meigs, "I shall follow him [Procter] as soon as I collect a few horses to mount the general officers and some of the staff. A miserable French pony upon which the venerable and patriotic governor of Kentucky was mounted, is the only one in the army."[11] Harrison was mistaken about the number of horses in Procter's army. They were actually very few. Procter's progress was slowed due to that fact, but more so by other circumstances and misguided beliefs held by the British General.

Harrison post-scripted his letter to Armstrong with, "The Aggregate amount of the force with me is about 5000 of which 2000 are regulars and the rest Kentucky militia, the Pennsylvania Regits., with exception of about 100 refused to cross the line."[12] It is an interesting historical footnote to realize that just as the New York militia a year earlier refused to move into Queenstown Heights because it was on Canadian soil, a handful of Harrison's army felt likewise when the time came to push into Amherstburg, Canada.

The British force now in retreat was upwards of sixteen-hundred men. This calculation came via the word of a few British-allied Indian deserters who spoke with Harrison and it was confirmed by residents who had remained at Amherstburg after Procter's retreat. Harrison told Armstrong, "Genl. Proctor has with him four hundred seventy five regulars of the 41 and Newfoundland Regiments, sixty of the 10th Regi-

Image courtesy of Parks Canada Agency - Fort Malden NHSC.

Painting - View of Amherstburg, by Magaret Reynolds circa 1813. A vessel is depicted under construction at the shipyard and Fort Malden is just beyond it.

ment of Veterans, 45 Dragoons and from six hundred to a thousand Indians"[13] Over the course of the next few days these numbers would dwindle due to sickness and death, as well as clusters of Indians who with each day of not stopping to fight decided to abandon the British.

Some of the American forces didn't follow Harrison into Amherstburg. General McArthur with about seven hundred men would be sent to Detroit to protect those townspeople from the hostile Indians in that region. A force of warriors led by chief Main Poc, who refused to partake in Procter's retreat, lingered in the Detroit area hoping to pillage a now defenseless American citizenry. Other men grew very ill as they traversed both land and sea. Some were left on the islands to fend for themselves while the main body of men proceeded on the offensive. It can be assumed that they had expected to have been recovered soon, in due course, since most thought the battle was imminent once they landed at Amherstburg. As it turned out, they were left to suffer for many days while their fellows pursued the enemy deeper into Canada.

It quickly became evident to the men who had marched up parallel roads leading into the town of Amherstburg that the enemy had dispersed. The ruins of Fort Malden were still smoldering. The few residents, mostly women who didn't follow behind the British in their retreat, had to be reassured of their safety by the American officers. Curiously, these women seemed long-hardened to the horror about them—a display which had immediately caught the eye of the arriving Americans. Scalps, American scalps, were skewered on posts by the Indians all along the streets. Terrence Kirby recalls:

> The British women showed me where the Indians had burnt the [American] prisoners under the liberty pole, and where they scalped them. They would run their scalps to the top of the liberty pole, one hundred and eighty feet high, and dance a war dance under them. The women informed me that the poor prisoners' moans and cries in death, under the devouring flames, was enough to extort tears from demons.[14]

The men also learned from the residents that when the British had retreated

> all had fled but the brave Tecumseh. The citizens told us that he sat on his faithful charger, at the head of the street, and looked till he saw the van of our army entering the suburbs below. He then turned his horse with a sigh, and as the Americans entered one end of the town, he slowly rode out of the other.[15]

As day turned to evening, the Americans settled down to sleep in and around the smoking ruins of the fort. Without their personal supplies they were already uncomfortable. Additionally they were left to sleep in the foul charred air. Two other circumstances would make a good night's rest an impossible feat. First was the looming fear of an attack before dawn from a contingent Indian force that was believed to be lingering in the area. Second was the rain—a long, hard, pounding rain. Alfred Brunson says:

> I lay on a piece of board, before the camp fire, to keep out of the mud, having no covering, with my cartridge-box under my head, and my gun-lock between my thighs, so as to keep it dry. In the night I awoke, and found my right, or upper, ear full of water, and my right, or upper, side wet to the skin, and turned over to let the water drain out of my ear. In the morning I found some men worse

off than I was, for they lay in ponds of water.[16]

Over the next day and a half, the army moved north along the east bank of the Detroit River until they reached the town of Sandwich (present-day Windsor, Ontario) directly opposite Detroit. At the same time, Colonel Johnson's regiment was moving north along the western bank of the same river until they made a grand impression upon the citizenry of Detroit.

> The entrance of the mounted regiment into Detroit presented a fine military spectacle. At 2 P.M. the advance of the column began to emerge from Belle Fountaine, and were visible at the distance of two miles from the town. The width and shortness of the road gave the military and citizens a full view of its approach. Both sides of the street for a considerable distance were lined with spectators. Suddenly our ears caught the thunder of 1100 horse in full motion. The whole regiment was rapidly approaching; and in a moment it was in the midst of us upon full speed and in admirable order.[17]

Throughout the day of October 1st, Colonel Johnson's regiment was ferried across the Detroit River and united with Harrison's army now situated at Sandwich. It was decided that evening, that the whole force would begin their pursuit of Procter at five o'clock the next morning. They would follow the shores of the Detroit River and Lake St. Clair until they reached the mouth of the Thames River which lay on the south shores of that lake. An alternate route of pursuit was briefly considered. They could have re-boarded the ships and sailed along the north shores of Lake Erie to Long Point which was due south of Chatham. A short march north would have brought them up to the point they expected Procter to settle upon for battle. It would have been a much easier route on the men physically, but the course ultimately chosen allowed Perry's ships, loaded with supplies, to sail alongside the marching troops much further inland and also kept them on a more certain trail of the enemy. General Cass's brigade and Lt. Colonel Ball's corps were ordered to remain at Sandwich until the men's supplies, blankets and knapsacks, which were left on the islands, were finally shuttled over to the mainland. Then they could follow behind the course of the main army.

Alfred Lorraine continued his service aboard the *Ariel* which was transporting supplies up to the point where the Thames empties into Lake St. Clair. Apparently the supplies his ship was carrying did not include foodstuffs.

We went on board hungry – we were hungry through the whole cruise, and were at last landed at the mouth of the Thames as ravenous as wolves. For several miles we marched through a mixed population of French and Yankees, and gathered up enough scraps to keep soul and body together. At last we encamped in a beautiful neighborhood that was settled by Scotchmen, who were more loyal [to the Crown] than the Englishmen. They would neither give nor sell to His Majesty's enemies. They acknowledged that we had ample power to take; that was one thing; but to collude with the enemy was another. . . . One of every mess took his tomahawk, and walking about the fields, brought in an abundance of pigs, turkeys, geese, etc.; and there was great feasting in the camp.[18]

Samuel Brown observed:

From Sandwich to the Moraviantowns is eighty-four miles. We found the roads for the most part good. The country is perfectly level. The advance of the troops was rapid; so much so, that we reached the river Riscum [Ruscom], twenty-five miles from Sandwich, in the evening [of the 2nd]. The enemy had neglected to destroy the bridge [over the Ruscom River]. Early in the morning of the 3d, the General proceeded with Johnson's regiment, to prevent the destruction of the bridges over the different streams that fall into Lake St. Clair and the Thames. These streams are deep and muddy and are unfordable for a considerable distance into the country.[19]

Samuel Brown, who was a volunteer in Colonel Ball's legion, continues to explain that later that day a handful of British dragoons were captured trying to destroy one such bridge and from them Harrison learned that Procter was surprisingly unaware of the Americans' whereabouts.

On October 2nd Robert McAfee was leading his company in the midst of Johnson's regiment. A part of the entry in his journal that day reads:

After marching about twenty miles up the border of Lake St. Clair over a fine sandy road, we were met by six deserters who informed us that Genl. Proctor and his army with Genl. Tecumseh & twelve hundred Indians were about 15 miles above the mouth of the River French, or Thames, that they had left him about one o'clock on yesterday, it was near sunset when we got this information but it infused new life into our Regt. and we marched on four miles farther. . . . Great exertions were made by the whole army to overtake the British and Indians. Three schooners loaded with provisions & about fifty boats accompanied us with a fine breeze in rear. Two of our large ships had passed up the day before & had anchored at the mouth of the River Thames, so that Providence seems to aid us in all our movements.[20]

So while the Americans spent the night at the Ruscom River, Procter and his troops, as well as the Indians, were camped at Dolsen's farm which was about fifteen miles up the Thames. The two forces were a mere twenty-five miles apart by the night of October 2nd.

As each day passed without a stance being taken against the Americans, Tecumseh and the Indians grew ever more anxious and skeptical of Procter. We learn through Procter's own report weeks later how the situation grew ever more intense. While camped at Dolsen's farm, a few miles downriver from Chatham, Procter had pledged again to the Indians

that we would not desert them, and it was my full determination to have made a stand at the Forks [Chatham], by which our vessels and stores would be protected; but after my arrival at Dover [Dolsen's] three miles lower down the river, I was induced to take post there first, where ovens had been constructed, and where there was some shelter for the troops . . .[21]

So Procter claimed that he wanted to hold out for a battle at Chatham, which was the original agreement he made with Tecumseh, but that he found the Dolsen's farm area a reasonable respite for his men because of its buildings and ovens, which provided both shelter and food for his troops.

Procter's strategies and competence up to this point were already suspect, but his actions in the last few days before the battle were so inexplicable that legitimate wrath from both Tecumseh and his own senior officers was warranted. As of October 1st the British and Indian force, instead of continuing their retreat toward Chatham, the agreed upon battle site, were ordered to remain at Dolsen's farm and did so for two additional days. Fearing that the Americans would gain on them, which was a distinct probability, they made some meager fortifications. However, Procter himself had abandoned his men with little explanation for his departure and even less instruction given to his officers. It wasn't long after his exit that trouble arrived.

Photo courtesy of U.S. Library of Congress.

The Dolsen Homestead as it appeared circa 1889-1892.

Colonel Elliott explains:

> On the morning of the 3d, shortly after which he [Procter] proceeded towards the Moravian Town, 28 miles distant, and about an hour after he set off, our scouts brought word that the enemy had crossed the forks and were rapidly advancing up the river . . .[22]

The Americans were indeed closing fast on Dolsen's. A British express was sent to catch up with Procter and alert him of the situation. At the same time, Colonel Warburton, who was left in charge of the British troops by default, started moving them out of harm's way toward Chatham. The Indians worked the rear of the British lines as they headed east. They would have a few minor skirmishes with the advance American guards along the way.

Procter simply dismissed Warburton's messenger when he had caught up with him and continued toward Moraviantown. Procter's motives were later discovered to be twofold. First he wanted to evaluate the area around Moraviantown which he had really preferred as the site for battle, even over Chatham; and second, he wanted to secure the safety of his wife and family who he made sure were sent ahead.

This continuing retreat and confusion infuriated more and more of the Indians. Larger groups gathered their families, who were following in the woods, and began making plans for a journey back to their homes. If not for Col. Elliott's coaxing, many more than already had, would have likewise abandoned the effort. Elliott stressed that they were just a few miles from Chatham where Tecumseh had been assured a stand would be made. This convinced some of the Indians to remain.

The Americans were only ten miles away when the British left Dolsen's on the morning of the 3rd. To slow their advance a British party of twelve, a Lieutenant and eleven soldiers, were sent back down the Thames to destroy another bridge. They were abruptly captured by members of Colonel Johnson's regiment. It was considered a fortuitous sign by the Americans that these spies were taken in total, leaving none to return a report of their location.

The American forces, still ravenous, had their appetites taunted by the harvest lying in fields all about them as they settled for the evening onto property owned by a man named Drake. They were about four miles south of Dolsen's farm. Governor Meigs tried to take the high moral ground and spare the local farmers' crops from his troops' hunger. "We have not come to molest the peaceable citizens," he told his men," but to fight those who are in arms against us."

However, General Trotter,

on hearing Gen. Meigs order, rode up in front of his men and said: "Boys don't go to bed hungry; if you can find anything good to eat, take it, and I will pay for it." It appeared that the whole army approved and followed Gen. Trotter's order. It was vegetables the men wanted, and they took them wherever found. The next morning Gen. Harrison sent for the men whose gardens had been invaded; the damages were estimated and paid to the satisfaction of all.[23]

The next morning the Americans were in for yet another edible surprise. "The British troops, in their hurry, left at Dolsen's Station several hundred loaves of bread which Mrs. Dolsen was selling to our men at twenty-five cents a loaf . . ."[24] Additionally, many of the residents in this part of the country had beehives, dozens of beehives, and when the men discovered this fact they were not shy about confronting the potential swarms in lieu of the delicious treat they defended. Mrs. Dolsen had severely scolded Gen. Harrison for his men's thievery of her foodstuffs. Harrison tried to appease her saying, "Madam, I will put a guard over the bees."[25] It was an idle promise and Harrison later paid Mrs. Dolsen and other farmers in the area for the honey. This treat of fresh baked bread and honey had nourished the Americans when it was intended for the British men who were now left ever the more hungry. Even cattle were left abandoned and half-butchered by the British because their flight came on so suddenly.

Perry's ships had been following the American troops up the Thames River, but here at Dolsen's the character of the river changed from a wide, slow-flowing current with low shores that stretched toward prairies into a narrow-flowing river winding its way through ever-rising high wooded banks.

> The Commodore [Perry] and myself [Harrison] therefore agreed upon the propriety of leaving the boats under a guard of one hundred and fifty infantry and I determined to trust to fortune and the bravery of my troops to effect the passage of the river.[26]

It was here that Perry left his fleet and may have been the first naval officer in American history to get his land legs by offering his military services in a battle fought upon solid ground.

As the two forces closed ranks, sniper shots and flurries of gunfire became more frequent. Colonel James Johnson concurs that

> from this time, some of our front were almost constantly skirmishing with the enemy, until the 4th we arrived at a bridge where Tecumseh had made a stand with 5-600 warriors; here we had a smart little engagement.[27]

As Johnson explains, the Americans had finally caught up to the British and Indians at the union of the Thames River and a large creek named McGregor. This was the site that Procter had repeatedly promised to Tecumseh as the place a stand would be made. The name of this village situated where the two currents met was known as Chatham. Having had this site embellished all these days by Procter as the superior location at which to do battle, can you imagine the fury Tecumseh must have felt as he surveyed this area upon his arrival? No fortifications, no additional artillery, and no Procter! Although it has been said that Tecumseh was sentimental about this place because it reminded him of his former village where the Tippecanoe River joined the Wabash, his disillusionment with the British had peaked. He decided that with or without Procter, he and his warriors would nevertheless make a stand here.

Photo courtesy of U.S. Library of Congress.

*"The Forks" in Chatham, Ontario - the meeting point of the Thames River
with McGregor's Creek as it appeared circa 1889-1892. As of 2010 this area
has become a local park named Tecumseh Park.*

This is how the 4th of October played out.

As dawn broke, the Americans became apprised of the geography
before them. The Thames River, whose southern bank they had been
following, now met McGregor's Creek, a large stream that flirted with
the idea of itself being deemed a river. The union of these waterways
created a wedge of land between them. Today the tip of this trian-
gular point is a small park appropriately named after Tecumseh, as
it was from this location that he and his Indian confederation made
a determined stand. Only two bridges provided easy passage across
McGregor's Creek. One was near the juncture with the Thames; the
other was a mile or so further east at Mr. McGregor's Mill.

The British version of the activities of the 4th are explained by the
British officer Colonel Matthew Elliott:

> The troops fell back opposite this place [Chatham] on the morning of
> the 4th October. The enemy advanced up to Chatham where a partial
> skirmish took place between the advance guards. At about 11 o'clock
> a.m. General Proctor arrived and found fault with Colonel Warburton
> for leaving Dolsen's. Yet he very soon after ordered the troops to re-
> treat to Moravian Town. From the manner in which this was conducted
> the greater part of the provisions and stores fell into the enemy's hands.

The Indians kept up a fire across the fork for some time after the troops moved off and then followed, after burning a house in which was a quantity of arms and stores. We halted this evening at Sherman's, five miles from the Moravian Town. The women and most of the baggage had been sent forward a few days previous.[28]

This was not the major battle history was about to record, but until it unfolded, Harrison was not sure how much of the enemy's force was stationed before him. For all he knew the full British and Indian contingent was lined up against him. Harrison told Armstrong:

Below a place called Chatham and four miles above Dalson's is the third unfordable branch of the Thames. The bridge over its mouth had been taken up by the Indians as well as that at McGregor's Mills one mile above. Several hundred of the Indians remained to dispute our passage and upon the arrival of the advanced guard, commenced a heavy fire from the opposite bank of the creek as well as that of the river. Believing that the whole force of the enemy was there I halted the army formed in order of battle and brought up our two six pounders to cover the party that were ordered to repair the bridge. A few shot from those pieces soon drove off the Indians and enabled us in two hours to repair the bridge and cross the troops.[29]

The repair of the bridges, and the crossing of them, was not without incident. That rugged old Indian fighter, William Whitley, was one who found his way to the front lines and was involved in repairing one of the bridges mentioned.

The British in their hurry had thrown down the plank from the bridge into the river, leaving the timbers, or frame standing, and had also set fire to a large log house on the opposite side of the river. Gen. Harrison on his arrival ordered the plank replaced and the fire in the log house extinguished . . . Col. Whitley, mounted on his spirited horse, was always with the advance guard of the army, and the order was given to cross the creek and extinguish the fire. The Colonel, rifle in hand, attempted to cross on the timbers of the bridge, but they got muddy, he slipped and fell into the water below, the fall being about twelve feet. He came ashore without assistance, and proceeded at once to clean his rifle, and when the army was ready to march he took his station with the advance guard. The army had not travelled many miles when they were fired on by the Indians as before stated. At the second assault of the Indians Col. Whitley got his eye on one of them, leveled his rifle and fired. He saw the Indian fall, and to ascertain whether he had killed him, swam his horse over the river, found the Indian dead, scalped him, swam his horse back, and took his station with the army.[30]

Whitley was certainly an energetic and animated man. James Bentley, a member of Johnson's regiment, says that Whitley passed the time in the evenings singing "war songs, & also a ballad of his own, narrating his experiences since leaving home for the Thames campaign."[31] Bentley provides an even more colorful description of the action at Chatham.

At McGregor's Fork, the British in their retreat had thrown the plank from the bridge, some twenty Americans in advance [William Bentley among them] crossed on the string pieces—Col. Whitley joining in this, as in all hazardous occasions—these skirmishers went thus ahead to protect a party engaged in gathering the plank from the river & replacing them on the bridge so as to cross the artillery. The Indians were within short gun shot in the woods ahead in the forks of the rivers, to dispute the passage. The advanced party of Americans took shelter after crossing, under the river bank—Whitley in there protecting himself, placed his old three cornered hat on the bank above him, & the Indians supposing it contained a human head shot at & riddled it with some twenty bullets, while the wary old colonel was watching his chances for good shots, which he was quite sure of securing.[32]

Later that evening Whitey would express to two of his closest friends his gut feeling that the morrow would be his last upon this earth. Joseph Desha, here in command of a full division, explains that he

for quite a number of years . . . remained with William Whitley at his station near Crab Orchard. Whitley became very much attached to him, and it was to General Desha, the night before the battle of the Thames, that he imparted his presentiment of death on the coming day . . .[33]

John Preston, another dear friend of Whitley was also there to hear Whitley's grim prediction. It was Preston who would "take his [Whitley's] effects to his wife at Sportsman's Hill in Kentucky. John Preston led his horse, Old Emperor, those hundreds of miles through the forests, on the saddle of which were tied his rifle, powder horn and belt."[34] This testimony comes from a direct descendent of William, Esther Whitley-Burch, during her 1943 speech sponsored by the Daughters of the Revolution of which she was the first elected regent of the Logan-

Photo courtesy of Joseph C. McClure and Stacy Thomason – William Whitley State Historic Site.

Portrait of William Whitley circa 1830-1850. Artist Unknown.

Whitley Chapter. These artifacts are preserved to this day and on view at Whitley's home which is still standing in Crab Orchard, Kentucky.

Like Whitley, Tecumseh would also have a premonition of death, but his would come on the morning of the 5th, as we will soon discover.

Meanwhile, Tecumseh was unable to withstand the Americans at Chatham. He disengaged and followed behind the already retreating British troops. This setback convinced even more Indians to leave the effort, or in the case of Walk-in-the-Water, to defect to the Americans.

> [This] Wyandot chief . . . had left the banner of Proctor with sixty warriors, came to Harrison and offered to join his army conditionally. The general had no time to treat with the savage, so he told him that if he left Tecumtha he must keep out of the way of the American army. He did so, and returned to the Detroit River.[35]

"In this attack [at Chatham], Tecumseh with five hundred warriors fought us and his loss amounted to twelve and ours to two . . ."[36] says Robert McAfee. It is believed that Tecumseh himself may have received a wound in his arm or wrist during this encounter. Samuel Boone, a nephew of Daniel, who was at the Thames battle told Lyman Draper that, "A young British officer said Tecumseh had received a wound in a skirmish the day before [the battle] across the wrist."[37] According to Boone, this particular wound would come into question on the day of battle as an identifying mark to be looked for when Harrison and others examined the many dead Indian bodies in search of Tecumseh. However, another witness, Major James S. Whitaker, who was also at the battle, says something quite the opposite. Whitaker states that Harrison dismissed a body that others had supposed to be Tecumseh's because:

> The Indian killed had a bandaged arm from a wound evidently not rec'd that day, as it was not fresh – & blood dry on the bandage, supposed to have been rec'd the day before at the bridge three or four miles below McGregor's Mills: And British officers said Tecumseh was not wounded when he went into the battle.[38]

Wait a minute. Who is to be believed here? One British officer told Sam Boone that Tecumseh was wounded at Chatham while James Whitaker heard other British officers say he was not. And, Boone says the presence of this wound proved to Harrison that the body was Tecumseh's; while Whitaker states that Harrison rejected a body as being Tecumseh because he had a day-old wound. So, here we glimpse the first of many, many details that seem to contradict each other in the controversy surrounding Tecumseh's death!

As the Americans finally crossed McGregor's Creek they found themselves in a small abandoned Indian village.

> We found several fine bear skins and many fine brass kettles & Indian plunder of all kinds and four or five barrels of flour. The Indians had poured out all the flour they had . . . [A mile up the Thames] we halted and found that the British and Indians had set fire to a fine schooner with two masts loaded with Muskets, cannon-balls & Military stores of an immense amount, which had all burnt down to the water edge, every eight or ten minutes a bomb would burst which the enemy supposed with injury [to] us but they were mistaken.[39]

With the retreat of the Indians from Chatham, the army paused briefly and allowed the horses to graze for a spell before continuing their pursuit eastward along the river. Soon they discovered an abandoned twenty-four-pound cannon. It was a sign that they were getting very close to the full British force, as such a weapon would not be left behind unless there was no time for them to move it forward.

McAfee and much of the mounted militia had been stretched out some distance behind the infantry who were leading the pursuit. When word came back from the front lines, that they were within three miles of the enemy, the mounted militia rode in haste to catch up as it was already late in the evening. They all settled together for the night, fed themselves and their horses and distributed the stored dried beef for use the next day. "Every preparation [was] made for an early start, with high anticipation of success, our watch-word being 'never fear' . . ."[40]

Tecumseh stopped for the night approximately six miles downriver from what would become the battlefield. He was invited by Christopher Arnold, owner of the largest mill in the region, to dine with him and spend the night. Arnold had fought as part of the Canadian militia alongside Tecumseh at the Fort Meigs battle just that past summer. Tecumseh shared one of his last meals with Arnold but, as usual, declined the indoor bed. Another significant mill in the area, McGregor's, had just been torched by the Indians on Tecumseh's order as they fled that site. It was done for fear the Americans would gain supplies from it. As a result many settlers would now be ever the more dependent on Arnold's provisions. In order "to prevent a similar act at Arnold's, he, Tecumseh, had slept near it and so guarded it through the night."[41] As it played out, it was in this humanitarian gesture toward the white, British/Canadian settlers that Tecumseh spent his last night reposing on Mother Earth.

The British had stopped for the night around eight o'clock a mile or so upriver from Arnold's Mill. Neither Tecumseh nor Procter made an early night of it. About midnight the two met up with each other and rode back to scout the position of Harrison's force. The discovery of their close proximity solidified the belief that there would be a fight tomorrow. Tecumseh returned to Arnold's Mill. Procter rejoined his men. One wonders how well each of them slept.

CHAPTER 8

Battle Lines Are Drawn

Heaven has smiled upon us beyond our asking – the very elements
conspired in our favor, so that Hull's dastardly surrender,
and Raisins Bloody field, and Fort Meigs Massacre
have in some measure been revenged by
the Kentuckians, and I most fervently hope that
a total separation has taken place between the British
and Indians and that Peace will once more smile
upon our North western frontiers
so long stained by the Blood of innocent
women & children . . .[1]

On October 5th Robert McAfee wrote in his diary that the American troops began to march at dawn. Little more than an hour into their renewed chase of the enemy, they would have an encounter with them. In fact the two forces would have several run-ins before they faced each other in formal battle. Just three miles out of their camp the Americans came to a deep chasm with a bridge that had been dismantled by a group of British regulars. The twenty saboteurs responsible were attempting to leave the scene in their single mast boat when they were captured. McAfee explains:

> My company soon filled the ravine with fence rails and passed over with Genl. Harrison, and going two miles farther we got another large boat loaded with women and children and ten or fifteen other boats and cannon with soldiers and plunder in them.[2]

Apparently not all of the British women and children had been sent ahead and out of harm's way by Procter, as he had made sure that his own wife and family had been.

A few more miles of marching brought the Americans to Arnold's Mill. It was here that Tecumseh had spent the previous night. The young Abraham Holmes, who lived a short way downriver from Arnold's, was at the mill this morning and saw, from a short distance, Tecumseh in conversation with Joe Johnston, a neighbor to Arnold who was well-versed in many Indian dialects. Holmes left before Tecumseh had, and was told afterwards by Johnston that Tecumseh remained guarding the mill until he spotted the advance guard of the Americans approaching. Only then did he rapidly mount his handsome and speedy bay-colored horse and ride ahead to join the rest of his Indian force.

When Holmes returned to his father's home that morning he explains,

> I found General Harrison, Col. Johnston [Johnson] and Col. Whitley breakfasting in company with my father, and a large number of their cavalry feeding their horses outside. As soon as breakfast was over, they resumed their march.[3]

When McAfee's company reached Arnold's Mill, Tecumseh was long gone, but they found a group of men including a British captain who was trying to get his own wife out of what was expected to become the battle area. They were promptly captured. The prisoners alerted Harrison that a stand was planned just a few miles upriver and that the Indians were lying in wait among the thick woods just ahead. This was a key piece of information. The mounted militia immediately formed for battle and, for a change, waited for the infantry, who were usually in the lead, to catch up to them. Harrison ordered that each horseman was to carry one footman on his horse as they crossed from the south to the north side of the Thames River. Yet again the Americans found plunder when they reached the opposite bank. Ten or fifteen abandoned cannons and a keel boat were left by the British and Indians in their haste. The boat helped the Americans to shuttle across the river in less than an hour.

At this crossing, Captain James Davidson relates yet another adventure of the incorrigible William Whitley.

> After we forded the Thames, Whitley caught site of four Indians on the opposite side of the river, and lingered behind, trying to get a shot at them. We went on, and when we had gotten about a mile on our road, we were overtaken by Whitley, who rode up with a triumphant air, holding aloft the scalp of an Indian. He gave me the account of his having killed the Indian in a singularly venturesome manner. I reprimanded him for it, and received the answer, "Don't fear Captain. The ball is not run, nor the powder made, that is to kill me." This was a favorite saying of the "old fellow." He was a complete fatalist . . .[4]

In the British camp, the day began with an alert. "Early on the morning of the 5th our scouts brought word that the enemy was advancing on both sides of the river rapidly and in force," says Lieutenant-Colonel Matthew Elliott. "The General [Procter] determined to halt and wait for their arrival."[5] Most sources state that Procter was the one to give the order to the troops to stop where the battle was ultimately fought. Although he may have given the order, the directive to issue it may have actually come from Tecumseh.

Colonel William Stanley Hatch was the Acting Assistant Quartermaster General of the Northwest Army at this battle. In 1872, some sixty years after the fact, he wrote a sketch of Tecumseh's life and a brief history of this battle and other events of this war. He apparently drew from several other historical sources, personal contacts he had made on both sides of the conflict over the years, and his own experience.

Although impossible to verify, Hatch concludes:

> Tecumseh saw that Proctor did not intend to fight; that instead of offering the Americans battle, his sole object was to escape from them; that his previous promises were false and deceptive; and knowing that all hope of success in his [Tecumseh's] cause – all prospect of achieving an advantage in his war against us; depended on the defeat of the American army, or obliging it to retire; after being harassed and fought in the wilds of Canada, he [Tecumseh] assumed the superiority that he possessed over him [Procter], again denounced him for his cowardice, as well as his evident treachery, declaring his intention from thenceforth, to act as the chief commander, to which his own force entitled him, prohibited Proctor's advance, proclaiming that HE would march in advance, select his battleground, and if Proctor would not fight the enemy, he would have him scalped!
>
> Tecumseh moved in advance, selected his ground, and it was well selected, fixed upon his plan of battle, put his forces in line, reviewed every rod of the field, and spoke to and gave orders to each of his chiefs; obliged General Proctor to occupy the position assigned him – and it was the proper one.[6]

This presumption by Hatch is plausible as Tecumseh had been documented in several accounts to have been angered with Procter ever since this forced retreat began with the burning and abandonment of the fort at Amherstburg. Procter obviously had his eye on Moravian-town from the beginning. He went there with little explanation just days before the battle in order to fortify it with several cannons. He also alerted the missionaries there that the troops would be using their shelters as blockhouses. The terrain was suitable for traditional British military defense. Even many of the British supplies were already on their way to Moraviantown per Procter's order. Therefore, Procter's sudden stop here, just a few miles short of his goal, seems odd.

Many historians claim it was the sudden proximity of Harrison's force that had allowed no more time for Procter to retreat. That was certainly a major factor in the decision to stop; but consider the report of the British Lieutenant Richard Bullock of the 41st Grenadiers:

> At daybreak the next morning [the 5th] . . . a few head of cattle were shot, but before the meat could be divided, the enemy were reported to be close at hand, and we were ordered to march. We proceeded to Moraviantown, and when within 1 ½ miles of it, were ordered to halt. After halting about 5 minutes, we were ordered to face to the right about, and advanced towards the enemy in files, at which the men were in great spirits. Having advanced about 50 or 60 paces we were halted a second time, at which the men appeared dissatisfied, and overhearing some, of those nearest to me express themselves to the following effect, "that they were ready and willing to fight for their knapsacks: wished to meet the enemy, but did not like to be knocked about in that manner, doing neither one thing nor the other," . . . About this time several of the Regiment came up without arms or accoutrements, who had escaped from boats cut off by the enemy's cavalry. From these men we learnt that the enemy was within a mile of us and had a large force of cavalry. We had halted about half an hour, when the Indian alarm was given that the enemy was advancing: most of our men were sitting on logs and fallen trees by the side of the road.[7]

So Harrison was close, within a mile, but that was after the troops had been sitting around totally disorganized for over a half an hour. They could have marched the 1-1/2 miles to Moraviantown in that amount of time. Maybe Tecumseh and Procter were in a power struggle over where to fight during this time period. Maybe Tecumseh won the debate because the fallen trees, wooded areas and swamps with heavy underbrush favored the Indian style of battle.

John Richardson, fighting with the 41st regiment, gives further evidence that the stop here was strange considering that Moraviantown was so close.

> The Moravian village, situated in a small plain, offered every facility of defense, being bounded on one flank by a thick wood, highly favorable

to the operations of the Indians, and on the other, by the river Thames, while immediately in front, a deep ravine, covered with brush-wood, and commanded by our guns, presented an obstacle peculiarly unfavorable to the passage of cavalry, of which, we were sufficiently informed, a large portion of the advancing columns consisted. Yet, notwithstanding the excellence of the position, from some singularly selfish motive, the project was entirely abandoned.[8]

Perhaps Richardson heard the rumors of Procter trying to protect his wife and children who may have still been at Moraviantown. Perhaps he saw how Tecumseh intimidated Procter to stop here for fear of his own life. William Caldwell, who was in company with Tecumseh and the Indians, states:

> Some of the Shawanoes said, throwing a cocked hat upon the ground & trampling it in the mud—[belonging to] one of Proctor's aid's—said they would thus treat Proctor if he did not fight. Proctor's orders were to retreat—not fight—but the Indians fairly forced him to it.[9]

Even though Richardson explains that the woods at Moraviantown were advantageous to the Indians, the swamps and undergrowth here at the battle site had to be even more to their liking. Regardless of who called for this location, the troops on both sides began to posture for battle.

The British Lieutenant Bullock shares some of the confusion experienced in forming the British battle lines.

> On the alarm being given we were suddenly ordered to form across the road. From the suddenness of the order, apparently without any previous arrangement, the manner in which we were situated when it was given, the way it was given, which was "form up across the road," and from the nature of the ground, the formation was made in the greatest confusion.[10]

Eventually two lines of British soldiers formed. They extended from the road to the woods, the second line about two hundred yards in the rear of the first. The men were not in the typical close formation.

> From the men of the Regiment who escaped from that line, I understand that they were not formed at regular extended order, but in clusters and confusion.[11]

Richardson concurs that this formation was used and laments the foolishness of again trying to fight a concealed enemy. Concealed because the view of the individual British soldier through the numerous trees was poor–twenty paces out at best. Yet it was here they were ordered to make their stand. Many other conditions favored the Americans and the British rank and file knew it. The absence of ground cover meant that the horses of Kentucky's mounted militia could glide through the trees unimpeded. And how was a British soldier to hide behind a tree when "the glaring red of the troops formed a point of relief on which the eye could not fail to dwell."[12] Contrarily, the American militia's clothing had at least somewhat blended with the bark and brush of the woods. It was about one o'clock in the afternoon when these tired, hungry, sickly and dispirited British men were ordered into this position. Two more hours would have to pass before they would finally be called to fight. If the axes and other supplies hadn't been sent ahead to Moraviantown, the men could have spent the time cutting down enough wood and branches to create an abattis preventing or at least slowing the enemy's passage. Tecumseh himself couldn't help but comment on the strange positioning of the Redcoats in the woods.

> He said to Billy Caldwell & his brother Capt. Wm. Caldwell: "See, these people are just like sheep, with their wool tangled & fastened in the bushes, they are trying to push aside to effect an entrance. They can't fight–the Americans will brush them all away, like chaff before the wind."[13]

Tecumseh would have more serious concerns to ponder this day. Less than an hour before the battle, similar to what William Whitley encountered, he would also have a premonition of his own death. According to William Caldwell:

> Col. Matthew Elliott, Capt. Thos. McKee, & a few other whites were present some twenty minutes before the firing commenced. While the men were getting their places, & awaiting the approach of the Americans, [and] while Elliott, Tecumseh, McKee, Wm. Caldwell & several others were sitting on a log, & [also] a young Shawonoe runner or aid of Tecumseh's–[when] all of a sudden, a noise came, like the sharp whizzing of a bullet. Elliott, Caldwell, & all heard it distinctly–no enemy in sight–no report of a gun–& Tecumseh jumped, & instantly placed one hand on his back & the other on his breast, as though wounded & in pain; presenting a strange & ghastly appearance. Capt. Caldwell asked

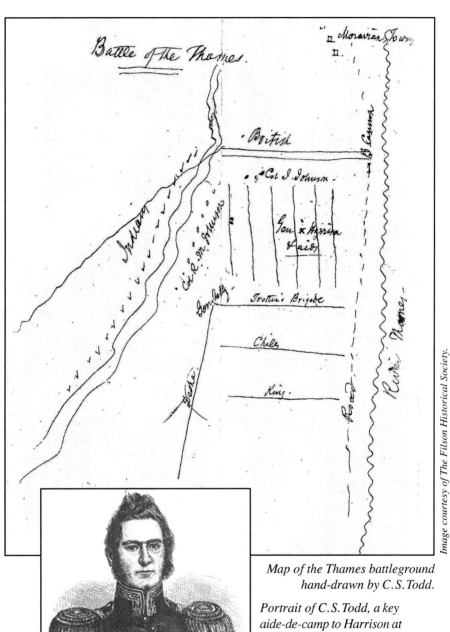

Map of the Thames battleground hand-drawn by C.S. Todd.

Portrait of C.S. Todd, a key aide-de-camp to Harrison at the Thames. Illustrated by Benson J. Lossing and shown here as it appeared in his Pictorial Fieldbook of the War of 1812 which was originally published in 1868.

Tecumseh, "What is the matter?" He said, "he could not exactly tell, but it is an Evil Spirit which betokens no good." Elliott said, "Capt. Caldwell, a precisely similar occurrence happened to your father–he fell, supposing a shot had passed through both legs just below the knees, but he found himself unharmed; the next day in a fight (about the last battle he was engaged in during the Revolution, & perhaps the year before peace), he was shot precisely as the singular presentiment & pain indicated the previous day–& that [therefore] Tecumseh would surely be killed."[14]

Shortly after this unsettling experience, Tecumseh gathered himself and reviewed his warriors and the British forces which were now positioned for battle. "He pressed the hand of each officer as he passed, made some remark in Shawnee, appropriate to the occasion, which was sufficiently understood by the expressive signs accompanying them, and then passed away forever from our view."[15] So says John Richardson as he was stationed in the woods with the 41st regiment. William Coffin, a Canadian historian wrote in 1864 that Tecumseh's last words to Procter were, "Father! Have a big heart!"[16]

In Procter's official report, written a few weeks after the battle, we see the reasons he gave for his actions up to and including the battle.

In the attempt to save Provisions and Ammunition we became encumbered with Boats not suited to the state of Navigation, The Indians and the Troops retreated on different sides of the river and the Boats to which sufficient attention had not been given became particularly exposed to the Fire of the Enemy who were advancing on the side the Indians were retiring on [the south side], and most unfortunately fell into the possession of the Enemy, and with them several of the men, Provisions, all the Ammunition that had not been issued to the Troops and Indians. This disastrous circumstance afforded the Enemy the means of crossing and advancing on both sides of the River; Finding the Enemy were advancing too near I resolved to meet him, being strong in Cavalry, in a wood below the Moravian Town, which last was not cleared of Indian women and children, or of those of the troops; nor of the sick. The Troops were formed with their left to the River; with a reserve and a six-pounder, on the Road near the River. The Indians on the Right. The want of Ammunition was unknown to the men, and but too few of the officers. My only anxiety was on that head, which I made an immediate attempt to procure a supply of, as well as Flour and Corn, and awaited the Result of the Attack with full confidence. The Gun which certainly should have produced the best effect if properly managed was in possession of the

Enemy immediately as the attack commenced, without having fired a shot.[17]

His only anxiety was over the loss of all his ammunition? What about all the food and other supplies lost to the enemy? What about the starving and sickly condition of his troops? What about the dwindling number of Indians who remained to fight? What about the fact that he had started to fortify Moraviantown with five cannons and still stopped just short of that location? And we could go on. Remember, this was an official report to his superior. Due care was certainly taken by Procter to put this defeat and all his miscalculations into the best light possible. He seems to justify his position for battle by claiming that the British and Indian women and children, as well as the sick, were still at Moraviantown. Why were they still there? Procter knew the enemy was very close for at least a full day. Why was word not sent up to Moraviantown to move the occupants eastward and out of danger? These questions do not have reasonable answers. One poignant example of the deception hidden in Procter's report is revealed by John Richardson. Procter seems to scold the 41st regiment for not even firing their lone cannon:

> General Proctor very gravely complains that the gun placed in the road on the left of the line, in the affair of the Moraviantown, and on which he so much depended, had been deserted "without an effort." What will be thought of the general conduct of the retreat, when it is known that there was not a single round of ammunition for the gun, it having by some unfortunate accident been left behind, on resuming our march in the morning![18]

Harrison explains how the situation unfolded in the American camp.

> Being now certainly near the enemy, I directed the advance of Johnson's Regiment to accelerate their march for the purpose of procuring intelligence. The officer commanding it, in a short time, sent to inform me that his progress was stopped by the enemy who were formed across our line of march . . . I soon ascertained enough of their position and order of battle to determine that which it was proper for me to adopt.[19]

Harrison had at his disposal about three thousand men. He placed Colonel Richard Johnson's mounted regiment on the front lines. Behind and aside them, Governor Shelby provided five brigades of infantry militia. Additionally, over a hundred regulars of the 27th regiment of Ohio were ready to fight. Having a keen understanding of the Indian's fighting strategy; Harrison used many of Shelby's militia to protect the flanks and the rear of the force from any surprise attack.

The natural characteristics of the battlefield have been described in some of the accounts already given, but an overall synopsis of the landscape is in order. The geography was quite varied for such a small area. As Harrison viewed the land he saw on his right the banks of the Thames which had grown high and steep. He explains that the whole area for miles approaching Moraviantown was

> a beech forest without any clearing . . . At from two to three hundred yards from the river a swamp extends parallel to it, throughout the whole distance. The intermediate ground is dry and although the trees are tolerably thick, it is in many places clear of underbrush.[20]

The *Detroit Road*, a fifty-foot wide trodden path used by the British for transport of goods between York (Toronto) and Detroit, continued to follow the banks of the Thames with a gap of about a hundred yards between them. To the left of the road was a span of approximately two hundred yards before the small swamp began. From the other side of the small swamp to the front edge of the larger swamp was a brief spell of dry ground. Behind the greater swamp was a dense wooded area.

If we begin at the river and work our way to what would be Harrison's left, we can detail how the factions of the opposing forces lined up against each other in this terrain.

A small contingent force of British regulars had gathered between the river and the road; a few were on the road behind that lone 6-pound cannon. Opposite them was an American group led by Colonel Paull who hailed from Ohio. Under his command were the hundred plus troops of his state's 27th regiment, of which Alfred Brunson was one. Approximately forty Delaware Indians also followed Paull's lead. William Conner the American interpreter was in their number. Harrison hoped the sight of Indians on the attack against them would cause the British much consternation, especially since they knew Walk-in-the-Water had already defected.

In the woods between the road and across to the lesser swamp was formed the main force of Redcoats; their long double lines broken only briefly by fingers of this swamp. Directly opposed to them was one half of the Kentucky mounted militia regiment. This portion of the regiment was led by Colonel James Johnson who reported in a letter to the

Missouri Gazette a few weeks after the battle:

> The regt. was formed, the footmen were soon up. The genl. Gave the command for the mounted regiment to attack the enemy, and if possible to go through his [the enemy's] lines, and they would be supported by infantry. The order was received with joy by the regiment–which was ready for the encounter in a few minutes: and in twelve columns of double files up near the enemy's line which lay concealed.[21]

What Johnson is describing is a decision of Harrison's that was as novel as it was successful–to storm the British troops using the mounted militia instead of the infantry. In his official letter to Armstrong, Harrison explains that he originally intended to have the whole mounted regiment turn toward the Indians who were positioned on his left and trailing down that flank from the small swamp and extending into the front edge of the greater swamp. The infantry was supposed to attack the British lines in the woods on Harrison's right. He says:

> A moments reflection however convinced me that from the thickness of the woods and the swampiness of the ground [in front of the Indians], they [Richard Johnson's mounted militia] would be unable to do anything on horseback and there was no time to dismount them and place their horses in security. I therefore determined to refuse my left to the Indians and to break the British lines at once by a charge of the Mounted Infantry. The measure was not sanctioned by anything that I had seen or heard of, but I was fully convinced that it would succeed. The American backwoodsmen ride better in the woods than any other people. A musket or rifle is no impediment to them, being accustomed to carry them on horseback from their earliest youth. I was persuaded too that the enemy would be quite unprepared for the shock and that they could not resist it. Conformably to this idea, I directed the regiment to be drawn up in close column with its right at the distance of fifty yards from the road, (that it might be in some measure protected by the trees from the artillery) its left upon the swamp and to charge at full speed as soon as the enemy delivered their fire.[22]

What isn't admitted by Harrison is that Richard Johnson was the one to alert him of the poor conditions in the Indians' area. Robert McAfee, whose company attacked the British under James Johnson, states that Harrison

> ordered the Colonel [Richard Johnson], "That as the infantry came up he must take ground to the left, and form two companies in a crochet, so

as to protect his flank and out flank the Indians." Col. Johnson replied that the ground was swampy, and the bush and fallen timber was so thick on his left, that it would be very difficult for mounted men to get with advantage. The General now seemed to hesitate for a moment & Col. Johnson was in the act of turning from him to execute his orders, when Maj. [Eleazar] Wood returned and told the General that the British were formed in an open order. The General immediately called to Col. Johnson and observed that he had determined to charge the British lines, and directed the Colonel to form his regiment in charging columns on horseback, ready to break through their lines and form in their rear, while he would return and bring up the infantry to support him.[23]

Samuel Brown gives a further explanation:

Colonel [Richard] Johnson had, however, a discretion either to attack the British with his full force, or with one battalion, reserving the other for the attack of the Indian line . . . Colonel Johnson perceiving that there was not sufficient room for his whole regiment, increased by fresh volunteers to eleven hundred men, to act advantageously against the British line only, determined to make a simultaneous charge upon the red and white enemy. Accordingly, he divided the regiment equally; gave the command of the first battalion, and the honor of charging the British line, to his brother, Lieutenant Colonel James Johnson; leading the other battalion [the second] in person against the Indians.[24]

We can glimpse a bit of Johnson's spirited leadership as Robert McAfee relates that Johnson

observed to some of the officers and men nearest him, "My brave fellows. I believe in my soul that we can whip the whole of them ourselves" and proceeded along his lines across the swamp to examine the situation of the 2nd battalion, and as he passed along he cheered and animated his men for the approaching conflict, which he observed was now certain.[25]

Harrison did bring forward the multiple divisions of the infantry and ordered them into various positions in support of the mounted regiment. Brunson recalls Harrison's pep talk to the regulars: "the General rode back to us and said, 'I don't know how these volunteers will act. If they give way, my whole dependence is on you, and if you fail me, I'll bury my head in sorrow and disgrace today.'"[26]

As Harrison viewed them, the Indian's force stretched from the point that the British lines had stopped and continued left well into the edge of the greater swamp. Benson Lossing a noted historian of the period states:

> The Indians were posted between two swamps, where the undergrowth was thicker, their right, commanded by the brave Oshawahnah, a Chippewa chief, extending some distance along and just within the borders of the larger marsh, and so disposed as to easily flank Harrison's left. Their left, commanded in person by Tecumtha, occupied the isthmus, or narrowest point, between the two swamps.[27]

This places Tecumseh, for all intents and purposes, smack in the middle of the battlefield where the Indian lines met those of the British.

There was one more special group of men who, as the battle played out, would suffer the most dead and wounded. It was called the *Forlorn Hope*. Samuel Theobold who was one of their members explains:

> Col. Johnson organized a small corps composed of the staff of his regt. which he denominated The *Forlorn Hope* which was designated to accompany him immediately in the event of a battle. And . . . to gratify old Col. Whitley who was a man of distinguished bravery & devoted service in the conflict with the Indians in the early settlement of Kentucky & then at the advanced age of 70 years or over, if I mistake not, had volunteered as a private in Capt. Davidson's company. He was appointed to head this little squad. Others who comprised it on the day of battle & charged immediately with Col. Johnson were Benj. Chambers–Robt. Payne, a nephew of the Col's, Joseph Taylor–William Webb–Garret Wall–Eli Short & myself.[28]

The additional men who deserve to be specially honored for volunteering for this most perilous duty include: John L. Mansfield, Samuel Logan, Richard Spurr, John McGunnigle, Hugh Offett, and Joseph Smith (also known by his Indian name of Dad Joe). Twenty men were supposed to comprise this group. If that number is correct, the names of the five others are, at least to date, lost to history.

Finally, the only infantry to be positioned on the American front lines were the men of General Joseph Desha's division whose formation began where the left edge of Richard Johnson's 2nd battalion had trailed off, and continued to the left and rear at an angle in order to protect that American flank. Harrison explains the positioning of the remaining key players.

> The Crotchet formed by the front line and Genl. Desha's division was

an important point. At that place, the venerable Governor of Kentucky [Shelby] was posted, who at the age of sixty-six, preserves all the vigor of youth, the ardent zeal which distinguished him in the Revolutionary War and the undaunted bravery which he manifested at King's Mountain, with my aids de camp the acting assistant adjutant General Capt. [Robert] Butler, my gallant friend Commodore Perry who did me the honour to serve as my volunteer aid de camp, and Brigadier General Cass who having no command tendered me his assistance. I placed myself at the head of the front line of Infantry, to direct the movements of the Cavalry and give them the necessary support.[29]

The hour drew near to three o'clock in the afternoon. It had already been determined by Harrison that "the sound of the regimental trumpeter should be the signal for a general charge of both battalions."[30] Each man on both sides of this conflict, whether officer, regular, militia, chief or warrior was in his assigned position; and each one waited for the certain break in the new silence about them.

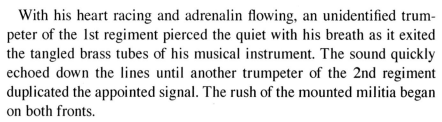

CHAPTER 9

The Battle of the Thames

*Col. Johnson, make the charge;
the infantry are ready and
will support you.[1]*

With his heart racing and adrenalin flowing, an unidentified trumpeter of the 1st regiment pierced the quiet with his breath as it exited the tangled brass tubes of his musical instrument. The sound quickly echoed down the lines until another trumpeter of the 2nd regiment duplicated the appointed signal. The rush of the mounted militia began on both fronts.

Robert McAfee, who led his company into the middle of the action against the British, was positioned between the two chief commanders in this area of the fight, Colonel James Johnson and Major Duvall Payne. He says that as their attack began they

> received a distant fire from the British lines; this somewhat frightened the horses, and caused a little confusion at the heads of the columns, and thus retarded the charge, giving the enemy time to prepare for a second fire, which soon followed the first. But the columns in a moment were completely in motion, and rushed upon the British with irresistible impetuosity. Their front line immediately broke in every direction; and their second about thirty paces in its rear, after giving us a fire, was also broken and thrown into confusion. Our columns having passed through, wheeled to the right and the left and began to pour a destructive fire on the rear of their disordered ranks – but in a moment the contest was over. No sooner had our horsemen charged through their lines and gained their rear then they began to surrender as fast as they could throw down their arms. And thus in a moment the whole British force, upwards of eight hundred strong, was totally vanquished and the greater part of it captured.[2]

Samuel Brown further describes the British regulars' reaction to the Americans' charge.

> Never was terror more strongly depicted on the countenances of men; with their pieces unloaded, their bayonets unfixed, broken, huddled in

confusion or trampled under the horses' feet, and surrounded beyond the possibility of escape, officers and men were seen throwing down their arms, and, with uplifted hands, exclaiming "quarter." So unexpected was the shock, that they were totally unprepared to meet it; the whole was the work of a minute.[3]

There was a pervasive assumption among the British that the Americans would give no quarter since their rage over the treatment of Kentucky POWs received at the Raisin River was still fresh in their minds. In fact many Americans cheered each other on with the call, *Remember the Raisin!* But quarter was shown, as over six hundred British soldiers were taken prisoner. A week after the battle Colonel James Johnson stated that, "We lost but one man on this part of the line . . . and killed 9 British, 3 Indians and took several hundred prisoners."[4]

In a speech delivered almost thirty years later, while he was vice-president of the United States, Richard Johnson noted:

When brother James charged through the British lines, they made no resistance at all. Brother James said it was less trouble to take them, than to know what to do with them after they were taken. They seemed anxious to give up their arms—one Irishman came to brother James and asked what to do with his arms; brother James said he had never thought of that, but the Irishman said if your honor pleases we'll stack them, and brother James ordered them to do so.[5]

As the cavalry had made their charge, Colonel Paull and his contingent of regulars and Indians had easily captured that lone British cannon which never fired a shot in their direction. The whole area of British occupation was secured within minutes. The only disappointment from the American perspective was that they had not captured Major-General Henry Procter, who had retreated, escaped, deserted—call it what you will.

The behavior of Procter is a story unto itself which will be only briefly summarized here. Understand that he was court-martialed several months after this battle for his questionable actions. One of those dubious deeds, his desertion, is reported in the diary of Robert McAfee who while surrounding the British regulars explains, "I wheeled to the right and pursued the road in full chase after a few horsemen who were making off with Genl. Proctor at their head, we continued on two miles to Moraviantown . . ." McAfee was then ordered back to the battle area and after meeting up with Major Payne, General Cass, numerous spies and more men of his company, he and others were ordered to re-pursue Procter

> and continued the pursuit six or seven miles on the road beyond the town which was full of waggons, coats, caps, valises, knapsacks and clothes all thrown off and lying in confusion; the enemy being routed had retreated in the utmost confusion, women and children were in every wagon; in about seven miles Genl. Cass ordered me to take charge of the women and children which I immediately did, directing each man to take a woman behind him & a child before, and bring them back to the town. I did not get back till after dark when I took up quarters in some of the cabins next to the river.[6]

Later, in his *History of the Late War*, McAfee explains further, "The pursuers [the Americans], however, at last pressed him [Procter] so closely that he was obliged to abandon the road, and his carriage and sword were captured by the gallant Major [Eleazar] Wood."[7]

In the British accounts, John Richardson concurs:

> General Proctor, mounted on an excellent charger, and accompanied by his personal staff, sought safety in flight at the very commencement of the action, and being pursued for some hours by a detachment of mounted Kentucky riflemen, was in imminent danger of falling into their hands.[8]

Speaking of that *excellent charger* upon whose back Procter fled – that steed had an interesting history of its own. About a year earlier in the Detroit area there was a Wyandot Indian named Jack Brandy who, though allied with the British, had befriended the American merchant Henry Hunt who lived in that vicinity. Jack was a high-spirited and fair-minded Indian who was always eager to demonstrate his good nature and humanitarian treatment of Americans. One day Jack happened to walk into Mr. Hunt's store just moments after Hunt discovered that his, *splendid, dapple grey horse* was stolen from his stable. Jack surmised from the tracks that some Pottawatomie Indians were the thieves.

> "Well," said Jack, "give me some bread and meat, and maybe I'll find him." Hunt gave him a liberal supply of provisions, and a few dollars in silver, and Jack started alone on his pony in pursuit. He easily tracked them by the horseshoe imprint, the Indian horses being unshod; and the second night when some forty or fifty miles on the route towards

Chicago, after dark, he came to the Indian's camp – there were several of them.

Jack was good at invention, when a plausible story was needed, so he told his new friends he was sent as a runner by Proctor to Chicago to rally the Indians to hurry forward and fight the hated Yankees. "They said they had a fine Yankee horse which they got at Detroit." "Ah! Me glad," said Jack; "may be in morning we trade, and me pay you some boot," slapping his hand on his match-coat pocket to show [by] the jingle of his dollars that he had means to make good his proffered exchange. They spent the evening pleasantly together before their camp fire in mutually recounting their adventures upon the war path, and Jack's were by no means the least brilliant or marvelous.

The next morning, after their simple repast, the fine dapple grey was produced. It was just such a horse, said Jack, as he needed, in order to accomplish in the least time possible the important public mission on which he was engaged. He now mounted the noble steed to try him, and at once boldly dashed off, leaving his own pony in exchange, and escaped, leaving his Pottawatomie friends perfectly astounded at Jack's adroitness in so completely outwitting them . . . Near night Jack reached Detroit and rode up to Hunt's with his horse all panting and foaming, and jumping off, said, "There, Harry Hunt, you see Jack Brandy no lie." Jack of course was liberally rewarded for the loss of his pony, and his own good service. Proctor soon after got his eye on this fine animal, and expressed a desire to purchase him; and Hunt knowing full well, if he did not sell him, the horse would be taken nolens volens [anyway], he sent word to Proctor that he could have him for a hundred guineas – much more than such a horse was really worth. Proctor unhesitatingly paid the amount, and his fleet dapple grey enabled him to escape captivity at the Thames when hotly pursued by the victorious Americans for several miles.[9]

A consensus of the most reliable accounts all paint this picture of Procter leaving the battlefield. He may have tried to briefly rally his troops but, as cited, the affair was over in a few minutes. On this swift horse, purchased a year earlier from the American Mr. Henry Hunt, he fled the scene very early stopping briefly at Moraviantown to switch to his carriage which was already laden with his belongings. Finally, a few miles out of Moraviantown, he decided to abandon the carriage and its contents and mounted one of the lead horses. This allowed him to get off of the road and ride through the trees to elude the ever closing American pursuers. And he did. In total he travelled over sixty miles in twenty-four hours, taking only a brief respite at Delaware, Ontario (near current London, Ontario) which was some thirty miles from Moravian-town. From Delaware, in a brief report to another officer, Procter's aid, Captain Hall, wrote very late in the evening of October 5th:

> An affair . . . took place with the enemy near Moravian Town this afternoon about 4 o'clock–one of the guns being deserted early in the action, the troops near it gave way and the consequence was a complete route–notwithstanding the exertions of the General to rally them, so much so that I thought it impossible he could escape being taken–we are just arrived here [Delaware]–The General is so fatigued by riding from the field of battle, on the other side [of] the Moravian Town, through the wilderness, that he cannot write and I am not much better.[10]

Procter himself wrote from Burlington a few weeks later, "Having in vain endeavored to call the men to a sense of duty and having no chance by remaining, but of being captured, I reluctantly quitted the ground, and narrowly escaped being taken by the enemy's cavalry."[11] At his court martial Procter was charged with various counts relating to his failures to use foresight and essential military skills throughout the retreat and the battle. He was convicted of only a few of the charges. His pay and rank were deferred for only six months, and he was held up to public scorn. Though considered a modest sentence, it squelched any further military career he may have desired. He died in England eight years after the trial at the age of fifty-nine.

As the British prisoners were being secured, some of the American cavalry, which had just made quick work of capturing this esteemed 41st regiment, remained in the area to help in the effort. Others were deployed to their left to catch the flank of the Indians nearest to them. They entered a fight that was already underway between Colonel Richard Johnson's regiment and Tecumseh's warriors.

The left front of the Americans' which battled the Indians was set into motion by the same trumpeters that triggered the right front into action against the British. The first movement in this line was of Colonel Richard M. Johnson and his band of twenty–dubbed the *Forlorn Hope*. In a speech he gave in 1840, the colonel elaborated on his thinking as regards the attack.

I selected 20 men that I knowed I could depend on as a forlorn hope. I was determined that we wouldn't play at long taw with them any more; and I was determined that we would make short work of it; so we charged upon them in three columns two abreast, so that we had the advantage of them. They could only shoot at two of my men, while my men could shoot at their whole line.

Then with a little braggadocio he expounded:

I placed the forlorn hope in advance of the rest, so that here was the charging columns, here was the forlorn hope, and where was I? Right here in front. (Cheers). Well, we charged on the enemy and in five minutes 19 of the forlorn hope had fell from their horses killed or wounded or thrown from their saddles. Some of their horses wouldn't stand fire, but my grey mare that I rode, would stand a cannon-shot and never start in the least. I was afraid that my horse that I generally rode wouldn't stand fire and so I changed him before the battle commenced for my grey mare that I knowed could be depended upon, but it is very few animals that would stand fire as she would; and so 19 of the forlorn hope was very soon either cut down or thrown from their horses.[12]

So the *Forlorn Hope*, on the right side of Johnson's regiment, was the first wave of attack, quickly followed by the columns of mounted militia. The left side of the line was commanded by Major Thompson, in whose battalion were the companies of Captains Stucker, Davidson, Combs, Rice and Coleman. One might wonder the need of the almost certain sacrifice of the *Forlorn Hope*. The strategic thinking seems to be that they were to provide a deception of sorts–drawing the first fire of the Indians. Then, while the Indians started to reload, the second wave–the columns of militia–would come rushing into the arena and overwhelm the enemy warriors by either killing them or causing them to scatter. It was hoped the action would be swift and complete, but regardless of its speed of execution, it really was a suicide mission for the *Forlorn Hope*. It is amazing to note that Johnson had to disappoint many young men who rushed forward volunteering for this deadly honor. Because he wanted it to be a small group, he unwittingly saved these gallant men's lives.

Samuel Theobold, in his letter to Ben Lossing (before Lossing wrote his much cited history of the battle), confirms that all of the *Forlorn Hope* were disabled. "I alone" says Theobold, "escaped without injury to myself & horse except a severe contusion of my leg from being set against a tree by the violent recoil of my horse."[13]

Up to this point of the battle, the facts set forth have had very little dispute among historians. For over two centuries these events have been generally agreed to be accurate. Yes, the numbers of participants in the battle have been occasionally skewed by both sides to embellish victory or save face in defeat. Also, there were some disputes years after the battle over which officer gave certain orders, or the wisdom of some of the tactics employed by said officers. All such disputes were to raise or lower the heroism of one over another. This can be seen in Procter's situation – his behavior had been excused by some due to extenuating circumstances, but still condemned by others. All of these types of disputes are nothing more than hindsight debate over how people could have acted or strategized differently.

When the *Forlorn Hope* took their first steps towards the Indians that day, a much larger debate was triggered that has yet to be settled. Tecumseh, in the next few minutes, would be killed. The fact that he fell that day is no longer questioned, though it was for the first week or two afterwards. But *how* he was killed, and by *whose hand*, has certainly been argued. The dilemma stems from too many supposed facts put forward by too many supposed witnesses to the event of this great chief's death. It is now these particular testimonies that need our thorough analysis; as we will discover how overwhelmingly contrary, ambiguous, self-serving, political and generally perplexing they are.

CHAPTER 10

Nothing But the Facts

Here the heroic Indian Chieftain, the greatest of his race,
doubtless fell. Yet no Indian that I have met,
has admitted the fact;
and no white man that I have seen,
has with certainty known it.[1]

One of the most reliable, simple and clear overviews of what happened as the *Forlorn Hope* made their move against the Indians, comes from Robert McAfee's diary. Although McAfee was chasing Procter toward Moraviantown while this action with the Indians was occurring, his information has obviously come from fellow men at the battle and his accuracy has rarely been disputed over the years.

> The battle on the left wing was against Genl. Tecumseh and his Indians and was much more obstinate, so much so, that the logs, brush and swamp prevented them from charging thro & the Indian's fired so hot that the companies had to dismount and fight from behind trees and logs in the Indian way; & repeated charges and repulses took place on each side. Col. Johnson was wounded in the first fire & Genl. Tecumseh it is said fell by the hands of our Col. The battle lasted near an hour and was fought entirely by Col. Johnson's Regt. and two companies of Gov. Shelby's troops which eventuated in the total defeat of the British & Indians.[2]

In his *History of the Late War*, written just three years later, McAfee elaborates:

> They [the Indians] reserved their full fire till the heads of the columns and the front lines on foot had approached within a few paces of their position. A very destructive fire was then commenced on them, about the time the firing ceased between the British and the first battalion.[3]

It all sounds so simple, and it would seem from this latter description that the plan for the *Forlorn Hope* to draw the first fire occurred as expected, but it took place a bit later than they would have preferred. The lead Americans were much closer to the Indians than planned when the firing began – only yards away. The columns of militia as well had already come up into the sights of the Indians. McAfee continues:

Colonel Johnson, finding his advance guard, composing the head of his column, nearly all cut down by the first fire, and himself severely wounded, immediately ordered his columns to dismount and come up in line before the enemy, the ground which they occupied being unfavorable for operations on horseback. The line was promptly formed on foot, and a fierce conflict was then maintained for seven or eight minutes, with considerable execution on both sides, but the Indians had not sufficient firmness to sustain very long a fire which was close and warm and severely destructive. They gave way and fled through the brush into the outer swamp, not, however, before they had learned the total discomfiture of their allies, and had lost, by the fall of Tecumseh . . .

McAfee elaborates further:

As soon as the firing commenced between the Indians and the second battalion, Governor Shelby, who was posted at the crotchet in its rear, immediately ordered that part of the front line of infantry, which lay between the first swamp and the crotchet, being a part of Colonel Donelson's regiment, to march up briskly to the aid of the mounted men. They rushed up accordingly into Colonel Johnson's lines, and participated in the contest at that point. This was the only portion of the infantry which had an opportunity of engaging in any part of the battle. The Governor also dispatched General Adair, his aide-de-camp, to bring up the brigade of General King to the front line, but before this could be accomplished, the enemy had fled from Colonel Johnson, and a scattering, running fire had commenced along the swamp in front of General Desha's division between the retiring Indians and the mounted men in pursuit who were now commanded by Major Thompson alone; Colonel Johnson having retired in consequence of his wounds. This firing in the swamp continued, with occasional remissions, for nearly half an hour, during which time the contest was gallantly maintained by Major Thompson and his men, who were still pressing forward on the Indians. Governor Shelby in the meantime rode down to the left of General Desha's division, and ordered the regiment of Colonel Simrall, which was posted on the extreme left, to march up on the right flank of the enemy, in aid of Major Thompson, but before this reinforcement could reach the scene of action, the Indians had given up the contest.[4]

The troop movements get a little hard to follow, but essentially McAfee reiterates that Johnson was wounded and off the field early.

As a result, Major Thompson took command and continued to lead the fight as the action became fluid and moved to the Americans' left for some time. As an example of what we are about to become involved in, a quick analysis of at least parts of McAfee's overview is in order. It will bring to light just a few of the many points of contention this seemingly straight forward testimony has with some of the other accounts we'll soon review.

In his diary McAfee writes, "& Genl. Tecumseh it is said, fell by the hands of our Col." Of course the truth of that statement is the focal point of our discussion. Since this quote is coming from McAfee's diary of October 5th, it seems like it should be believable and it shows that the apparent belief in camp was that Colonel Johnson had indeed killed Tecumseh. We will soon see many legitimate cases made in support of this opinion, and even more against it; as well as claims for several other men to have been the perpetrators. Even the reference to rumors of any sort flying through the camp suggesting that someone, let alone Johnson, had killed Tecumseh, we will soon see as controversial.

"The battle lasted near an hour," says McAfee. Well, that's his conclusion from his experience. But, from the handful of other people who commented on the length of the battle, the time ranges from a few minutes to two hours. The length of the battle is important when the issue of Johnson leaving the battlefield early is addressed – especially by those who claim he killed Tecumseh.

One other important point cited in numerous other accounts is that a loud bone-chilling Indian yell was heard when Tecumseh fell, and that this cry signaled the remaining Indians to retreat thus ending the fight. If we throw this one item into the mix of McAfee's facts, well, things get complicated.

Let's try to add it up. McAfee says Johnson killed Tecumseh and was "wounded in the first fire," and "retired in consequence of his wounds," but the battle continued "for nearly half an hour, during which time the contest was gallantly maintained by Major Thompson and his men." If Johnson killed Tecumseh in that first fire and Tecumseh's death in turn signaled the Indian yell which ended the fight, how does one explain the additional half-hour of fighting? What if Johnson had killed another Indian, not Tecumseh, as many others claim? Then the fighting would have continued until someone else killed the chief and the yell was heard. Should the truth of the Indian yell at Tecumseh's death be questioned? If so, then Johnson could have killed him, but so could anyone else! If the Indian yell is true, then someone else had to have killed him sometime after Johnson was off the battlefield if the length of the battle per McAfee is to be believed.

Are you beginning to see how one questionable fact feeds on another? How an assumption becomes a fact? And, this example is just from reviewing a couple of the points brought up by others and measured against McAfee's. Witnesses, friends of witnesses, people who heard this or that from someone – all sorts of people have cherry-picked assumptions and facts and made them into their own story of what happened to Tecumseh on October 5th, 1813.

Before we delve deeper into this mystery, let's be clear about one fundamental thing – this was a battle in a war. The point of war is to kill your enemy. Killing of your enemy is not a crime, and the man who killed Tecumseh was not a criminal. As fair-minded, humane, dignified, brave, righteous, and admired Tecumseh may have been, on this day he was the enemy of the Americans. Likewise, Harrison, Shelby, Johnson, and all the rest of the Americans were the enemy of Tecumseh and his Indians. In our effort to determine who it was that did this deed, however; we'll need to take an approach somewhat similar to the proceedings of a criminal trial. That is, presenting the evidence and then allowing you, the jury of readers, to decide who did it.

It's time to present the long list of facts in question regarding Tecumseh's death. With our goal being to determine who killed Tecumseh, these questions have to be asked. The simple truth is that there are many, many conflicting answers to them and weeding through them all is unavoidably tedious.

We've already mentioned that the length of the battle is disputed as well as whether or not it ended upon Tecumseh's death. Additionally the questions at hand are:

Did Johnson kill Tecumseh, or another Indian who appeared to be a chief?

Was Johnson on horseback when he killed the Indian attacking him, or had he and his horse fallen?

What color was Johnson's horse – white, grey or spotted?

Was Johnson's horse killed on the battlefield? Or did it die later after carrying Johnson off?

Who removed the wounded Johnson from the battlefield?

Were there other Indians killed in the vicinity of where "Johnson's Indian" was killed?

What were the rumors, if any, circulating in the American camp? Was there talk of Tecumseh being dead? If so, was the belief that Johnson had killed him? Did anyone else's name come up as the slayer?

What weapons were at Johnson's disposal? A Rifle? A Sword? Pistols? All or some of these?

Did Tecumseh target an officer with his final attack? Was it the dress, or horse, of his opponent that signaled Tecumseh that his opponent was an officer? Was Tecumseh targeting Harrison?

What weapons did Tecumseh bring into the battle? A tomahawk? A sword? A knife? A rifle? A musket? Or was it any number or combination of these?

Was Tecumseh on horseback or on foot at the time of his death?

What was Tecumseh wearing the day of the battle? Was it the very ornate dress of a chief or the simple buckskin garb of a common warrior?

Did Tecumseh wear a medal, a sash or any other British military ornamentation?

Did Tecumseh wear any war paint? If so, what color?

Did Tecumseh wear a single or multiple ostrich feather plume in his headdress? Did he wear a turban?

What weapon killed Tecumseh? Was it an axe, a rifle, a musket, a pistol, a bayonet, a tomahawk or a sword?

Where on his body did the fatal wound land? Was it in the face, the leg, the hip, the back, the breast, or the head?

If he was killed by firearms, what type of ammunition killed him? Was it two balls, two balls and buckshot, a single rifle ball, a single musket ball, a small rifle ball, a pistol ball or a pistol ball with buckshot?

Was Tecumseh's body left on the field of battle after he was killed? If so, for how long? If not, when was he removed? Immediately? A few hours later? The next morning? Never? Did Americans bury him?

If he was removed early from the battlefield by the Indians, how could he have been identified as slain?

Who identified the body that was concluded to be Tecumseh's? Were they qualified to identify him? Had they ever seen Tecumseh before?

Did any of the British soldiers have an opportunity to identify Tecumseh's body?

How badly distorted were the features of the body that the identifiers claimed was Tecumseh? Wouldn't any disfiguration make it difficult to identify him?

What known markings were used to ascertain Tecumseh's identification? Was it scars on his leg, hip, thigh, face, or back; a leg shorter than the other, a recent wound on the arm or wrist, a blue tooth or acne?

Was William Whitley's dead body found near Tecumseh's? Could Whitley have killed Tecumseh? Could they have killed each other?

Could a young private named David King have killed Tecumseh?

Did anyone else independently claim to have killed Tecumseh?

What have the Indians said about Tecumseh's death? Who do the Indians believe killed him?

And finally, was Tecumseh's body skinned after death? It is certain that an Indian body was skinned by vengeful Americans. They bragged that they had cut the strips off of the Indian's back and thigh to later be used as razor strops or just as souvenirs of their nemesis. But was it Tecumseh's skin or someone else's?

As you can now see, the intermingling of all these questions is what builds this mystery. The majority of accounts about this event favor three men to be the most likely ones to have killed Tecumseh. They are Colonel Richard M. Johnson, William Whitley, and a private about whom little is known, named David King. Several other individuals have claimed that they killed Tecumseh, and they may have, it will be up to you to decide if their claims are valid.

CHAPTER 11

History's Perspective

Rumpsey Dumpsey,
Colonel Johnson killed Tecumseh![1]

History books as a rule contend that Colonel Richard M. Johnson was the man who killed Tecumseh at the Battle of the Thames. Some declare this as undisputed fact. Most acknowledge that it is the most probable scenario, though impossible to prove. There is good reason for this conclusion. Much of the testimony given, especially within the first few years of the event, cites Johnson. Further, much of it is given by eye-witnesses. Yet, even many of these early first-hand accounts have their share of speculation and contradiction. When we look at the accounts of the people even further removed from the event, we see, as expected, even more discrepancies. Yet, true or false, history has repeatedly decided to give the credit, at least conditionally, to Johnson.

One might have expected that the news of Tecumseh's death would have warranted screaming, extra-bold headlines in newspapers across the country. Not quite. A general review of newspapers of the early 1800s quickly illuminates the fact that the use of large sensational headlines was an idea whose time had not yet arrived. Events of the day were simply reported. Often heroic events were cited almost in passing in the body of the text. The fact that Mrs. Smith was holding a family reunion on the morrow, seemed as newsworthy as the troops winning a battle over the British. The victory at the Thames and Tecumseh's death trickled into the newspapers in a fragmented fashion.

The very first published accounts of the battle itself only sometimes mentioned Tecumseh's death. They did not cite his slayer. Initial knowledge of either of these facts, as we will see, is disputed even among those closest to the action. The earliest newspaper account came on October 19, 1813 in the *Kentucky Gazette* when they published a letter written on the day of the battle by John J. Crittenden. From, "Camp on the River Thames, 67 miles from Sandwich, October 5, 1813," Crittenden reported, "The British colors no longer wave in this part of Upper Canada, nor have they one yard of canvas on Lake Erie or its waters." Only as a postscript did Crittenden add, "P.S. I believe we have not had a single officer killed. It is said Tecumseh is killed."[2]

In the same issue, of the same newspaper, we learn that General Duncan McArthur, who was defending Detroit while the Thames conflict took place, had received word of the battle results as quickly as the day after it was fought. He did not make mention of Col. Johnson but did note, "General Tecumseh is said to be among the dead."[3] Although we will see many people claim otherwise, these first two accounts reveal that Tecumseh was in the least rumored to be dead.

Major-General Henry Procter didn't make his first official communication to his superiors until two and a half weeks had passed. Near the end of his letter, Procter states, "with deep concern, I mention the Death of the Chief Tecumthei who was shot on the 5th Instant."[4]

Another American account appeared in the *Ohio Republican* newspaper on October 25, 1813. Major Thomas Bodley, who was in the action, said:

> Colonel Johnson received 5 wounds in the engagement but is now considered out of danger–Gen. Tecumseh after having been frequently and severely wounded, at last fell with one hundred of his red brethren on the field of battle–thus makes his quietus, perhaps the greatest Indian General, that ever lifted a tomahawk.[5]

No connection is made between the Colonel and Tecumseh.

Just a day later, in the *Kentucky Gazette*, a letter from Col. George Trotter was published. It was written just a day after the battle and highlights the confusion over Tecumseh's death. Trotter said, "Elliot, Tecumseh and Proctor fled at the commencement of the action."[6] Yet Col. James Johnson stated in a letter dated October 12th, "As yet, I have not heard officially, our number of prisoners in all–but it is said about 600 including officers. Tecumseh is killed–Proctor and Elliot made their escape . . ."[7] Two officers of high command who were fully engaged in the conflict tell the newspapers two different stories regarding Tecumseh.

Harrison never mentioned Tecumseh in his report to the Secretary of War, written just a few days after the battle. The first official reference to Tecumseh came from General Lewis Cass to the Secretary on

October 28, a full three weeks after the fight. Cass reports, "There is little reason to doubt but that the celebrated Tecumseh was killed in the battle. His body was seen by us all, and recognized to have been that of the Indian chief; and subsequent information confirms the identity."[8]

The first connection between Tecumseh and Johnson comes from the colonel's hometown newspaper in Georgetown, Kentucky. As reprinted in November in the *Missouri Gazette*, the Georgetown editor reports:

> In consequence of the unpredictability of passing thro' the thicket and swamp on horseback, after passing into the lines of the enemy at the head of his men [Johnson] receiving five wounds . . . which were severe, and shooting Tecumseh deliberately with his pistol—he ordered his volunteers to dismount and fight the savages in their own way; which was instantly obeyed.

The writer goes on, bringing up a contentious point that we touched upon earlier—the length of the battle after Johnson left the field. He says:

> Col. Johnson, being covered with wounds and unable to remain in the field from the loss of blood, the command of that part of the Regiment devolved entirely upon Major Thompson, who sustained the action with about 500 men against 1000 or 1500 savages for one hour and forty minutes.[9]

The debate over who killed Tecumseh ebbed and flowed over the years, usually argued out through public letters like these to the editors of newspapers. Kentucky and Ohio had the keenest interest in this topic since the majority of the combatants at the battle were from those states. But it was a national curiosity as well. The confusion begins within moments of Tecumseh's death. Some accounts claim that there were rumors in the camp that night suggesting Tecumseh was killed by Johnson, others say by King, still others by Whitley. But additional reports say that there was absolutely no speculation in camp over who killed Tecumseh; because it was controversial enough at that point to suggest that he was even dead.

A few years after the battle, the debate settled down, at least for awhile. The majority of the general public concluded that Johnson was the probable slayer. Some, however, still believed it was either William Whitley or David King. After some twenty years of rela-

Image courtesy of U.S. Library of Congress.

Portrait of Lyman C. Draper, the renowned historian who tirelessly travelled and corresponded with the pioneers of 19th century America. Samuel Sartain-Engraver.

tive dormancy, the topic became newsworthy again – and for several reasons. Historians, interested in writing biographies of Tecumseh, or chronicles of the War of 1812, began doing their research. Veterans were being called upon to give their accounts to historians like Benjamin Drake, who was writing his *Life of Tecumseh, and his Brother the Prophet, with a Historical Sketch of the Shawnee Indians*. His work was published in 1841. Shortly thereafter, for his upcoming book, Lossing's *Pictorial Field Book of the War of 1812*, Benson Lossing began writing to men who participated at the Thames, asking for their take on what happened there. Lossing's book was published in 1868. And Lyman Draper, for decades the wandering historian without whose effort much of the understanding of the American frontier life would have been lost; wrote letters to, and visited veterans, friends and descendents of Thames participants. His archive of interviews and personal letters are a treasure trough of information which never made it to book form before his death in 1891. So we see that the topic was one that sparked a lot of public interest, but was never fully resolved. In waves of time, over the seventy-plus years after the event, accounts appeared in the publications of the day as one man's conclusions weighed in against another's.

When this topic resurfaced in the 1830s, the reason was politics. Richard M. Johnson was already a military hero and a beloved politician in Kentucky. But soon, in 1836, he would be seeking the second highest office in the land, vice-president of the United States. Johnson was running on the Democratic Party ticket with Martin Van Buren. Their opponents, from the Whig party, were none other than William H. Harrison for president, and his running-mate Francis P. Granger. *Spin* as we use the term these days in political circles is nothing new. It was a public relations tool actively employed even back in the 1830s. The question as to whether Johnson really did kill Tecumseh could make or break this candidate so supporters embellished this at least *probable* truth and made it appear to be fact. Detractors, of course, scoffed at the claim, but had to tread lightly since Johnson was revered in both parties for his overall bravery. Additionally, his opponent, Harrison was quite heroic at the Thames himself. How precious it was for the supporters of Johnson to take this supposed truth and use it to raise Johnson to greatness for having bested the greatest Indian warrior of their generation.

In 1824, upon Colonel Johnson's return from Congress, he, in conjunction with his neighbors, gave a general invitation to assemble at Blue Spring on July 3, 1824, "to celebrate the birth of their liberty" On this occasion, a splendid table was prepared, three hundred feet in length, and suitable accommodations were provided. At an early hour on the third, "the whole country seemed to be in motion." People were on their way to accept the Colonel's invitation, "their bosoms swelling with rapture." The Georgetown Light Infantry was on its way, "waving the standard of their country" and supporting the emblem of freedom – "the cap of liberty." The Light Infantry halted in full view on descent of the hill and fired a salute, which was answered by the artillery planted at the spring. At eleven o'clock the cannon gave signal for the concourse to assemble around the spring, "the rude cliffs of which, forming a kind of amphitheater" enabled crowds to hear the speakers of the occasion. Attention was commanded and the drums and fifes played "Yankee Doodle," after which Colonel Johnson read and commented upon "the testament of our liberties," the Declaration of Independence. This was followed by an oration, after which Doctor Richard Emmons recited a "poem" including the words, "Rumpsey Dumpsey Colonel Johnson killed Tecumseh." The

The Blue Spring where many 19th century citizens refreshed themselves as guests of Richard M. Johnson. Shown as it appeared in 2008–now on private property near Georgetown, Kentucky.

Photo courtesy of Georgetown & Scott County Museum -Andrew Green, Director

The program cover to Richard Emmons' play celebrating Johnson's slaying of Tecumseh at the Battle of the Thames.

Image from microfilm files at Bowling Green State University

Music written by I. B. Woodbury celebrating the victory at the Thames.

Image courtesy of U.S. Library of Congress.

A Broadside from the Democratic-Republican party's 1840 presidential campaign, promoting Martin Van Buren for President and Richard M. Johnson for Vice-President. Episodes of Johnson's military prowess are depicted along the bottom, the central image being the lithograph of John Dorival highlighting Johnson's slaying of Tecumseh.

Image courtesy of U.S. Library of Congress.

Death of Tecumseh. Battle of the Thames Oct 5th 1813. 1841.
Nathaniel Currier-Lithographer.

stanzas, whatever their literary quality, were received with unbounded applause. Following Emmons' offering, the large number of people enjoyed a dinner, lasting two hours.[10]

Blue Spring, so named for the deep-water pool of said hue, was on the property of Richard M. Johnson's farm and home just outside of

Image courtesy of U.S. Library of Congress.

Death of Tecumseh – Battle of the Thames Oct: 18: 1813. 1846. Nathaniel Currier-Lithographer. Note the surprising misprint of the date of the battle.

Georgetown, Kentucky. Johnson was a wealthy but generous man, always looking out for the poor and unfortunate in society. His home was frequented often and by people of all walks of life. Distinguished political figures as prominent as President Monroe, small and large business owners, and people of society all visited Johnson's resort; but orphans, widows, veterans and poor farmers, whom Johnson had a fondness for, were also invited for a respite at his residence.

This particular Indepedence Day celebration of 1824 on Johnson's property was a grand event indeed. Imagine a buffet table the length of a football field! Imagine the delight of hearing live music resonating in the hollow when such harmonies were rarely heard on the quiet frontier. Imagine the dramatic multi-gun salutes echoing off rolling hills! Imagine the genuine joy these people felt as they celebrated their freedom – freedom bought at such a high cost. Certainly, the elder partiers reminisced about the sacrifices they, their friends and their family had made during the Revolution for the privilege of being able to meet safely here today. The middle-aged and younger guests, as well, had experienced the growing pains of this country and had known the tales of their parents' and grandparents' adventures. It wasn't a fireworks show or a day off from work that motivated this celebration. It was an authentic appreciation of what they had; what they or their parents had fought for; what many of their kinsmen had died for. This was a very pure celebration of their forty-eighth year of liberty.

And it was here, while Johnson was a U.S. senator, and still a dozen years away from seeking the office of vice-president, that his future campaign slogan was given birth to by his long-time friend and poet, Richard Emmons. The *Rumpsey Dumpsey* jingle most likely had been used sporadically in the interim years of Johnson's political life, but it matured to become a nationally-renowned slogan in his 1836 campaign with Martin Van Buren for the top seats in the land. The verse has since been recorded in historical accounts with only slight variation. One reads, "Rumpsey Dumpsey, *Hickory Crumpsey*, Colonel Johnson killed Tecumseh!"[11] In all likelihood, the original verse from Emmons' poem was used as is, with only the words Rumpsey Dumpsey repeated in the first line. If a campaign ribbon or card should ever come to light, in all probability it would read:

> "Rumpsey Dumpsey, Rumpsey Dumpsey,
> Colonel Johnson Killed Tecumseh!"

Its blunt declaration that Johnson slew Tecumseh solidified the event as fact in supporters' minds. It stirred controversy in his opponents'.

Richard Emmons, and his brother William, were life-long friends of Johnson. In 1834, Richard would write a play titled *Tecumseh, of the Battle of the Thames – A national drama in five acts.* In it, he depicted Johnson gallantly slaying the famed Tecumseh. His brother William published a biography of Johnson just a year earlier, and was also involved in publishing two engravings of the event – one coincided with the printing of this biography. Both Emmons brothers' efforts were undertaken to gain political attention for Johnson just before his run for the vice-presidency.

Tecumseh and his death have been written about in books ever since the event took place. But beyond all the books, many other venues have been used to remember this man, and in particular, how he was killed. There have been plays, like the one written by Emmons, but additionally poems, political cartoons, early posters (referred to as broadsides), engravings, and even songs. If any of these works mentioned or depicted Tecumseh's foe, they generally cited Johnson.

One poem was written by a Canadian author, John Richardson, the same Richardson who fought at the Thames. An avid admirer of Tecumseh, Richardson wrote *Tecumseh: Or the Warrior of the West* in 1828, and names Johnson as the slayer. Another poet, G. A. Aynge of Dartmouth, wrote *The Death of Tecumesceh; and poetical Fragments on Various Subjects* in 1821. Aynge adds, via a footnote in his book, a statement recounting the traditional scene of Johnson shooting Tecumseh, but includes a caveat, "the Col. [Johnson] was discovered severely wounded when Tecumesceh fell, but whether by Tecumesceh or not, is not known."[12] So in Aynge's circle of knowledge, Johnson certainly killed Tecumseh; but in a twist, the fact of whether any of Johnson's multiple wounds were received from Tecumseh is the question.

Other plays written on the topic of the Thames, cautiously evade the issue of *who* killed Tecumseh. Besides Emmons drama of 1834, another, titled *Tecumseh* was written in 1886 by a Canadian named Charles Mair. In it, Mair manages to dodge the issue by having the chief lead a fight scene between the Indians and Americans only to have him temporarily fade from view and then reappear mortally wounded. Likewise, near the area of Tecumseh's birth in Chillicothe, Ohio, a contemporary outdoor drama titled *Tecumseh!* has been performed seasonally since 1973. In this play, its author, Allan Eckert, similarly skirts the issue. The chief falls in the general melee of the fight scene with no particular character singled out as firing the fatal shot.

During Johnson's campaign years for the vice-presidency, political cartoons and broadsides often included at least a subtle reference to the battle. One cartoon cleverly used a painting of the Battle of the Thames, which depicted Johnson shooting Tecumseh, as a backdrop on a wall. More obvious was the National Democratic-Republican campaign broadside which prominently featured a painting of Johnson shooting Tecumseh and text referring to Johnson which read:

At the Battle of the Thames, Oct 5th 1813 [Johnson] commanded the regiment of Kentucky mounted men and in their charge on the enemy, led his battalion against the Indians headed by Tecumseh in which daring movement his horse was killed under him. Several balls passed through his clothes, and three (severe) wounds brought him to the battleground, weltering in his blood, but not till he had slain & with his own hand, their Indian chief, roused the army of Proctor, and obtained for Harrison and Shelby, an easy victory . . .[13]

As cited earlier, numerous pieces of art, mostly engravings, have been created since the event. The last and most prominent painting is in the frescoed frieze circling the rotunda of the U. S. Capitol (see cover art.) It was completed in 1889 and depicts Johnson killing Tecumseh as part of the timeline of American history. All the works of art which portray the death of Tecumseh imply that it was by the hand of an American officer, if not Johnson himself.

At least one song was officially composed celebrating the battle. Titled, *Battle of the Thames*, the song is full of patriotism, but makes no specific mention of how Tecumseh was killed.[14] Certainly, other poems, lost to history, were set to music amongst friends and neighbors of the frontier who had reaped the peace benefit that resulted from this battle along the Thames.

A few facts surrounding Johnson's actions at the Thames are indisputable. He did lead the charge of his regiment against the Indian contingent. He was severely wounded in the engagement, proven by the scars he bore the rest of his life. He did kill an Indian in the fight. He did leave the battlefield at some point earlier than others due to his injuries. Beyond these facts, certainty ends. Through all the nineteenth century forms of cultural expression, be it visual arts, music, or the written word, history has nodded its head toward Johnson as the man that killed Tecumseh.

CHAPTER 12

The Forlorn Hope Testifies

*On first view, Shane pronounced it not the body of Tecumseh,
but on a particular survey and examination,
he was rather of a different opinion,
and eventually thought it was.[1]*

Let's begin the investigation with the testimony of those who were physically positioned very near Johnson on the battlefield – the *Forlorn Hope*. If Johnson was the most likely slayer, then it seems a logical extension that these men would have key testimonies regarding both his actions and Tecumseh's fate. Furthermore, any eye-witness inherently tends to be the most credible source of information, right? Well, as you will see, such is not always the case. There is often just enough conflicting detail presented causing the investigator to utter an involuntary "hmmm". Just wait, you'll see.

Beyond making a case for any one person to have killed Tecumseh, most witnesses bring in other circumstantial evidence to support their story. This peripheral information will be dealt with as it appears or as it becomes important to the reader's fundamental understanding of the event. Therefore, some brief side-trips away from an original account will be required on occasion in order for the reader to gain these foundational reference points regarding any given issue. It will inevitably get a bit messy, but that's why this event is such a mystery.

The *Forlorn Hope* was the first group of men to charge into the action. Since they were led by Colonel Johnson, they were the closest men to him when contact was made with the Indians. One of the few surviving members of the *Forlorn Hope*, Samuel Theobold, wrote several letters recounting his participation at the Thames. Theobold was a medical doctor, lawyer and well-educated in other studies as well. In Johnson's regiment he served as a judge advocate (what would become commonly referred to today as a JAG – Judge Advocate General's Corps). While most of today's JAGs spend their time in military courtrooms, or reviewing strategic rules of engagement, Theobold was literally up front and in the heart of the action. He was the only member of the *Forlorn Hope* to have his horse and himself come out of the action unscathed.

Theobold's first public account of the event appeared in the *Kentucky Gazette* on December 9, 1816, just three years after the battle. In it, he explains how several men of the *Forlorn Hope* were fired upon at nearly the same time:

> Just before the charge was blown, colonel Whitley exclaimed to colonel Johnson, "Our motto today, colonel, is victory or death"–The brave old fellow first met his fate–He received a mortal wound through the breast, and expired soon after. I have no doubt colonel Johnson received several wounds almost at the same instant–Joseph Taylor esq., Robert Payne and Eli Short, who were immediately before me, were all wounded nearly at the same time and dismounted. By this means a considerable space was made between colonel Johnson and myself–I halted my horse just at this period near a large tree, and from this circumstance, together with the density of the smoke from the enemies fire, which was then very considerable, [I] lost sight of colonel Johnson for a few minutes. Whilst in this position I saw an Indian rather indistinctly, spring briskly forward to my right, in the attitude of striking. I changed my horse's head from left to right of the tree; colonel Johnson presented himself full in my view very near me, approaching me from that direction [the right]. He was then literally covered with wounds, having received five, four of which were deep and severe–his horse was likewise wounded by seven or eight balls, but the faithful animal bore him through a deep and almost impassable swamp, to the arms of his surgeon, and [his horse] expired not long after.[2]

Theobold didn't expound on his helping Johnson off the battlefield in this early letter, but forty-five years later he did. At the request of Ben Lossing, who was soliciting information for his now distinct history of the war, Theobold furnished many more details surrounding Johnson's removal from the battleground.

> Col. Johnson approached me bleeding & wounded, as I have stated, and requested me to conduct him from the field. I saw no one near us at the moment. I think he said to me as we met, "I am severely wounded, which way shall I go?" I replied, "follow me," which he did without a word further being spoken, and fortunately without knowing anything of the position occupied by the surgeon. I conducted him across the

slough, into the road & passing some 2 or 3 hundred yards, came directly upon a stand occupied by Dr. Mitchell, Surgeon General of Shelby's
corps. I was assisted in taking him from his horse and laying him on
the ground. He said not a word and appeared very exhausted & faint. I
inquired if he would have water, to which he answered affirmatively. I
[looked] about immediately for some but found none at hand & nothing better than a common funnel which I saw lying on the ground in
which to bring it. I seized it and ran hastily to the River Thames, stopping the extremity with my finger, conveyed him a draught of water. He
was then given over into the hands of the surgeon. Directly afterwards,
Garret Wall, one of the Forlorn Hope, came to me and requested me to
accompany him back to the ground on which we had charged, to aid
him in the recovery of his [Wall's] lost saddle bags, to which I assented.
We passed from the road & crossed the narrow slough along which we
had charged, whilst a scattering fire was still kept up on the left by the
retreating Indians . . . we came upon the body of our brave & venerable comrade, Whitley—near him & some 10 or 15 steps in advance, I
noticed immediately with exultant feeling & exclamation, the body of a
dead Indian and but *a short distance in advance of that, another, which
I shall notice hereafter as having been fixed on as the body of Tecumseh*, Neither Wall or myself gave any attention whatever, that I recollect,
to the dress or anything else about these fallen Indians.[3]

Now that we understand how Johnson was led off, we can return to
Theobold's first letter in which he gives us a matching report to this
letter regarding the position of the fallen bodies, a fuller description of
Johnson's part in the action, and his experience with the identification
of Tecumseh's body. He states:

I found the body of old colonel Whitley . . . Not far in advance of it,
and somewhat to the left, I found the body of an Indian, and more to the
right, and in my opinion nearer the spot where I saw the Indian spring
forward, I found another. I cannot doubt from what I saw, and from
other corroborating evidence, that this Indian fell by the hands of colonel Johnson. The colonel discharged one of his pistols at an Indian that
approached him, and was satisfied for his own part, that he had lodged
its content in his side.[4]

Theobold goes on in his first letter to explain how Anthony Shane,
an Indian interpreter working for the Americans, did a flip-flop on his
identification of Tecumseh's body.

The body had been found which general Harrison himself recognized to be that of Tecumseh. From these reports, the curiosity of almost every man in the army appeared to be highly awakened and excited to see the body. Anthony Shane, the interpreter and guide of the . . . mounted regiment, coming to our markee on the morning of that day, the subject was spoken of—Shane said he had been intimately acquainted with Tecumseh for several years before he deserted his native tribe the Shawnees, and although it had been a long time since he had seen him, doubted not but he should be enabled to recognize his features under almost any circumstances. I was happy to find this opportunity of having my curiosity fully gratified, and proposed to accompany Shane to examine the body—we went. By this time it required no better guide than a plainly trodden path to direct us to the spot; we soon reached it, and I found it to be the body of the Indian [I] have before mentioned, to have been the preceding evening somewhat in advance and somewhat to the right of colonel Whitley, and the one which I can't but believe fell by the hands of colonel Johnson. On the first view, Shane pronounced it not the body of Tecumseh. But on a particular survey and examination, he was rather of a different opinion, and eventually said he thought it was.

Theobold concluded this first letter, "From this evidence, and from evidence more positive of his having fallen in this engagement and about that place, I never hesitated to believe that this was really the body of Tecumseh."[5]

By the time Theobold wrote to Lossing in 1861, however; he had become aware of a key new account of the affair. During this forty-five year interim, Theobold's friend, Capt. Benjamin Warfield, also a participant in the battle, related that he

commanded a company belonging to the mounted Regt. and was ordered by Genl. Harrison, immediately after the surrender of the British, to recounter the ground and take up any wounded & stragglers of the enemy that could be found. In the discharge of his duty, Warfield found a man mortally wounded, but entirely sensible and able to speak, who being interrogated, told him his name was Clark, that he belonged to Proctor's army as Indian interpreter. Capt. Warfield inquired if he could tell him anything in regard to Tecumseh. He answered that he was killed, but the Indians had carried the body off. I might add that whilst on a visit to Frankfort, KY, in Octo, last, I had the great invitation to meet with my old & highly valued friend, Col. Charles S. Todd, who was in the service on that occasion [at the

Portrait of Samuel Theobold. Illustrated by Benson J. Lossing and shown here as it appeared in his Pictorial Fieldbook of the War of 1812 which was originally published in 1868.

Thames], as aid to Gov. Shelby, with whom I had long ago freely communicated on the events of the battle & particularly as to Shane's failure to recognize Tecumseh's body. I mentioned to him the statement of Col. Warfield, as derived from Clark, which I supposed he had in all probability heard from him personally; but he said he did not recollect ever to have heard him mention the circumstances. But, informed me in *further* conversation of the same fact, that the celebrated Chief Black Hawk had stated, on the occasion of a treaty with the Indians after the close of the war with us, that it was a fact known to him [that Tecumseh was removed], he [Black Hawk] having been present & participating in the Battle of the Thames. To that, I think there is scarcely room to doubt in this point.[6]

So according to Theobold, two people of the day had believed that Tecumseh was removed from the field very quickly – Ben Warfield and Black Hawk. Theobold's original belief of 1816 was now challenged by these new testimonies. In question, was a critical point which would either give Johnson the credit or not. Was the Indian body, identified as Tecumseh, which lay ahead of Whitley's and to the right of another, really Tecumseh? If not, then Johnson did not kill Tecumseh. If so, what do we make of Warfield's and Black Hawk's testimonies which say Tecumseh was removed from the field?

Theobold goes on to tell Lossing:

> Altho I did not see Col. Johnson shoot an Indian, I know that he was in close contest with them & the statements made by several of our comrades of the *Forlorn Hope*, who as myself were near him in the charge, but favored with a better opportunity of seeing him at the moment, went fully to sustain his [Johnson's] own account, given to his friends the morning after the battle; which was that in the charge, an Indian charged toward him with his tomahawk upraised, where only at a distance of 5 steps, as he judged, he shot him down with his pistol.

He continues:

> There was contradiction & conflicting statements at the time & have been ever since as to who killed the two Indians I have mentioned as lying near Col. Whitley, one to whom was fixed on as Tecumseh–being found immediately on the ground & at the very point where Col. Johnson & the *Forlorn Hope* came in direct conflict with the Indians. He and many others then believed that one of them was killed by him [Johnson]; but now the statement of Capt. Davidson, a gentleman of veracity, who commanded a company of mounted regt., [makes it appear] that the Indian fixed on as Tecumseh was killed by David King, a private of his own company, *after* Johnson left the ground; & that the one nearest Col. Whitley was killed by Lieut. Massey of Capt. Stucker's company; or, according to the statement of John (Herndon), a private in the same company & a gentleman of equal veracity; [this Indian was killed] by J. Harrod (Holeman), also a private of that company. The probability is, I think, that both these brave men [Massey and Holeman] . . . shot at the Indian [closest to Whitley] about the same moment . . . Then it would appear that if Col. Johnson killed an Indian on or near that ground, he must have been taken off immediately. The facts I have stated show that Tecumseh was killed and carried off.[7]

To sum up, Theobold's final conclusion is that two soldiers named Massey and Holeman simultaneously killed the Indian lying a few yards directly in front of Whitley's dead body, and that Indian was *not* Tecumseh. David King killed the Indian lying ahead and to the right of Whitley–the same one that Theobold believed in 1816 to have been killed by Johnson, and apparently subsequently misidentified as being Tecumseh. Johnson killed Tecumseh, but Tecumseh was removed from the battlefield immediately.

His conclusions seem to be quite reasonable and believable based on the facts he knew. His conclusions could be exactly what happened. But his conclusions are also based on some questionable assumptions as well as some other people's further questionable assumptions. It is necessary to review some of those other accounts that deal with Theobold's details before we go on with the testimonies of other *Forlorn Hope* survivors.

General Harrison and Anthony Shane, assumed to be the only two men in the American camp that could identify Tecumseh due to their previous contact with him, each had some things to say about their involvement in the identification of the body, as well as who they believed killed Tecumseh.

Harrison, Theobold claims, had already recognized a body as that of Tecumseh by the morning after the fight. Perhaps there were rumors circulating around the camp, many other participants say there were, but *officially*, Harrison *never* made such a statement. In fact he was publicly taken to task by a British critic for not immediately reporting that Tecumseh was killed. Harrison's official report of the battle, addressed to John Armstrong, the Secretary of War, on October 9, 1813, just four days after the fight, gave a clear, lengthy, detailed account of the conflict; but had absolutely no mention of Tecumseh's death, let alone who may have killed him.

The repeated taunting in the American newspapers from the self-proclaimed *friend of the truth* (British historian William James) eventually unnerved Harrison enough to cause him to vent to his friend General Tipton in an 1834 letter. Harrison explained to Tipton his frustration with his personal friends who suggested that he not give any credence to James by responding to him publicly; and he begged Tipton, "I must enjoin it upon you my dear Gen. not to publish this letter nor anything in it in any manner or shape"[8]

Among other things, James claimed that "Comdr Perry & several other American Officers, as well as British officers who knew Tecumthe, saw and recognized his body." Harrison retorted:

> Now, I will venture my head if Comdr Perry or any of the American officers, or any American Soldier who was in the action, had ever seen Tecumthe in their lives, myself only excepted. I would make the same

venture that no officer of the British Regular army saw the body that was
supposed to be T—e. For early in the morning after the action I sent them
down the river to a farm house . . . I was persuaded, too, that none of
them heard any thing certainly about the death of T—e until after their
arrival at Detroit [several days after the battle] & then only as a rumour.
The British troops forming the left wing of their army could not see, &
could not possibly know, what passed between the Indians & those who
were opposed to them in the swamp on their right . . . in this I am supported by Colo. [C.S.] Todd who was the Asst. Inspector Genl. Of the
army . . . & to whom the charge of the British officers were committed,
& by Colo. O'Fallon & Major Chambers; the former one of my regular
Aids de Camp & the latter a volunteer Aid de Camp.[9]

This identification, or lack thereof, is one of the key recurrent facts
referred to in numerous accounts. Harrison went on in his own defense
and added some additional obscure facts surrounding the event.

In the morning after the action, I understood that a Canadian who had
been captured in the retreat had asserted that T—e was killed. I went to
see this man & he told me that he had seen Tecumthe wounded mortally
& that the Indians had wounded him. If I am not mistaken, this man [the
Canadian] died of a wound he had received.[10]

What? This Canadian, per Harrison, just said that the *Indians* mortally wounded Tecumseh! This is the only such accusation of its kind
against the Indians themselves ever to come to light. Could Tecumseh
really have been accidently shot by his own warriors? It would certainly
be an embarrassment to the Indians if such was the case. Consider how
mortified citizens of any country feel to this day when a military effort
goes astray, leaving men killed by *friendly fire*. Is this report credible?
It seems extremely unlikely; maybe that is why this Canadian's words
are totally overlooked in history books to date.

Harrison continues:

Another Canadian informed O'Fallon that he was told on the retreat
that T—e was killed. He said he would easily recognize T—e & I directed O'F to take the man & examine the bodies which were left on
the ground. He reported to me that the man recognized a body as T—
e, & declared that another body which lay near it was the Prophet's.
But that body had two eyes. The Prophet was known to have but one
& the Canadian acknowledged he was mistaken. Toward the evening
of that day I took Comer. Perry & several other officers & went to

examine the body which had been thus designated as T—e. I found it in the situation described by Chambers [skinned] & was very much mortified & irritated. I was certain that I had seen the person before but I could not determine whether it was T—e or a Potawatimi Chief who had always been with him whenever I had seen him.

The face was much swollen & it appeared to have had a stroke with a tomahawk or something else over the top of the head. O'Fallon says that he had on a cotton hunting shirt when he saw him [earlier]. I think, however, the body was either naked or the shirt was rolled up above the breast when I saw it. The British writer [*a friend of the truth*] says that he [Tecumseh] was "distinguished by wearing a leather shirt". Now although you [James] were many hundred miles from the Thames at the time, yet from your knowledge of the predilection of the N. A. Indians for that article of dress, you would no doubt give it as your opinion that out of the 1800 or 2,000 Indians who were in the action (or near it, for nine tenths of the whole number did not fire a gun), there must have been some hundreds who were thus "distinguished".[11]

Harrison establishes the fact that he could not definitively identify the body as Tecumseh. We are additionally introduced to yet another key point of contention, what was Tecumseh wearing? We will soon review others' opinions on his dress, but keep in mind that Harrison made an astute observation. The plain leather (deerskin, buckskin, etc.), which many said he was wearing, was the same dress worn by hundreds of Indians that day. It was as common as denim blue jeans are to American society today.

Harrison also mentioned his irritation with the fact that this body was mutilated. He reveals further some surprising feelings about the fallout of this action which was perpetrated by his soldiers.

Greatly vexed & mortified at the mutilation of the body, I would not suffer any person who had been attached to the British army to be called to examine it, & was desirous that it should be attributed to *our* Indians, who would, I knew, suffer no loss of honour by it. But yet, I was morally certain that they [our Indians] had not committed it.[12]

Apparently Harrison was so embarrassed that his men had committed such an atrocity to another human being; that he hoped the scuttle-butt of the day would point the finger of blame on the Indians who were fighting against Tecumseh. Harrison's assumption that the Indians opposed to Tecumseh would feel no shame in committing such a deed is certainly problematic. Tecumseh may have been on the opposite side of their fight, but the Indians who allied with the Americans, in large part, admired the man personally as well as his effort, even if they disagreed with its chance for success. For them to have mutilated his body is implausible.

The failure to report Tecumseh's death is further justified by Harrison:

> I prepared my official dispatch on my arrival [at Detroit] but as the death of Tecumthe still remained in a great degree uncertain, I did not mention it. I was now ever morally certain that he was killed, but as one account states his being wounded & taken off, I was unwilling to run the risk of having my report contradicted by the best evidence viz. that of his presenting himself alive . . . I knew indeed that Colo. J—n had been wounded by Indians, for he told me so & added that he had killed one of them when I visited him shortly after the action. I have been endeavoring to recollect when it was I first heard that it was supposed that T—e was killed by Colo. Johnson. I am satisfied that it was not until my return to Ohio in the Febry. following, & I believe not until some time in the spring. Chambers (who went immediately home after the action) says that he is satisfied that he did not hear it for several months & so say both Todd & O'Fallon . . . When ever the circumstance was mentioned in my presence, I always referred to the fact that Colo. Jn. had informed me immediately after the action that he had killed an Indian, & before he could have heard that T—e was killed, & having heard from good authority that T—e had said to Genl. Proctor a few days before, at Chatham Creek, that he [Tecumseh] was determined to conquer or die. (His expression was, "Here Genl. Harrison or I shall lay our bones.") I concluded that it was most probable that seeing from the position of Colo. Jn. that he was the (Commander) of the party which was about to assail him. T—e had singled him out, rushed upon him, & fell in the contest. This opinion I have always expressed.[13]

We now have a better understanding of why Harrison never made a definitive identification of the body in question as being Tecumseh's, even though many said that he did.

Another instrumental person in this matter of identifying the body was the Indian guide and interpreter, Anthony Shane. Many testimonies base their further assumptions on the supposed fact that Shane said the body in question was Tecumseh's. But, as Theobold explained, Shane first said the body was not Tecumseh then changed his opinion over a non-specific time period. Was that change in opinion valid? Let's see what has been said by a few others about Anthony Shane's observations.

Shane was born of a French-Canadian father and Shawnee Indian mother and so raised by Shawnee through his youth. His wife was a relative to Tecumseh. He switched his allegiance to the United States shortly after the Battle of Fallen Timbers which occurred on August 20, 1794 (in present-day Maumee, Ohio, just south of Toledo). Toward the end of that fight, as the Indians were retreating to the nearby British Fort Miami for protection, the British refused entrance to him and his fellow Indian allies. His loyalties tainted, he soon thereafter, being well-versed in many Indian dialects, became an interpreter for the United States. He served over the years at several American forts and in many battles before finding himself at the Thames confrontation.

For all the weight Shane's identification of the body seemed to carry in many accounts, there are few direct records of his opinion. Beyond Theobold's observations, we find this report from the son of a man named Abraham Edwards who had served in the battle:

> As the Indians denied that Tecumseh was killed, Gen. Cass sent an old Frenchman, by the name of Schien [Shane], who was well acquainted with Tecumseh; and, upon looking on the face, he pronounced it Tecumseh, and said he has a scar on his back plainly to be seen, and turned the body over, and (sure enough) there it was.[14]

In 1833, William Emmons, Johnson's friend and biographer wrote:

> [I] inquired of Shane, what he knew of the death of Tecumseh. He answered, that immediately after the battle of the Thames was ended, he went to the spot where several of the men had seen Col. Johnson kill an Indian commander, and there he saw Tecumseh lie dead upon the ground; that he examined the body, and observed that he must have been killed by a person on horseback, for a ball and three buck shot were shot into his breast, and the ball passed through his body and came out at the lower part of his back. While looking at the body he was asked if he was certain it was Tecumseh. Shane told them he was certain, for he had known him from childhood and that if they would examine his thigh they would discover a remarkable scar, occasioned by the misfortune of Tecumseh having his thigh broken many years before; that, on examining, they found the scar as he had described.

Based on Shane's comments, Emmons comes to this conclusion:

Shane knew this person to be Tecumseh, and his body was found where Col. Johnson had killed an Indian commander. He was killed by a person on horseback; and Col. Johnson was the only person in that part of the battle who fought on horseback. He was shot with a ball and three buckshot; and the pistol with which Col. Johnson shot the Indian chief was charged with a ball and three buckshot. These circumstances establish the fact beyond all reasonable doubt, and as conclusively as any historical fact can be established, that Col. Johnson, in this chivalrous act, slew Tecumseh . . .[15]

The scars on Tecumseh's back and thigh were critical evidence introduced by Shane. Only in the course of several interviews with the historian, Benjamin Drake, does Shane explain that Tecumseh broke both of his thighs when he was about nineteen years old. He says Tecumseh was thrown from his horse while on a buffalo chase. Stephen Ruddell, who knew Tecumseh very well at the time of the accident, told Drake the same story but with the more accepted detail of only one broken thigh.[16]

Christopher Miller, an American who was captured by the Shawnee in his youth, knew Tecumseh and spent several years with the Indians. He concurs that Tecumseh had a broken leg as a result of a fall from a horse in his younger days. The injury deeply affected Tecumseh, as Miller's most intriguing footnote to the story tells us that "he [Tecumseh] had tried once to kill himself because he said 'he could not be a warrior or a hunter.'"[17]

Captain James Coleman, another participant in the front lines of the battle, confirms this scar as well as Theobold's description of Shane identifying the body. He states:

Anthony Shane (our guide) doubted it [being Tecumseh] on his first examination, but on reflection, recollected a scar, which he examined for and found, after which from Shane's description, I have no doubt it was Tecumseh, and I believe this was the Indian killed by Col. Johnson.[18]

How Coleman became knowledgeable of his information is unknown, but it was published in 1816, just a month after Theobold's letter was printed in the same Kentucky newspaper. Soon, we'll see how years later Coleman's opinion of Johnson's role took an intriguing turn.

In 1834, as Johnson's vice-presidential campaign was kicking off,

Drake received an account from the Rev. Obediah B. Brown. In it, he cited Shane's opinion that Tecumseh was killed by a ball and three buck shot to his left breast. Brown felt this was solid evidence for Johnson killing Tecumseh. A long-time friend of Johnson, Brown gave a very detailed, albeit often contradictory, account to Drake in support of Johnson. Drake, in his history, gives a point-by-point analysis of Brown's claims and does an admirable job of pointing out the incredulity of much of it. So why would a man of the cloth give an account that was viewed by most serious analysts as partisan and full of more zeal than facts? Consider the connection of Brown to Johnson, and an interesting historical footnote as well, as discovered in a news clip from the *Washington Post* in 1900. The article was debating the end of mail delivery on Sundays in Washington D.C. and read:

> The measure to stop the mails on Sunday was introduced and advocated by Col. Richard M. Johnson—who killed Tecumseh at the Battle of the Thames, which act made him Vice President—under the inspiration, it was said at the time, of Rev. Obediah Brown, with whom he lived in the double house on the south side of E. street, between Eighth and Ninth. Parson Brown, as everybody called him, built the church which stood where Ford's Theater was built.[19]

Drake received one additional letter which quoted Anthony Shane. It came from Major William Oliver in 1840. Oliver had withstood the spring and summer sieges of Tecumseh and Procter upon Fort Meigs. In fact, he was the runner who risked his life during that fight to deliver Harrison's critical instructions to General Green Clay as Clay approached from up the Maumee River with Kentucky militia reinforcements. Of Shane, Oliver says:

> In 1819, I lodged with Anthony Shane, at what was then called "the Second Crossing of the St. Mary's." I had known Shane intimately for a long time, indeed, from my first settlement at Fort Wayne, in 1806. In speaking of the battle of the Thames, and the fall of Tecumseh, he [Shane] said, the most authentic information he had obtained upon this point, was from two brothers of his wife, who were in the battle, and near the person of Tecumseh when he fell. They stated, in positive terms, that Tecumseh was shot by a private of the Kentucky troops; and Shane seemed so well satisfied with the truth of their statement, that he informed me *it was entitled to belief.*[20]

Per Drake's interviews, this change of opinion by Shane was also disclosed to John Johnston, the reputable Indian agent. Lyman Draper's notes reveal an even fuller account directly from Shane both of the event and Tecumseh's part in it.

> He [Tecumseh] went into the battle with but little hope of success, and a fixed determination not to survive a defeat. He placed his sword in the hands of a brother Chief, for safe keeping, with the remark, "When my son becomes a noted warrior and able to wield this sword give it to him." He then threw off all his dress of an English officer except the plume, & entered the battle arrayed in the ordinary Indian costume. From the moment the battle commenced, his powerful voice was distinctly heard along the Indian lines, roaring, to use the expression of Shane, like a mad bull, giving orders & exhorting his men to deeds of renown. The moment that voice ceased to be heard, that moment, the Indians under Tecumseh ceased to make battle. His fall seemed to be the signal of discomfiture. It paralyzed all further resistance . . . about 10 or 15 steps from where he fell, lay his principle chieftain and brother-in-law, Wasegoboah [Stand Firm]–top front of his head blown off–Te_ was shot by a ball and three buckshot–and from the place they entered and came out it was evidently done by a horseman–the charge entered the breast near the center and came out close to the backbone between his hips–no other wound–laying on his back–the skin on his left thigh was taken off for about 1 inch in breadth and 7 or 8 in length.[21]

At this point we can make some summarizations of Harrison's and Shane's involvement.

Harrison went to the body supposed to be Tecumseh, but never *officially* concluded it was Tecumseh. Never-the-less, rumors seem to have flown through the camp that he had. Perhaps, although he didn't admit it in his own words, Harrison alluded that it *might* or *probably* was Tecumseh upon viewing the body. As for who killed Tecumseh, Harrison claims that it was months after the fact before he began hearing reports that Johnson may have done it. At that point, and on that point, he did agree that it was *likely* to be so.

Anthony Shane at first found it difficult to identify the body. Later he apparently remembered the scars Tecumseh bore on his leg and back. He re-examined the body and upon finding them changed his mind. One wonders why, considering the important nature of his determination, he wouldn't have checked for the scars on his first examination.

This body was wounded by a ball and three buck shot which entered its breast at a downward angle. This logically meant it had to have been fired from an elevated position, a horseman, and Johnson was supposed to be the only one in the area not on foot at the time. Years later, Shane was persuaded by relatives who were near Tecumseh in the fight, that an American private killed him. The private, it is assumed, would have had to of been on foot, thus making the downward angle of the observed wound problematic.

Because Harrison and Shane were the only men believed to have known Tecumseh before this event; their identification, or not, of the body, was substantive. Many men afterwards would use what bits and pieces they desired of these two men's accounts in order to build their own cases.

Returning to Theobold's account, we find Johnson himself reporting that he had shot an Indian and "was satisfied for his own part, that he had lodged its content *in his side*." When used as criteria in the attempt to identify the body, the location of Johnson's shot becomes a more significant point. As we will see, numerous accounts assert all types of fatal wounds. The majority of them favor Tecumseh being shot in the breast, which might be construed as the *side*. There are a couple accounts, however, still in support of Johnson, which say that he killed Tecumseh with a shot to the head.

William Gaines, the ordinance sergeant for the army was at the battle and claims, "Colonel Johnson's Pistol Ball broke his skull." [22] Likewise, Isaac Hamblin, who was in the fight, gave a similar but fuller opinion to Lyman Draper:

> [Hamblin] says he was standing but a few feet from Col. Johnson when he [Tecumseh] fell, and in full view, and saw the whole of that part of the battle. He was well acquainted with Tecumseh, having seen him before the war, and having been a prisoner seventeen days, and received many a cursing from him. He thinks that Tecumseh thought Johnson was Harrison, as he often heard the chief swear that he would have Harrison's scalp, and seemed to have a special hatred towards him. Johnson's horse fell under him, he himself being also deeply wounded; in the fall, he lost his sword, his large pistols were empty, and he was entangled with his horse on the ground. Tecumseh had fired his rifle at him, and when he saw him fall, he threw down his gun and bounded forward like a tiger, sure of its prey. Johnson had only a side pistol ready for use. He aimed

at the chief, over the head of the horse, and shot near the centre of his forehead. When the ball struck, it seemed to him that the Indian jumped with his head a full fifteen feet into the air; as soon as he struck the ground, a little Frenchman ran his bayonet into him, and pinned him fast to the ground.[23]

Gaines and Hamblin just stated that they witnessed Tecumseh take a ball to the head. Does that mean the body Shane identified as Tecumseh was not Tecumseh because it was shot in the breast? *Hmmm.* Perhaps we can get a clearer picture from the other surviving members of the *Forlorn Hope.*

Garret Wall was obviously in the thick of the initial charge, as testified to by Theobold. Wall wrote a letter to a Kentucky historian named Mann Butler in 1834. Not so coincidentally, Johnson's vice-presidential campaign was blossoming just about this time. Wall says:

> Colonel R. M. Johnson selected Colonel Whitley and myself to be near him during the battle of the Thames. Col. J. commanded twenty brave men, chosen by himself, to make the charge upon the Indians. This select corps was placed in front of the two charging columns at the point formed by two companies, commanded by Captain James Coleman and Captain Davidson . . . the fighting became very severe, each party mingling with the other. Col. R. M. Johnson and Dr. Samuel Theobold, of Lexington, were all that remained on horseback. The remainder of the forlorn hope were all, in a few minutes, either killed, wounded, or had their horses shot from under them. The whole battalion now dismounted by order of Colonel Johnson, and fought the Indians, at this point, on foot for probably near half an hour.

Wall goes on to report how he encountered Johnson on the battlefield.

> Near the close of the firing, I was engaged in carrying Lieutenant Logan from the field. He was my neighbor and mortally wounded. At this moment I discovered Colonel Johnson, who had been all the time in front, passing by me on horseback into the lines; [now] very bloody, apparently weak and exhausted: one of the volunteers was leading his horse by the bridle. When I was carrying Lieutenant Logan into the lines, I discovered Colonel Johnson lying at the root of a tree, bleeding and languid. I laid Logan by the side of the Colonel and perceived him to be mortally wounded. He died the next day. After lying him down, I gazed for a moment on these two officers, doubting which would die first. The firing had not yet entirely ceased; a scattering fire continuing

on the left of the ground on which we fought. Colonel Johnson raised his eyes and said—"My brave men, the battle continues, leave me, and do not return until you bring me an account of the victory."—I immediately returned to the field of battle, including to the left; by passing over the dead Kentuckians, Canadians, Indians and horses, until I came to the ground occupied during the battle by the forlorn hope.

On first read, this account doesn't seem to mesh very well with Theobold's account. A closer analysis, however, would suggest that Wall *might* have witnessed Theobold leading Johnson off the field. When he later laid Logan down next to Johnson, it *might* have been at the spot off the battlefield where Theobold had helped Johnson down from his horse. Since Theobold said that Wall asked him to go back on the battlefield, perhaps that occurred at this point in time—the scene being that Wall arrives with Logan just as Theobold is finishing attending to Johnson. Further, Johnson's quote, albeit seemingly romanticized, addresses "my brave *men*" which would imply someone besides Wall was present.

In his letter, Wall additionally relates his observations surrounding the identification of the body when he returned to the battle area.

The men by this time had collected in groups. It was remarked that Colonel R. M. Johnson was dead; but I contradicted the report; also that the great Indian commander, Tecumseh, was slain. I asked by what authority? I was told that Anthony Shane, who had known him from a small boy, said so, and had seen him among the slain. In a short time I saw Shane with a small group of men, walking towards a dead Indian; as he approached the body I asked him if he knew that Indian. He said it was, in his opinion, Tecumseh; but he could tell better, if the blood was taken from his face. I examined the Indian. He was shot in the left side of the breast with several balls or buckshot, and entering near and above the left nipple. There was also a wound in his head too small for a rifle ball to make. The ball in his breast inclined from the left side towards the centre and downwards. I have no doubt the shot was from an elevated position. The Indian was afterwards recognized as Tecumseh. He was at a small distance in advance of the ground on which lay dead horses of the forlorn hope. His wounds were bleeding when I first saw him. On returning, Col. Johnson's pistols were examined, one was empty, the other loaded. It was the common talk, and generally understood, that Col. Johnson's pistols had been loaded a few days previous by Capt. Elijah Craig with a ball and three buckshot. It was soon reported that Tecumseh was the Indian that the Colonel had shot in a single handed encounter . . . The ground

Image courtesy of U.S. Library of Congress.

Portrait of Garrett D. Wall while he was U.S. Senator from New Jersey 1835-1841.
Charles Fenderich - Artist.

on which Tecumseh lay, the manner in which he was shot, the distance of the place on which lay the dead horses of the forlorn hope, all went to satisfy me that he fell by the hand of Colonel R. M. Johnson.[24]

Wall cites Shane as identifying the body to be Tecumseh, but doesn't mention any of the criteria that Shane used to do so, such as looking for the scars. Further, he notes that Shane said he could be more certain if the blood were washed off his face – but he does not report that it was cleaned off. Taking logic one step further, how could Shane say it was Tecumseh, when the blood hadn't been removed yet? Wouldn't cleaning the face be one of the first steps to a surer identification? When and if the blood was removed it *could have* revealed someone else's face.

Wall gives a clear, first-hand observation of the type of wound the body in question received, and he makes a good case that Johnson's pistols were loaded with appropriate ammunition to fell this Indian. His final conclusion that Johnson killed Tecumseh, however; is based on his putting these pieces together, not on an eye-witness account of the shooting.

Benjamin S. Chambers was another *Forlorn Hope* member to voice his opinion on this event in the same issue of the *Kentucky Gazette* as Theobold voiced his in 1816. Chambers' account was a rebuttal to William G. Hunt, the editor of the *Western Monitor*, who made several accusations against the accepted role of Johnson in the event. Mr. Hunt boasted "that no man of intelligence, in Kentucky, believes that Col. Johnson killed Tecumseh." Chambers retorted:

> I don't claim the merit of being intelligent, but I will state that I saw colonel Johnson discharge his pistol (and I believe) at the very Indian, that was said to be Tecumseh by general Harrison and Anthony Shane (an Indian interpreter), at a distance not more than ten feet, and the Indian fell to the ground; therefore I believe that Johnson killed Tecumseh.[25]

Chambers goes on in his letter to debunk several other points of attack made by Hunt against Johnson's claim by pointing out that:

> Samuel Theobold esq. Judge Advocate to the regiment, and myself, took colonel Johnson off the battle ground, and had frequently to hold him upon his horse, on account of his extreme weakness and sickness from the loss of blood. Colonel Johnson's horse was but barely able to bear him off the battle ground; as soon as Johnson was taken from his horse, it immediately lay down and died. After Mr. Theobold and myself had got a surgeon to dress the wounds of Colonel Johnson. I returned to the point where the charge was made by Johnson and his little squad of 8-10 men that followed him (the *Forlorn Hope*), for the purpose of pro-curing my saddle bags, which contained some valuable papers to me, and found them not more than ten paces from where Tecumseh lay and at the spot where my horse fell. I then believed that the Indian, that afterwards was proven to be Tecumseh, was the very one that col. Johnson shot down, for immediately after colonel Johnson discharged his pistol, my horse was shot & fell near the same place and AT THAT PLACE I found my saddle bags, and AT THAT PLACE, colonel Johnson shot an Indian, and AT THAT PLACE, Tecumseh was found dead.[26]

A brief analysis of Chambers' report shows him validating most of Theobold's story. Johnson was helped back while still upon his horse, but now Chambers is assisting. Theobold didn't mention others being involved, but neither did he claim to lead Johnson back alone. Theobold did say that Garret Wall wanted to go back to the battleground for his saddle bags, not Chambers. Could this simply be a name mistake? Perhaps. Wall said he went back, but implied it was to fight on the left where the battle had drifted. Wall never stated that he needed to recover his saddlebags, Theobold said that. Chambers' narrative rings true. The low number of *Forlorn Hope* members, eight to ten, does not square with all other sources, but could be attributed to the fact that many were already killed at that point in time. His conclusion for Johnson sounds impressive especially given that he is one of the few who actually saw Johnson shoot the Indian identified as Tecumseh. The only possible hole left in his story is whether the body identified as Tecumseh actually was Tecumseh.

The last member of the *Forlorn Hope* to get his two nickels worth of opinion in on this event was Richard Spurr. It came late in the game via his great nephew's affidavit in 1895. It is a fascinating account of what transpired.

About thirty men volunteered and stepped to the front and among them Col. Whitley, my old uncle Richard Spurr, and John McGunnigle. They were ordered to advance to attract the Indians, to keep well in line with spaces of twenty to thirty feet between them. When formed in line, McGunnigle was on the right of Richard Spurr and Col. Whitley on his left . . . Almost simultaneously they were fired upon by the Indians from the opposite side of the slough. Mr. McGunnigle fell dead shot thru the heart. Col. Whitley instantly threw himself behind the body of a large tree that had fallen diagonally to the slough, its branches reaching it. Spurr threw himself behind the stump of the fallen tree, and near, as he thought, to the dead body of Col. Whitley, supposing himself to be between two dead men. Very soon he saw an Indian start from the opposite side of the slough to scalp Col. Whitley. Just as the Indian got near the log Whitley raised his gun and shot him dead. Then turning on his back he reloaded his gun. After doing this he crawled along behind the log to its end near where the dead Indian lay, as supposed to scalp him.

While doing this another Indian broke out of the brush at the farther side of the slough. When he got about half way across Col. Whitley jumped up, threw up his gun to his face and the Indian seeing him raised his gun and both fired sounding like the report of one gun, and both fell dead. At this time Johnson's Batallion came up in force, a charge was ordered and a sharp skirmish ensued. The Indians retreating scattered in the bushes and this part of Battle of 1813 was over . . . Richard Spurr, an officer, was ordered to take a squad of men and bring in the dead to the camp, which he promptly did. He found the body of McGunnigle in a thicket of briars, and the body of Col. Whitley lying where he saw him fall, with the two fresh Indian scalps at his belt. Just over the log he found the Indian Whitley had slain, lying on his back and having a piece of skin two inches wide and more than a foot long taken from the middle of his back. These four they carried into camp and laid side by side. Gen. Harrison was present and looked at the four bodies and stated "That body with the strip of skin taken from its back was that of Chief Tecumseh" as he had seen him often and knew him well.[27]

What a colorful account of Whitley's part in the battle. Apparently Spurr believed that it proved Whitley had killed Tecumseh because at the end of this statement was added that he [Spurr] "was a devoted friend of Johnson's and forbade giving this statement publicity while Johnson lived."[28]

This testimony, though it was given by a relative two generations away from its author, is the only direct report of William Whitley's actions in the battle. Others tell us where his dead body was found and its relationship to other dead Indian bodies on the field. Some state whether his rifle was loaded or not, whether he was scalped or not, and how badly he was shot up. So this man, Richard Spurr, is a unique witness. He even claims to have silenced himself for years to save face for his friend Johnson. Most of his story is plausible but for a few points. One puzzling observation is that Spurr says only one single strip of skin was taken off Tecumseh's back. Except for a few people who claimed that the whole body of Tecumseh was flayed, most say the strips of flesh were taken from his thigh. Was this a simple gaffe in his statement, or was further souvenir taking done after Spurr saw the body? More troublesome is the fact that Spurr says he carried Tecumseh's body into the American camp. Most other narratives acknowledge that American bodies were brought back into camp to be nursed or buried, but none speak of Indian bodies being moved off the battlefield. This makes his claim of Harrison's identification dubious. As we have seen and will see many more times, when Harrison was called upon to make an identification he rode to the body in question. Still, this story on the whole rings true as to Whitley's confrontation with the Indians. Perhaps Spurr tried just a little too hard to make certain Whitley's Indian was Tecumseh.

We now have seen four survivors of the *Forlorn Hope* testify to the event. Theobold and Wall were in the thick of the action and near Johnson, but did not actually eye-witness Johnson shooting the man later identified as Tecumseh. Yet, they concluded for Johnson having done so. Chambers directly observed Johnson firing at the man later identified as Tecumseh. Spurr, likewise, was only a few feet away as he watched Whitley shoot, and be shot by, the man later identified as Tecumseh. Three of the *Forlorn Hope* supported Johnson and one endorsed Whitley as the slayer of Tecumseh. Let's see how a couple more key testimonies stack up against the word of these brave men.

CHAPTER 13

Two Key Testimonies

I heard a fellow named Clarke, exclaim:
"Look out King! An Indian is aiming at you!"
Whereupon, the Indian turned to fire upon Clarke,
thereby exposing his left breast to King's aim,
who instantly fired, and as the Indian fell,
King exclaimed: "I've killed one d____d yaller
Indian booger!" [1]

Like cream in a bottle of fresh milk, the accounts of two particular men rise to the top of the stack of testimonies begging to be examined before the others. The reason – they are referred to in many of the other men's testimonies, and as well, by most historians over the past two hundred years. We've already met these men; their names are Robert McAfee and James Davidson. Both were respected men of their day and each made significantly more detailed reports than most, of what they knew concerning the death of Tecumseh.

McAfee, a captain from whom we have already gleaned much information leading up to the battle, continued fighting in the war effort even after the conflict at the Thames. Within a few years, he wrote a history of the war and later served in the government of Kentucky as a representative and as Lieutenant Governor. Although he was on the other end of the battlefield under James Johnson at the Thames, and therefore not an eye-witness to Tecumseh's death, he has been considered thorough and forthright by those who have evaluated his account over the past two centuries.

Like McAfee, Davidson was also a captain at the Thames and led the company of mounted militia who followed directly behind and to the left of Richard Johnson and his *Forlorn Hope*. He was in the thick of the fight. From his position on the field, he did not visually witness the killing of Tecumseh – but he may have heard it! Based on his own involvement and the reports of four other specific witnesses, Davidson came to some distinct conclusions, the key one being that David King had killed Tecumseh. Some of his details appear contradictory, never-the-less, they are often cited. After the Thames, Davidson went on to become a senator and then Treasurer of the State of Kentucky. He was always considered to be an honest and fair-minded man.

As well-acquainted as these two men had to have been with other eye-witnesses and participants in this affair, and as trustworthy as they were said to be; it is surprising that even they have both left themselves open to scrutiny on a few details in their testimonies.

Let's begin with McAfee. His words come from three sources, his diary, his history book and his letters published in newspapers. The entry of October 5th in his journal reads:

> The battle on the left wing was against Genl. Tecumseh and his Indians, and was much more obstinate, so much so, that the logs, brush and swamp prevented them from charging thro, & the Indians fired so hot that the companies had to dismount and fight from behind trees and logs in the Indian way, & repeated charges and repulses took place on each side. Col. Johnson was wounded in the first fire & Genl. Tecumseh it is said fell by the hands of our Col.[2]

This simple diary entry seems to innocuously describe the setting of the conflict as it unfolded. The last twelve words, however, state two bold facts. First, Tecumseh is rumored to be dead, and second, Johnson is believed to have been the man that killed him. Consider that this diary entry is from the day of the battle and already McAfee has logged the fact that these rumors are flying through the camp. Granted, this diary entry might have been made a little while after the fifth of October. After all, that day was quite a long one for McAfee, but it certainly was not written months later. Didn't Harrison say he first heard rumors that Johnson had killed Tecumseh in February? That would be four months out from the event. Could Harrison have been that far out of the loop of common gossip on such a highly-charged topic?

In 1816, at the prompting of his longtime friend Colonel Johnson, McAfee wrote his *History of the Late War in the Western Country* in which he summarized this whole event. Certainly the opinions given in his book were molded by conversations with many of the participants since McAfee gives many particulars he could not possibly have witnessed directly. In it he states:

Portrait of Robert B. McAfee as it appeared in The Register-Kentucky State Historical Society, January, 1927, Vol. 25. Image courtesy of Jenny Tenlen whose 4th-great grandfather was Robert's brother, Samuel McAfee.

The colonel was shot through his thigh and in his hip, by the first fire of the Indians, and shortly afterwards he was shot through his left hand, by a ball which ranged up his arm, but did not enter his body. He continued, however, in front of his men, gallantly fighting the enemy, as long as the action lasted at that place. The white mare on which he rode was also shot so severely that she fell and expired soon after she had carried her rider within the lines of the infantry.[3]

The wounds of Johnson, his horse and the fact that his mare carried him off the field are all in agreement with most other accounts. However, McAfee adds a statement that Johnson continued to lead his men *after* he was shot in the wrist. That wrist wound, according to most testimonies was received from Tecumseh, and within a moment or two, Johnson supposedly shot back, killing Tecumseh. The insinuation that Johnson remained on the field for any length of time after receiving his wrist wound, and lingered to rally his men as well, is contradictory to most who say Johnson left the field, faint, very soon after he made his shot at Tecumseh.

McAfee continues:

> Tecumseh was found among the dead, at the point where Colonel John-
> son had charged upon the enemy in person; and it is generally believed
> that this celebrated chief fell by the hand of the colonel. It is certain that
> the latter killed the Indian with his pistol, who shot him through his
> hand, at the very spot where Tecumseh lay, but another dead body lay at
> the same place, and Mr. King, a soldier in Captain Davidson's company,
> had the honor of killing one of them.[4]

Even though he was a friend of Johnson, McAfee left the door of
credit open to David King. That speaks to McAfee's integrity, but confuses anyone trying to arrive at a firm conclusion. Up to this point in
time McAfee had sounded convinced that Johnson had done it. The
dilemma gets more confused when we look at further comments made
by McAfee.

As we have already seen, in the winter of 1816 Benjamin Chambers
and Sam Theobold had publicly responded to attacks against the military merits of Colonel Johnson as put forth in the *Kentucky Gazette* by
a Mr. Hunt, editor of a *Federalist* newspaper. (Johnson was a *Demo-
cratic/Republican*). McAfee, who had just published his history, also
boldly defended his colonel in the newspaper at this time. His observations in regards to Johnson firing at Tecumseh, as well as other details,
elaborate on his own earlier statements, as well as those of Theobold,
Chambers and even Wall.

McAfee writes:

> The Colonel [Johnson], with Col. Whitley and his select corps, had not
> advanced far before a heavy fire was poured upon them from almost ev-
> ery direction, which mortally wounded Col. Whitley, and wounded Col.
> Johnson in several places, as well as the *white* horse on which he rode, and
> [wounded] nearly every man of his forlorn hope. He still pressed forward,
> and several Indians [were] discovered . . . one of which leveled his gun at
> the Colonel, who drew his pistol and both fired, nearly at the same mo-
> ment. The Indian fell and his ball passed through the Colonel's left hand
> and tore it very much. The colonel now growing faint with loss of blood,
> retired slowly on horseback toward the right within the line of infantry,
> and soon after was helped off his horse; she fell and shortly died.[5]

Here we are presented with a scene from McAfee that is a bit different than the one he delineated earlier. He now says that Johnson and

Tecumseh fired at each other simultaneously. It is this shot by Tecumseh that wounds Johnson's left wrist. It is this shot by Johnson that takes down Tecumseh. Soon thereafter, Johnson is faint and drifts off the field on horseback. However, didn't we just read from McAfee's earlier testimony that Johnson rallied his men even after his wrist wound? Further, what if we compare this to what Isaac Hamblin said previously? Hamblin was the eye-witness that also knew what Tecumseh looked like. He said that Johnson was shot in the wrist by Tecumseh, and *then* Johnson's horse buckled under him and trapped Johnson on the ground, and *then* Tecumseh charged him with his tomahawk, and *then* Johnson shot him with his pistol. *Hmmm.*

> Capt. Davidson who was at the head of his company with Capt. Coleman, and his [Coleman's] 2nd lieutenant, Lieut. Logan, being close in the rear, soon came up. Capt. Davidson himself pushed forward and saved Col. Whitley from being scalped with his sword, keeping off an Indian who was making the attempt. In this act, Capt. Davidson was wounded through the thigh and soon after fainted with the loss of blood and helped off by his men as soon as he came to. Lieut. Logan was in the meantime mortally wounded, and Capt. Massie (of Capt. Stucker's company) killed the Indian that was attempting to scalp Col. Whitley. About the same time, Mr. King of Capt. Davidson's company killed an Indian near the place where the one had fallen by the hands of col. Johnson; and [because] a part of Col. Donalson's regiment of infantry, [was] now advancing to the support of the line, the Indians fled from this point and pressed down on the left, [it was as the action moved left] when Capt. Rice and Combs, with Major Thompson at their head, bravely fought them, four to one, for a half hour longer . . .[6]

The number of officers and regiments referred to tends to make this passage quite difficult to sort through. The most important piece of information to be gained from this segment of McAfee's account is the sequential movement of the companies into the action. The *Forlorn Hope*, with Johnson, led the charge. Johnson had his encounter and was lead off the field. The two companies of Kentucky militia who were on horseback—Captain Davidson's and Captain Coleman's—soon came into the area of the *Forlorn Hope*, continuing the fight. Before long the Indians fled toward the left pursued by other companies. This is all in agreement with the fragmented chain of events offered by the *Forlorn Hope* members.

Image of James Davidson as it appeared in the "200 Years of the Kentucky Treasury" brochure as part of "1792-1992 Kentucky–The Celebration".

Another item to note from this account is the timing of Lieutenant Logan meeting his fate. McAfee's story states that Johnson had already vacated the area when Logan was mortally shot. This concurs with Garret Wall's account which stated that he had carried Logan off the field and finding Johnson already on the ground somewhere distant from the battlefield, had set Logan beside him.

Finally, as detailed earlier, one needs to keep in mind McAfee's statement that the fighting, further to the left, continued for an additional half-hour. Therefore, from this account, there appears to have been a good deal of fighting for some time *after* Johnson left the battleground.

Davidson's testimony is a significant one, but it brings up even more points of contention. And, it is only through Davidson's words that we get anything even close to an actual quote from David King himself. To date, no direct opinion of the event from King has come to light.

Captain James Davidson led a company of Kentucky militia which included both William Whitley and David King. Whitley as we know, volunteered for service in the lead charge with Johnson, but King saw action just behind him within Davidson's company. Davidson made two public testimonies about the event. The first came in 1831, as a result of an interview that his brother Michael and he had given to the editor of *The Commentator*, a Frankfort, Kentucky newspaper.

The editor begins by confirming the fact that Davidson himself was severely wounded.

> He soon received a rifle ball, which twirled through his thigh; another bullet passed across his abdomen just under the skin; a third, the most distressing wound of all was a contusion upon the breast from a half spent ball, which penetrated to the bone.[7]

The story continues with a description of the injuries that Johnson had incurred. "Col. Johnson was wounded–his left hand, the bridle hand, was struck by a ball and shot to pieces–yet, to his honor be it spoken, he kept his seat upon his horse and continued to discharge the duty of a commander." Davidson backs up McAfee as we again hear that Johnson continued to lead his men after receiving the wrist wound.

The next segment of the interview brings a bit more controversy.

> Having the use of one hand only to manage his horse and wield his sword–is it likely that, in this condition, he carried a pistol as well as his bridle and sword all in one hand, or drew one from his holsters and shot down Tecumseh or anybody else? It has been said that after the action, his pistols were examined and found not to have been discharged; if it were so, it was nothing to the discredit of Col. Johnson.[8]

Well. Captain Davidson seems to have made an assumption that Colonel Johnson could not have shot his pistol since it would be impossible to juggle a sword, the reigns to his horse and a pistol all in his right hand. Johnson did in fact carry a sword, but Hamblin said he lost it when his horse fell. It is also possible that Johnson had put his sword in its hilt or lost it before he fired his pistol at Tecumseh. This point struck by Davidson seems to be pure innuendo to discredit Johnson. No one else claims that Johnson was wielding his sword, brandishing his pistol and controlling the reigns of his horse all with one hand and at the same time. Johnson himself, as we'll see, attested that he managed to use his disabled *left* arm above the wrist area to control the reigns of his horse, thus allowing him to use his right arm to defend himself.

Davidson also states that Johnson's pistols were never fired! General Leslie Combs believed it. He was so sure that he sent a note to the editor, as an addendum to Davidson's story of 1859, Combs said:

> Dr. Theobold states that he was Surgeon's mate of Col. Johnson's regiment; when with him in his charge, and saw him wounded at the first fire of the enemy. Afterward took his holsters and pistols from his saddlebow when his horse fell and died, and carried them back to camp; both of the pistols being loaded. This being so, it is certain Co. J. did not shoot Tecumseh, or any other Indian in the battle. Davidson and Theobold are men of unquestionable veracity, and are still alive. I knew nothing myself of the facts. The Johnsons [Richard and James] were both brave men.[9]

If Theobold ever said that Johnson did not fire his pistols, it is lost to history or was the result of a private conversation. In fact, Theobold said just the opposite, "the colonel discharged one of his pistols at an Indian that approached him."[10] Combs' opinion is probably based on his brother Sam's experience, who had led a company in the area where Tecumseh was killed. (Leslie was not at the Thames.) Sam simply said that he "did not think he [Tecumseh] was killed by Col. Johnson, although the Col. was badly wounded near that point. It is now, and ever has been, perfectly uncertain whose finger pulled the fatal trigger."[11] In an interview with Lyman Draper, Major Thompson, who led the left flank of Johnson's front lines, was another person who "thinks Col. Johnson's pistols were not shot off–(& so says Mark Haidin, who had it from a physician on the campaign)–& hence [Johnson] could not have shot any Indian."[12] We have now been alerted that there were at least a few people who thought Johnson never even fired his pistol!

Further in Davidson's account, we learn that his company came on the scene quite quickly behind the *Forlorn Hope*, themselves receiving some of the very first fire. After Johnson had vacated the area, David King became involved in the action as the density of men in this quarter had dissipated momentarily. It was then that

> Clarke . . . suddenly called out to his comrade, David King, to 'take care of the Indian that was near to him. The warrior turned toward Clark, at the same instant King fired at him with Whitley's gun and lodged the two balls, which he knew it was loaded with, in the Chieftain's breast, for when Whitley fell, King threw away his own gun and took the better one, and the powder horn of the old Indian fighter–The Indian dropped upon King's fire–'Whoop, by G__,' exclaimed King–he was every inch a soldier–'I have killed one d_____d yellow bugger' . . . the voice of the

Indian commander had been distinctly heard and observed by our soldiers – about this time it ceased and was heard no more – Tecumseh was
dead – presently a cry of 'How! – How!' was raised among the Indians,
upon which they turned and fled – pursued by our soldiers.[13]

Davidson clearly states how King happened to kill his Indian. Further, Davidson brings up the issue of Tecumseh's voice resonating
through the battle. He claims it was no longer heard after King made
his shot. Others claim that it was no longer heard after Johnson made
his shot! None-the-less, Davidson agrees that the Indians shouted upon
Tecumseh's death and fled.

In Davidson's second account, some twenty-eight years later, he more
fully describes how King managed to acquire Whitley's rifle and use it
to kill Tecumseh.

I will now proceed to tell you who I think did kill Tecumseh. In my
company was a private of the name of David King. He was a splendid
specimen of back woodsman, brave as Caesar, an honest man, and an
unerring marksman. Whilst we were awaiting another charge from the
Indians, King, in loading his gun, put in his ball, forgetting the powder,
and had no means of drawing the ball. He was much vexed, and told me
about it, saying: 'Captain, what shall I do?' I told him Whitley had a fine
gun, but it was hazardous to attempt to get it. He immediately crawled
toward Whitley, keeping the body between him and the Indians, and succeeded in getting his gun and shot-pouch, and regaining his tree. The Indians peppered the spot with balls, but fortunately none hit him. He, and
some five or six of his comrades, asked permission to go a little farther
to the right, as they wished to prevent the Indians flanking us. They outnumbered us so far that it was with great difficulty we could keep from
being surrounded. I detached them a short distance to the right, but their
eagerness to get to the Indians made them move faster than the left wing,
on perceiving which, I started toward them to warn them. I was afraid
they might be cut off from the rest of the company. When I got about half
way to them I heard a fellow named Clarke exclaim: 'Look out, King, an
Indian is aiming at you.' Whereupon the Indian turned to fire on Clarke,
thereby exposing his left breast to King's aim, who instantly fired and the
Indian fell. King exclaimed: 'I've killed one d_____d yaller booger.'
(I should have mentioned above that it was Whitley's custom to load his
gun with two bullets, and that when King got the gun it was cocked, but
had not been discharged. He therefore used the charge Whitley put in.)
I got the men in the right place and returned to my other men. I was

soon after severely wounded three times and saw no more of King and his comrades until after the battle.[14]

Several things need to be addressed from this part of Davidson's story. Yes it concurs with his first account, and with more detail, on how King acquired Whitley's gun. As well, the movement of his men seems rational. But two claims are intriguing. He says that Whitley's rifle was loaded and cocked, but not fired. That will contradict a few other stories, as well as some we have already seen, which state that Whitley and his Indian may have killed each other simultaneously. Second, Davidson gives quite a flattering description of King, even comparing his bravery to Caesar's! The one attribute Uncle James overlooked mentioning was that David King was the son of his sister.

Perhaps the most controversial point cited by historians in Davidson's accounts is the seemingly contradictory description of "King's Indian's" dress since it is described differently from one letter to the next. Specifically, the question is: *Did he look like a chief or not?*

In the early account, Davidson explains that King went back to see the Indian he had killed because he "wanted to get his fine leggings . . ." He goes on to describe how King and his friends, including Sam Davidson, who probably was King's cousin, found the body.

It was lying behind a tree, face downward, "There he is," said (Sam) Davidson, "but I see no wound upon him"–"Roll him over," said King, "and if it is my Indian, you will find two bullet holes in his left breast." It was done, and there were the two bullet holes, an inch apart . . . *The Indian from his dress was evidently a chief*–His fanciful leggings (King's main object in hunting out the body), his pasty colored worsted sash, his pistols, his two dirks, all his dress and equipment were the undisputed spoils of King–He kept one of the dirks, the sash & moccasins for himself, the rest he distributed as presents among his messmates.–Now it was this very Indian which was afterwards identified by those who had known him, as Tecumseh, this and no other . . . King himself, Clark, Sam Davidson, Giles, Von Treece and others knew that the corpse which was afterwards discovered to be that of Tecumseh, was the same that King had hunted for and found and stript–the spoils. The same (spoils) which he had claimed without controversy or dispute–because he had slain the former owner . . . *No one* on that day, the memorable 5th Oct 1813, or at that place, ever thought of attributing the fall of that most extraordinary savage to a personal encounter on the field of battle with

*Image of James Davidson's second "Letter to the Editor" as it appeared
in the Louisville Daily Journal, November 3, 1859.*

Richard M. Johnson—The volunteers had travelled scores of miles on the
way to their respective homes, when they met this "Camp News" for the
first time in a public print—It was strange news to them.[15]

Before we tackle the issue of the slain chief's attire, a couple other
observations need to be made. First, Davidson's cites several of King's
friends as eye-witnesses to this event. It would have been great to
have heard from any or all of them directly. Unfortunately, history to
date has no documented public comment on this event from any of
them. Second, we are introduced to another version of the rumor mill
in camp. Davidson says everyone knew Tecumseh was dead, and that
they believed King had done it. McAfee said there were rumors, but
for Johnson. And again, remember how Harrison said there were no
rumors until well after the battle. *Hmmm.*

Davidson mentions that they rolled the body over to see the bullet wounds. Consider that if they were indeed the first men on the scene, then others, like McAfee, can still be supported in their statements that Tecumseh was found lying on his back. King would have already rolled the body over. King could have been the first one to view the body since Davidson was rescued by him immediately after the fighting had ceased. Perhaps this could be taken a step further by suggesting that if King was there first, and he took all the "fancier" clothing and weapons as Davidson describes them; then when the others finally arrived to see the body it had to of appeared simply dressed–probably barely dressed at all. As well, all the fine weapons would have been gone, already in the possession of King and his friends. Harrison alluded to the scant clothing when he viewed the body, which probably occurred some time after numerous others had viewed it and taken what they wanted from it, even its skin.

This part of Davidson's storyline, that he was lying wounded on the field after the battle when a group of his men, including King, arrived to take him back to camp, is consistent in both of his accounts. But, King wanted to see if he could find *his Indian*. Davidson wasn't much interested at first, since he was in serious pain, but King explained that it would be on the way back to camp so Davidson acquiesced. Clearly, in his first letter, Davidson felt the dress identified the body as a chief. Analysts seem to believe Davidson contradicts himself on this point in his second letter. This is how Davidson describes finding the body, and its appearance, in the latter account:

> When we got there, we found the Indian behind the tree. They turned him over and sure enough, his left breast was pierced by two balls, about a half an inch below the nipple. The Indian was plainly, but more comfortably dressed than the rest of the Indians, having on the finest wampum belt I ever saw, and his knives and arms were superior to those of the Indians around. I mentioned to Davy I thought he 'might be a chief.' . . . I was informed that next day, Mike (my brother) and Charles A. Wickliffe, of Bardstown, determined to have a look at "King's Indian." They went to the spot and found the Indian. Whilst they were looking at him, General Harrison and two British officers came up and one of the latter exclaimed: "I believe this is Tecumseh." The other also thought it was him. They reported that Tecumseh had a scar on his left cheek and one leg shorter than the other. They agreed that this was Tecumseh. It

was soon noised aloud that the body was found, and the skin was taken by soldiers to make razor straps.[16]

Contradiction to his first account is attributed to the fact that he now describes the body's dress as plain and comfortable. But in the next sentence he describes some pretty impressive attire and weaponry, such as a distinctive wampum belt and superior knives. Davidson clearly states in both accounts that he believed it was a chief. In the first interview he said, *"The Indian from his dress was evidently a chief."* In the second story he said the Indian was *"plainly, but more comfortably dressed"* but quickly adds, *"I mentioned to Davy I thought he 'might be a chief."* Contradiction?

The sash in the first story changed to a wampum belt in the second. This fact is difficult to dismiss. It is unlikely, but a wampum belt worn over a shoulder might be referred to as a sash. Davidson also states in both accounts that the weapons were extraordinary; so there is no discrepancy on that point. He mentioned the fine leggings in both accounts as well, again no discrepancy. Any blatant contradiction, except for the sash/wampum belt point, doesn't seem to exist.

What does exist is a difference in perception as to whether this Indian was a chief or not. And the discrepancy that exists is not all within Davidson's own words, but in comparing Davidson's account with many others' who described Tecumseh's dress on that day as being that of a common warrior. So let's ask, what specifically would have made a white American soldier come to a conclusion that any particular Indian was a chief? One has to wonder how many of these men had even seen a chief before this day. It's possible that the fine weapons alone were enough to convince King and his friends that he was a chief. Tecumseh most likely still used his own knives that day, except for the sword he gave away for his son. Perhaps Tecumseh's leggings were inherently just a bit fancier than the common warrior. It's possible that fringe alone may have made them appear distinctive to young Americans. Yet leggings are still in keeping with most other accounts of Tecumseh's "simple" dress. To one man a fancy weapon, to another fringe on common leggings, and yet to a further something else may have been the trigger to conclude that the bearer was a more important Indian than the next. In this instance it all seems to fall into the lap of the beholder as to what distinguished a warrior as a chief.

The only lingering problem in Davidson's story is that he says two British officers identified the body along with Harrison the next day. Harrison made it clear that no British soldiers were anywhere near the battlefield after the fight. Even putting that aside, Davidson is yet another person on a growing list to say that Harrison himself verbalized that he at least *thought* the body was Tecumseh's.

Davidson concludes:

> Because Tecumseh was killed where Johnson made his charge, Johnson got the credit of killing him, and as there was a great rivalry between Shelby's and Johnson's corps, we were glad that the Colonel of our regiment got the credit of it. King never cared a cent for it. It is only at the request of friends that I make this public. King brought Whitley's gun home and restored it to his family.[17]

Is this a renege on Davidson's part concerning who the men believed had killed Tecumseh? Probably not. In his earlier report he said that everyone in camp believed it was King who killed Tecumseh. This second report was written so many years later, it seems to be a summarization by Davidson of how history viewed the event in Johnson's favor over time.

A correct identification of the body is critical to all these stories. McAfee doesn't say who identified the body, but certainly a body, still on the field, was determined to be Tecumseh. Davidson says Harrison and others made the identification. It was speculated by many that only Harrison and Shane could have made such a declaration as they were supposed to be the only two in the American camp who had ever seen Tecumseh before this battle. But Harrison's and Shane's conclusions were, well, inconclusive. None-the-less the camp generally ran with their supposed identification. Unbeknownst to Harrison, there seem to have been others present at the Thames who knew and could identify Tecumseh. Isaac Hamblin, as we've seen, was one. Let's discover which other participants had previously known Tecumseh, and what they had to say about his death.

CHAPTER 14

I Knew Tecumseh When...

*At that time Col. Miller came upon the scene
and said it was the Chief Tecumseh. Miller told
the parties to examine the calf of the leg, and that
they would find there a scar, as the chief had been wounded
in that part of his person at the battle of Brownstown.
The examination was made, and the wound found
as Col. Miller described it.[1]*

Although Charles Wickliffe was not personally familiar with Tecumseh, he brings to us his personal testimony backed up by the word of Christopher Miller who did know him. Wickliffe was at the Thames serving as an aide-de-camp to General Caldwell. He was in the fight, but not on the very front lines. It seems that upon trying to attach himself to the *Forlorn Hope*, he realized that his Canadian-bred horse could not keep up with the Kentucky-bred horses of his fellow riders. Therefore he fell back a short distance to his original station in Caldwell's brigade near Shelby's position. As the battle progressed he soon became engaged with the enemy. In 1859, he was solicited by the editor of the *Bardstown Gazette* to verify the testimony recently published by James Davidson. In his response, Wickliffe relates his own remembrances of the event and his involvement in them.

After the fight, as soon as he could be relieved of his duty, Wickliffe went to the area where the dead and wounded were gathered. He was searching for his brother whom he believed to have been in the heat of the fight and was relieved to find him not dead. He recalled seeing Davidson among the wounded and proceeded to Colonel Johnson's tent to check on his condition. There he talked with James Johnson who was at his brother's side.

Col. James Johnson in reply to a question put by me as to the manner and circumstances attending the wounding of Col. Rick Johnson, [he] stated to me what the Col. had told him, viz., that in the charge made by my command and by the first fire from the Indians, he was shot in his bridle hand [the left hand]. His horse "or *gray* mare I believe he rode"

Image courtesy of Kentucky Historical Society.

*Image of Charles A. Wickliffe, as he appeared while Governor
of Kentucky 1839-1840. William Besser-Artist.*

whirled with him at which moment he was then shot in his thigh and his mare, it also was shot. An Indian rushed up with his tomahawk raised. Johnson having his pistol in his right hand raised and shot and the Indian fell. This statement was made before it was announced that Tecumseh was killed.

We see the classic story here but with a notable twist. Johnson told his brother that he was wounded in the wrist in the first fire. Then, he says, he was struck in the thigh, before he fired upon the attacking Indian. Also, Wickliffe states that Johnson was riding a *gray* mare. McAfee said it was white, so did many others, as we will see.

Wickliffe observes Tecumseh's voice being heard repeatedly and finally ceasing.

The battle from the first gun to the time of the Indian shout for retreat totaled fifty-five minutes by my watch. I am satisfied that the Indians did not retreat until after Tecumseh was killed. I can remember that preceding each Indian yell which accompanied their fire, to have heard the sound of an Indian voice, loud–it was a command to the charge or to fire. I heard this where the heavy . . . charge was made in an angle formed by

Chiles and Trotter and [E___] Brigade. After that struggle I heard that voice no more and the body of Tecumseh was found near that point.

So Wickliffe timed the battle at fifty-five minutes. Johnson was already off the field for some time. If the voice referenced was truly Tecumseh's, obviously someone else killed him later in the fight. Wickliffe was in the area of the field which Harrison referred to as the *crotchet*. It was an inverted *V* shape of men moving forward toward the area Johnson had fought in. Shelby led from the center point where the lines met. These men saw heavy fighting toward the end of the battle.

On the morning after the battle Wickliffe was parading the area with others counting the dead.

> We came to the Indian which had been examined by some persons, and I suppose the one Gen. Harrison had looked at. He was lying on his back. He had on his leggings and a hunting shirt. Some one had deprived him of his moccasins or shoes. He was barefoot.

At this point in the letter, Wickliffe explains that he had served previously in the war with a man named Christopher Miller. The two had once discussed Tecumseh because Miller had known him. Miller's brother and he were kidnapped at an early age by Indians. As he grew up he worked as a spy for them, but was finally re-captured by the whites and persuaded to remember his original family. He knew Tecumseh while captive and told Wickliffe in the course of their discussion that Tecumseh's leg was broken in his youth by a fall from his horse and that "one of his legs was shortened by the wound. [And] that he had the small pore and was pock-marked slightly when he [Miller] saw him last."[2]

With this memory, Wickliffe proceeded to observe the body. "I stript off the legging of this Indian [and] distinctly saw the wound in his leg . . . there was a difference in the length of about one inch." Wickliffe went to the area where the British prisoners were being held and asked if anyone of them knew Tecumseh. One replied that he knew him well, so Wickliffe tried to let the guard to release him so he could take him to identify the body. The guard did not cooperate, but Wickliffe received a good description from the prisoner.

> He said I would find his face painted different from the other Indians, one half red, the other black. He described this chief and said that he had some marks of small pore in his face. He stated also that on the day

before the skirmish between the two enemies, at the bridge [Chatham], he was slightly wounded in one of his arms and it was bandaged.

Wickliffe continues:

I returned to my camp, took my shaving soap and a cup of warm water and some friends with me, Col. Davidson says it was his brother Capt. Mike Davidson (who accompanied me) . . . I found the Indian dressed as the British sergeant had described. I found the wound on his arm bandaged, his face painted as described. I washed the paint from the face and saw the pock-marks distinctly, but not many of them.

We have learned a good deal from Miller and Wickliffe. Apparently, to some degree, Tecumseh had at least a slight acne problem which few people ever mention. And we have yet another person who is testifying to Tecumseh's shortened leg caused by his fall from a horse. Wickliffe verifies Harrison's report that the British prisoners were held some distance from the battlefield. And, Harrison's truthfulness is even further strengthened by the fact that the American guard would not release a British officer to Wickliffe's charge. Security was tight.

Surveillance of the battleground continued and others came to view and identify the body. Wickliffe says:

I returned to the camp and reported to Gov. Shelby and conducted him and others to the same Indian. Gen. Harrison also went, saw and recognized him to be Tecumseh. He was shot in the breast just below the nipple. I think there were three ball holes, I know there was more than one.

Wickliffe is yet another witness to state that Harrison identified the body as Tecumseh. The description of the wound from three balls concurs with Shane and some others. But wait. Wickliffe is not finished giving us some vital information and his own conclusion.

There was lying about 40 yards from Tecumseh a dead Indian near the same size and dressed very much in the same style of Tecumseh. This was the Indian I always believed Col. Johnson killed. He was killed by a single ball in his forehead, just above his eyebrow. His eyebrows & hair & skin powder burnt, [showing] that his head must have been very close to the muzzle of the instrument that killed him. I was satisfied of the fact, by the statement [said] of Col. James Johnson, that his brother Richard Johnson killed this Indian.[3]

Wickliffe concludes, based in part on some undisclosed reasons provided to him by James Johnson, that Richard killed the Indian shot in the head (the one who was not identified as Tecumseh). Did James Johnson perhaps reveal to Wickliffe some comments of Richard which might have suggested that he shot his Indian in the head? We don't know. Contrary to Wickliffe, most men believed that the body identified as Tecumseh by Wickliffe, Shane and others, the one who was shot in the breast, was the one killed by Johnson.

Confusing matters even further, Wickliffe also notes, "I have read Mr. Hamblin's account and like Col. Davidson, I do not concur in his statements of the facts given by him."[4] This means that Hamblin, who said Johnson was fallen under his horse when he shot Tecumseh *in the head*, is not to be believed. Didn't Wickliffe just a few sentences earlier say that he believed Johnson had shot the other Indian, the one who was near Tecumseh, the one that was shot *in the head*? *Hmmm.*

Surprisingly, there were still several more men who were both participants in the fight and claimed that at some point in their lives they had known Tecumseh. Thus they felt qualified to identify his body. Most of these alleged acquaintances with Tecumseh seem plausible. However, some encounters were so brief, or so long before this event occurred, that one wonders if a valid identification based upon them could have been made.

Simon Kenton, the well-known frontiersman of the day, was certainly one who was very familiar with Tecumseh. Kenton, as we saw earlier, knew Tecumseh, both as a participant in treaty negotiations, and as an opponent in battle, but always as an admirer of his integrity. By the time the Thames battle occurred, Kenton was an aged man and had seen more than his fair share of confrontations. Yet, as his descendent Edna Kenton explains, "Kenton's nostrils dilated daily with the smell of war and when Governor Shelby came through Urbana [Ohio] on his way to the Thames, with hundreds of Kenton's old friends among his troops, he simply joined in."[5]

He served, as his contemporary Whitley had, *on his own hook* not having to answer to any particular superior. His family did not want him to go. "Shelby urged him to go along as counselor and advisor, but Kenton's family getting wind of it, objected vehemently. He was fifty-eight years old; he had a broken leg; he could not stand the hardships and exposures of a long campaign."[6] But, Kenton had a mind of his own.

> So Kenton, always amiable and considerate and always averse to "contrary talk" when his own mind was made up, saw Shelby's forces off without tears. His family sighed with relief when the last company marched out of Urbana; they thought the matter settled—and so it was. A few hours later, Simon saddled his horse, flung a blanket and a sack of corn across it, mounted it, and rode casually off, presumably to the neighborhood mill. Falling in with a neighbor a few miles out on his journey, he sent back word to his family that he was on his way to Proctor's Mill. He went there indeed. He easily caught up with Shelby's troops and marched on to the Thames. . . .[7]

Another inducement for Kenton to partake in this adventure was to hopefully learn something of his son, Simon Ruth, whose whereabouts had been unknown since he was involved in Hull's surrender over a year previous.

The road to the Thames was especially hard on Kenton. Along with the younger men, he was marching thirty miles a day while enduring the pain of an unhealed leg and rheumatic knees. As they closed in on the site, Kenton found himself acting as a spy ahead of the troops. He was not in the area where Tecumseh was killed but was called later to identify the body believed to be his.

> He always asserted that the Indian displayed as the great dead chief was not Tecumseh; said he has seen him too often and knew him too well to be mistaken . . . He insisted that the Indians, with their reverence for the dead, would never have left the body of their chief behind them in their flight.[8]

Samuel Baker relates a story told to him by Simon Kenton:

> He [Kenton] stated that at the battle of the Thames in which he took part, an Indian warrior fell and was supposed to be Tecumseh, and that the men cut strips from his legs and back for razor strops, much to his chagrin & most of the officers. But Kenton asserted positively that it was not Tecumseh, but that he was mortally wounded and died shortly after at Long Point [Long Point is on the northern coast of Lake Erie about a hundred miles from the battlefield].[9]

In Lyman Draper's notes, is found this reference to Kenton:

> Kenton said that the Britishers fired, but shot among the tree tops clear

Image courtesy of U.S. Library of Congress.

Portrait of Simon Kenton, (1755-1836). Lithographer and date unknown.

over our heads–were poor marksmen at best, & when they shot & found their lines broken, they called for quarters. Kenton thought they purposely fired high, as they were ordered to fire & had to obey, & did so expecting to be taken, & fearing they would be ruthlessly slaughtered by the Kentuckians, [who were] exasperated by the inhumanity of [the] British and Indians at the River Raisin & Dudley's defeat–& not wishing to provoke them farther. But K. said it was not Tecumseh whose body was pointed out as such–for Tecumseh had a fine set of teeth, & this fellow had not. (as K. had not seen him for six years, Tecumseh might have changed some in this particular–L.C.D.)[10]

Kenton again insisted that the body said to be Tecumseh's, was not. This time he based it on his teeth, which even Draper noted to himself (L.C.D.–Lyman Copeland Draper) Kenton could have been wrong about, since teeth can deteriorate over time. Perhaps the body truly was not Tecumseh, but some have speculated that Kenton purposefully claimed it was not in order to spare the corpse any further mutilation.

William Conner was the interpreter who had been on this campaign ever since Harrison requested his presence, back in the summer of 1813. Conner was well acquainted with Tecumseh. As noted earlier, they were neighbors for years along the White River in southern Indiana. William's son, A. J. Conner confirms this fact in a letter to Lyman Draper in 1891, "My father knew Tecumthe and the Prophet quite intimately." He continues:

> The Democrats universally claimed that "Col. Johnson killed Tecumthe." One of their campaign songs repeated these words over and over. But my father often declared, that this could not be, that an old Indian fighter and camp follower was probably entitled to the honor, if such a thing could be counted as an honor. His name was Wheatley [Whitley]; he was a bitter Indian hater and a crank, so much so that he was never mustered into the military service. He went into the battle on his own account, and was slain in the fight. Tecumthe was shot through the breast, and the wound plainly indicated that he came to his death from the effect of a shot from a small bore rifle, such as the frontiersmen usually carried. A few feet from the body of Tecumthe was found that of Wheatley, who had pressed forward to the front of the battle. He was armed with the kind of rifle described above. At that time it was the universal belief with the soldiers, that Wheatly had made the fatal shot that killed Tecumthe, and there was no mention made of Col. Johnson. Johnson was mounted, and had for arms his sword and horse pistols, and could not have fired the fatal shot. Col. Johnson was a brave soldier, and does not need the distinction. Public rumor without basis, sometimes misleads the historian, and then history misleads for all time.[11]

Perhaps Conner's opinion was based solely on ballistic analysis, but the fact that his son makes a point of saying that it's the Democrats who believe Johnson killed Tecumseh raises some eyebrows. Conner was a Whig. Be that as it may, Conner says that Tecumseh was shot in the chest, but unfortunately he doesn't note how many holes were there. He is convinced that the wound was from a rifle which is small-bore (meaning the barrel had a small diameter). The pistols of the day were large-bore and thus would have fired a larger ball. By this observation Johnson is ruled out as the shooter since he only carried pistols. Also, Conner is yet another person added to the list of those who say that rumors were running through the camp. This time, however, they were not for Johnson or King, but for Whitley.

A. J. continues:

> My father was summoned to the quarters of Col. Johnson, who stated to him, that it was rumored that Tecumthe had been slain in the bat-

tle. The Colonel directed him to take some of the friendly Indians and search the field for the great warrior's body if it was indeed true that he had fallen. My father selected five or six Delawares, and at once began the search which was successful. When the body was found, there was some doubt whether it was Tecumthe or the Prophet . . . there was a very striking resemblance between the brothers. One of the Indians stooped over the body, and turned up one of the eyelids, and at once declared that the body was that of Tecumthe. One of the brothers had a spot or defect on one of his eyes, and had often been recognized by that mark. It was then indeed Tecumthe, the great Indian chieftain, whose body they were looking at. Someone had cut and peeled off the skin from one of his thighs . . .[12]

Conner is the only one to claim that Johnson had sent him out to look for Tecumseh. Others were sent by Harrison or went on their own accord. With the Indians concurring, Connor obviously agreed that they were looking at the body of Tecumseh. It is surprising to see that someone again confused Tecumseh with his brother the Prophet, especially since Conner had plenty of contact with both of them. Perhaps, besides the damaged eye, they did closely resemble each other, but most people who describe them through history suggest that Tecumseh was much more fine featured. History has one legitimate portrait of the Prophet, and it is exquisite. On the other hand, there was never a likeness of Tecumseh done from life. All existing depictions of Tecumseh are speculative and were created after his death.

One more relative of William Conner has given an opinion. His name is Flavius Maximus Finch. He was William's brother-in-law and stated in a letter to Lyman Draper that

Mr. C. always insisted that T. was killed by a rifle ball—not a large bored pistol as was alleged. He examined the body naked and saw the wounds that killed T. Said there was a small piece of skin cut from the top of the head, as by a sabre. Another man named Whitley, who had a rifle carrying such a ball as killed T. was lying dead about 20 feet from the body of T. and he always insisted that that old man shot T. and was afterwards killed himself. Mr. Conner knew Tecumseh and his brother well, long before this war, met him at his trading post . . .[13]

To sum up, William Conner believed that the body on the field was Tecumseh. Further, due to his ballistics observation, and the position of Whitley's body in relationship to Tecumseh's, he concludes that Whitley killed him. It seems that this is more of a case *against* Johnson, because of the pistol versus rifle argument, than it is a solid case *for* Whitley. Being frontiersmen and hunters, at least some of the militia men in this area of the fight had to have been firing rifles as well as muskets and pistols.

A particular area of the *Northwest Territory*, generally stretching from Fort Meigs to the Raisin River (present-day Perrysburg, Ohio to Monroe, Michigan), was home to several men who both knew Tecumseh and fought at the Thames. One of them was James Knaggs. We read one of his tales earlier, showing Tecumseh's generosity to a young boy. In 1853, Knaggs signed an affidavit, at the request of B. F. H. Witherell, an attorney who was making a case for Johnson having killed Tecumseh. Witherell sent it off in a letter to General Lewis Cass, declaring that this affidavit proved that no one but Johnson could have done it.

James Knaggs deposeth and saith as follows: I was attached to a company of mounted men called Rangers, at the Battle of the Thames in Upper Canada in the year 1813. During the battle we charged into the swamp, where several of our horses mired down, and an order was given to retire to the hard ground in our rear, which we did. The Indians in front, believing that we were retreating, immediately advanced upon us, with Tecumseh at their head. I distinctly heard his voice, with which I was perfectly familiar. He yelled like a tiger, and urged on his braves to the attack. We were then but a few yards apart. We halted on the hard ground, and continued our fire. After a few minutes of very severe fighting, I discovered Colonel Johnson lying near, on the ground, with one leg confined by the body of his *white* mare, which had been killed, and had fallen upon him. My friend Medard Labadie was with me. We went up to the colonel, with whom we were previously acquainted, and found him badly wounded, lying on his side, with one of his pistols lying in his hand. I saw Tecumseh at the same time, lying on his face, dead, and about fifteen or twenty feet from the Colonel. He was stretched at full length, and was shot through the body, I think near the heart. The ball went out through his back. He held his tomahawk in his right hand, (it had a brass pipe on the head of it,) his arm was extended as if striking, and the edge of the tomahawk was stuck in the ground. Tecumseh was dressed in red speckled leggings, and a fringed hunting shirt; he lay stretched directly towards Colonel Johnson. When we went up to the Colonel we offered to help him. He replied with great animation, "Knaggs, let me lay here, and push on and take Proctor." However, we liberated him from his dead horse, took his blanket from his saddle, placed him in it, and bore him off the field. I had known Tecumseh from my boyhood; we were boys together. There was no other Indian killed immediately around where Colonel Johnson or Tecumseh lay, though there were many near the creek, a few rods back of where Tecumseh fell. I had no doubt then, and have none now, that Tecumseh fell by the hand of Colonel Johnson.

James Knaggs

Sworn to, before me, this 22nd day of September, 1853.

B.F.H. Witherell, Notary Public[14]

In many respects, this affidavit paints a very different picture from what we've seen from most witnesses so far. That is except for Isaac Hamblin's account. The scene of Johnson on the ground, under his horse, concurs with Hamblin. But that is where the similarity ends. There are many other discrepancies that have to be reconciled.

First, Knaggs says that Johnson's *white* horse was dead. Remember how others said Johnson was led off upon his horse, and that the horse hadn't died until Johnson was removed from it? Second, it seems a bit too convenient to state that Tecumseh had his tomahawk, and Johnson had his pistol still in hand when found. Third, Tecumseh is described as wearing "red-speckled leggings." We now have another color of his dress which is unique to this testimony. Fourth, the conversation with the wounded Johnson seems a bit romanticized in its language. Further, Knaggs says that Johnson spoke with much animation. Everyone else testifies that Johnson was so severely wounded and faint that any energetic discourse with the colonel seems quite improbable. Fifth, Knaggs says that there were no other fallen Indians close-by. Everyone else acknowledged that at least one, if not more, Indians were killed in the immediate area; one in particular appearing similar in appearance to Tecumseh. And most accounts acknowledged the position of Tecumseh's body in relation to Whitley's. Knaggs makes no mention of Whitley.

Knaggs was born in Roche de Bout, (present-day Waterville, Ohio) and later settled on a farm about a mile north of the Raisin River. Early in his life, he became so well-versed in Indian dialects and French, that his allegiance to the American effort was sometimes questioned. He proved his loyalty boldly, however; through various stints of service during the War of 1812, including as a ranger at the Thames. The scenes of horror that had occurred in his very own backyard during the Raisin River massacre haunted him all his life and fueled his patriotism.

In the excitement of the political campaign when Johnson was elected vice-president, the question, "Who killed Tecumseh?" was widely discussed . . . During that time, General Cass "stumped" the State [of Michigan in support of Johnson] accompanied by Knaggs and Labadie, whom at a proper juncture in his address, he introduced as witnesses to the truth of his statement of the occurrence.[15]

This campaigning for Johnson, by Knaggs and Labadie is attested to again by James Bentley of Monroe, Michigan who says that these two men

were placed on a platform with Col. Johnson as his companions in the day of trial, who had borne him from the field of battle. Knaggs and Labadie may be regarded as backers of the colonel in more senses than one, as they, after the battle of the Thames, alternately carried him on their backs from Malden to Monroe.[16]

Just a minute, please. Did Bentley just say that on their way home these two men *literally* carried the wounded Johnson on their backs for a distance that would have been over fifty miles? Considering the seriousness of Johnson's many wounds, this is as implausible as it gets. In the least, Bentley could have suggested that they carried him on a stretcher!

Medard Labadie is often mentioned in association with Knaggs. They fought side-by-side at the Thames. They also were brothers-in-law. One obscure note in Lyman Draper's papers comes from Joseph Bisseau, another brother-in-law of Labadie, who also lived in the Raisin River area. Bisseau claims, "He [Labadie] was in the battle of the Thames, and seeing Tecumseh shoot Col. Johnson, and the latter fall, *Labadie shot the chief who immediately fell.*"[17] Apparently only Labadie's inner circle of friends and family knew this truth, and Labadie must have been too humble to take any credit away from Johnson. He even swallowed this truth to boost Johnson's claim to it.

James Bentley himself was at the Thames with Knaggs and Labadie. He as well lived in the Raisin River area. One day in 1812, Bentley says he saw Tecumseh with other chiefs as they were eating lunch. The Indians were on their way to talk with General Hull in Detroit. Bentley told Lyman Draper that he

> did not see him again till he saw his dead body at the Thames. Bentley was then in Col. Johnson's mounted regiment – saw Tecumseh's dead body, recognized it – stretched upon his back, with his plain blue surtout [knee-length frock] coat on, and thinks blue leggings, with breech-clout; afterwards in showing the body to others, found the coat gone – and finally saw where his thighs had been skinned for razor straps. His body lay near where Col. Johnson fell, as though the Colonel might have killed him; and Col. Wm. Whitley's body (who went into the fight mounted) was within a short distance near a tree.[18]

It is very curious that Bentley, who knew, spoke of, and lived near both Knaggs and Labadie, paints such a different picture of the event. He first verifies that he was qualified to recognize Tecumseh because he saw him once, momentarily, a year earlier. Then he says that Tecumseh was wearing blue clothing. Knaggs just swore in an affidavit that Tecumseh was dressed in red-speckled attire. Bentley goes on to describe Tecumseh's body in close proximity to Whitley's, the most referred to location in other accounts as well. But how does that mesh with Knaggs's picture of Tecumseh lying alone in the area?

The last resident of this region who had something to say was Peter Navarre. He lived most of his life at the mouth of the Maumee River, in an area known as Presque Isle (present-day Oregon, Ohio). He often travelled throughout the area of the Northwest Territory, especially during the war years while he was serving Harrison as a spy and messenger. He was at the Thames acting in that capacity in advance of the main body of troops. Navarre met with Lyman Draper several times over the years since and Draper recorded his remarks concerning Tecumseh.

According to Navarre, "Tecumseh could and did talk English – often visited the Navarre's on the Maumee, giving and receiving presents." Draper further notes what he learned from Navarre:

> Tecumseh – Had sixteen bullet holes in his body in his last fight – at the Thames – was tomahawked, and bayoneted in the face. Peter Navarre, who knew him well, helped bury him, but could not with certainty recognize him, his face was so disfigured; and sent for Gen. Harrison, who

*Portrait of Peter Navarre. Illustrated by Benson J. Lossing
and shown here as it appeared in his Pictorial Fieldbook of the War of 1812
which was originally published in 1868.*

said Tecumseh had a scar from a burn received when young, nearly the whole length of his left hip; and finding this, Harrison was satisfied as to his identity, and told Navarre, Medard Labadie, James Knaggs and two or three others, to give him a decent burial, as he was a brave and honorable antagonist. "Had I been taken prisoner," said Harrison, "I know he would have saved me." Tecumseh had on buck-skin leggings. His body was not skinned–that was another's. He was buried on the battle-ground–found near where Col. Johnson was wounded. A grave was dug amid the trees, with sticks and axes, some three feet deep, and covered with dirt and logs on top.[19]

Several details, which we have not seen from anyone else, make this a very quizzical account. Navarre claims that Tecumseh's face was severely cut, that's new. He says that Harrison was called for, by him, to identify this body and that Harrison knew of Tecumseh's burn scar, that's new. He states that Harrison ordered Knaggs, Labadie and himself to bury Tecumseh, that's new. Neither of these other two men ever made a similar claim. In fact, you would expect that if such was the case, Knaggs might have mentioned burying Tecumseh in his af-

fidavit. And, Navarre says that this body, identified as Tecumseh, was
not skinned, that's new. Since the skinned body is the one most men
identified as Tecumseh–hence the reason it was skinned–Navarre is
claiming something quite opposite by saying that Harrison identified
an un-skinned body as Tecumseh's.

With this account already difficult to digest, Navarre made another
statement in the *Toledo Blade* newspaper in 1872.

> At the battle of the Thames, on the 1st [5th] of October, Navarre was
> under Johnson, in the immediate vicinity of Tecumseh, of whose death
> he speaks as follows. "He was standing behind a large tree that had blown
> down, encouraging his warriors, and was killed by a ball that passed di-
> agonally through his chest. After death he was shot several times, but
> otherwise his body was not mutilated in the least, being buried in his
> regimentals [uniform], as the old chief desired, by myself and a com-
> panion, at the command of Gen. Harrison. All statements that he was
> scalped or skinned are absolutely false.[20]

For a second time Navarre states that he buried the un-skinned body
of Tecumseh. Additionally, he reports that Tecumseh was buried in his
British uniform. Few historians believe Tecumseh had ever worn British military garb of any sort, except for possibly a medal he had been
presented with.

Navarre took his story to an even more ludicrous level just a few years
before his death. In his memoirs, he claimed to have slain Tecumseh
himself. Navarre was already a celebrity in the Toledo, Ohio area, and
when a local historian, John Gunckel, came along requesting his life
story for a book he was writing (*The Early History of the Maumee Valley*, 1902), apparently Navarre decided to embellish his memory of the
Thames event. His most interesting quote on the claim reads:

> Colonel (Richard Mentor) Johnson under whose command I fought,
> was wounded and had his horse killed under him. While he was down,
> Tecumseh sprang from a tree to tomahawk and scalp him, and I fired
> upon him. He fell and the war cry of Tecumseh was heard no more.[21]

Abraham Holmes was the sixteen year old boy who, as we had learned
earlier, had seen Tecumseh at Arnold's Mill just before the fight ensued
on the morning of October 5th. He says:

> On the day after the battle I visited the scene having in the meantime

heard of the death of Tecumseh. Although quite a number were reported killed, I discovered only two bodies, neither of which that of the chief, and I am of the opinion that his body was taken by his friends, along with others who fell, and buried. It was said at the time that the fatal shot was fired by Col. Johnson but of this, or of the final disposal of his body, nothing was known certainly.[22]

Holmes had made only one observation regarding Tecumseh's dress that day. "He remembers nothing noteworthy about Tecumseh's head gear and thinks it was a small shawl worn as a turban."[23] There is little detail in Holmes' account but that is for good reason—he did not see Tecumseh's body after the fight. There would seem to be little reason for the young Holmes to lie, unless he was trying to avoid history recording that his hero's body had been abused in death.

It was Joe Johnston who Holmes had witnessed talking to Tecumseh at Arnold's the morning of the battle. Johnston, who obviously knew what Tecumseh looked like, had his own tale to tell of the event. Apparently his story was the stuff of local legend until it was promoted publicly in the Canadian newspaper *The Chatham Planet*. Johnston claimed to have been "one of the six who formed Tecumseh's body guard, and who helped to bury him."[24] Johnston further claimed that Tecumseh was wounded and sitting on the ground still rallying his braves when a stray bullet killed him. Keep this version of Tecumseh's last moments in mind as we soon move ahead and review some Indian testimonies.

As we learned earlier through Sam Theobold's account, C.S. Todd had heard a story from Ben Warfield who had talked with an Indian aide of Tecumseh named Clarke immediately after the fighting had ceased. In a letter from Warfield to Todd in 1840, we hear the story in Warfield's own words.

> I was ordered by Genl. Harrison to count and examine what might be found on the battle ground with my company. In making that examination, I discovered a man concealed in the root of a hollow tree. I had him dragged out & it proved to be a man by the name of Clarke who represented himself as to be the British Indian Interpreter, very badly wounded. I conversed with him on our way with him to Genl. Harrison's quarters & he distinctly informed me upon my interrogation as to what had become of Tecumseh, that he had been shot down by his side & I think killed, but that the Indians had taken him off the ground.

When I carried him to Genl. Harrison, he made to him the same statement, the truth of which I never doubted.[25]

These words of Clark are referred to in several testimonies.

A lingering question is whether any of the British officers had gotten to the body in question in order to identify it. There are a few more reports in Lyman Draper's notes that point to the fact that they were solicited to identify the body in question which is contrary to Harrison's report.

A person identified as Judge Todd told Draper that he

was on the Thames campaign. The next day after the battle of the Thames, the British Col. Chambers & other British officers, looked at the body designated as Tecumseh's—with straps taken off by the American soldiers—& they unhesitating identified it as Tecumseh's.[26]

Another entry in Draper's notes relates a brief account from Col. John O'Fallon who was Harrison's aide at the Thames. O'Fallon was referred to in Harrison's story as being the person who found the Canadian militiamen that had identified Tecumseh. Perhaps it was when he learned from John Richardson, then a young British prisoner, who had heard from some Indians that Tecumseh was dead, that O'Fallon himself "got a British interpreter to go & show the body [on] the night of the battle—[He] did so; the body was plainly dressed in a fringed dark shirt or dress—was subsequently stripped, & skinned for strops & by the Am. Soldiery,"[27]

Captain Samuel Boone, as we learned earlier, tells Draper of another anonymous young British officer who had cited Tecumseh's wrist as being wounded the previous day. Boone goes on:

So Harrison, Shelby & other [American] officers & this young British officer went to view the body—& Harrison said he should know Tecumseh by a scar on the face—he examined it & found it & the wound on the wrist also, & the leather, nicely fringed hunting shirt, as the young British officer had described. Harrison pronounced it Tecumseh. This was toward evening & a large crowd of soldiers followed . . . (Sam among them). Next morning Harrison & Shelby again examined the Indian, and repeated their conviction that it was Tecumseh's . . . it was not then thought that Col. Johnson killed him—[Sam] thinks it could not be known who shot him. Tecumseh's thighs had been skinned.[28]

Here we see yet another person who says Harrison did recognize the skinned body as Tecumseh's, in fact twice, and apparently there was no talk in camp of Johnson having killed him. These testimonies of Todd, O'Fallon and Boone mark three more contradictions to Harrison's report that no British officers were involved in the identification.

Samuel Baker already told us how Simon Kenton didn't believe the body identified was Tecumseh. Over the years, Baker provided further accounts from which we learn of another Col. Miller's involvement. This is not the same Christopher Miller that Charles Wickliffe told us about. This is Colonel James Miller who would go on after the Thames battle to become acclaimed as the Hero of Lundy's Lane. A *Cincinnati Daily Gazette* reporter who interviewed Baker says:

> At that time Col. Miller came upon the scene and said it was the Chief Tecumseh. Miller told the parties to examine the calf of the leg and that they would find there a scar, as the chief had been wounded in that part of his person at the battle at Brownstown.[29]

The reporter continues:

> When the charge was made Col. Johnson was wounded, and near him lay an Indian dead. Mr. Baker informs me [the newspaper reporter], that he was upon the ground in a few minutes after the wounding of Johnson and the killing of this Indian occurred . . .[30]

In an article in the same newspaper thirteen years later, and seventy-three years after the battle, Baker has a few even more striking contradictions, and embellishments, to his own story.

> I remember it as if it were yesterday, seeing Tecumseh brandish his tomahawk, and jump at one of our men with fiendish activity and a glare of hate in his eyes. Just then a tall officer dashed up, followed by a lot of Kentuck soldiers. It was Colonel Richard M. Johnson of Kentucky. He took deliberate aim at Tecumseh, and the Chief fell. Then our victory was easy. The red devils fled, and we all gathered around the yet warm body of the noted Indian. The blood was oozing out of a bullet wound in his breast, and was soaking the sash which he wore indicating his rank as a Major-General in the British Army. There was no doubt as usual to his identity, but Colonel Miller, who had led the successful charge at Lundy's Lane, came up and said: "Look at his right leg. Tecumseh was shot at Fort Meigs. See if there is a scar." Sure enough as we took the off

the leggings there was the scar, and everybody rejoiced.[31]

Baker is consistent from one account to the next about Col. Miller arriving on the scene, but little else. It is strictly coincidental that both Millers knew Tecumseh via his scars, albeit different ones. That leg scar referred to here becomes a problem because in the first story Miller said it was received at Brownstown, in the second it was at Fort Meigs. Also in question now is whether Baker came on the scene a few moments after the fact, per the first story; or did he see Johnson take deliberate aim, as told in the second? Baker is the second person to reference a sash, Captain Davidson was the first, but there is no telling if that helped identify the body. And finally, the reporter of the day tells us that Baker proudly showed him something special in the course of his interview. "Here is a strip of Tecumseh's flesh." Baker said. "It is old and used up, but it is genuine."[32]

Aura Stewart claimed that his father who had fought at the Thames could recognize Tecumseh. After the fight, Aura's father was still another of the many who had walked the battlefield with comrades looking for wounded.

In their search they first came to Colonel Whitley, and about four rods distant lay Tecumseh, both dead on the battlefield. My father had seen Tecumseh often at Detroit and pointed him out to the officer [with him] who never saw him before. The shout that Tecumseh was dead, brought all of the [search] parties together to see him, and he was soon stripped of his dress and ornaments; but how and where Tecumseh was buried, father did not remain to see; but he could have taken his turban, and has since often expressed a wish that he had. Who killed Tecumseh is a question that cannot be answered, but . . . Colonel Whitley went into battle with a desire to meet Tecumseh, and it is possible that he killed him.[33]

Apparently Stewart was one who made a personal identification which in-turn drew the men to the area. He points out that the body had at least some ornamentation. It also seems that Stewart was inclined to believe that Whitley was as likely as anyone else to have killed Tecumseh. He states further that

here Col. Johnson had that desperate encounter with an Indian chief–not Tecumseh . . . and my father had good reasons for believing [this], from the fact that the Indians fought at least three quarters of an hour after

Col. Johnson had returned wounded and disabled. . . . He saw the Col. when he returned, badly wounded, his horse pierced by seven balls, and falling immediately after the Colonel was taken from him. . . . It was the opinion of those acquainted with Indian warfare that the Indians fought until Tecumseh fell, and no longer. But all admit that Col. Johnson had, while wounded and disabled, a dreadful encounter with some daring Indian chief, not-withstanding all awarded to Col. Johnson the honor.[34]

So we see that Stewart concludes it could not have been Johnson since he witnessed Johnson off of the field for forty-five minutes before the battle ceased. His detail of Johnson's removal from his dying horse does concur with Theobold's account.

One final testimony, from someone who claimed to have known Tecumseh, comes from General George Sanderson. His story delivers some believable, but even more incredible details. Sanderson says:

I remember Tecumseh. I saw him a number of times previous to the war. He was a man of huge frame, powerfully built, and was about six feet two inches in height. I saw his body on the Thames field before it was cold. Whether Colonel Johnson killed him or not, I cannot say. During the battle all was smoke, noise and confusion. Indeed, I never heard anyone speak of Colonel Johnson's having killed Tecumseh until years afterward . . . In the evening, I was appointed by Harrison to guard the prisoners with my company. The location was near a swamp. There is no doubt about the fact the Kentuckians skinned Tecumseh's body. I saw them in the act. They would cut strips about a half a foot in length and an inch and a half wide, which would stretch like gum-elastic. I saw a piece two inches long, which, when dry, could be stretched nearly a foot in length. That it was Tecumseh's body which was skinned there can be no question. I knew him, and the Indian prisoners under my charge continually pointed to his body, which lay close by, and uttered the most bewailing cries at his loss. By noon the day after the battle, the body could hardly be recognized; it had been so thoroughly skinned. My men covered it with brush and logs, and it was probably eaten by wolves.[35]

Apparently, Sanderson had not read or heard of anyone else's account of this event over the fifty-seven year span leading up to his own testimony. If he had, he would have learned from people who *really* had known Tecumseh; that he was five foot eight to ten inches tall at best, and did not have a huge frame. The incident of Indian prisoners pointing to this large body as Tecumseh's, which was being flayed by Kentuckians, had to be a ruse on their part; if indeed they ever behaved in this manner at all. Finally, Sanderson teaches us a science lesson: that human flesh, in particular Tecumseh's, was so hearty it could be stretched to six times its original size!

The testimonies just reviewed are from of the Americans, Canadians, and British men who have claimed to have known Tecumseh by appearance. There is one more group of men who knew Tecumseh better than any of these—the Indians. Let's see if they agree on how this event transpired along the Thames.

CHAPTER 15

Shaubena... At His Side

Tecumseh was a very brave but cautious man.
He had, however, been wounded in the neck and became desperate.
He thought his wound was mortal and told his warriors
that as he must die, there would be no risk in rushing
forward to kill Col. Johnson. He did so, and Sha-ben-eh saw
him when he fell. His object was to strike the Colonel
with his tomahawk before he saw him, and a moment more
of inattention and the Colonel's head would have been
sundered. He was shot just as his arm had reached
the full height to strike the fatal blow.[1]

One might assume that Tecumseh's fellow Indians, with whom he had shared his life and fought alongside until his death, would be the most reliable source of information available to relate how he met his fate. Well there are in fact several accounts from the Indians. Some claim to have been eyewitnesses, at his side, at the time of his death. Others had heard what happened from fellow Indians who were near him and repeated their stories. However, it is surprising to note that a review of these Indian accounts spotlights the fact that they do not agree with each other any better than the American or British testimonies had. One Indian was cited by numerous sources and called upon more often than others to tell his story of Tecumseh's death. His name was Shaubena, a close friend and aid to Tecumseh.

Shaubena was an Ottawa Indian who married into the Potawatomie tribe and eventually became one of their great chiefs. A loyal friend and supporter of Tecumseh, his name had almost as many variations in spelling as Tecumseh's. They included *Shaubenee, Shabonay, Shabbona, Shabene, Shawbeneh, Shabonee, Shabonis,* or *Shabehnay*; and the French interpretation was written as *Chambly, Chamblee, Chaboneh, Chaubenay,* or *Chaubenee.* All translated to English as *built like a bear, burly shoulders,* or *the coal burner,* depending on who you cite for a translation. Although it is disputed among historians, Shaubena was probably born along the Maumee River in northwest Ohio in 1775 or 1776 to the Ottawa village occupying the area at that time. He was a grand-nephew of another famous Indian leader–Pontiac.

Shaubena has always attested to the fact that he was positioned next to Tecumseh at the Thames conflict. No one seems to dispute it simply because of his status at the time and his intimacy with Tecumseh. He was kind of a right-hand-man or aid-de-camp to Tecumseh so it makes perfect sense that he would be at his side in battle. The only inherent problem with his testimony of how Tecumseh was killed that day is that it kept changing over time.

In 1832, John Kingston listened in as Shaubena told tales of his Thames exploits to his father and a group of other men. Kingston recalls Shaubena's story:

> Tecumseh, and several other Indians, including Sha-bo-nis were concealed in the top of a fallen tree. The first Sha-bo-nis noticed of the "white man" was, when he came around the root of the same tree–in falling, the roots of the tree had turned up considerable earth, enough to conceal both horse and rider from view when coming in the direction the tree was lying. The horse was *white*, and both horse and rider appeared to be wounded; the man in particular appeared to be faint, hardly able to keep the saddle.–When they came in sight, but a few feet from the Indians, Tecumseh quickly rose to his feet and fire; his aim was too low, however, the ball striking the horse. He then sprang forward with uplifted tomahawk. The white man, at that instant drew a pistol, and fired, exclaiming, at the same time, "you d____d Indian." The ball took effect, killing Tecumseh instantly; both horse and rider fell to the ground. During the battle the voice of Tecumseh was heard commanding and cheering his warriors in the fight; but now that voice was heard no more. "And then," said Sha-bo-nis, in peculiar Indian style, "I saw all the other Indians run, and thought it was time for Sha-bo-nis to run too." "That white man," continued he, "is now a great chief at Washington,"–meaning Col. R. M. Johnson, who was then a member of Congress, and since Vice President of the United States. "I knew him," said he, "the moment I saw him." "Sha-bo-nis never told a lie," was the proud boast of that good Indian, and no one that knew him, ever doubted his word.[2]

Keep in mind a few key points from this relatively early account. First, note the position of the combatants: Shaubena and Tecumseh were positioned at one end (the top) of a fallen tree, in line with the oncoming Johnson who was somewhat hidden behind the large uprooted end. Second, note the fact that Johnson yelled, "You d____d Indian." And third, note that Shaubena went to Washington and recognized Johnson.

Thomas L. McKenney was for many years Superintendent of Indian Affairs in the United States. Along with James Hall, he is responsible for soliciting artists of his time to do beautiful portraits of Indians from numerous tribes. The image we have to this day of the Prophet is due to McKenney's urging. In his memoirs he relates an account as told to him by General Clark, presumably William Clark of the *Lewis and Clark Expedition* fame. Clark interviewed a Pottawattamie Indian in St. Louis in 1816. Though anonymous in the story, circumstantial details suggest that this Pottawattamie was probably Shaubena. If so, this is the earliest account received from Shaubena given just three years after the fact.

The interview was recorded as follows, beginning with Clark asking the Pottawattamie:

"Were you at the battle of the Thames?"

"I was." [responded the Indian]

"Did you see Tecumthe in the battle?"

"I did."

"Did you see him shoot?"

"I did."

"Where were you when he fell?"

"Close by him."

"Who killed him?"

"Don't know."

"Did you see the man who killed him?"

"Yes."

"What sort of a looking man was he?"

"Short, thick man."

"Was this short, thick man, on horseback?"

"Yes."

"What was the color of the horse he rode?"

"White."

"How do you know the short, thick man, on a white horse killed Tecumseh?

"I saw him shoot him."

"When did you first see the man on the white horse?"

"When he was galloping up in front of where Tecumthe stood, his horse got tangled in the top of a tree that was blown down; and while he was there, Tecumthe raised his rifle, and fired. Saw the man go so – (reel on his horse, imitating the motion) – came galloping up – came close – Tecumthe raise his tomahawk, just going to fling it – white man raise pistol – fire—Tecumthe fell – we all run away.[3]

McKenney heard this account directly from Clark and took the initiative to write to Col. Johnson asking some pertinent questions. He tells us how this transpired.

(Without him [Johnson] knowing my object) [I asked] what was the color of the horse he rode at the battle of the Thames? To which he answered, a *white* mare. Where were you, when you received the rifle-ball in the fore-knuckle of your bridle hand? To this he replied, in substance, (I have not his letter in hand), "my mare was at the time entangled in the branches of a tree that lay across the line of my advance to the British line; and while there, I saw an Indian aim at me and fire. I received the ball near the upper joint of the fore-finger of my bridle hand. Getting out of the difficulty, I spurred the mare, drawing a pistol from my holster with my right hand, having thrown the reins of the bridle over my left arm, and, as I neared the line, the same Indian raised his tomahawk, when, with what little strength I had left, I raised my pistol, and fired – and from that moment lost all sense of what was going on." Colonel Johnson knew nothing of the effect of his fire. His mare, he was told, wheeled with him, at the moment of the discharge of his pistol, galloped to the American lines, and fell, being pierced by many balls. The Indian further told General Clark, that Tecumthe was hit in the forehead, or near the corner of one of his eyes, with a ball. I learned afterwards, that, besides the bullet wound, near the eye-brow, there were three oblique cuts on the person of Tecumthe, as if made by a knife – one down his thigh, and two others in other front parts of his body. To the question put by me to Colonel Johnson, how was your pistol loaded? He answered, "with one ball, and three buck-shot." The ball, therefore, took effect in the head of the chief, and the buck-shot, scattering, cut his flesh, in a descending line, as they must needs have done, as stated, Colonel Johnson's position being above Tecumseh's. The foregoing are the circumstances which furnish the proof – to my mind amounting to demonstration – that Colonel Richard M. Johnson killed Tecumthe.[4]

McKenney was convinced by this story that Johnson was the killer. It makes sense since Shaubena described the shooter as a short, thick man; which Johnson was. As well, this account coming only three years after the fact, Shaubena may not yet have heard of credit being given to Col. Johnson. We do learn two additional significant details from McKenney: Johnson said his horse was *white* and Tecumseh was shot in the *head* by the main ball in Johnson's pistol while his chest was wounded by the three buck-shot.

Perry A. Armstrong, a historian of the mid 19th century, shared his interview of Shaubena with Lyman Draper in an 1881 letter. Armstrong says:

> He [Shaubena] was second in command of the Indian forces in the battle of the Thames and was close by the side of Tecumseh when he fell. As nearly as I can now remember the statement of this old ... Chief, it is about this: "After the fight had been going on for a considerable time, Tecumseh ordered a charge of his braves upon the center of the pale faces' line, and that his braves responded with alacrity, when with tomahawks and spears the Indians had virtually cut their way through the pale faces' line, near the center, a counter charge was made by the palefaces from the right on horseback, led by a white Chief riding a large white horse. In a moment this white horse was severely wounded by spear thrusts, and became unmanageable, and that Tecumseh made a rush at this white Chief, and when almost within striking distance, the paleface Chief pulled from his horse's back a small "speaking thunder," and fired it full in the face of Tecumseh, who fell dead on the spot. That thereupon he, Shaubenee, exclaimed ... and ordered an immediate retreat, and added, suiting the action to the words—"Indians scattered like little wild turkeys when hunter scares them." This I have always held determines the fact that Col. R. M. Johnson killed Tecumseh.[5]

This story is consistent with what we have learned so far from Shaubena's other testimonies. Tecumseh was shot in the head by a pistol ball of Johnson's while he was on his white horse. And, Shaubena and the Indians fled as soon as Tecumseh was killed.

After the defeat at the Thames, Shaubena allied himself with the United States. Per Armstrong, we glimpse how Shaubena's spiritual life influenced this decision.

> Shaubenee also told me that from the moment Tecumseh fell, he made up his mind that the Great Spirit had created the paleface to be the con-

querors of the Indians. That he had given the palefaces equal courage, and greater wisdom, than to the Indians and from that day to the time of his death, July 17, 1859, Shaubenee was the Sauganash (English-speaking) or whiteman's friend, and never took the war path against them.[6]

Another historian of the early Chicago, Illinois area, Nehemiah Matson, gives us the account he received from Shaubena.

The Indian rifles were fast thinning out the ranks of the Americans, when a large body of horsemen were seen approaching on a gallop. These troopers came bravely on until they approached the line of battle, when Tecumseh and his warriors sprang forward with the Shawnee war-whoop to meet the charge. For a moment all was confusion, being a hand-to-hand fight, and many were slain on both sides. Tecumseh after discharging his rifle, was about to tomahawk the man on a *white* horse (Col. Johnson), when the latter shot him with a pistol. The tomahawk, missing its deadly aim, took effect on the withers of the horse, while Tecumseh, with a shrill whoop, fell to the ground. Shaubena said he was standing by the side of Tecumseh when he received the fatal shot, and sprang forward to tomahawk the slayer of the great chief; but, at that instant the horse reared and fell, being pierced with many bullets, and the rider, badly wounded, was thrown to the ground, but rescued by his comrades. The warriors, no longer hearing the voice of Tecumseh, fled from the field, when the battle ended.

That night, after the battle, Shaubena accompanied a party of warriors to the fatal field, and found Tecumseh's remains where he fell. A bullet had pierced his heart, and his skull was broken, probably by the breech of a gun; otherwise the body was untouched. Near Tecumseh's remains lay the body of a large, fine-looking warrior, decorated with plumes and paint, whom the soldiers no doubt mistook for the great chief, as it was scalped and large portions of skin stripped from the body. On the day of the battle Tecumseh was dressed in plain buckskin, wearing no ornaments except a British medal suspended from the neck by a cord.[7]

This story begins in agreement with the others Shaubena has told, but soon steers off the established course. Here he states that Johnson's horse had fallen, throwing its rider to the ground. Only by the fortuitous presence of fellow American soldiers was Johnson spared Shaubena's wrath. This actually adds some credibility to the stories of Hamblin and Knaggs, where Johnson is found pinned to the ground by his horse. This time, however, Tecumseh is shot through the *heart*, not the *head*. His head is severely wounded, but probably as a final blow by a passing soldier. Here also, we are introduced to three new details. First, Shaubena says that he went back to the battlefield *that night*. Second, he states that a body near Tecumseh with more decorative attire was the one skinned. And third, Tecumseh was in *simple dress* but he did wear a *medal*.

In a footnote, Matson tells us that he often overheard Shaubena and Dad Joe (who was a soldier in Johnson's regiment fighting against Shaubena) discuss the battle years later and both agreed Johnson killed Tecumseh. Matson goes on to say:

> Years after (post-1836), when Colonel Johnson was vice-president, Shaubena visited Washington and called on the colonel, and together they talked over the incidents of the Thames campaign, after which the vice-president took the old chief by the arm, and introduced him to the heads of the departments. On leaving Washington, Johnson gave him a heavy gold ring as a token of friendship, which he wore on his finger to the day of his death, and by his request it was buried with him.[8]

In a lecture given by John Wentworth, a U.S. congressman and editor of the *Chicago Democrat* newspaper, we see how a passionate Shaubena had once acted out his version of the story. Wentworth told his audience:

> You ought to have seen old Shabonee, at this part of his narrative. No professed tragedian can do him justice. An Indian talks much more with his countenance than the white man. Up to this point his countenance bore marks of gloom, doubt, despair. He knelt down and defined Col. Johnson's position. Then he ran back some distance, turned, seized a club, and with the countenance of a fiend incarnate, he gave Tecumseh's last rallying yell, and brandished his club like an Indian tomahawk, in one hand, and his knife in the other, as if to scalp, he rushed towards the spot where Col. Johnson was supposed to be suffering from his wounds, but suddenly placing his hand upon his sides, as if shot, he fell, and imitated the dying Tecumseh.[9]

A newspaper account in 1859 gives us another peek at Shaubena's candor.

> Immediately after the death of Tecumseh, he says he looked around and saw not only the Indians, but the red coats flying in all directions. "And what did you do?" asked the person to whom he was narrating the

occurrence on one occasion. "Shabene puckashee!" (Shabene run too) was his blunt reply.[10]

In an 1839 letter to the historian, Benjamin Drake; Robert Anderson, who years later would be in command of the Union's Fort Sumter at the beginning of the Civil War, shared his memories of a conversation he had with Shaubena. Anderson says:

> He [Shaubena] stated that he was very young, and was at the battle of the Thames, and near Tecumseh, when he was killed. He represented Tecumseh as engaged in a personal re-encounter with a soldier armed with a musket, that the latter had made a thrust at the Chief, who caught the bayonet under his left arm, where he held it, and was in the act of striking his opponent with his tomahawk, when a horseman rode up and shot Tecumseh dead with a pistol. The horseman, he stated, had a white and red feather (plume) in his hat, and that he was mounted on a *spotted* horse – the colour as described by my interpreter, from the Indian language, was perhaps what is called a *red roan* – Chamblee (or as called by some Chabonnie) said he saw Tecumseh's body a day or two after the battle and that it was not mutilated . . . Tecumseh was plainly dressed, he wore a leather hunting shirt.[11]

Hmmm. Suddenly Tecumseh is engaged in hand-to-hand combat with a *musket-bearing regular soldier* who just missed Tecumseh's chest with his bayonet, getting it stuck in his buckskin shirt. Tecumseh had his tomahawk raised, but now he is aiming it at the foot soldier when he gets shot by an on-coming horseman. The horse color is described as *red roan and spotted*. Red roan can have either a white or chestnut appearance in horses, so there is a chance that this is consistent. Finally, we learn that it was *a day or two* after the fight, not later that night, before Shaubena returned to the area of the fight. Even after this longer stretch of time, Tecumseh's body remained on the field and again is reported to not be mutilated.

It is interesting to note here, that the general *uniform* of the Kentucky mounted militia at the Thames, according to the *History of the United States Cavalry*, was, "hunting shirts of jeans fringed with red, wearing round hats with long plumes of white tipped with red."[12] Shaubena mentions that the mounted shooter had just such a plume in his hat.

Another very early account is given by Thomas Forsyth, an Indian agent to the Fox and Sauk tribes. He heard about Tecumseh's death in

Image courtesy of Chicago History Museum-JCHi-62619.

Portrait of Shabbona–Near forty years of age.

1816 from an anonymous Pottawatomie. It is contemporary and concurs with William Clark's story as told to McKenney, but adds far more
detail. Forsyth did not seem to recognize Shaubena by name as the Pottawattamie he was talking with, but the Indian's information, of having
lived in Prophet's town and knowing Tecumseh while there, makes it
plausible that he was indeed Shaubena.[13] Forsyth's story reads:

> At Fort Clark [near present-day Peoria, IL.], I met a Pottawattamie
> who was in the engagement on the Thames, that took place between
> the American and British armies in the fall of 1813, who saw Tecumseh
> killed. His story as respects the death of that Indian is as follows: "The
> Indian spies came in with accounts of the American Army being near at
> hand and where I and others were, we would be opposed to the American
> horsemen; a Pottawatamie Indian named Kichekemit was on my right,
> Nesscottinnemeg on my left, and on his left stood Tecumseh armed with
> a sabre and a pair of pistols. We had agreed to fire on the Americans,
> seize the reins of the bridles and knock the riders off, but the horse-
> men came up with such rapidity and in such numbers that I had time
> only to fire (but missed) and hide myself in some brush. Kichekemit fell,

Nesscottinnemeg run away. I then saw Tecumseh engaged with a foot soldier having run his bayonet through Tecumseh's leather coat near the hips, and the latter trying to disengage himself from the Bayonet with his sabre in his hand when a horseman rode up and shot him through the head, and he fell over. An opportunity offered and I made off into the woods where I remained the best part of three days and then returned to the battle ground. I there found Kichekemit and Tecumseh lying and the whole skin of their heads taken off.' On my asking this Indian if he was sure it was Tecumseh he saw lying on the battle ground, and if he was not otherwise cut or disfigured not to be known, he observed to me that he lived with his uncle (who was taken on board of the British Fleet by Capt. Perry) at Prophets town on the Wabash for three years, and was in habits of intimacy with and knew Tecumseh well: that he was not cut nor disfigured except his being skinned and the breadth of about three fingers and about a foot long of skin and flesh taken from his right thigh. This Ottawa Indian had nothing in view to tell me a falsehood, it was he who commenced the conversation, and I believe he told me the truth.[14]

We learn here that the four Indians referred to lined up (from their point of view) with Tecumseh on the far left, Nesscottinnemeg (also known as Bad Sturgeon) on his right, Shaubena next to the right, and Kichekemit farthest right. The encounter between Tecumseh and a foot-soldier with a bayonet is repeated, except Tecumseh is now brandishing a sword instead of his tomahawk. This time Shaubena stayed away from the battleground for *three days*, not returning that night, one night or two nights later as reported in previous accounts. Also note how the term *disfigured* is apparently a subjective one, for Shaubena implies that the removal of Tecumseh's scalp, as-well-as a three-inch by twelve-inch strip of his thigh, did not qualify him to be so designated.

Years later in a letter to Lyman Draper, Forsyth relates another account. It can't be definitively attributed as coming from Shaubena, but in it we find another new twist. As the fighting ensued,

among the retreating Indians was a Pottawattomie brave (who on perceiving an American officer–supposed to be Col. Johnson) on horse close upon him, turned to tomahawk his pursuer but was shot down by him with his pistol. . . . The fallen Pottawattamie brave was probably taken for Tecumseh by some of Harrison's infantry and mutilated soon after the battle.[15]

So this Pottawattomie's account says it was a case of mistaken identity–an anonymous Pottawattomie warrior was at the end of the line of retreating Indians being chased down by Johnson when he turned back upon Johnson in the same fashion we've been told Tecumseh engaged Johnson. *Hmmm.*

Forsyth's son, Robert, gave Draper a brief account of the event that his father told him he heard in 1824. He says "that an American on a *dark dun* or *elk colored* horse, shot Tecumseh–& saw the horse running away without a rider."[16] So here we have another color of the horse introduced, dun (a pale red hue), and we learn this time that it rode off without Johnson.

Lyman Draper has notes referring to a conversation he had with Alexander Robinson, a Pottawattamie chief, who knew of another intriguing Shaubena account.

> Col. R. M. Johnson appeared on a *white* horse–Tecumseh, Chau-be-nay, & 3 or 4 other Indians remained near together–some of the Indians shot Johnson, when Tecumseh ran up to tomahawk the Colonel, then Johnson shot him. Chau-be-nay said he hadn't time to re-load his gun–& his gun was empty when Tecumseh fell. Subsequently Chau-be-nay visited Washington in company with my informant, Robinson, & they called on Col. Johnson, & Chau-be-nay said to the Colonel, referring to these incidents connected with Tecumseh's fall–"If my gun had been loaded, I would have shot you." Col. Johnson smiled.[17]

In 1839, the *Niles Register* in Washington City published an account given by Shaubena to a gathering at the United States Hotel.

> Tecumseh was a very brave, but cautious man. He had, however, been wounded in the neck and became desperate. He thought his wound was mortal and told his warriors that, as he must die, there would be no risk in rushing forward to kill Col. Johnson. He did so, and Sha-ben-eh saw him when he fell. His object was to strike the Colonel with his tomahawk before he saw him, and a moment more of inattention and the Colonel's head would have been sundered. He was shot just as his arm had reached the full height to strike the fatal blow.
>
> He described the Colonel's horse very minutely. He was very large and white, with occasionally a jet black spot. Another Indian in company, whom Shaw-ben-eh said was but a boy at the time of the battle, interrupted him to say that his mane and tail were black. The next day he with many others and this boy, went upon the field of battle, and saw Tecumseh's body there, and by the side of it another Indian whose skin had been

taken off. He said he had heard of this skin's having been exhibited as that of Tecumseh. They might think so. But it was not. Tecumseh's body had not been touched.

Here someone asked where and how they buried him? This aroused the Chief from his seat, and he was eloquent in the extreme! "None but brave warriors die on the battlefield. Such afraid of nothing when alive, don't care for dogs, wolves, eagles and crows when dead. They want the prairie to lie upon. Lo, Tecumseh, the bravest man that ever was, whom the Great Spirit would not let be killed by the common soldier, but sent Col. Johnson to be killed [by], wanted no grave nor honors. He let every animal come and eat his flesh, as he made every Red Man love, and every White Man fear him.[18]

This time we learn that Tecumseh was wounded in the neck, before he lifted his tomahawk toward Johnson. But, perhaps the most fascinating part of this version of Shaubena's testimony is how it changed so drastically to state that Tecumseh was left on the field forever to be eaten by the wild animals. And Shaubena spins this story to make such an action, if it were true, appear honorable!

Even though it seems impossible, two descendents of Shaubena confused his story even further. A nephew, David K. Foster says Shaubena was

with Tecumseh on the day he was killed; he [Tecumseh] was stooping scalping a soldier—while he was in that position, another soldier came on horseback with his musket and fired at him the same time he could almost touch him on his back—he then ran his (bayonet) through him so the Great Warrior was slain on the spot. The soldier who killed him was killed on the same spot and the Brave Warrior was hid under a brush heap till next morning—then they took his body and carried away for burial. Shaubena says on reaching the spot where he was killed I saw one of our braves had been skinned; they had skinned a wrong one, instead of Tecumseh.[19]

Just a few weeks later he wrote to Draper again repeating a shorter version of the same story, but adding, "Col. Johnson might stood off distant at the time. This is a story of Shaubena personally (told) to me at his home near Morris, Ill."[20] Seems Foster picked and chose from various accounts given by Shaubena, but focused on the *ordinary soldier with a musket* theme and deliberately made a point that Johnson was not directly involved in the event.

Joseph Bourassa was a grand-nephew of Shaubena and tells a little different story.

In the fight, Tecumseh was among the foremost and did as he counseled others, that when the Americans fired, they would fire too high, and then for the Indians to rush up and use the tomahawk. While Chau-be-nee was thus engaged, he saw Tecumseh in his plain buckskin coat, and no medal on – the coat with buckskin fringe along the upper part of the arm or sleeve where sewed together and a similar fringe up and down in the back where sewed together; Chau-be-nee did not say – did not know who shot the man on the *white* or *cream colored*, and *somewhat spotted*, mare (Col. Johnson said to informant [Bourassa] when at Choctaw Academy more or less from 1830-1837 – that he rode a mare and she corresponded to this description) – that he appeared pale and apparently in a badly wounded condition – horse unguided and quartering off, when the Brave (Johnson – as they termed the leader on the white mare) with his right hand and without seeming to be fully aware of what he was doing, put his small rifle, or holster pistol – over his horse's neck, and fired aimlessly and the ball penetrated through Tecumseh's head – the temples and he fell – advancing as he was with tomahawk in hand, and fell backward on the ground, with his tomahawk clenched, and the Brave fell under his horse, dead as Chau-be-nee believed. He said if there had been any doubt of it on the part of the Indians, they would have rushed up and finished so distinguished an antagonist and taken his scalp.

O-ketch-gum-mee, The Fish who represents the Earth, a noted Pottawattame brave, rushed up with uplifted tomahawk and was in the very midst of the whites and was killed. Three days after the battle, Chau-be-nee said he went in company with Tecumseh's son, to see and find the body; and they found Tecumseh's body lying on his back as he fell, with his tomahawk still in his hand – in a low spot, full of caves; and not far off they found Tecumseh's nephew, nearly as old as Tecumseh, a large, finely formed man and who had been mistaken for Tecumseh and had on his uncle's medal with "General Tecumseh" engraved on it (can't tell particularly about his dress) apt to wear claws or feathers, to appear more terrific, and had skinned his thighs. So Chau-be-nee frequently related. When he saw Tecumseh fall, the cry went forth, "our chief is fallen, let's retreat" and all quickly fell back except O-Ketch-gum-mee.[21]

Bourassa stresses the *Johnson on the white horse* theme. He seems to go out of his way to prove that it was Johnson who killed Tecumseh and that the Americans skinned the wrong body. He eagerly points out that Tecumseh's nephew was wearing his uncle's medal. It is disputed whether Tecumseh ever had such a medal, and is a further stretch to suggest it was engraved with the title "General Tecumseh." Many reports had circulated by the time of Bourassa's story citing that Tecumseh was found dead wearing such a medal.

John Hunt happened to be at a hotel in Columbus, Ohio in 1836, when Shaubena and his friends passed through on their way to Washington City. Hunt talked with Shaubena both on his way down and upon his return.

> I was introduced to an Indian who was with Tecumseh when he was killed, this Indian said where they received the charge from the Americans, he was with Tecumseh, acting as his chief . . . or confidential war chief. They came behind a fallen tree, (they raised) and fired against the advancing enemy. Tecumseh fixed at an officer on a *white* horse, and supposing that he had killed or mortally wounded him, drew his tomahawk and ran down upon the log to kill him when he was shot by this officer with a pistol. Thereupon the retreating whoop was given. Upon the return of the party from Washington City they told me they had seen and talked with Colonel Johnson, and from comparing notes, they believe from the fact that Johnson rode a *white* horse and other incidents of the fight they had no doubt but that Colonel Johnson did kill Tecumseh.[22]

Notice that the fallen tree reappears in this account, but now it is a more spirited Tecumseh who strides down its length before being shot. And, concurring with his other stories, the identity of Tecumseh's killer is confirmed to be Johnson after their meeting.

William Hickling and Gordon Hubbard were residents of the Illinois area and both had personal contact with Shaubena. From Hickling's conversations with him, he concluded:

> To the day of his death, Shab-bo-ne was in the firm belief that a bullet from the pistol of Col. Johnson was the cause of Tecumseh's death. Shabbone said that he was only a few yards distant from Tecumseh, at the time when the colonel dashed forward on his "*white* horse" several yards in advance of his men towards a number of Indians who were clustered around Tecumseh, that the colonel's horse stumbled & nearly fell, seeing which Tecumseh advanced towards Johnson with his tomahawk raised ready to strike, that then Johnson drew his pistol & fired the fatal shot, at the same time in a loud voice, heard distinctly by Shabbone uttering the soldierly words of "God damn"–upon receiving his death wound

Shabbone states that Tecumseh leaped up from the ground some two feet & then fell down apparently dead – Shabbone could not tell whether or not he saw, during the action, any other white horses ridden by Col. Johnson's men, but he insisted upon it that when Tecumseh fell, that the action had been going on for some little time . . .[23]

Gordon Hubbard's many conversations with Shaubena led to a slightly different conclusion.

He [Shaubena] was no doubt convinced of the truth of the current story that Johnson shot Tecumseh, as he was in the habit of taking for granted reports of that fact to him. To my questions often repeated "How could you tell that the man riding on the white horse did fire the shot that killed (Tecumseh) when so many were firing?" & was there not more than one white horse rode by the Americans, his replies were always that no one could so say & no doubt more than one white horse. You Americans say Johnson killed him & he Johnson should be beleaved – somebody killed him & I saw a man on a white horse fire and Tecumseh fell. Someone else may have shot him, this was the purpose of his answer when particularly questioned he has always told me that he was by him when he fell. I never understood him to say that Tecumthe advanced on seeing the horse stumble . . . Shabonee may have pointed out Johnson when he visited Washington, if so, no doubt Johnson was first in some way been (made) known to him, & whom he pointed out after being informed. It is hardly probable that seeing him, if he did, in the excitement of battle, that he could have noticed his countenance at any time after the fight, especially after so long a time & the probable change in Col. Johnson's appearance.[24]

We hear different stories from two people who lived near each other, knew each other, and knew Shaubena. Especially note that when pushed, Shaubena admits that his opinion is at least in part formed by the general clamor he had been hearing from the Americans that Johnson did it.

How is one to sort through all the variations in this one person's account? In part, they might be attributed to confusion brought on by his age and the forty-six years over which he repeated his stories. The friendship he developed with the Americans certainly could have influenced his story-telling. Perhaps he wanted to politically appease the right people in high places. Johnson had the second-highest station of anyone in the United States when he was visited by Shaubena.

His stories did turn to favor Johnson more stridently after this visit to Washington City in 1836. Maybe it was just the flamboyant side of Shaubena's personality that wanted to tell a more compelling story. Perhaps he just had tired of hearing everyone say it was Johnson so he deferred to their conclusion. Whatever the cause, Shaubena's story remained consistent on only a few specifics: Shaubena was near Tecumseh, Shaubena fled when Tecumseh was killed and Tecumseh was not skinned.

A comparison of Shaubena's many accounts to those of other Indians may produce some clarity. Then again . . .

CHAPTER 16

We Knew Him Best

Tecumseh ordered his warriors to rally and fight the
Americans once more, and in this very spot one of the American musket
balls took effect in Tecumseh's leg so as to break the bone
of his leg, that he could not stand up. He was sitting on
the ground when he told his warriors to flee as well as they
could, and furthermore said,
"One of my leg is shot off! Be quick and go!"
That was the last word
spoken by Tecumseh.[1]

Of the hundreds of Indians in the fight that day, only a handful of them have been documented to have had an opinion of how Tecumseh was killed. We just reviewed the major discrepancies that exist in Shaubena's numerous stories alone. Let's see if the remaining Indian accounts can stand on their own merit.

Do you remember Andrew Clark? He was the man found mortally wounded by Ben Warfield just after the battle who said he was next to Tecumseh when he was killed and saw him removed from the field. Clark was a white man but had grown up with the Indians and served as an aid and interpreter with Tecumseh. Lyman Draper had conversations with relatives of Clark; one who was a half-brother states that he

> was also with Tecumseh on this day. He pronounced it impossible to declare who gave the fatal shot which brought down the Chief. When the latter [Tecumseh] was mortally wounded, as he was upon his hands and knees unable to fire, the Kentucky light infantry horse came up and dispatched him.[2]

This scenario of Tecumseh being down and seriously wounded before the fatal blow came from an American horseman has already been seen in a few other accounts.

Alfred Brunson was in the area where the wounded were being treated after the fight. He happened to find himself near to Andrew Clark as the surgeons had concluded that there was little they could do for him. Brunson says:

While standing by the dying man, knowing that he was aid and interpreter to Tecumseh, the conversation between the surgeons naturally turned upon the report of the death of the chief. The Americans insisted that he was dead; while the British thought that he was a wily old dog that he had made his escape.

At this the interpreter [Clark] spoke and said, "He is dead, he fell when I did," and then related as follows: "Tecumseh swore that if Harrison was in that battle, he would kill him or lose his life; for he had owed him great hatred since the battle of Tippecanoe. Seeing a man on a fine horse, with a cocked hat on, and a wide wampum belt over his shoulder to which his powder-horn and bullet-pouch were hung, and being thus distinguished from every other man in the army, he supposed that it must be Harrison, and advanced from the line of the Indians to get a shot at him. In his advance he was followed by other Indians in the form of a harrow or triangle.

At the same time the white chief seeing this movement, having dismounted with the others, moved forward to meet him, being followed by his men in the same form. They both leveled their rifles at the same moment, but Tecumseh got the first fire and the white chief fell. At this Tecumseh rushed up to get the scalp, followed by the interpreter [Clark], and a number of other Indians, when a volley from the white men brought the chief himself and many others to the ground. Tecumseh being still intent upon securing the scalp rallied again, though badly wounded, when a youth who had discharged his musket, drew a pistol from his belt and shot the chief dead." In half an hour after relating this, the aid and interpreter died.[3]

This scene has been recorded by others but usually with the specific identity of the American on the fine horse being William Whitley. It seems that Clark, and Tecumseh per Clark, assumed that the garb worn by this attacker identified him as Harrison, but in fact he was probably Whitley. The dress and regalia as described here fits with what we know of the old Indian fighter. As well, other accounts tell of an Indian and Whitley shooting at each other simultaneously and then the Indian trying to scalp Whitley. Two points are unique and suspect in this account as Brunson relates it: the use of the word youth and the said youth shooting Tecumseh with a pistol. Although we have and will see cases made for David King, a youth of eighteen, having done the deed, most of those accounts tell of King firing a musket or rifle not a pistol. Brunson may have manipulated this story from Clark to match accounts he heard years later from two other men, James Gentry and John Booth. Let's take a look.

In 1848, Gentry told Brunson that when he was twelve years old, he heard the report of the battle as given by the adjutant of Col. Johnson's regiment. Though he was child, Gentry recalled hearing that a "young King, of Captain Anderson's company, shot Tecumseh with a pistol."[4] The name Anderson is obviously mistaken for Davidson, but he does mention a *young* man with a *pistol*.

In 1861, Booth, who was in Johnson's regiment and a friend of King, tells Brunson his story of examining the Indian that King killed and the fact that it was not being doubted in the camp that King had killed Tecumseh. Brunson adds that, "Booth, like Gentry, was a personal and political friend of Johnson's, but could not sacrifice truth to honor their friend."[5] Brunson, understanding that King was believed the killer, may have confused the matter by labeling Clark's shooter as a youth and giving him a pistol since others had attributed credit to Johnson based on the wound on Tecumseh from such a weapon.

As for the rider who Tecumseh killed which triggered this chain of events, Brunson explains why he was certain that he was William Whitley:

> The white chief who fell by the fire of Tecumseh was recognized at once by the Americans, as being Colonel Whitley. The Colonel could, it was said, have commanded a regiment under Governor Shelby, but he declined, preferring to "fight on his own hook;" and he was permitted to go when and where he pleased. If he heard a gun on either wing, front or rear of the army, his fleet horse he put upon the run to see what it meant, and if a fight, to share in it. He was clad in Kentucky jeans, hunting-shirt and pants. He had on his left shoulder a white wampum-belt, which held his powder and bullet-pouch, as above described; a leather girdle round his waist, to which was attached a tomahawk and scalping-knife. His rifle was long and highly mounted with silver. His horse was a tall bay, slim legged, and looked like a racer.[6]

This description of Whitley's garb mirrors the reports of others who detailed Whitley's appearance, and it reinforces Clark's sketch. Believable, yes; but troublesome as well because both descriptions are coming from Brunson who has possibly manipulated Clark's description of the rider with his own belief that it was Whitley.

The Caldwell brothers, William the elder and Billy the younger, were present with Tecumseh at the Thames. They were both half-breeds, children of a Pottawattamie mother and Irish father (who had served as a British officer). Billy would become more popular than his brother as time went on, acquiring the status of chief, and was known as *The Sauganash* or *The Britisher*. Both brothers gave an account of Tecumseh's death. William's was lengthy and somewhat questionable, given late in his life to Lyman Draper. Billy's was brief and recorded by only a few sources.

In Draper's notes we see William portraying a pessimistic Tecumseh just before the battle.

> "What's the matter," asked Capt. Wm. Caldwell of Tecumseh, at the same time tapping him on the shoulder. "No one," replied Tecumseh sorrowfully, "will stand by me + fight today." Caldwell replied, "Yes, Tecumseh, one man will–I am that man; I will stand by you till the last–I will pledge myself not to run till you set me the example." Then Tecumseh, holding up three fingers said, 'Yes–you, I + Billy Caldwell I know will fight–but what can we do alone?" [7]

William continued; detailing the behavior of the British troops as the battle began:

> The firing soon commenced at a distance on the right, but saw no enemy–except a rush along the main road; & the British regulars intimidated, broke + ran away– + Capt. McIntire, one of their captains, vexed at their conduct, said he hoped they would at least fire off their guns before they went–so many of them fired with their guns on their shoulders + backs to the foe, aimless + without a purpose.

This is an interesting picture of what happened in the British ranks. We saw a similar account from Simon Kenton. Both stories allude to the fact that the British regulars were quite wary of the Kentuckians who were eager to avenge the massacre at the Raisin. They imply, therefore, that perhaps they fired randomly to appease their officers and their enemy. The latter, they hoped, would treat them less harsh as prisoners for their gesture. William explains what happened next:

> While Tecumseh + Capt. Caldwell were three or four yards apart, in the rear of these runaways, watching the Americans + the retreating British regulars, Tecumseh exclaimed "Waugh!" clasping one hand behind + the other before, indicating a wound through his body, but clasping

his rifle in his hand. Caldwell asked him if he was wounded, he said "yes" + at the same time pointing to the flying British regulars as having shot him in the back + out at his heart. Caldwell asked if he could walk–he replied he could. "You had better go on, if you can, + I'll walk behind," said Caldwell. Tecumseh at once started, + only went about a rod, when in stepping over a large fallen oak, apparently weak + attempting to sit down as though he could go no further, he fell his back upon the tree–dead. He then had on a dirty linsey hunting shirt, belted around the middle–had a sort of cap, + buckskin leggings–a very good small silver mounted rifle, tomahawk, knife, pouch + horn. This was something like 300 yards off from the road– + beyond the road from the river. Tecumseh had not fired a shot–nothing to shoot at–except the Americans did make a momentary dash in that direction . . . + then retreating. Caldwell picked up Tecumseh's rifle which laid in his open right hand; + then thinking he might be charged with killing the chief for his rifle, stood it up against the tree + left it + retreated. Soon met Col. Elliott–helped him to disentangle his (riding) horse–told him of Tecumseh's fate, which he said was nothing more than he had suspected. Elliott escaped. Capt. Caldwell had met young Tecumseh (Paukeesaa), a youth of perhaps seventeen, + told him of his father's death which by his expression seemed to effect him–his hands trembled badly as he tarried briefly to hear the sad news, + reload his empty rifle–then all hastened away. Tecumseh was (as my informant [William] believes) skinned, on back + thighs.[8]

Apparently the anonymous Canadian's testimony given to Harrison was not one of a kind after all! William claims that he was with Tecumseh *behind* the British lines and as they were retreating Tecumseh received his fatal shot in the back from an unknown British or possibly Canadian soldier! Although outlandish on the surface, William says that he and Tecumseh were some three hundred yards from the road. This would place them at the far end of the British line, where it met the Indian line. Most sources agree that this is where Tecumseh was positioned, though the other reports place him in front of his forces, not in back of them. All of this would have happened very early on in the fight, as Col. Elliott is cited by William as escaping immediately after he made contact with him. Elliott did in fact escape with Procter and this flight infamously came within the first few minutes that it took for the British regulars to surrender.

William gives a full description of Tecumseh's dress which is in line with others who said he wore simple buckskin. The weapons he describes Tecumseh to be carrying do not seem extraordinary in number, only his knife, tomahawk and rifle. William does not say whether the body was recovered from the field after he left it. The implication is that he did see it again because he claims to know that it was skinned.

Billy Caldwell's account comes to us through two sources who repeated it to the third: Lyman Draper. Here is how the story travelled. Draper heard it from John Kinzie, a trader in the Chicago area where Caldwell had settled, who heard it from Thomas Forsyth (the Indian agent from whom we earlier read an account attributed to Shaubena). Forsyth says:

> A half Indian, half white, named William [Billy] Caldwell whilst retreating after the last encounter overtook and passed Tecumseh who was walking along slowly using his rifle for a staff–when asked by Caldwell if he was wounded he replied in English "I am shot"–Caldwell notes where a rifle bullet had penetrated his breast through his buckskin hunting coat. His body was found by his friends where he had laid down to die, untouched, within the vicinity of the battleground.[9]

The question begs to be asked: *Why didn't Caldwell help Tecumseh off the field?* And where was William Caldwell at his time if, as he had said in his testimony, he was by his side until he fell dead?

One other letter found in the Draper collection from an unknown source, states:

> Tecumseh and [Billy] Caldwell were behind a large down tree . . . Tecumseh said: "We must leave here; they are advancing on us." The lines, at this time were quite close together. Caldwell said he did not wait for a second invitation (for he was very much frightened), but ran. That was the last time he ever saw Tecumseh alive. Tecumseh was found lying where he had left him. He thought Tecumseh must have been killed within two or three seconds after he left him, or he would have followed.[10]

Obviously, we have two different accounts attributed to Billy. In both cases, it seems Tecumseh was abandoned as Billy left the scene in fear.

Stephen Ruddell was the close childhood friend of Tecumseh who we met earlier. He was not in the battle, but heard the particulars of Tecumseh's demise a few years afterwards from an interpreter, Joseph

Parks, who was in the fight. Draper notes:

> Capt. Joseph Parks & other Shawnees visiting S. Ruddell in Ky after the war of 1812-15, told him in response to his inquisitive inquiries about his old & much loved friend Tecumseh, that at the Thames Tecumseh had singled out a mounted officer, shot at & made a dash at him, & himself received a pistol shot at the hands of the officer, & was carried off by his Indian friends, & died that night. That several other Indians fell in that vicinity, & one of them was mistaken for the Shawnee chieftain. S. Ruddell believed this version of his death & so repeated it.[11]

This is a simple account that is in accord with several other tales. It depicts the classic scene of an officer on a horse shooting the charging Tecumseh and the body being taken off the field. It even matches the few consistent points in most of Shaubena's stories.

One might expect that Tecumseh's own brother, the Prophet, would be one of the surest sources for the truth. Unfortunately, there is no direct testimony from his brother that has been given to any reporter or historian in his day. A few secondhand accounts, however; have been preserved.

A letter to Lyman Draper from G. C. Johnston of Piqua, Ohio in 1872 is one such indirect testimony. Johnston states, "I know nothing about the story of the skin marks on Tecumsegh's body for when Tecumsegh's body was shot down by the Kentuck melish [militia] the Wyandot chief Menoncue said to the Prophet, 'let us run or we will be killed.'"[12] This brief referral to the situation does establish one fact; the Prophet *was* in the battle. (Menoncue was a known Wyandot chief as well as a Methodist minister believed to have been at the Thames).

C. C. Trowbridge was a historian who collected volumes of information regarding the Indian culture of his time, especially their numerous fanciful stories. He travelled with Lewis Cass who had a lot of interaction with the Indians after the war. Trowbridge wrote to Draper in 1874.

> His [Tecumseh's] brother, Elskwatawa, or the Prophet, was invited to make a visit to Detroit, and was requested by General Cass to relate the events of Tecumseh's life, which the chief fully proceeded to do. I was the scribe. When we came to the battle of the Thames, the Prophet ridiculed the idea of identifying the man who killed Tecumthe. He said he fell in a melee, and was shot by a musket ball by an unknown hand.[13]

Portrait of Tens-Kwau-Ta-Waw, the Prophet.
One of numerous exquisite portraits of Indians commisioned by
Thomas McKenney in the mid-1800s. Drawn, printed and coloured at L. T. Bowens
Lithographic Establishment. Published by F. W. Greenough.

The son of Abraham Edwards gives another opinion of the Prophet's. Edwards served in the military under Lewis Cass for many years. His story reads:

> Gen. Cass said he had not the least doubt but that Col. Johnson was the one who killed Tecumseh. The Prophet, Tecumseh's brother, was in a canoe with Gen. Cass, Col. George Croghan, Col. Johnson, and my father [Abraham], going to Mackinaw to attend a conference with the Indians. The colonel was pointed out to the Prophet as the man who killed Tecumseh; but the Prophet replied that the man was not living who killed his brother, for Tecumseh had killed the man who shot him at the same time. Col. J. told my father about that time, or soon after, that he did not know whether he had killed Tecumseh or not; but he was sure he had killed a big chief from his dress.[14]

What a moment in time this had to be! Can you imagine being introduced to the man that everyone believes killed your brother? And, then bluntly telling him, to his face, that he shouldn't flatter himself so, for Tecumseh killed the man that had slew him?

There is a last twist to the meager amount of testimony attributed
to the Prophet. In 1852, while Lewis Cass was serving as a senator
from Michigan, he became a participant in a discussion on the Senate floor regarding an appropriations' bill to benefit the Shawnee Indians. Cass took the opportunity to clear up the lingering controversy of
Tecumseh's death. After giving his opinion that at the Thames it was
Johnson's idea, not Harrison's, for the mounted militia to charge the
British lines, he continued:

> Now, as to the other historic but disputed point: Who killed Tecum-
> seh? (Laughter). I will tell you what I know. Tecumseh fell in the battle,
> as we are all aware; but in the following year the Prophet, Tecumseh's
> brother, and his son, young Tecumseh, a very intelligent young man,
> often came to see me, and we had several conversations respecting the
> series of events in which his father was engaged. The young man was
> near his father's side in the battle, but his uncle, the Prophet, was in
> Creek country. The young man described the battle very graphically – the
> persons, the parties present, and the incidents, without hesitation from
> the beginning to the end, and I have no more doubt from his narration,
> than I have that I am here, that Col. Johnson was the person who killed
> his father. There were three of the Johnson's in the battle, and they were
> as brave men as ever followed the standard of their country to war.[15]

Nice of Cass to pat the Johnson brothers on the back, they really
did deserve it. But, what is the point of being so brazen as to suggest
that the Prophet was not even at the battle? Creek country was quite a
distance from Upper Canada – it was in Alabama. After years of being
the second most visible person striving to convince the Indians to form
into this coalition, does it seem plausible that the Prophet would abandon this effort, and his brother, by not even fighting at the Thames?
Besides, a number of Creeks themselves are known to have been participants. Perhaps Cass recognized the political snag of having people
hear Tecumseh's own brother say that no one could know who killed
Tecumseh? How could one more easily discredit the Prophet than to
claim that he wasn't even at the battle to have known such a fact? Keep
in mind that it was Cass, along with Knaggs and Labadie who stumped
nationwide for Johnson in the 1836 campaign for vice-president, using
Johnson's hero status for having killed Tecumseh as a key credential
for the office. Although these comments of Cass came sixteen years

after Johnson's campaign, the fact is that by declaring the Prophet as not present, his conflicting opinion is summarily dismissed. As a result, all of Cass's opinions and stories from the time of the battle to the time of this speech remain trustworthy. Cass takes this even a step further when he brings Paukeesaa into the tale. With no specifics whatsoever supporting his statement, Cass steers the listeners to believe that even Tecumseh's son was convinced that Johnson had killed his father. Maybe you thought slick politicians were something new?

Another *brother* of Tecumseh gives a very interesting testimony. George Ironsides was a British trader at Amherstburg who is often claimed to have been a half-brother of Tecumseh, though according to his grandson, he became a relative to Tecumseh by marrying his niece.[16] Dr.C.C.Graham, a renowned personality of the 1800s, tells us what Ironsides related to him.

> He said that no white man had laid sight on his brother, till he detected three Yankees taking him out of his grave to exhibit his skeleton, which, to them, would have been a fortune; but he took the body from them and buried it under the floor of his own house. He said his brother fell by a musket-shot, the ball passing through his heart, and he fell across the trunk of a fallen tree, near the roots. The top of this tree was very large, and pointed towards where the whites made the charge. Taking all circumstances into consideration, he was of the opinion a random shot killed him. In answer to the Doctor, upon being asked if his brother had been mutilated by knives, and whether the rumor was true, that his back had been skinned for razor straps, he replied, that no white man in that battle could have touched him, for he was instantly picked up and borne off. He said, however, that there was an Indian chief killed, and literally skinned, who was much like his brother, that they were often taken for each other.[17]

We are starting to see a few more common threads in these stories. Tecumseh is often at the root end of an up-turned tree, he has fallen over a log a few times, and many Indians are saying it was a random shot that killed him. But Ironsides provides a very unique twist—he protected his relative's body from any further desecration by re-interring it under his own home! *Hmmm.*

An article about William Whitley and his home, published in the *Louisville Times* of 1893, makes a reference to Dr. Graham and

Image courtesy of U.S. Library of Congress.

Portrait of Lewis Cass, circa 1855-1865

Mr. Ironsides. It reads:

> The late C.C.Graham, of Louisville, several years before his death, visited with Maj. Ironsides [who] positively confirmed the statement that Tecumseh was shot from *a rifle loaded with two balls.* Besides this it will be remembered that several recent sketch-writers of primitive events have credited to "Whitley, an Independent," the killing of the great chief.[18]

It is possible that this account is true. But if so, it shows that Ironsides changed his story much like Shaubena changed his over the years. In particular, Ironsides is now supposedly claiming two rifle balls, not the previously attested to single musket ball, took down Tecumseh. A more likely explanation for the alteration to this tale is that the writer of this article about Whitley did it to solidify his obvious prejudice for Whitley, who shot a two ball load.

The second in command of the Indian force was Oshawahnah. He, like others, had his name pronounced and spelled various ways. A few of these were *Shawanwannoo, Shahwahwannoo, Ooshawanoo,*

Portrait of Oshawannah. Illustrated by Benson J. Lossing
and shown here as it appeared in his Pictorial Fieldbook of the War of 1812
which was originally published in 1868.

Shawano, and the English name *John Naudee*. He commanded the right side of the Indian line. After the battle at the Thames, he settled on Walpole Island about forty miles northwest of the battleground. Per the missionary of Walpole Island, Andrew Jamieson, Oshawahnah was with

> Tecumseh at the Battle of the Thames, where Tecumseh was killed. I asked him if he could give me any account of the last hour of the great hero, but he said he could not, as he and his . . . were so panic stricken, that each individual sought his own personal safety & could think of nothing else.[19]

John Richardson, who visited Shahwahwannoo at Walpole in 1848, recorded a statement from him. In it, Shahwahwannoo deferred to his fellow chief, Shawanabb's testimony.

> Brother, I promised to send you a few particulars concerning the death of the great Tecumseh. Shaw-an-abb, an old Indian resident on the Island, and an intimate friend of the lamented Hero, and who was with him in his last moments, told me the following, touching the manner and

circumstances of his death. Tecumseh was riding on horseback, encouraging his Indians to engage the enemy, when a shot from the Yankees struck him under the fifth rib. Tecumseh, aware of the fatal character of the wound, and resolved not to die unavenged, advanced towards the enemy–threw himself off his horse, and being armed with three pistols, took one in each hand, and fired, and having discharged the third, he drew his sword, which he used efficiently, as long as strength remained. Being soon exhausted with loss of blood, he fell to the ground, and an American dispatched him with a stroke of an axe; and as proof that he had killed the renowned Tecumseh, cut a piece out of his [Tecumseh's] thigh, to show to his superiors.[20]

Certainly a lot of particulars are introduced by Shawanabb, and they are new ones, unseen in any other account. If he knew so specifically that Tecumseh was shot under the fifth rib, than he must have seen the body after the battle. However, the picture of a frantic wounded Tecumseh charging and wielding three pistols and then a sword before being struck by an axe; seems to be a romanticized version of the truth probably used to show that his hero fought to the last.

Shawanabb's story includes one other side-note. He says:

Tecumseh was buried under a large tree–the tree having been previously cut down–the stump was six feet high. It was hewn on four sides, and there was written on these, in characters well understood by the Indians, the number of persons whom he had killed with his tomahawk.[21]

One needs to look closely at the map of the battleground, as drawn by Ben Lossing for his pictorial history book (see page 5). On it is depicted a tree stump with no explanation of its purpose or significance. Perhaps Lossing believed in this account from Shawanabb and deliberately added this image of Tecumseh's grave marker to his map?

Among the Wyandot Indians of southern Ontario, the traditional belief of how the event transpired is handed down in an 1870 book written by their chief, Peter Dooyentate Clarke. In it, Clarke states that after the first encounter between the British soldiers and the Americans:

A second encounter took place between the Kentucky mounted riflemen, led by Colonel Johnson, and the Indians, who had pursued them in their retreat, on foot. The latter were soon overpowered and routed. Among the retreating Indians was a Potawatamie brave, who, on perceiving an American officer (supposed to be Colonel Johnson) on horse, close upon him, turned to tomahawk his pursuer, but was shot down by him with a pistol. Thus closed the second or last encounter. The fallen Potawatamie brave was probably taken for Tecumseh by some of Harrison's infantry, and mutilated soon after the battle.[22]

Interestingly, as Chief Clarke goes on with his explanation of what happened to Tecumseh, he provides an almost word-for-word reiteration of the account received earlier from Forsyth, which was part of the testimony Forsyth had received from a Pottawattomie supposed to be Shaubena. Could Shaubena's story have trickled into the Wyandot's history?

John Norton, an Iroquois leader in Upper Canada, was many miles east of the Thames battleground when the fight occurred. He says:

Ev'ry report that had reached us respecting the unfortunate Affair of the 5th of October being confused and contradictory as to the fate of the Indians who had accompanied the retreat . . . determined me to go in search of them. In a few miles we met many [retreating Indians and their families after the battle] and learnt . . . the following particulars of the late unfortunate events . . . The Americans made their appearance,–and advancing forward rapidly, overwhelmed the Troops [Indians]. The Indians on the right for a little time sustained the assault, but were finally obliged to retire with some Loss. Among the killed was the intrepid Tecumthi,–he was seen rushing boldly forward upon the hostile ranks, when victory seemed to incline to their Side. Few of the Women or Children fell into the hands of the Enemy, notwithstanding the little time they had to effect their escape,–but some of these which they took they inhumanely butchered,–and they barbarously skinned the Body of the gallant Tecumthi.[23]

From these retreating Indian families, just days after the battle, we learn only the general story that Tecumseh was killed while running into the American lines and that his body was skinned.

Andrew Blackbird was an Ottawa Chief and later an interpreter for the U.S. government. In 1887 he wrote a history of the Ottawa and Chippewa Indians which is considered unbiased since it was one of the first books of its kind authored by an Indian instead of a white man trying to interpret Indian culture. This is what he says about

Tecumseh's death:

> "Even in the history of the United States, I think there are some mistakes concerning the accounts of the Indians, particularly the accounts of our brave Tecumseh, as it is claimed that he was killed by a soldier named Johnson, upon whom they conferred the honor of having disposed of the dreaded Tecumseh. Even pictured out as being coming up with his tomahawk to strike a man who was on horseback, but being instantly shot dead with the pistol. Now I have repeatedly heard our oldest Indians, both male and female, who were present at the defeat of the British and Indians, all tell a unanimous story, saying that they came to a clearing or opening spot, and it was there where Tecumseh ordered his warriors to rally and fight the Americans once more, and in this very spot one of the American musket balls took effect in Tecumseh's leg so as to break the bone of his leg, that he could not stand up. He was sitting on the ground when he told his warriors to flee as well as they could, and furthermore said, "One of my leg is shot off! Be quick and go!" That was the last word spoken by Tecumseh. As they look back, they saw the soldiers thick as swarm of bees around where Tecumseh was sitting on the ground with his broken leg, and so they did not see him any more; and, therefore, we always believe that the Indians or Americans know not who made the fatal shot on Tecumseh's leg, or what the soldiers did with him when they came up to him as he was sitting on the ground.[24]

Blackbird introduces a new type of wound, to the leg, but we see some similarities with other accounts. Here Tecumseh doesn't fall over a log, but he does end up on the ground with the severely injured leg and once again bids his fellow Indians to flee. It does seem incongruous that his fellow Indians would leave the chief helpless in the face of the on-coming Americans, but Blackbird makes it clear that they fled at Tecumseh's command.

Word of Tecumseh's demise reached Fort Mackinac, (present-day Mackinac Island) by December of 1813. Fur trader John Askin, grandfather of John Richardson, wrote in a letter:

> An engagement took place one mile below the Moravian Village, which lasted for two hours, when our army was compelled to make a precipitate retreat towards Queenstown, leaving all their baggage behind. Our loss is said to be two subaltern officers and one hundred privates killed, two interpreters, and twenty-two Indians. Capt. Muir and one hundred

privates of the Forty-first regiment prisoners; also one hundred and fifty
Delaware woman and children which the enemy took. I am sorry to say,
that Antoine Brisbois, and Lewis Campau, interpreters, and Tecumseh,
are among the number slain. The latter fought bravely to the last, sword
in hand; the enemy skinned him after he was slain.[25]

This general account tells us that the word had gone out among the
British and Indians that Tecumseh was in fact dead. As well, it was
accepted that he had been skinned and had his sword (perhaps tomahawk) in hand when he fell.

In William Hatch's history, it is explained that over the years since the
Thames conflict he and many other white men had befriended scores
of Indians.

Yet with all this comparative intimacy and evidently friendly feeling, we could never obtain from them any information as to Tecumseh's
death; all appeared unwilling to admit that he was slain by the white
man, that he fell at the "Thames," or was dead; pride of feeling, pride of
race, previous devotion to him, always prevented any explicit replies to
questions on the subject.[26]

Another celebrated chief who gave an account of the event was Black
Hawk of the Sauk tribe. In 1838, a contributor to the *Baltimore American* newspaper who signed his story only as *W*, told Black Hawk's story
as he knew it.

He [Black Hawk] was fond of recounting his earlier exploits, and often
boasted of his being at the right hand of Tecumseh, when the latter was
killed at the battle of the Thames. His account of the death of this distinguished warrior was related to me by himself, during an evening that
I spent in his lodge some winters ago. In the course of our talk, I asked
him if he was with Tecumseh when he was killed. He replied–
"I was and will now tell you all about it. Tecumseh, Shaubinne and
Caldwell, two Potawattimie Chiefs, and myself, were seated on a log
near our campfire, filling our pipes for a smoke on the morning of the
battle, when word came from the British General that he wished to speak
to Tecumseh. He went immediately, and after staying some time rejoined
us, taking his seat without saying a word, when Caldwell, who was one
of his favorites, observed to him–my father what are we to do? Shall
we fight the Americans? 'Yes, my son,' replied Tecumseh, 'We shall go

Image courtesy of U.S. Library of Congress.

Portrait of Ma-Ka-Tai-Me-She-Kia-Kiah, Black Hawk.
One of numerous exquisite portraits of Indians commisioned by
Thomas McKenney in the mid-1800s. Drawn, printed and coloured at L. T. Bowens
Lithographic Establishment. Published by F. W. Greenough.

into their very smoke – But you are now wanted by the General. Go, my son, I never expect to see you again.' Shortly after this (continued Black Hawk,) the Indian spies came in, and gave word of the near approach of the Americans. Tecumseh immediately posted his men on the edge of a swamp which flanked the British line, placing himself at their head. I was a little to his right, with a small party of Sauks. It was not long before the Americans made their appearance; they did not perceive us at first, hid as we were by the under growth, but we soon let them know where we were by pouring in one or two volleys as they were forming into line to oppose the British. They faltered a little, but very soon we perceived a large body of horse (Col. Johnson's regiment of mounted Kentuckians) preparing to charge upon us in the swamp. They came bravely on, yet we never stirred until they were so close that we could see the flints in their guns, when Tecumseh, springing to his feet, gave the Shawnee war cry, and discharged his rifle. – This was the signal for us to commence the fight. But it did not last long; the Americans answered the shout, return-ing our fire, and at first discharge of their guns I saw Tecumseh stagger forwards over a fallen tree near which he was standing, letting his rifle drop at his feet. As soon the Indians discovered he was killed, a sudden fear came over them, and thinking the Great Spirit was angry, they fought no longer, and were quickly put to flight. That night we returned to bury our dead, and search for the body of Tecumseh. He was found lying where he had first fallen; a bullet had struck him above the hip, and his skull had been broken by the butt end of the gun of some soldier, who had found him perhaps when life was not yet quite gone. With the exception of these wounds his body was untouched, lying near him, however, was a large fine looking Potawattimie who had been killed, decked off in his plumes and war paint, whom the Americans no doubt had taken for Tecumseh, for he was scalped, and every particle of skin flayed for his body. Tecumseh himself had no ornaments about his person, save a British medal. During the night we buried our dead, and brought off the body of Tecumseh, although we were within sight of the fires of the American camp.'"

This is somewhat different from the account which is commonly given of Tecumseh's death, yet I believe it to be true; for after hearing Black Hawk relate it, I heard it corroborated by one of the Pottawattimie Chiefs mentioned by him.[27]

Comparing this account with others we are starting to see a recurring report of Tecumseh being shot and then in some fashion ending up on the ground near or over a fallen tree. Additionally, another hotly-contested issue, whether Tecumseh wore a medal or not, was often based on this testimony of Black Hawk's. One tidbit of proof that Tecumseh may have worn such a medal is found in a letter from J. D. Butler to Lyman Draper, who was apparently prodding Butler for certain evidence of the medal's existence. He tells Draper:

Two facts I took great pains to ascertain. 1.That T. wore a medal when he was killed. Proof by Black Hawk who stood by him then. 2.The identity of the T's medal with our Phila mint. Letter [assumed to be included] from head of mint on the credibility of Snowden who preserved the medal.[28]

This short letter to Draper seems to prove that Tecumseh did have and wore a medal given to him by the British. Archibald L. Snowden was superintendent of the Philadelphia mint in the 1880's. Butler states that Snowden had the medal in safe-keeping at the mint at that time. The whereabouts of this medal today is unknown at this time. Unfortunately, Butler bases the fact that Tecumseh was wearing this medal at the Thames on Black Hawk's account, for we are about to see there is another controversy to be evaluated.

Black Hawk wrote an autobiography in 1833. Well, maybe. Whether it is truly a work dictated by Black Hawk to the editor, J. B. Patterson, or not, has been an argument ever since it was published. It is perplexing to note that Tecumseh is not even mentioned in this book. If Black Hawk was so close to Tecumseh as to share a smoke with him and an intimate group of friends on the morning of the battle, it seems incongruous that he makes no mention of that day, let alone Tecumseh himself, in this autobiography.

What Black Hawk does say in his life story is what was noted earlier–he was disgusted with the British after the defeat at Fort Stephenson. Black Hawk says that following this incredible defeat, "I took about twenty of my braves, and left the British camp for home." [29] That means he abandoned the British on one of the first few days of August. Could he have rejoined the fight in Canada by late September? It's possible, but his autobiography describes several adventures he undertook upon his return to Rock River in Wisconsin, and going to the Thames is not one of them.

Reuben Gold Thwaites, a renowned historian from Wisconsin, who took up recording history where Lyman Draper left off, explains the controversy over the legitimacy of the autobiography.

> In his Autobiography,–probably authentic in the main, but written in a stilted style which we doubtless owe to the editor, Patterson . . . Ford [another author] . . . questions the accuracy of the autobiography; he says that "Black Hawk knew little, if anything, about it;" that it "was written by a printer, and was never intended for anything but a catch-penny publication," and that it is a "gross perversion of facts." Later historians, not as strong Indian-haters as Ford, have taken a more favorable view of the book.

So it seems that Thwaites validates the authenticity of the autobiography, yet it is perplexing that Thwaites in the same book in which he gives this opinion, states:

> Black Hawk–who had, in company with the Pottawatomie chiefs, Shaubena and Billy Caldwell, been near Tecumseh when he fell–at once hurried home [after the Thames battle].

Thwaites had to know that Black Hawk himself never claimed such in his autobiography. In fact, the autobiography implies that soon after

Black Hawk's return to his village, he went down the Mississippi river to the Fort Madison area of Iowa to fight Americans, avenging the death of his adopted son. If the autobiography is accurate, then Black Hawk could not have been at the Thames, for he was at Fort Madison. If Black Hawk was at the Thames, than, the autobiography is false. Why Thwaites would seem to contradict himself in this fashion is inexplicable.[30]

Perry Armstrong also wrote a history of the Sauk nation and the Black Hawk War. In it he explains the relationship between Tecumseh and Black Hawk which might clarify why Tecumseh is not mentioned in Black Hawk's autobiography:

> Erroneous is the somewhat general belief that he [Black Hawk] participated in the battle of the Thames, October 5, 1813, as aid-de-camp to the celebrated Tecumseh, or Couchant Tiger. While he was a great admirer of Tecumseh from the information he received of the dash and push of that renowned Shawnee chief, their territories were so far apart that he had but a slight personal acquaintance with Tecumseh, and was never his ally, although engaged in the war of 1812-14, on the same side, and participated with him in two or three battles. Inordinately vain, Black Hawk undoubtedly became jealous of the attention paid Tecumseh by Gen. Procter, and mortified at the terrible drubbing Maj. Croghan and his little band of heroes administered to the British and their Indians at Fort Stephenson, he became disgusted, and really deserted the British cause before the battle of the Thames was fought. It will be remembered that immediately after the attack on Fort Stephenson, at Lower Sandusky, Black Hawk, with only twenty of his braves stole away from the British camp in the night and returned to Saukenuk on Rock river. Hence, he was hundreds of miles away from the place when the battle of the Thames was fought.
>
> Elskwatawa (Tecumseh's brother–the Prophet) visited the Sauks to enlist them in Tecumseh's great confederacy scheme, but they declined. This declension was no doubt largely influenced by Black Hawk's inordinate vanity and aversion "to play second fiddle to any man." He never brooked the idea of a superior officer, and boasted that he had won an hundred battles and was never defeated. Had the Couchant Tiger offered to make him commander-in-chief of the confederacy, he and his band would doubtless have joined it.[31]

Here we see that Black Hawk may have had a bit of an ego. He didn't really have a lot of faith in Tecumseh's confederacy, and seemed to loathe all the attention Tecumseh was receiving. Black Hawk was certainly at the battles of Fort Meigs and Fort Stephenson, but it seems reasonable to conclude he may not have been at the Thames.

Henry Schoolcraft, a noted geographer and student of the Indian cultures, accepted the autobiography of Black Hawk as authentic and in his memoirs gives an interesting footnote to Black Hawk's life – his burial. Schoolcraft says:

> Black Hawk, who was buried, agreeably to his own request, by being placed on the surface of the earth, in a sitting posture, with cane clenched in his hands. His body was then enclosed with palings [fencing] and the earth filled in. This is said to be the method in which Sac chiefs are usually buried. The spectacle of his sepulcher was witnessed by many persons who were anxious to witness the last resting place of a man who had made so much noise and disturbance.[32]

Another historian of the early 1800s was Caleb Atwater. He also was an interpreter working with the Indians. Atwater tells us:

> In this action, Tecumseh . . . was killed, which circumstance has given rise to almost innumerable fictions – why, we can hardly tell, but it is so. The writer's [Atwater's] opportunities for knowing the truth, is equal to any person's now living [circa 1838]. He [Atwater] was personally, very well acquainted with that celebrated warrior. He accompanied Tecumseh, Elsquataway, Four Legs and Caraymaunee (Nawkaw), on their tour among the six nations of New York, in 1809, and acted as their interpreter among those Indians. In 1829, at Prairie Du Chien, the two latter Indians, both then civil chiefs of the Winnebagos, were with the writer, who was then acting as commissioner of Indian Affairs in the United States service. From the statement of these constant companions of Tecumseh, during nearly twenty years of his life, we proceed to state, that Tecumseh lay with his warriors at the commencement of the battle in a forest of thick underbrush, on the left of the American army. That these Indians were at no period of the battle, out of their underbrush; that Nawcaw saw no other officer between them and the American army; that Tecumseh fell the very first fire of the Kentucky dragoons, pierced by thirty bullets, and was carried four or five miles into the thick woods, and there buried by the warriors, who told the story of his fate. This account was repeated to me three several times, word for word, and neither of the relaters ever knew the fictions of which Tecumseh's death has given rise.[33]

Atwater added that the Winnebagos apparently felt a little cheated of the notoriety to which they deemed themselves entitled to. He tells us:

> Carrymauny, the elder, three times repeated to me his history, and requested I write it in a book. He complained to me that in all our [American] accounts of Tecumseh, we had only said of him that, "Winnebago who always accompanies Tecumseh," without calling the Winnebago by his name – Nawkaw Carrymauny.[34]

Another Indian, an Ottawa chief named Noonday, has given a documented testimony. It comes via D. B. Cook, the editor of the *Niles Mirror*, in 1885. Although compelling, it has been viewed with some skepticism for some very understandable reasons. It reads as follows:

> Mr. Cook's father, Phineas Cook, was an early settler in the region near Gull prairie. He says: "I had in 1838 an interview with Noonday, chief of the Ottawa tribe . . . Noonday was at the Thames." Mr. (Phineas) Cook's diary runs thus: "After rehearsing the speech which Tecumseh made to his warriors previous to the engagement, and how all felt that they fought to defend Tecumseh more than for the British, he was asked:

"Were you near Tecumseh when he fell?"

"Yes, directly on his right."

"Who killed him?"

"Richard M. Johnson."

"Give us the circumstances."

> "He was on a horse and the horse fell over a log, and Tecumseh with uplifted tomahawk, was about to dispatch him, when he drew a pistol from his holster and shot him in the breast and he fell dead on his face. I seized him at once and with the assistance of Saginaw, bore him from the field. When he fell the Indians stopped fighting and the battle ended. We laid him down on a blanket in a wigwam, and we all wept, we loved him so much. I took his hat and tomahawk."

"Where are they now?"

"I have tomahawk and Saginaw his hat."

"Could I get them?"

"No; Indian keep them."

"How did you know it was Johnson who killed him?"

> "General Cass took me to see the Great Father, Van Buren, at

Washington. I went to the great wigwam, and when I went in I saw the same man I see in battle, the same man I see kill Tecumseh. I had never seen him since, but I knew it was him. I look him in the face and said: 'Kene-kin-a-poo Tecumseh,' that is, you kill Tecumseh. Johnson replied that he never knew who it was, but a powerful Indian approached him and he shot him with his pistol. 'That was Tecumseh; I see you do it."

Noonday finished his story of Tecumseh by telling his noble traits, the tears meanwhile trickling down his cheeks. There is no doubt of the truth of his unvarnished tale.[35]

Well, Mr. Cook is convinced, but then again, he is telling the supposed story from his father's diary. The account is strangely similar to one of Shaubena's. Noonday says he was on Tecumseh's immediate right, where Shaubena said Nesscottinnemeg was positioned. Cook also mimics Shaubena's conversation with Johnson during the trip to Washington City, but he makes it seem that Noonday made the connection with Johnson, not Shaubena. Could Noonday have been in Shaubena's entourage on the trip to Washington? It's possible, but there is no other reference to it being so. Additionally, this story did not surface until 1885, several decades after Noonday's death. There is no obvious reason for the delay. Noonday is documented as a genuine Ottawa chief who lived in the area of present-day Grand Rapids, Michigan. In defense of this account, Noonday is known to have travelled to Washington to sign a treaty ceding large tracts of Michigan land to the United States in 1836. This fact shines the light of possibility on Noonday's supposed conversation with Johnson in Washington at this point in time.

A final Indian word on this topic comes from Thomas Wildcat Alford—Tecumseh's great-grandson. Alford doesn't tell us *who* he believed killed Tecumseh, but he does make it clear that the body which was skinned and believed by the Americans to be his; certainly was not. Alford's account reads:

Tecumtha entered this battle convinced that he would there lose his life. He divested himself of all clothing and insignia which might identify his body to the enemy, and dressed for the battle in plain tanned buckskins, frock shirt, leggings and moccasins. He carried no arms or ornaments of any kind. He fell in the thick of the fight, but his body was retrieved by his warriors, and later taken to a point well marked on the banks of a distant creek and buried there. After some years, a band of Shawnees who knew the burial location, journeyed to the grave to disinter the body and bear it to their western reservation for re-interment suitable to the greatest leader of their race. This party, selected because it knew the spot of the interment, found that the creek, at flood times, had washed away all evidences of the great warrior's last resting-place.[36]

One of the most curious points in Alford's statement is that Tecumseh took no weapons into the battle. Isn't it just a little hard to believe that one of the noblest and fiercest Indian warriors in history would enter a fight empty-handed?

We have now digested what those closest to the event and closest to Tecumseh have had to say. However, we have not yet heard from the key survivor of this confrontation, the one man who should know what really happened since much of the talk surrounds him – Colonel Richard M. Johnson. Let's take a look at his comments on this event.

CHAPTER 17

Colonel Johnson Says...

The Indian supposed he had mortally wounded me;
he came out from behind the tree and advanced upon me with uplifted tomahawk.
When he had come within my mare's length of me, I drew my pistol
and instantly fired, having a dead aim on him.
He fell and the Indians shortly after either surrendered or had fled.
My pistol had one ball and three buckshot in it, and the body
of the Indian was found to have a ball through his body
and three buckshot in different parts of his breast and head.
("Thus fell Tecumseh", cried someone from the audience.)
Col. Johnson said he did not know that
it was Tecumseh at that time.[1]

In 1901, Dr. John O. Scott, a noted Kentuckian, gave a speech to a crowd of Dallas, Texans, who were all gathered together that day as a group of displaced Kentuckians. His topic was, *The Orators of Kentucky.* Scott recalled for the assembly how as a youth at White Sulphur Springs, Kentucky, he heard Richard M. Johnson speak.

> All through life, his [Johnson's] charming eloquent voice has ever rung in our ears like the sweet-toned music of the midnight serenade of the gay Trubadour. Mr. Johnson's oratory was not like Marshall or Crittenden to gather wreaths of rhetoric from the sunlit clouds that deck the horizon with brilliant beauty and gorgeous grandeur, or paint the dying acts of heroes in colors as brilliant as the resplendent rainbow. Often his oratory was a conversational kind. He could weep with one eye and laugh with the other. At one time his audience would be bowed down in tears, at another the welkin [sky air] would ring with shouts of laughter for his amusing anecdotes.[2]

Obviously Johnson was no ordinary orator. According to Scott, Johnson spoke of the Battle of the Thames that day, but primarily in praise of the bravery of William Whitley, not his own.

> We never will forget the pathetic, heart-searching oratory of Mr. Johnson, when he related how, at the battle of the Thames, General Wm. Whitley led the forlorn hope of the Kentuckians . . . to glory and victory, through the dense undergrowth of the dark forest and down into

the swampy river bottom to the jaws of death, to the jaws of hell . . . The war-painted Indian, with bloody tomahawk and scalping knife in hand; could be seen darting from tree to tree, hiding in the thickets, crawling through the long grass and giving no quarter to the brave Americans he met in his merciless pathway . . . where death held high carnival, could be seen the lordly form and waiving crest of General Whitley, with bloody falchion [sword] in hand, soaring above the battle tide . . . although mortally wounded, he still clung to the star-spangled banner, given him by the ladies of Kentucky . . . On the spot where Tecumseh fell, and from whence the Indians fled, the flag of the Stars and Stripes all tattered and rent with ball and stained with dying heroes' blood, was found beneath the cold pale body of General Whitley, and a score or more of brave Kentuckians . . .[3]

Whether Whitley actually carried the U.S.Flag into the battle is dubious, more importantly this speech paints a picture of Johnson's romantic style of speaking.

The first official word from Johnson himself regarding the battle was in a letter he wrote to John Armstrong, the Secretary of War, in November of 1813. Keep in mind, Johnson was seriously wounded and it would take him several weeks to recover to the point where he could communicate coherently to his authorities. Johnson states that the battle against the Indians was

fought solely by the M. Regt. at least so much so that not fifty men from any other corps assisted . . . I crossed with the 2nd under Majr Thomson 500 men & fought the Indians, 1200 or 1500, one hour and twenty minutes drawing them from the extreme left of my line.[4]

This letter made no mention of Tecumseh being killed or of Johnson's involvement beyond the general movement of his men. From the time of the battle in 1813, until the beginning of his campaign for high office in the 1830's, Johnson usually let others speak for him regarding the event, never specifically claiming it was Tecumseh he had killed. On one occasion, however, when asked directly about the subject, he gave an intriguing blunt and brusque response:

They say I killed him; how could I tell? I was in too much of a hurry when he was advancing upon me, to ask him his name, or inquire after the health of his family. I fired as quick as convenient, and he fell. If it had been Tecumseh or the Prophet, it would have been all the same.[5]

Johnson gave speeches across the country throughout his life. Most of the few that have survived to this day are from the 1840s, either during his stint as vice-president or recently thereafter. In 1840, at Lafayette, Indiana, Johnson addressed his audience with his version of the Thames affair.

> Well now I'll talk a little about myself again. It has been published in some of the papers that I was taken off the ground at the commencement of the action; this is not true, I never left the ground til the British was taken and Tecumseh killed: as soon as it was known that Tecumseh was killed the fighting ceased.

From all the previous accounts, neither Johnson, nor anyone else was aware of Tecumseh's death until quite some time after the battle had ceased. Johnson continued:

> I fought it out, but I was pretty badly wounded. I received one ball in my left leg which makes me limp a little, and I received another ball in my thigh which is there yet, and another in my arm which went in here and came out there (holding it up and showing).
>
> When I was about to bring on the attack some of my men would keep getting ahead of me, but I told them if they would only keep up with me I would lead them into danger enough.
>
> I selected 20 men that I knowed I could depend on as a forlorn hope. I was determined that we would make short work of it; so we charged upon them in three columns two abreast, so that we had the advantage of them, they could only shoot at two of my men while my men could shoot at their whole line; I placed the forlorn hope in advance of the rest, so that here was the charging columns, here was the forlorn hope, and where was I? Right here in front. (Cheers) Well, we charged on the enemy and in 5 minutes 19 of the forlorn hope had fell from their horses killed or wounded or thrown from their saddles. Some of their horses wouldn't stand fire, but my *grey* mare that I rode, would stand a cannon shot and never scare in the least. I was afraid that my horse that I generally rode wouldn't stand fire & so I changed him before the battle commenced for my grey mare that I knowed could be depended upon, but it is very few animals that could stand fire as she would, and so 19 of the forlorn hope was very soon either cut down or thrown from their horses.
>
> I told them to take it on foot, and so fought on for a while, but I soon saw a large but likely looking Indian who seemed to be a master spirit among them. Some said it was Tecumseh. I cannot tell whether it was or not, but many of my friends think it was . . .

Image courtesy of U.S. Library of Congress.

Portrait of Richard M. Johnson as Vice-President of the United States, 1840.
Charles Fenderich - Lithographer.

I advanced toward him but there was a fallen tree between us, which I had to ride around before I could get within pistol shot of him. I started to go around the tree top; my mare stumbled and fell to her knees for she had been wounded, but with some difficulty she rose again and I started on up the tree or log, and as I paced up the log, he paced down; but re-member my pace was a walk for my mare could not go out of a walk. I let the Indian have the first fire, he fired and I received his shot in my arm the ball going in here and coming out here, but it did not disable me much for I run my arm through the bridle rein: you know we often tie a knot in the rein anyhow, and so I just run my lame arm through the rein and when I came within pistol shot I found he was flourishing his tomahawk, but before he got ready to throw his tomahawk I fired my pistol and shot him right through here, and his heels flew up and he came down like a to-bacco hogshead. I never saw a man fall so heavy in my life. (Cheers.) The fighting ceased immediately, except by Gen. Thompson about a fourth of a mile off and this was what may have misled Capt. Davidson to suppose that I was taken off the ground early in the action.[6]

It seems that Johnson told the standard story we have heard from several others. The consistent points include the fallen tree; his and his horse's severe wounds; Tecumseh approaching with his tomahawk; and his pistol shot which killed Tecumseh. He does disagree with Davidson's account on many points. When he says that the battle essentially ended with his shot he is in conflict with Theobold and many others who claimed to have seen Johnson leave the field well before the fighting ended in the area Johnson was in. Also keep in mind that the Indian accounts repeatedly pointed to an officer on a *white* horse. Johnson just said he switched to his *grey* mare who could better withstand the clamor of the fight. And finally, we do not know where "right through here" is, as Johnson obviously pointed to a body part during his speech to show where he had shot Tecumseh. If we knew it was the head or the chest, it might have helped to arrive at some reasonable conclusions when compared to other accounts. Then again . . .

Three years later, in April of 1843, Johnson's story retained a number of the same points, but there were a few notable changes. It was in a speech delivered to the good people of Oswego, New York that he spoke of the Thames battle once again. A portion of the published address reads:

"And first, allow me to say that history is all wrong as to the details of this affair. I have never seen a correct account of it in any history or official report . . ." He then went on to explain the geography of the battlefield and how the forces were positioned.

"I proceeded through the swamp at the head of my Battalion. We soon discovered the Indians, peeping their heads from behind trees in every direction, horribly painted, and invested with all the habiliments [attire] of savage warriors. My own men were armed with a rifle, a hatchet and a large knife. At this moment, with a view to make the Indians waste their fire, and to give my men an opportunity of rushing upon them, before they had time to reload, I told my men that I wanted twenty brave fellows who were willing to doom themselves to certain death. More than sixty immediately presented themselves, and so would have done the five hundred, had it been necessary. I selected twenty men at random, and putting myself at their head, gave the signal for the sound of the bugle. It was soon heard. I led these men to the attack. In one instant at least five hundred rifles were discharged at us. Nine out of the twenty of this 'forlorn hope' fell dead, ten more were either wounded or had their horses shot from under them; one escaped unhurt. I was myself badly wounded and my mare, a fine white animal, shot through and through. I turned and called to my men to dismount, and fight the Indians in their own way. They did so, and the Indians gave way, but were soon rallied by their chief, whose voice I could distinctly hear, urging his braves to fight. I knew that I was near him. I was near the branches of a fallen oak, and the bushes thick around me. In turning my horse slightly to the left, in the direction of the roots of the tree, my horse fell on its knees. I felt for the moment that I was a lost man. If my horse should fail me, I could neither walk nor stand, nor even spur my horse, so completely was I disabled. I suddenly jerked my horse by the bridle, and it had strength to recover and slowly moved in the direction of the roots of the tree. I had reserved the fire of one of my pistols loaded with ball and buckshot, keeping it close to my right side, in case of emergency. At this moment I saw Tecumseh, who had discovered me, and was deliberately taking aim at me with his rifle. He fired, and the bullet struck my bridle hand, which occasions the appearance of the hand which you see." (Here Colonel Johnson held up his withered hand showing his wounds.)

"I was for a second stunned by the shock it gave my nervous system. The savage perceived the effect of his fire and felt sure of me. He came toward me with a gentle, leaping trot, with his tomahawk. Whilst in the act of raising it to throw at me, I suddenly fired my pistol at him, and he instantly fell. The Indians set up a loud cry and retreated. My men came up, took hold of me, and guided my horse slowly from the field. After going a little distance, they took me off, laid me in a blanket on the ground, and my noble animal fell down dead, pierce by fifteen balls."[7]

In this speech, one contradiction has to be noted again – the color of his horse. It was challenging enough having to reconcile the Indian accounts saying he rode a *white* horse with his own statement (which we read first) that he rode a *grey* one. In fact, in his earlier speech Johnson made clear that he had deliberately chosen to ride his *grey* mare into battle because she could better handle the confusion of combat. Now, three years later, he says he rode a *white* horse. *Hmmm.*

Keep in mind that Johnson's full description of being led off of the battlefield wounded and on his dying horse does concur with the testimonies of both Garret Wall and Sam Theobold which we reviewed much earlier.

A month after giving this speech in New York, Johnson was received by the people of Springfield, Illinois with unbounded admiration. People lined the streets and hung from windows waving their handkerchiefs as the colonel paraded passed them. He gave a two hour speech to the multitude, which at least one attendee found so compelling that he remarked it seemed to have only lasted minutes. In this address Johnson did not deviate from his latest description of his part in the battle of the

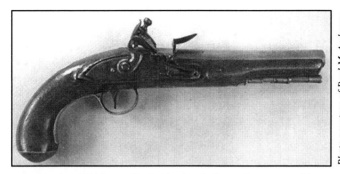

Photo courtesy of Paul M. Ambrose
www.ambroseantiques.com

An example of an 1812 era flintlock pistol - the style presumably used by
Colonel Richard M. Johnson in the Battle of the Thames.

Thames. He did omit the color of his horse this time, and as well, other incidents of the fight are given in more general terms. This was probably not deliberate, but merely an oversight on the reporter's part who admitted that the speech he had published was written from memory.

After repeating many of the incidents already reviewed in his other speeches, Johnson got to the heart of the matter.

"I noticed an Indian chief among them who succeeded in rallying them [fellow Indians] three different times. This I thought I would endeavor to prevent, because it was by this time known to the Indians that their allies, the British, had surrendered. I advanced singly upon him keeping my right arm close to my side and covered by the swamp he took a tree and from thence deliberately fired upon me. Although I previously had four balls in me this last wound was more acutely painful than all of them. His ball struck me on the knuckle of my left hand, passed through my hand, and came out just above the wrist. I ran my left arm through the bridle rein, for my hand instantly swelled and became useless. The Indian supposed he had mortally wounded me; he came out from behind the tree and advanced upon me with uplifted tomahawk. When he had come within my mare's length of me I drew my pistol and instantly fired, having a dead aim upon him. He fell and the Indians shortly after either surrendered or had fled. My pistol had one ball and three buckshot in it, and the body of the Indian was found to have a ball through his body and three buckshot in different parts of his breast and head." (Thus fell Tecumseh, cried out someone in the audience.) Col. Johnson said he did not know that it was Tecumseh at that time. (Circumstances have rendered this a matter of certainty. No intelligent man, we believe, now pretends to doubt the fact.)

It is interesting to note how the reporter, whose comments were in the parentheses of this quote, decided that there could be no other conclusion, than for Johnson.

We can sense the attention Johnson garnered from his audience by way of the further description of the occasion provided by the reporter:

> As Col. Johnson described these thrilling incidents, the vast hall was so still as to render the fluttering of one of the window curtains distinctly heard all over the room. Some one cried out, 'Huzza for the Hero;" and the simultaneous shout which instantly arose from a thousand voices might have waked the dead.[8]

Over time, a few other people have commented on what they had heard at a particular speech of Johnson's or what someone else had told them they had heard from Johnson directly. Rev. William Bouton, in his *History of Concorde* (New Hampshire), reports on comments heard at a dinner party which Johnson had attended in that city circa 1840. He says:

> Mr. William Low proposed the question to Col. Johnson, "Did you or did you not, in your opinion, kill Tecumseh?" Col. Johnson then minutely related the circumstances of the battle, and closed by saying, "In my own opinion, I did kill Tecumseh."[9]

Willa V. Johnson was a nephew of Richard Johnson. He too recalls hearing the story direct from his famous uncle.

> When a boy, uncle Richard M. Johnson visited my father in Scott county, Kentucky. I was left to entertain him on the porch "and asked uncle Dick to tell me of the killing of Tecumseh, the Indian chief." He said, "My horse was killed and in falling caught my left leg under his body pinning me down. The Indians were charging down on us. I drew my pistol from the holster–Tecumseh saw I was alive and drew back his tomahawk to throw at me, being only a few feet away on the other side of my fallen horse. I laid my pistol across my saddle, took aim and fired, the chief pitched forward dead, his head on or against my dead horse."[10]

Here we go again with Johnson contradicting himself. Granted this is *Uncle Dick* telling his tale to an impressionable young relative but it does not correspond to his other accounts. This telling says that Johnson's horse fell and Johnson was pinned beneath him as we have seen both Knaggs and Hamblin describe. Could Johnson's nephew have been influenced by other reports over the years about his uncle's feat, so that by the time he made this story known, the facts were confused? Or, did Johnson really change his story?

R. B. Duncan wrote to Draper to tell him that he was once in conversation with William Conner and a few other gentlemen, who had heard Johnson during a campaign speech in Indianapolis claim to take credit for shooting Tecumseh with his holster pistol. Duncan recorded Conner's reaction.

> William Conner who was at the battle at which Tecumseh was killed, in command of friendly Indians, and who was well acquainted with Tecumseh, was called on to recognize the distinguished dead Indian, and found there lying dead Tecumseh. An officer of the U.S. Army and a boy who was acting as his aid – all dead. Tecumseh was shot by a gun carrying a very small ball as shown by the hole in his body, and just such a ball as must have been shot from the gun in possession of the boy – and the only gun found carrying such a ball. All holster pistols carrying large balls. Thus the belief of Conner was that the boy shot Tecumseh, in fact, he [Conner] had no doubt in his own mind but that the boy killed the great chief.[11]

We can note a couple interesting points from this account. First, Johnson supposedly did claim to have killed Tecumseh in his speech. Second, Conner is consistent in his relying on ballistic evidence to come to his conclusion. However, this time Conner is certain a young boy who fell in the fight had fired the shot which killed Tecumseh. We saw earlier where Conner testified repeatedly that it must have been Whitley who fired the fatal ball.

In 1885, in an open letter to *The Century* magazine, Benjamin Griswold explained what he heard Johnson say during a campaign speech.

> About the year 1842 I happened to be present where Colonel Johnson was giving a graphic account of the whole battle, and in particular of his hand-to-hand conflict with a powerful Indian whom he finally killed. The colonel then remarked that for some time a doubt had existed whether the Indian killed was really the formidable chief or not; but he added, in terms entirely unqualified, that recently developed circumstances *had removed all uncertainty* as to this fact. He gave no information showing *what circumstances* had determined his question but simply spoke with positiveness on the subject.[12]

While Johnson was serving in Washington, Elisha Whittlesey worked as a Controller in the U.S. Treasury department. Whittlesey had frequent contact with Johnson through this position and claims that

he heard Johnson say that he did not know whether he killed Tecumseh or not. Johnson said he killed an Indian but whether Tecumseh or not he did not know. The circumstances under which he killed the Indian were as follows. Johnson was wounded in the right arm which was disabled, and his horse killed under him. The horse fell against a log and so caught Johnson's leg as to hold him, a big burly Indian seeing his condition rushed upon him with his tomahawk. Johnson seeing his danger, with his left hand drew a pistol & shot the Indian when within a few feet of him.[13]

This story from Whittlesey is a bit skewed. The wounded left and right hands are confused and the description of the Indian as burly seems misplaced. This may not be Whittlesey's doing, however; for this account came through Alfred Brunson who was very old and ill at the time he made it. Brunson's daughter, who took this dictated letter from her father added a sad postscript before she sent it on to Mr. Draper. "He is so stupid from morphine to quiet the excruciating pain – he can neither think nor talk connectedly."[14]

In summary, Johnson seems to be reasonably consistent with his story over the years. He does contradict himself as to whether he remained on his horse or whether it fell and pinned him to the ground. The color of his horse as well, is an issue. But beyond those two points his story doesn't change too much. He did kill an Indian but the *elephant in the room* question is whether it was Tecumseh or not. It seems reasonable to assume that he really didn't know. It's no excuse, but try to imagine the pressure Johnson faced. What could vault you to hero status faster than to have killed such a valiant enemy as Tecumseh in nothing less than hand-to-hand combat? Over the years of political campaigning, everyone in his camp either believed that he really had killed Tecumseh or they told him that since so many people already believed it, that he should accept it and use it to his political advantage. It must have taken quite a bit of restraint for Johnson to wait until the 1840s, after serving as vice-president, to let it occasionally slip from his own lips that he did believe he killed Tecumseh.

With Johnson's own words now on the table, it's time to see what some of the people who were a little further from the heart of the action had to say about Tecumseh's death and Johnson's part in it.

CHAPTER 18

More Evidence For and Against Johnson

"Who killed him?"
I replied, "Why, who but Dick Johnson,"
for Johnson was lying in his tent, badly wounded in
several places; none of us believed he could recover,
and I thought he might as well have the credit
of Tecumseh's death. [1]

The case for Richard Johnson having killed Tecumseh has been made by many participants, himself included. But there are still more people who may or may not have been near Johnson or Tecumseh on the battlefield, yet they have offered firm opinions and observations about Johnson's part in the event. An examination of these accounts will help determine if they are valid.

Samuel Brown was a participant, though not a direct witness to Tecumseh's death. In his history book, written immediately after the battle, he states:

The colonel most gallantly led the head of his column into the hottest of the enemy's fire, and was personally opposed to Tecumseh.—At this point a condensed mass of savages had collected. Yet regardless of danger, he rushed into the midst of them, so thick were the Indians at this moment, that several might have reached him with their rifles. He rode a *white* horse and was known to be an officer of rank; a shower of balls was discharged at him—some took effect—his horse was shot under him—his clothes, his saddle, his person was pierced with bullets. At the moment his horse fell, Tecumseh rushed towards him with an uplifted tomahawk, to give the fatal stroke, but his presence of mind did not forsake him in this perilous predicament—he drew his pistol from his holster and laid his daring opponent dead at his feet. He was unable to do more; the loss of blood deprived him of strength to stand. Fortunately, at the moment of Tecumseh's fall the enemy gave way, which secured him from the reach of their tomahawks; he was wounded in five places; he received three shots in the right thigh and two in the left arm. Six Americans and twenty-two Indians fell within twenty yards of the spot where Tecumseh was killed and the trains of blood almost covered the ground.[2]

From Brown we receive the classic description of the charging Tecumseh with his raised tomahawk and Johnson's pistol shot to take him down. Brown does agree with the fewer accounts which state that Johnson fell from his horse. He makes clear that the Indians retreated as soon as Johnson took his shot, but makes no comment on what happened to Tecumseh's body.

The uncle of Dr. John Richardson, Dr. Samuel B. Richardson, was a surgeon to Col. Johnson's regiment of volunteers at the Thames. John Richardson tells us of his uncle's adventures in a letter he wrote for the reading to the Filson Historical Club of Kentucky in 1901. Sam Richardson told his nephew:

> I not only acted as a surgeon to Col. Johnson's regiment, but with gun in hand fought as a private in this particular encounter . . . I was at a certain moment standing near Colonel Johnson (who was mounted, I was on foot) and engaged in reloading my gun after firing at the enemy, when my Commander called to us and said. "Doctor, observe that black devil, how desperately he is fighting. Hand us your gun, we can see him better than you, and can hit him from where I sit . . ."
>
> I did as he desired, watching intently the Indian he had pointed out, to see the effect of his shot. Aiming very deliberately he fired and at that moment Tecumseh, (as it was afterward discovered to be) fell.
>
> Doctor (Samuel) Richardson said he had never entertained but one doubt that the shot fired by Col. Johnson killed Tecumseh, and that was the possibility that some other shot simultaneously fired with that of Col. Johnson's might have killed him, and that Col. Johnson believed, and had expressed the same opinion, to and in his hearing.
>
> Doctor (Samuel) Richardson in describing Tecumseh to me said, "He was much above the average height of the Indian. About the most perfect specimen of Indian manhood I have ever seen. Quick in action and he fought as though entirely devoid of fear."[3]

Richardson's story is unique, plausible and yet unlikely. Johnson is supposed to have gone into battle with a sword and pistols. He could have asked Richardson to hand him his gun for a better shot, assuming this gun was a rifle or musket, but if Johnson had pistols available it's not clear why he would not have used them in a situation like this.

Also, Richardson's description of Tecumseh as "much above average height" is contrary to what is known of Tecumseh's physique.

General Joseph Desha, who led a division of men at the Thames, made his opinion of the battle known but not until 1840. It came in a letter he wrote to a fellow officer. The purpose of Desha's correspondence was primarily to respond to what he felt were unfair charges which impugned his men and his leadership at the conflict. His division was the left wing of the front lines which formed the wedge referred to as the *crotchet*. In due course of his defense, Desha makes a few critical observations:

> The firing where Col. R. M. Johnson fought was in front of my right. I commanded my men to march towards the firing line but so as not to break their ranks. We had gone but a short distance when the firing ceased & Col. Johnson passed through the vacancy on my right . . . after he had been cut up by wounds.

Desha continues to explain that he made sure the *crotchet* was defended, as it was a key area of the fight, but that the majority of the fighting after Johnson departed had moved to his left. He concludes:

> From the time the firing commenced when Col. *James* Johnson charging the British, until it ceased on our left, did not exceed three quarters of an hour. I understood after the affair was over, that the firing on our left was not produced by the left of my Division, as I supposed . . . but by Major Thompson's men, part of Col. Johnson's Regiment with whom the enemy fell in with after they had left the right.[4]

So Desha presents us with the facts that Johnson was seen leaving and that the fighting continued, but to the left of where Johnson had fought. Also, he makes clear that Major Thompson was involved in this later fighting. Desha's timing of the whole engagement was about forty-five minutes.

The son of William H. Harrison, Scott, wrote a letter to Draper in 1873. He expressed what he gleaned from his father over the years. Scott's letter reads:

> I am very sure that my father believed that Tecumseth was killed at the battle of the Thames and probably by Col. Richard M. Johnston.
> I have frequently conversed with my father on this subject and never

heard him express a doubt on the subject. I have heard him say that he waited on Col. Johnston directly after the battle and found him severely wounded, that in the course of conversation, Col. Johnston remarked that he had killed an Indian Chief . . . and that his impressions were it was Tecumseh. In relating this incident my father remarked that a celebrated Winnebago War Chief–a man of very powerful frame & imposing appearance, was the constant companion of Tecumseth and it was reported, always fought at his side. My father added that it was possible–the Indian killed by Col. Johnston was this Winnebago & not Tecumseth.

I am of the opinion, however, that my father believed that both these Indians fell in the battle and one of them, by the hand of Col. Johnston.

I do not know that my father saw the body of either these Indians after death. I am inclined to think that he did not–as he would otherwise have most probably alluded to his recognition of his old enemy Tecumseth, whom you are aware he knew very well. But be this as it may–I am entirely certain, that my father never doubted that Tecumseth was killed at the Thames and most likely by the hand of Col. Johnston.[5]

Harrison gives us a repetitive endorsement that is not based on any facts, but is an endearing nod toward Johnson. (His mental vacancy from the event is evidenced by his misspelling of the name Johnson as Johnston throughout this letter.) He does present an opinion similar to that of Robert McAfee by pointing out that a larger though comparable looking Indian lay nearby and Johnson had to of killed one of them.

Lyman Draper, who collected much of the information we have read concerning this event, never divulged his own conclusion of it. He visited Johnson several times over the years. On one occasion, he recorded his impression of Johnson as he was being shown the pistols he used in the battle.

Colonel Johnson was invariably modest about claiming the honor of having slain Tecumseh. When I paid him a visit, at his residence at the Great Crossings, in Kentucky in 1844, while collecting facts and materials illustrative of the career of Clark, Boone, Kenton and other Western pioneers, he exhibited to me the horse pistols he used in the battle of the Thames and modestly remarked, "that with them he shot the chief who had confronted and wounded him in the engagement."[6]

Only twenty years after the battle, an early historian named Samuel

Drake, wrote a book laden with the biographies of over two hundred Indian chiefs of the era. Regarding the death of Tecumseh, Drake states:

> After withstanding almost the whole force of the Americans for some time, Tecumseh received a severe wound in the arm, but continued to fight with desperation, until a random shot laid him prostrate in the thickest of the fight* (*The story that he fell in a personal recounter with col. Johnson, must no longer be believed. Facts are entirely opposed to such a conclusion. Indeed we cannot learn that the colonel ever claimed the honor of the achievement.)[7]

By 1832, when Drake's book was published, there must have been rampant reports giving what Drake considered to be unfounded credit to Johnson. Obviously he felt strongly enough about the issue to include this footnote which he hoped would end what he believed was an erroneous conclusion.

Marcia Harlan wrote to Draper in 1884, that her father was at the Thames and even brought home Tecumseh's tomahawk. She explains:

> I have heard him say that history did not give a true account of the battle of Thames: he said no one knew who killed Tecumseh. He said it was a hand-to-hand fight; he and the chief were engaged in a struggle; the chief struck at his head with his tomahawk; he missed his aim, and hit father on the arm before he could make another lick he was shot falling against my Father; he took the ax from the dead chief's hand. He said the chief was a formidable man to fight with–said he was fully six feet tall, with high forehead and piercing black eyes. The tomahawk has been missing many years, when we was children we would have it to play with, we would loose it and then again would find it. . . .[8]

Harlan provides another unique story by citing her father going one-on-one with Tecumseh until an anonymous shooter took him down. The description of Tecumseh as a large man is once again contrary to popular belief; so although the scene could have played out as told by Harlan, it certainly was not Tecumseh he was fighting. But it is interesting to see that with few toys available in the 1800s, children were allowed to play with deadly weapons, and supposed legendary ones at that!

Nancy Wright was a lady who had a husband, brothers and cousins serving in many of the conflicts of the war, including the Thames. In a rambling and disjointed letter, probably due to her age, she manages to make a few key observations in the course of sharing her cousins' opinions about the event.

> I heard all of them talk about the battles—what I heard them say is stampt in my memory like a book—and R. M. Johnson never claimed the honor of killing Tecumseh, and I have read in a book since I rote to you that Johnson's bullet went right straight to Tecumseh. Now in a battle and the bullets flying, how can any one tell where or who these bullets hit? I have seen it in books that Johnson was covered with wounds, and know he had but two flesh wounds my mother dressed his wounds, he was cousin to my husband.[9]

Well, one might have to agree with Wright's opinion that with bullets flying everywhere no one could tell who struck who. Her mother may have tended to Johnson's wounds, but he did have more than two. Perhaps the others healed by the time her mother became involved, or perhaps Ms. Wright's memory was a little fogged by the sixty-six years since the event occurred.

In 1859, Thomas Woodward wrote a book of his experiences with the Creek Indians. In it he re-tells the account he heard from Col. Clever who served at the Thames. Woodward states:

> It will be recollected by those who knew Col. Clever that he was a great friend of Col. Johnson, but denied him credit of killing Tecumseh. He said Tecumseh was killed some time after Col. Johnson was wounded and disabled; that he was killed at least three hundred yards from where the Colonel was shot.

Woodward went on to note that Clever's story matches one that he heard previously from two other acquaintances. He then continues:

> He [Clever] said, from the way the Indians rallied and fought around a certain Indian until he was killed, and a small trinket found on his person, that he was supposed to be a Chief. And there being but few if any among the whites that had known Tecumseh, except Gen. Harrison, it was some time after the close of the fight before it was ascertained that the dead Chief was Tecumseh; and it was only ascertained through the General. The circumstance of the bold stand made by the supposed Chief being communicated to Gen. Harrison, he visited the spot where

the dead Indian lay; the body was much mangled, and as the General approached the spot a soldier was in the act of taking off a piece of skin from the Indian's thigh. The General ordered the soldier to stop, and said he regretted to know that he had such a man in his camp, and reprimanded him severely. He had some water brought, had the Indian washed and stretched his full length, examined his teeth and pronounced it to be Tecumseh. One of Tecumseh's legs was a little shorter than the other, and the foot on the short leg a little smaller, and he had a halt in his walk that was perceptible, and he had a tooth, though not decayed, of a bluish cast. This was Col. Clever's statement, that I heard him make a hundred times. . . .[10]

This story from Clever has a lot of similarities to Charles Wickliffe's. Recall that with several others, Wickliffe told us that he had washed off the war paint from the face, found the shorter leg, and that Harrison was present and identified the body as Tecumseh's. However, Clever had no prior personal acquaintance with Tecumseh, so he had to be basing this story on other's knowledge or he was one of those others present when Wickliffe cleaned off the body. As well, Clever boldly declares that Johnson was quite a distance from where Tecumseh fell and that he was killed well after Johnson was disabled. Unfortunately Clever does not substantiate how he knows this information.

Two brothers, the Endicotts, fought together at the Thames, but per their grandsons, they told two different stories about Tecumseh's fate. Will Davis, Joseph Endicott's grandson, relates:

Grandfather lived near us and often came to see us and spend the night. He enjoyed telling the grandchildren tales. I remember he told us about shooting at Tecumseh during the battle in which he was killed. He said there were (sic) a number who shot at the Indian and that it was never positively known whose bullet hit him.

The other grandson of the other brother, John Blakely, wrote:

My grandfather, John A. Endicott and his brother, Joseph, enlisted in Kentucky in Col. Richard Johnson's regiment of mounted infantry . . . Col. Johnson was the man who killed the noted Chief Tecumseh, and my grandfather said it happened this way: Col. Johnson had his horse shot under him and in falling caught his leg under it. Tecumseh, seeing his plight and thinking to get an easy scalp, rushed out, but the Colonel drew his dragoon pistol from his saddle holster and killed him.[11]

Two brothers, two different observations, but the list of accounts for Johnson having fallen under his horse is growing longer.

William Gaines, the Ordinance Sergeant of the regular army, gave a full account of his experience at the Thames to Draper in 1882. In it, he brings to light even more contradictory pieces of the puzzle.

There were not only one, but a number of dead Indians lying around, but I am very positive about Tecumseh as he was pointed out to me by a Quarter Master Sergeant of the British Army, whom we had as a prisoner & who said he had been acquainted with him for two years. That he [Tecumseh] had been in the habit of visiting Fort Malden and associating with the Officers more or less every week, attending then Balls & parties and that he received the pay of a Brigadier General from the British Government. I am satisfied that this Sergeant was well acquainted with him. He was a fine honorable man, well-educated, & I believe what he said in reference to him was true. The Americans were not mistaken in the man.

He had on no ornaments but a British Medal & three silver half moons.

This body was not taken off till the next day as I was "on post" all night within fifty yards of where he lay. He was shot about the hip. I can say precisely the locality, but part of his hip was taken away

Colonel Johnson's Pistol Ball broke his skull. The body was on the ground the next day after the battle, when we left–about 9 o'clock; & there was a party left to bury the dead and Tecumseh was buried by our troops.

The body appeared in my judgment from 5 ft 11 in to 6 ft tall. There was no feather nor plume on this body only the Medal & three silver moons I have spoken of–I do not know what became of either.

His dress was of the finest Buckskin & scalloped all round the bottom.[12]

In an earlier letter, Gaines had noted:

The body that was pointed out as Tecumseh after the Thames battle was the identical one that was skinned and made into razor-strops. It was very near where Col. Johnson was wounded, perhaps 10 or 15 yds & Col. Whitley was killed about 100 yds from the spot as near as I can remember. . . . I did not see any disfiguration in the body (Tecumseh), but I heard it spoken of afterwards. It was talked about commonly among the men.[13]

And, in yet another letter, Gaines contradicts his observation of Tecumseh's disfigurement when he relates that he

> saw Tecumseh dead on the battlefield. He was pointed out to me by a British prisoner who said he had known him well for two years or more. He was so disfigured & covered with blood that it would be impossible to give a description of him. He lay among the other dead Indians with his limbs drawn up, he was very strong & athletic in form and build, He was dressed in Buck skin, Indian style, decorated with beads and half-moons and a red sash.[14]

Gaines provides observations that we have seen before and, as well, presents new ones. He is the only one to mention half-moon decorations. He is one of a few to cite the red sash. He claims, as others have, that a British prisoner helped identify the body – again contrary to Harrison's claim. He is one of the few to point out a hip wound aside from the Indian accounts that mention it. He also sounds sure that it was Johnson's pistol ball that landed in Tecumseh's head, but he does not explain how he came to that conclusion.

Courtesy of Joseph Sullivant, who wrote a family history and who was related to Colonel Joseph McDowell (the Adjutant General to Governor Shelby at the Thames), we learn the tales of two more participants. One story comes from a man named Elkins and the other from a friend of the family, James Coleman.

The reporter of the *Mobile Register* says he interviewed Elkins, who was at the Thames.

> As for the story of Colonel Johnson killing Tecumseh, Mr. Elkins said it was commonly reported and not questioned at the time; he himself was in another part of the engagement, being under Lieutenant Colonel James Johnson . . . the day after the battle the troops were marched out by companies to gratify their curiosity by viewing the scene . . . His company was the first that reached the ground where Tecumseh fell, and they found his body, from the back of which "razor-straps" (that was his expression) had been cut . . . We think Mr. Elkins said that on the morning after he saw the body, it had disappeared.[15]

Elkins provides another simple testimony citing only that Tecumseh was skinned and taken off overnight. James Coleman, however; provides a much more intriguing story. We referred to James Coleman earlier as one who was present when Anthony Shane was struggling to identify the body as Tecumseh's. Coleman, in his early 1817 letter to the editor of the *Kentucky Gazette*, had stated:

> I saw Col. Johnson fire his pistol at an Indian who was advancing (and within 12 feet) rather on the left with a sword in the attitude of striking. The Indian fell and I have no doubt was killed by Col. Johnson as the execution was done by a ball and several buck' shot and Col. Johnson's cartridge were composed of such material. Our troops immediately . . . in that part of the line, were armed principally with U.S. rifles which carried a single ball.

Regarding Shane's identification of the body, Coleman says, "I have no doubt it was Tecumseh, and I believe this was the Indian killed by Col. Johnson."[16]

A few years later, however, Coleman told his relatives quite a different story. Per Joseph Sullivant we learn:

> I put here upon record what I never doubted was the true version of this celebrated affair: In June, 1823, Colonel James Coleman, of Cynthiana, Ky., was on a visit to my father, and spent the day, which was Sunday, the same on which the great rain fell which produced the memorable flood of that month and year. They spoke of many things, of old times and old friends, and discussed some of the men and events in the late war, among others the battle above referred to, and on my father alluding to Dick Johnson and Tecumseh, Coleman burst into a loud laugh and said, "Why, Sullivant, I started that story myself!" He made the following statement: "After the battle myself and another person were on the field looking for Captain Whitley, who was reported missing. In our search we came to a number of dead bodies, both of Indians and soldiers, showing there had been a sharp contest at that spot. We found a dead Indian lying on his face, who, from his dress, we thought might be a Chief; as we stood over him I discovered a young Indian who was badly wounded, and in a sitting posture supporting himself against a tree, and who seemed intently watching us. I touched the dead body with my foot, and at the same time pointing at it with my hand, asked the young Indian Who is it?" Understanding my signs at last he replied, "Tecumseh." We returned immediately to our camp, and spread the report of the death of the great Chief. It excited great interest, and the question was asked, "Who killed him?" I replied, "Why, who but Dick Johnson," for Johnson was lying in his tent, badly wounded in several places; none of us believed he could recover,

and I thought he might as well have the credit of Tecumseh's death. Turning to my father, he said, "I give you my word this is the simple truth in the matter." Coleman was asked about the skinning of the dead body and the razor-strop story. He said there was not a word of truth in it, except that one man said he would like to cut a strip of skin from Tecumseh's thigh for a razor-strop. The body, turned over on the back, was found pierced with two bullet-holes in the chest. Coleman further said, "Whitley was found dead close by, and from the concurrent testimony of the camp, it was conceded that Whitley had killed Tecumseh; although," said Coleman, "Dick Johnson will always retain the honor given him by the story I myself started as a joke."[17]

Hmmm.

Alfred Lorrain will have the last word among these random observations. He states:

To finish his [Tecumseh's] history at once, we will add, that he fell in the battle that followed, in the midst of his people, that were stationed in the swamp, and, as they say, pierced with many balls; and was buried four miles in the rear. There we suspect he remains to the present day. And the razor-strops, and other precious relics, that will be handed down to future generations, as samples of his hide, are all, as the old chief himself would express it, "ec-shaw." And we believe if his resurrection should take place tomorrow, it would interrupt nobody's shaving utensils in Kentucky or elsewhere.[18]

CHAPTER 19

The Cases for Whitley, King and Others

*I helped kill Tecumseh
and helped Skin him and brought two pieces
of his yellow hide home with me
to my mother and Sweet Hart.*[1]

The people of the United States had spoken and declared their independence just three years before William Whitley had gathered up his wife and his very young children to lead them on a journey along the old Wilderness Road from Virginia to Kentucky. In 1779, near a branch of Dick's River, Whitley staked his claim and settled into a new life within the wilds of Kentucky. He built a simple fort to protect his family; for his was one of the furthest probes into the Kentucky backwoods since the Bloody Sevens. (In July of 1777, the British government authorized Henry Hamilton to direct numerous Indian tribes allied with them, to assault the frontier people of Pennsylvania and Kentucky. The scalps returned by the warriors to Hamilton caused him to be referred to as the *hair-buyer general*. The slaughter of innocent pioneers was long remembered.)

With determination, Whitley defended his family and neighbors from on-going Indian attacks. Over the next few years, he would build the first brick house and thus architecturally and personally declare the advance of American civilization and culture.

The Kentuckians' everlasting affection for equestrian activities can be in part traced to Whitley, who loved his steeds as much as he loved the companionship of his friends. Within sight of his fine home was a clearing punctuated by a small knob hill. Whitley saw the potential. He transformed the knob into the first American race track for horses. Notable friends visited him to relax, sing, dance, feast on fine foods; and to race their horses. His brother-in-law, George Rogers Clark, Governor Isaac Shelby, and Daniel Boone were just some of his distinguished visitors. Of course, by Whitley's deliberate design, the horses competed in a counter-clockwise direction around his knob – dubbed *Sportsman's Hill*; a protocol which has remained uniquely American. It was Whitley's way of thumbing his nose at the Tories whose race tracks had, and still do, run their horses in a clockwise direction.

William has already been described by several who were at the Thames as an impetuous and aggressive man, and that he was. Before the Thames battle, he had fought in at least twenty conflicts which were directly or indirectly a part of the Revolutionary War. He never disguised his disgust for the Indians or the British. Too many brutal attacks had been made by both upon his family and friends over the years. Samuel Theobold described him thus: "Col. Whitley was tall, his features strongly marked, hair sandy, light eyes, prominent aquiline nose – somewhat vain." [2]

But to linger on the aggressive side of Whitley's personality is to miss the whole man who was high-spirited, competitive, funny and romantic. He was known to often sing songs of his own composition and joke with his fellows. A premier example of his full personality can still be witnessed to this day by reading the poem he etched into his powder horn. It reads:

> *Wm. Whitley I am your horn*
> *The truth I Love a lie I Scorn*
> *Fill me with best of powder*
> *Ile make your rifle Crack the Lowder*
> *See how the dread terrefick ball*
> *Make Indians bleed and Toreys fall*
> *You with powder, Ile Supply*
> *For to defend your Liberty* [3]

We have already seen a few people testify that they believe it was this die-hard patriot, William Whitley, who killed Tecumseh. There were several others who felt the same – some with questionable stories, others with seemingly accurate information. Let's take a look.

In 1859, Captain Ferguson told the *Louisville Daily Journal* that after the fight, he was ordered to take fifty men and cover part of the battle-field attending to the wounded and burying the dead. The article states:

Among these [dead Indians] he [Ferguson] discovered the body of

Tecumseh, well known personally to several of his company, killed by a rifle ball. Directly in front of, and but a short distance from him, lay Major Whistler (Whitley), with his rifle in his hand, which had evidently been discharged the moment before he fell. He was pierced by several balls showing most conclusively that Tecumseh had fallen by his hand, and at that moment [when] he fired and Tecumseh fell, several Indians had discovered and fired upon him.

This point, Mr. Ferguson said, was full half-a-mile from where Colonel Johnson made his charge, was wounded, and carried from the field. Besides, Colonel Johnson's pistols were smooth bored, and Tecumseh was killed by a *rifle* ball, as the jagged and open character of the wound, peculiar to the rifle ball, showed. This was closely examined at the time.

Furthermore, there were no Indians in that part of the British line which was charged by Colonel J. and the mounted volunteers; and he was wounded in the very commencement of the charge before the two lines had come in close contact, and immediately borne from the field; his brother, next in command, then leading the charge, and commanding the regiment during the remainder of the day.

The fact that Tecumseh was directly across from Whitley has been recorded by several others, as well as the ballistics analysis pointing toward a rifle ball. These two points make a solid case for Whitley, but Ferguson went on in his statement to incorrectly assert that there were no Indians in the area that Johnson fought in, and that James Johnson came as the backup force behind Richard. He implies that Richard Johnson was involved against the British line, not the Indian line. All of these claims are incorrect.

It is also suspect that Ferguson would have had friends with him who could recognize Tecumseh, unless they included Shane, Miller or the other handful of people who have testified that they had known Tecumseh. He further claims that "he took the body of Tecumseh to headquarters, where nearly the whole army saw it. . . ."[4] Again, this was a highly unlikely action.

Even though it was riddled with discrepancies, a couple weeks after Ferguson's account was published S. B. Nisbet felt compelled to endorse it with his own. Nisbet told the newspaper readers of Louisville:

Col. Whitley, to my judgment, was some fifty or sixty years old, and

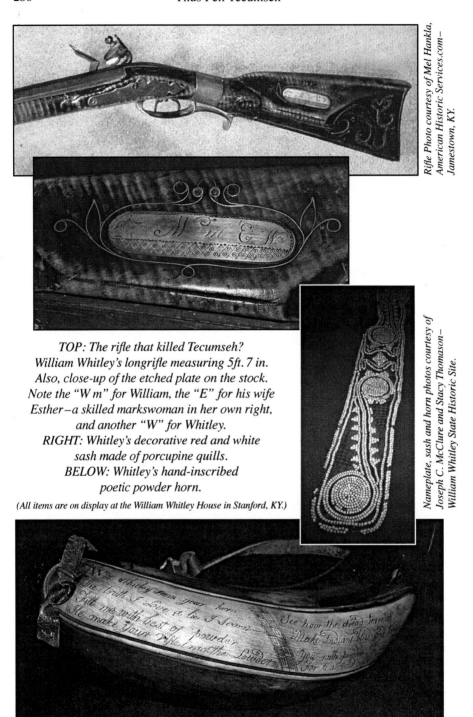

*TOP: The rifle that killed Tecumseh?
William Whitley's longrifle measuring 5ft. 7 in.
Also, close-up of the etched plate on the stock.
Note the "W m" for William, the "E" for his wife
Esther – a skilled markswoman in her own right,
and another "W" for Whitley.
RIGHT: Whitley's decorative red and white
sash made of porcupine quills.
BELOW: Whitley's hand-inscribed
poetic powder horn.*

(All items are on display at the William Whitley House in Stanford, KY.)

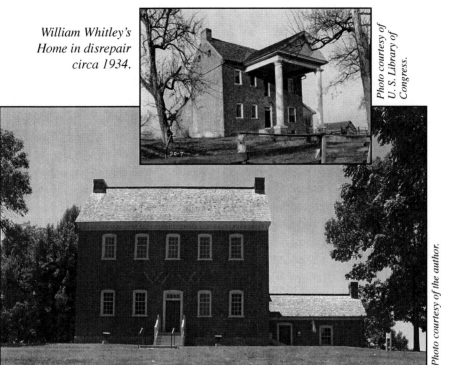

William Whitley's Home in disrepair circa 1934.

Photo courtesy of U. S. Library of Congress.

Photo courtesy of the author.

The refurbished William Whitley Home as it appeared in 2008. Note the owner's initials fashioned into the brickwork.

Photo courtesy of the author.

Sportsman's Hill as seen from the Whitley Home in 2008. Around this knob hill Whitley established the first American horse-racing track. He also began the practice of running the American horses in a counter-clockwise direction to spite the British practice of running them clockwise. Both traditions are still upheld.

wore a continental three cocked or cornered hat. Now we find him next after the battle was over, lying dead behind a lynn stump about fifteen inches through and broken off about ten feet high, and some sproats grown up close on the left or west side of it, with a ball shot in his left breast and perhaps other wounds, but unnoticed by me. Tecumseh was lying dead direct across the line of the battle about thirty or forty steps from this place, and nearly direct between where Whitley and Tecumseh were killed were two little black Indians, one still nearer Whitley's concealment than the other, as though they had been advancing on him in revenge for their chief, and in my opinion was, and often expressed, that he likely killed all three of them and a fourth Indian killed him. The bullets were shot into the stump, where they said he was killed like some person had been shooting at a target. Whitley took his own position in the line of battle, and Tecumseh no doubt was his aim. I saw Whitley the evening he was brought into camp, and Tecumseh the next day lying where he was killed with all his clothes off, the front part of his thigh and each side of his back skinned for razor strops.[5]

In Nisbet's attempt to make his case for Whitley, he gives an account similar to Ferguson's but with new details. Whitley is now found behind a stump but still directly across from Tecumseh and there are two additional Indians between them. Nisbet's projection that Whitley killed all of them is plausible but still pure speculation. A contradiction to Ferguson's story arises when Nisbet says that he viewed Tecumseh's body on the field, not back in camp, as Ferguson had alleged.

A colonel named Ambrose Dudley spoke of the Thames on at least two occasions. Dudley was serving in Trotter's brigade which was charging behind James Johnson's regiment against the British. Since their surrender was almost immediate, Trotter ordered Dudley to the left in order to aid the troops fighting in the engagement with the Indians.

Dudley says:

Col. R. M. Johnson's men, at that point called the crotchet, were driven back, and the infantry were warmly engaged with the Indians. As I passed the left, near the Crotchet, after the firing had ceased on the right, I met Col. R. M. Johnson passing diagonally from the swamp towards the line of Infantry, and spoke with him: he said he was badly wounded—his *grey* mare bleeding profusely in several places. The battle continued with the Indians on the left. The Infantry, with some of Col. R. M. Johnson's troops mixed up promiscuously with them, continued the battle for half an hour after Col. Johnson was disabled, and had ceased to command his men. . . .[6]

About six months later, Dudley gave further details of what happened as he heard it from an anonymous spectator. Dudley relates:

The morning after the battle of the Thames, in company with several other persons, I walked over the ground, to see the bodies of those who had been slain in the engagement . . . we came to a place where some half a dozen persons were standing, and three dead Indians were lying close together. One of the spectators remarked, that he had witnessed that part of the engagement which led to the death of these three Indians and two of our troops, whose bodies had been removed the evening before for burial. He proceeded to point out the position of the slain as they lay upon the ground, with that of our men. He said old colonel Whitley rode up to the body of a tree, which lay before him, and behind which lay an Indian: he [the Indian] attempted to fire, but from some cause did not succeed, and then Whitley instantly shot him. This Indian was recognized by one of the persons present as Tecumseh; the next Indian was pointed out as having killed Whitley; then the position of another of our troops who killed that Indian, and the Indian who killed him, with the position of the man who shot the third Indian – making three Indians and two Americans who had fallen on a very small space of ground . . . The Indian pointed out as Tecumseh, was wearing a bandage over a wound in the arm, and as it was known that Tecumseh had been slightly wounded in the arm the day before, while defending passage of a creek, my conviction was strengthened by this circumstance, that the body before us was that of Tecumseh.[7]

Bang, bang, bang, bang, bang! Five dead within moments and the first one down is Tecumseh by the hand of Whitley. It's plausible.

The colorful Tarrance Kirby, from whom we have heard earlier, tells us:

Dick Johnson led his men to the charge like a hero, as he was, cheering and encouraging them; Tecumseh met him with twelve picked warriors, and they shot seven balls through Dick, who fell across his horse; at that instant, old Colonel Whitly rode up and shot Tecumseh dead, whereupon the Indians all fired upon Whitly, who fell dead the worst shot man I ever saw. I make this statement in order to do justice to the dead and the living. I know it has been said that Dick Johnson killed Tecumseh, but I know the facts are as here detailed.[8]

Another participant at the Thames, William Greathouse, says:

None but Colonel Johnson and two or three (others) were able to make their horses stand the fire of the enemy, and in their retreat back, Johnson received five wounds. I passed over his feet or legs. He seemed in great pain and calling for water. I saw close by some men running with a hat full of water for him. His *gray* mare was close by, badly wounded, and was very bloody and died that night.

Greathouse must have almost tripped over Johnson as he was lying wounded near the river. This is possible since the battle had ended so quickly on the right that Greathouse would have likely returned from the British lines to the origin of the charge which was near the banks of the river.

He continues:

The Captain ordered me to take a file of men and take charge of the [British] prisoners. I begged to be excused as the Indians were firing sharply and I wanted to have a hand in it. My Captain ordered me to obey. I took the file of men and went about fifty yards and I handed the prisoners over to one of my men and told him to take good care of them and I returned to my Captain and by that time the Indians had outflanked my company and we wheeled to the left and passed the Indians. By that time their Chief fell and they gave the loudest yells I ever heard from human beings, and that ended the fight. . . . Tecumseh fell by some man, but it was not known by whom. It was thought he fell by the hand of an old man. We called him Colonel Weekly. They lay close together . . . I intended visiting Tecumseh but learned that the boys had taken several razor strops from his person, so I did not go where he lay.[9]

Even though Greathouse acknowledged that no one knew who killed Tecumseh, he states that it was generally assumed Whitley had. He also verifies that it was the yells of the Indians which signaled the end of the fight. Since Greathouse had seen Johnson off the battlefield some time previous his statements support the notion that someone besides Johnson had killed Tecumseh.

A private named Abraham Scribner threw his support behind Whitley but with little concrete evidence. He says:

I had never seen Tecumseh, until the body was shown to me on the battle ground on the river Thames; by whose hand he fell must always be an uncertainty. My own opinion was the day after the battle, and is yet, that Tecumseh fell by a ball from the rifle of colonel Whitley, an old Indian fighter; two balls passed through colonel Whitley's head, at the moment that Tecumseh fell; he (colonel Whitley), was seen to take aim at the Indian said to be Tecumseh, and his rifle was found empty.[10]

A few brief comments endorsing Whitley are found here and there in other historical records. William Watts, in his application for a veteran's pension as late as 1882, makes note:

Was at the Battle of the Thames on the 5th Octr. 1813. Saw Tecumseh as he was identified by the Prisoners, and also Col. Whitley, as they laid near to each other & from all the circumstances is satisfied that they killed each other.[11]

Another random remark in Draper's notes comes from a judge named Sebastian. He told Draper that "it was generally thought Whitley killed Tecumseh – they were found dead only 14 paces apart."[12]

A curious anonymous account comes via the renowned author Nathaniel Hawthorne who states:

"An old gentleman has recently paid me a good many visits,–a Kentucky man, who has been a good deal in England and Europe generally without losing the freshness and unconventionality of his earlier life . . . He fought through the whole War of 1812, beginning with General Harrison at the battle of Tippecanoe, which he described to me. He says that at the beginning of the battle, and for a considerable time, he heard Tecumseh's voice, loudly giving orders. There was a man named Wheatley in the American camp, a strange, incommunicative person,–a volunteer, making war entirely on his own book, and seeking revenge for some relatives of his, who had been killed by the Indians. In the midst of the battle this Wheatley ran at a slow trot past R——— (my informant), trailing his rifle, and making towards the point where Tecumseh's voice was heard. The fight drifted around, and R——— along with it; and by and by he reached a spot where Wheatley lay dead, with his head on Tecumseh's breast. Tecumseh had been shot with a rifle, but, before expiring, appeared to have shot Wheatley with a pistol, which he still held in his hand. R——— affirms that Tecumseh was flayed by the Kentucky men on the spot, and his skin converted into razor-straps. I have left out the most striking point of the narrative, after all, as R——— told it, viz. that soon after Wheatley passed him, he suddenly ceased to hear Tecumseh's voice ringing through the forest, as he gave his orders.[13]

Hawthorne's visitor, (R---), obviously confused the name of the battle as Tippecanoe instead of Thames, and the name Wheatley for Whitley, but the rest of the details are believable, albeit romanticized.

Only two descendents of Whitley are on the record stating their opinions of the event, unfortunately they too are based on little evidence beyond their opinion. The earliest comment is from William's granddaughter, Sallie Ann Higgins. In a letter to H.C.Whitley, from whom she was trying to ascertain H.C.'s relationship to William, she says:

> Grandpa was in Nineteen battles and [was] killed, the day Tecumseh was killed. He killed Tecumseh. He always loaded his gun with two Bullets, he [Tecumseh] was Shot with a gun that was loaded with two bullets, 5th day [of] October 1814 . . . I have my Grandpa's Gun & Powder Horn & Indian Belt. It is beaded; the one that killed Tecumseh – the gun.[14]

The only other descendent documented to speak of the event was Miss Esther Whitley Burch, founder of the Lincoln County Historical Society, at a meeting in 1943. She says:

> Whitley often said the death he craved to die was in his country's defense. At the spot where the Forlorn Hope had received the concentrated fire Whitley's body was found, his trusty rifle in his hand, his horn over his shoulder, his hunter's knife in its sheath, his body pierced with bullets, and near were the others who had so gloriously fallen. About twenty yards away were the bodies of the Indians and that of Tecumseh . . .[15]

Later in her speech, Miss Higgins only cited the opinion of an early historian, Lewis Collins, who said, "In our view it is conclusive that Col. Richard Johnson did not kill Tecumseh, that David King might have done it, but that Col. Whitley probably did kill him."[16]

A final testimony comes from William T. Sterling in a letter he wrote to Draper in 1886. The aged Sterling, the founding settler of Utica, Wisconsin, had grown up in Kentucky. He was only 5 years old when the Thames battle occurred but he confided to Draper his memories.

> I knew Col. Johnson intimately when a boy; he obtained a scholarship for me in Georgetown Univ. in Kentucky. I have heard him say

repeatedly that he did not kill Tecumseh; but that it was Col. Whitley who killed him. Col. Whitley's mother lived near my house in Versailles, Woodford Co. Ky. Col. Whitley was killed at the battle of the Thames; about 3 hours before his death he killed an Indian concealed in a pile of driftwood across the Thames, and then swam his horse across and brought back the Indian's body. Gen. Harrison remarked to him that he was too venturesome; and that he would be killed. Soon after that Whitley killed Tecumseh and shortly after was himself killed by the Indians. It was claimed by old settlers in Ky. that Col. Whitley had fought in 62 different Indian battles and skirmishes before his death. Gen. Harrison presented Whitley's wife with a small brass cannon about a foot long and every anniversary of the Battle of the Thames she loaded and fired it until the time of her death.[17]

Sterling was not an eyewitness to the event, but he was witness to the after-effects of it in the communities through which he circulated.

The third person most often referred to as the slayer of Tecumseh is David King. Unfortunately very little is known of King. It is certain that he grew up in Lincoln County, Kentucky, probably in Crab Orchard where Whitley lived. His father was married to Captain James Davidson's sister. When he enlisted, he was a mere eighteen-year-old, red-headed youth. Most likely he was as fine a young man, and marksman, as his proud uncle had described him earlier. The county records show that a David King married a Jane Leeper on June 29, 1816. There is no way to be absolutely certain that this was the same David King we are discussing, but it is very probable. A search of Tennessee records shows a family surnamed King, with David, Jane and four children listed as living together in Henry County circa 1840. In the 1850 census, however, David is missing from the family rolls. James Davidson reported that he lost track of his nephew but believed he passed away in Tennessee in 1847.

As for the credit of killing Tecumseh, it must have been as Davidson said, "King never cared a cent for it,"[18] for he never made a documented comment on it.

C. S. Todd, who was a key aid to Harrison, publicly stated in the *Louisville Daily Journal* that:

> After the date of general Harrison's dispatches . . . it was ascertained from the enemy, that Tecumseh was certainly killed; and even then the

opinion of the army was divided as to the person by whose hands he fell. Some claimed the credit of it for colonel Whitley, some for colonel Johnson; but others, constituting the majority, including governor Shelby, entertained the opinion that he fell by a shot from David King, a private in captain Davidson's company, from Lincoln county, Kentucky.[19]

We already heard a great deal from Alfred Brunson, but he did make one more observation toward David King. Brunson brings up the fact that Clark, Tecumseh's aid who died shortly after the battle in the American camp, said a youth fired the fatal shot. He explains that on the way back to Detroit after the fight:

> Some anxiety began to be manifested as to who was the fortunate indi-vidual–the youth or young man [referred to as the shooter by Tecumseh's dying aid, Clarke]–who had done the deed. But we were taken all a-back, when the papers from the States brought the General's report of the battle, in which he gave credit of killing Tecumseh to Col. Johnson. I think he gave it as a rumor, but he seemed to favor the idea, and it went over the world as a fact. It was said, and probably correctly, that Col. Johnson did kill an Indian, who was supposed to be a chief, and someone *guessed* it was Tecumseh. But Whitley and Johnson were not so close together as to make the latter the youth [referred to by Clarke] who killed the daring chief . . . Whitley and Johnson were in different parts of the battle. Tecumseh fell by or near Whitley, therefore the Indian whom Johnson killed could not have been Tecumseh.[20]

Most accounts state that Whitley and Johnson *were* near each other as they were both leading the *Forlorn Hope.* Also, Harrison hadn't even given an *official* opinion on Tecumseh's death or slayer, let alone one to the newspapers that the men could have read a few days after the fact at Detroit. Perhaps excerpts of opinions from other people and from other newspapers were read by the men, but certainly not from General Harrison.

Another declaration for King is made by John Hedges, a soldier serving at the Thames. Hedges says:

> I saw Tecumseh's remains, and saw the fatal bullet hole. His mortal wound was on the left side–directly through the heart–and it was so small that a soldier tried to penetrate it with his little finger but found it impossible to do so. There were several other wounds in different parts

of his body, some of which would have proved fatal. Tecumseh was distinguished by a real silk sash wound about his waist, which no doubt had been procured from some British officer; as such an article in those days was real costly. After the battle, I was informed that the soldiers mutilated the body of Tecumseh, cutting several strips of his skin for the purpose of using as razor strops . . . It has been the general impression that Tecumseh was killed by Colonel Johnson. Such is erroneous. There is no doubt that he met his death by the hand of a private soldier by the name of King. . . .[21]

The sash has only been mentioned by a few others, but the ballistics – the small hole wound – points once again to a rifle over a pistol shot.

William Galt took timeout of his life one day in 1866 to affirm a previous article published in *The Historical Magazine* regarding Tecumseh's death. He tells us that his close friend Colin Spiller was at the battle and told him:

He walked over the field with a Kentuckian, a *red-headed* man; and I am very sure that he said that his name was King. As they went on, they came to three Indians lying dead. The Kentuckian remarked, "I killed that fellow," pointing to the Indian lying between the two others. King did not know who the savage was, and it was not until afterwards that he was identified as Tecumseh. The conversation was introduced by my own assertion that I believed that Col. Johnson had killed the Indian chief, as was then the general opinion, and M. Spiller gave me the above account to prove that I was mistaken.[22]

Lyman Draper notes information he learned from Thomas Shelby, the governor's son. Thomas relates that his father "said Gov. Harrison recognized Tecumseh; & both Gov. Shelby & his son Evan Shelby [aid to his father – also acting as a scout at the time] thought King killed Tecumseh."[23]

Draper received a further observation from Major James Whitaker. Draper's notes read:

The Indian killed there (Thames), & called Tecumseh, Mr. Whitaker measured – he was 5 feet 10 inches – looked like Tecumseh only shorter & smaller every way, & became satisfied he was not Tecumseh. This was the one whose thighs were skinned for razor strops. It was reported by the officers that Gen. Harrison said, "he first thought it was Tecumseh, but the body was too small – that it must have been a nephew of his, who much resembled him, though smaller in size." . . . One Thompson of Johnson's regiment said he thought he shot – dismounted – through the fork of a tree, with two balls, & shot the Indian [in question] in the left side. This Indian was shot in the left side, about an inch a half apart. One King of Davidson's company claimed to have shot him. But [Whitaker] thinks Col. Whitley quite as likely to have done it – Whitley was killed not more than ten or fifteen steps off from this Indian, with his head towards his foe in open ground, & his gun in his right hand empty, & his knife in his left arm, with the left side of his face on the ground.[24]

This account favors Whitley but mentions a potentially new slayer of Tecumseh, Major David Thompson. Thompson was second in command under Johnson. His name has appeared periodically in reports for his participation in the fight. Here, it appears that Major Whitaker must have heard Thompson make the claim as he described it.

Robert McAfee describes Thompson's part in the fight:

The enemy had fled from Colonel Johnson, and a scattering, running fire had commenced along the swamp in front of General Desha's division, between the retiring Indians and the mounted men in pursuit, who were now commanded by Major Thompson alone, Colonel Johnson having retired in consequence of his wounds. This firing in the swamp continued, with occasional remissions, for nearly half an hour, during which time the contest was gallantly maintained by Major Thompson and his men, who were still pressing forward on the Indians.[25]

Joseph Desha earlier supported this role of Thompson.

The Thompson family paraphrased some of the contents of David Thompson's diary (which is in a private collection and inaccessible for verification):

On the 20th of May 1813, [Thompson] started on a campaign in a mounted regiment commanded by Richard M. Johnson and on the 5th of Oct we fought the British and Indians on the banks of the river Thames, where he commanded the 2nd battalion. The engagement lasted one hour and forty minutes when the enemy, who were three to one in number, were completely routed and between five and six hundred of the

British were taken prisoners with large quantity of stores.

Major Thompson was the commanding officer who lead the charge against the Indians after Colonel Johnson had been wounded. There was fierce hand to hand fighting in the swamps where the American troops were obliged to dismount. Here Tecumseh was killed and the Indians routed.[26]

Although not cited from his diary, the Thompson family legend is that David did kill Tecumseh. They say he never sought the honor because he was a neighbor of Johnson in Georgetown, Kentucky, they were friends, and they were distant relatives through marriage.

We heard from Sam Theobold that a soldier named John Herndon had explained that one J. Harrod Holman was involved in the thick of the fight near Whitley. Theobold concluded that Holman had shot the Indian lying dead in front of Whitley, but *that* Indian was not Tecumseh. In the actual letter of Herndon we read:

> Harrod Holman and myself were close together and near the spot where Col. Whitley was lying dead, say 30 or 40 steps, and an Indian advanced on Whitley and was scalping him, when Holman leveled his gun and fired and killed the Indian who was scalping Whitley, and Holman ran and obtained the pistols of the Indian, which he kept until his death, and the British soldiers whom we had taken as prisoners told us that was Tecumseh whom Holman had killed, and it was understood and believed . . . that J. Harrod Holman was the man who killed Tecumseh.[27]

Nat Crain was a volunteer in Robert McAfee's company, fighting against the British lines at the Thames. Crain states that after the fight:

> We turned back and camped with our prisoners–about 600–about two miles from the battlefield, and it was here just after dark that we first learned that our other battalion, under Colonel Dick Johnson, had routed the Indians, and that Tecumseh was killed. We returned and buried our dead the next morning. I went over the Indian battleground and saw Tecumseh's dead body, then partly stripped of clothing, where he fell about forty yards from the edge of the swamp. He was wounded in three places, the fatal shot being in his right breast. It was reported that Dick Johnson killed him, but a comrade, John Lamb, and myself, who made a close examination of everything on the ground, thought that Brown, from

Stanford, Kentucky, who lay dead near Tecumseh, had killed him.[28]

Joshua Brown is on the roster of Captain Davidson's company.

Nancy Wright, whose somewhat confused account we discussed earlier, communicated further with Draper recalling her brother's memories of the Thames. She says:

> I had a brother with Colonel R. M. Johnson at the Thames. Col. Johnson got the credit of killing Tecumseh but he did not kill him, the one that killed Tecumseh was name[d] Alfred Pennington; he put two bullets in his gun just before he went into battle and the two bullets were found in Tecumseh's wound.

Apparently Whitley's trick of double balls in his rifle was not a secret, Alfred Pennington did likewise. Unfortunately, Mrs. Wright may have been a bit confused in her recollections as she continued, "I got this from history; but the rest from reliable sources . . ."[29]

Another testimony comes anonymously out of an Irish history book for a man named Mason. The account reads:

> Tecumseh was supposed to have fallen by the hands of Colonel Johnson, of Kentucky; but that veteran soldier has himself said, that all he could say was, when attacked by the chief, he fired, and when the smoke cleared away, the Indian lay dead before him. The popular account attributes the deadly aim and wound to one Mason, a native of the county of Wexford, Ireland . . .

A footnote in the history book tells, "In a contemporaneous view of the battle, he is represented as firing at Tecumseh, over Colonel Johnson's shoulder, with a rifle, while Johnson is discharging a pistol."[30]

In a quite robust account, *The Bourbon News* of Paris, Kentucky states a case for Mr. Jerry D. Lillard, who uncannily took down the chief in a fashion very similar to Mr. Mason. The article reads:

> The *Owen County Democrat* spoils history, after this fashion: For nearly a century there has been a controversy among historians as to who ended the life of the redoubtable Indian chieftain, Tecumseh. The death of Uncle Kimbo Thomas, on Cedar Creek, Owen county, developed the fact that Colonel J. D. Lillard of Owenton, sent the soul of the great Sachem to the happy hunting ground. Uncle Kimbo was a soldier in Col. Dick Johnson's regiment

in the battle of the Thames and he was wont to recount, rarely, however, the stirring scenes of that sanguinary conflict. Uncle Kimbo said that amidst the clash of arms, when foot to foot and hand to hand, the savage and the white man fought for life, he saw the noble Indian and Colonel Dick Johnson front each other. Johnson raised his pistol to fire, while the chieftain brandished aloft his deadly tomahawk. The flint-lock of Colonel Johnson flashed in the pan. Just behind the heroic Johnson stood Jerry D. Lillard, then a boy of fifteen, and ere the hatchet of the Indian sped from his hand a musket ball from Lillard's gun laid him dead upon the field.[31]

Hmmm.

The final account is fittingly anonymous in both author and story. In was published late in 1859 in the *Louisville Daily Journal*. It snuck in among the flurry of stories which appeared in that newspaper at that time testifying to Tecumseh's demise. This is the article in its entirety:

The Death of Tecumseh – A New View. As the question of Tecumseh's death is again upon the tapis, a gentleman of very distinguished intelligence has obligingly handed us the subjoined statement of the substance of an article from the *United Service Magazine* which he read many years ago:

Some 20 years since, there appeared in the *New York Albion* an article republished from the *United Service Magazine* purporting to be from the journal of an English officer.

This officer states that in 1813 he was attached to Tecumseh's spy corps; that on the day of the battle of the Thames, he with Tecumseh and others was grouped on the field, with no troops in sight, except a body of Canadian militia; that Tecumseh fell dead, shot; and that immediately his party left the ground, in consequence of the rumors that the Americans were advancing, leaving the body of their chief on the spot.

The narrator writes of the event as though he was ignorant that the mode in which Tecumseh met his death had ever been mooted. He infers that he met his death from an accidental shot fired from the body of Canadian militia before alluded to.

Whether or not a skillful collation of the British Officer's account, as thus succinctly stated, with the various attestations, theories, and speculations which we have recently laid before our readers will throw new light on this curious question, we leave to the determination of these who feel more interest in it than we can possibly do.[32]

CHAPTER 20

And the Slayer Is...

Thus fell Tecumseh.[1]

It's been quite an investigative ride. The testimonies surrounding the death of the great chief Tecumseh have been numerous, tedious, contradictory, ludicrous, obvious, and sometimes humorous. So what kind of conclusion can one come to? This debate has raged on and off for nearly two centuries and very few new facts have surfaced in the past one hundred. Even if they had, what impact would they have upon all the existing contradictions? And how could anyone's story be verified so long after the fact. It seems truly impossible to definitively prove that any one person killed Tecumseh.

Just for fun, let's first try to come to some small understanding of the facts and scenarios. Perhaps in doing so we can arrive at our own overall conclusion, or at least produce a conjecture.

Perhaps the best place to start is with the body identified as Tecumseh. Can we definitively determine whether or not this body was in truth the person known as Tecumseh? If we can decide this, it will affect the next conclusion which is based upon it. But even as we begin to re-hash this single point, it is easy for one to become stymied. There are so many pieces to this part of the puzzle alone, that one's synapses can begin to fire erratically.

Remember? We saw that many men identified one particular body, left on the battlefield, as Tecumseh's. This was the body that was scalped, skinned and/or mutilated in some fashion. While many accepted this body *as the one*, some other witnesses scoffed at the notion. They insisted that Tecumseh's was one of the other bodies in the area; one that was not skinned, or one that was dressed in a particularly different manner. We saw that some of these opinions were held firm by their owners, while others seemed to be more of a hunch. There were many

criteria available to each person in their attempts to determine whether
or not this was the actual Shawnee chief. Some men only used one or
two of them to make their cases, while others employed several.

Let's dig a little deeper. Keep in mind; we are still just trying to
determine if the body identified as Tecumseh's was indeed his. Only
one of the many criteria used by the witnesses to make this determination was Tecumseh's attire. Even this simple point is one of contention
because there were so many varied opinions. Many said that he was
dressed simply. Some, at least assumed, he was dressed as a chief. Both
of these are relative terms. Red leggings seemed ornate to one man,
yet simple to the next. Some considered fringe along the seams of any
buckskin garb to be elaborate, while others viewed it as usual. If one
cannot determine whether the assumptions are wrong in the first place,
how can a conclusion be reached?

We need to linger on this one facet, Tecumseh's dress, for a moment
because we will unfortunately see a trend that repeats itself in most of
the men's accounts – an uncanny number of contradictory observations
of the very same item or event.

We have already seen the testimonies, which describe Tecumseh's
attire on the day of his death, but a stroll through them in succession
will highlight the dilemma that they present. The reports have stated
that he: had no ornaments or arms; had ornate dress; was dressed like
a chief; had an ornate sash and arms; wore a sash; wore a belt; wore a
simple shirt and leggings; wore tanned buckskin, a frock, leggings and
moccasins; wore a buckskin coat; wore the finest buckskin with fringe;
wore buckskin with fringe on the arms and back; wore plain dress and
a fringed dark shirt; wore a hunting shirt; wore usual deerskin; wore
a blue surtout (frock) coat; wore blue leggings with a breech clout;
wore a deerskin coat and pantaloons; wore red speckled leggings and
a fringed hunting shirt; wore simple buckskin; wore beads and half
moons; wore a medal; wore a silver medal; did not wear a medal; wore
a turban; wore a cap of sorts; wore a plume; and, did not wear a plume.
Hmmm.

How can anyone come to a conclusion of what Tecumseh was wearing that day; let alone if the body left on the field and believed to be
Tecumseh fit any of those descriptions. Consider that we haven't even
talked about the other criteria, just as individually diverse as this one

is. These others include: Tecumseh's wounds and scars – and whether any particular observer identified them correctly; his face paint or lack thereof; his weapons and their allure or not; his state of undress – depending on when any said observer viewed the body; and whether or not he was skinned for souvenir razor strops, scalped, or otherwise mutilated. All of these points multiply upon themselves to such a ridiculous degree that it is seemingly impossible to come to a firm conclusion even on this one simple piece of the puzzle.

What makes this whole discussion almost absurd is that Tecumseh *may* have been carried off the battleground long before anyone identified the body that was left behind. For all that anyone knows, that body identified as Tecumseh could have been his brother-in-law, Wassakekabows – known as Stand Firm or Firm Fellow; or Kitchekemit – who Shaubena said was near him; or any other Pottawattomie, Ojibwa, Ottawa, Munsie, Delaware, Nanticoke, Sac, Musquake, Wyandot, Winnebago or Shawnee involved in the fight.

Several of the Indians who gave a testimony on how Tecumseh fell, made no mention of what became of his body afterwards. But, of those who did comment on what happened to his body, the vast majority says that it was removed from the battlefield. Two key witnesses, who should have had the best credentials for stating the truth, incredibly changed their stories over time. Anthony Shane and Shaubena each gave testimonies of Tecumseh being both left on the ground and being removed.

So, we are left not being able to confirm if the body left behind was Tecumseh's or not. Yet the position of this body was crucial in many accounts. Sometimes the body was directly across from Whitley, so many concluded that surely Whitley did it. Some said the body was where they saw Johnson engaged with the enemy, so surely Johnson killed him. Others said they saw or heard that David King had shot Tecumseh. Surely King killed him because the body fell near Whitley's and they knew that King was in Whitley's vicinity.

The type of wound suffered by Tecumseh was yet another key point of contention. Witnesses used it to determine in favor of their particular hero or against another. It is cumbersome, but a listing of the multiple wounds supposedly suffered by Tecumseh is just too intriguing to resist. How one body could be viewed by so many men, with each one observing something different from the other, would make a premier case-study of human behavior.

Here is a synopsis or what they reported. Tecumseh was killed: by a bullet; by two balls and buckshot; by only two balls; by only one rifle ball; by only one musket ball; by only one pistol ball; by only a small rifle ball; by a pistol ball and buckshot; by a tomahawk or saber; by a bayonet wielded by an American soldier; by a Frenchman's bayonet which pinned him to the ground; and by a shot to the head while struggling to be free from a soldier's bayonet stubbornly snagged in his clothing. The next logical step is to recall where the reports have claimed that the shot or blade landed. They state he was shot: from above (by a horseman); in the face; in the back; in the neck; in the head; in the breast; in the leg; in the hip; in the side; and of course, any combination of these locations.

A final blow to one's attempt to reason through these discrepancies is the fact that *if* the body was taken off, especially immediately, most of these descriptions of wounds are moot. The greater numbers of reports are indeed from men who viewed the body that was left on the battleground and identified as Tecumseh's. If the body was removed, then no one, except an eye-witness who was very close to Tecumseh at the moment of his death, could have observed the weapon used against him. No one, except a member of the group who removed Tecumseh from the battleground, could have known where on his body he was wounded. Of those who claim that Tecumseh was removed, we have seen that there are but a few who claim to have been that close to him or involved in removing him.

In spite of all these obstacles, the majority of the testimonies point toward one of three men to have done this deed. They are Richard M. Johnson, William Whitley, or David King. A re-cap of the accounts for each should tell us what little we can be absolutely sure of, and what has to be left to speculation.

Richard M. Johnson:

Yes, he road into the battle heading up the *Forlorn Hope*. Yes, he was severely wounded. Yes, he was either the only one, or one of the very few of the *Forlorn Hope*, to be left on horseback after the first fire of the Indians. Yes, his horse died of its wounds. Yes, he killed at least one

Indian. Yes, it is most probable that he killed his Indian with his pistol since he was armed with only pistols and his sword. The idea that he never fired a shot strikes of incredulity since he was positioned in the thickest of the fight. Yes, his pistols were most likely loaded with a ball and buckshot. These few facts are the only ones which can be verified by multiple sources to be certain.

Many points in support of Johnson fall into the category of plausible and probable, yet not provable. Here are some of them:

Did Johnson's Indian charge him with a tomahawk raised? It's very likely.

Did Johnson ride a white mare or grey mare? Even Johnson reported a different color depending on which speech one cites. Is there a reason for this? Possibly. A dun color horse, as Johnson's horse was at least once referred to, can appear white, albeit with a slight grey or cream hue. Considering it was viewed only briefly, in the heat of battle, and in a smoke filled woods; whether it was called white or grey may after all be another moot point. With this in mind, the Indian testimonies of an officer on a white horse *could* describe Johnson. But remember it was over time and some nudging from American stories that the officer astride the white horse was labeled as Johnson.

Did Johnson shoot his Indian while straddling his horse or from the ground while pinned beneath his fallen steed? It's impossible to say. Accounts cite both versions. It becomes important only when a witness refers to the angle of the shot found in the body left on the battlefield.

Did Johnson shoot his Indian in the head, breast or elsewhere? It cannot possibly matter. As we just reviewed, there are too many accounts for all sorts of locations of the wounds Tecumseh suffered. Cases have been made for Johnson because of a head wound on his Indian, as often as they have been made due to a breast wound. Johnson himself, most likely, could not have known for sure where his shot landed considering the dire wounded condition he was in as he fired.

Did Johnson leave the battlefield early? It seems very probable. The majority of the testimonies report that Johnson was seen leaving in some fashion shortly after the first firings. This point, however, is interwoven with several others: the length of the battle, the end of Tecumseh's voice being heard, and whether these two items are even related to each other. Many claimed that Tecumseh's voice was heard rallying his warriors for varying lengths of time. Some further state that when this voice ceased, the battle likewise ceased. A few accounts state that this occurred when Johnson killed his Indian. Others argue it was much later.

Did the claim to have killed Tecumseh hold political clout for Johnson? Do we really have to think very long about this one?

Did Johnson's political opponents try to discredit his, or at least his promoters', claim to this feat? Most assuredly, yes.

Did Johnson kill Tecumseh?

It is possible.

William Whitley:

Yes, he was a member of the charging *Forlorn Hope*. Yes, he was daring and likely to risk his life for a shot at an Indian or British soldier. Yes, he carried a rifle, not a musket. Yes, he was known to load his rifle with two balls. Yes, he was dressed with a three-cornered hat, a red sash beaded in white, his hunter's knife, his fine rifle, and his powder horn. Yes, he was killed early in the fight.

Several other assumptions can be deemed probable, but again, not provable. Keep in mind that very few men claim to have eye-witnessed Whitley firing his rifle at the Indians.

Did Whitley kill an Indian? It is most likely that he did, possibly more than one.

Was Whitley in the vicinity of Tecumseh? It is almost certain. Most accounts that mention this fact say that they were directly across from each other at a distance of as little as a few steps to many yards. Other reports allude to them being at least in close proximity to each other. This is, of course, if the body being cited were Tecumseh's.

Was Whitley's gun empty or loaded when found? It is impossible to say. Testimonies conflict, but favor it being found empty.

Did Whitley kill Tecumseh?

It is possible.

David King:

Yes, King served in Captain James Davidson's company as a private. Yes, Davidson's company was in the thick of the fight, coming up from behind and left of the *Forlorn Hope*. Yes, King was Davidson's nephew and only eighteen years of age. Yes, King had several eye-witnesses to his shooting the Indian later identified as Tecumseh. Yes, accounts for King say he fired a double ball shot. Yes, King's Indian was found killed by a double ball wound in his breast.

There are fewer details and hence fewer points of contention in the case for King, but two interesting observations can be made and left to consider.

One: of all the accounts, only two report something audible, rather than strictly visual, happening at the moment Tecumseh fell. They both state that the American aiming at Tecumseh shouted loud and clear enough for others to hear, as he fired his weapon. Shaubena stated that the white man, who he assumed was Johnson, fired his pistol and exclaimed, "You damned Indian!" While Captain James Davidson reported that when David King felled his Indian he shouted, "I killed one damned yaller booger!" These cries have a similar ring to them. Could there be a connection between these two reports? Could Shaubena actually have heard David King's exclamation, but attributed it to Johnson?

Two: Did King use Whitley's rifle as Davidson had stated? It's possible since his Indian was found with two balls in his breast; but yet, it's un-provable. Whitley was not the only man to use a double ball load. And, isn't it odd that no one who testified for Whitley said that his rifle was missing? They said it was either loaded or discharged. If King took his rifle, would he have put it back down next to the dead Whitley and continue to fight unarmed? The point gets more involved when one considers that Davidson claims King returned Whitley's rifle to his family. Other reports say that Whitley's close friend, John Preston, returned his rifle, his belongings, and even his dear horse, *Old Emperor*, to his widow, Esther.

Did David King kill Tecumseh?

It is possible.

We have a dozen or so accounts for other men who could have killed Tecumseh. Generally, they have been passed over for serious consideration by historians. And rightly so, most are obvious false claims. There is, however, something to be said for one of them – Major David Thompson. Some of the evidence is circumstantial and some is easily considered prejudiced; but it is conceivable that Thompson did this deed. Let's see if a legitimate case can be made for him.

Robert McAfee, the participant and trusted early chronicler of this event, left his conclusion open to any of the big three candidates. He never suggested Thompson had a part in Tecumseh's death, but he does, in due course of his history, recount the movement of the battle to the left and Major Thompson participation in that area of the fight. Thompson was second in command, taking charge of the regiment after Johnson was taken off. Joseph Desha, who was major-general in charge of a division of the Kentucky militia, is documented as verifying McAfee's account of Thompson's position and involvement. So, yes, Thompson was definitely in the thick of the fight for at least a half an hour–maybe longer–after Johnson had been taken off.

The only account for Thompson, which we have reviewed, came from a Major in the battle, James Whitaker, who reported to Draper what he had heard and concluded. He surmised that King, Whitley or Thompson could have killed the Indian identified as the chief. The problem with Whitaker's testimony is that he actually measured the dead body. Even though it was 5 foot, ten inches tall; he decided that was too small to be Tecumseh, which is contrary to most accounts which state Tecumseh was about that height. This identification snafu confuses the issue, because Thompson had told Whitaker that he thought he had shot at this Indian who he just measured.

Additional information comes from the family of David Thompson. As already cited, they had reason to believe that Thompson really did think he killed him, but that he had kept mum on the point because of his friendship and kinship to Johnson.

If the battle did not end until the rallying cries of Tecumseh were silenced, then Thompson was in position to have had a hand in the conclusion of the engagement. Some said that the voice, assumed to be Tecumseh's, was still being heard during this latter time of the fight.

Did David Thompson kill Tecumseh?

It is possible.

Now you may be thinking that this case for Thompson is presented on very little evidence. And so, why is it even suggested? The point of adding Thompson to the list of most likely slayers is to make yet a larger and hopefully obvious point. *Anyone* who had a desire to make a case for who killed Tecumseh could do so by simply picking and choosing what they deemed pertinent. They could hang their opinion on one single point or employ numerous details. Disproving can be as difficult as proving. Hence we have so many differing accounts of one event.

There is a final thought to keep in mind and that is the physical atmosphere of this fight. Bullets were flying everywhere that afternoon. The men on the front lines were at the very most the distance of a run from home plate to first base away from each other, sometimes only a few feet apart. They had to be this close because most of them were firing muskets which were inherently inaccurate and positively useless at further distances. Bayonets are referred to because the fight was often hand-to-hand. Smoke from all the shooting clouded their view and stung their eyes. Horses were reeling from the noise and confusion. Men were thrown from their horses, both usually wounded. The fighting continued over the dead and wounded bodies of fallen comrades and horses in a mostly swampy land already covered with the obstacles of fallen trees and brush. The men were in a life and death situation. The adrenalin was flowing. Can you hear the simultaneous din of the dozens of gun shots consistently popping all about, the shrieks of the horses, the shouts of the American soldiers, the war cries of the Indian warriors and the screams of the wounded and dying? In all this chaos, with certain attention to their individual precarious situation, could anyone have been expected to have accurately been following Tecumseh's every move?

We saw three accounts on this journey that seemed unreasonable at first glance, but they do warrant a final mention. An anonymous Canadian reported to Harrison, shortly after the battle, that Tecumseh was shot by a stray bullet from the Indians themselves. Hard to imagine, but we've heard a number of wild testimonies. Then, we reviewed the account of William Caldwell, who stated that Tecumseh was positioned at the rear of the British and Indian forces at the point where they met. Again, a random bullet from the guns of the aimlessly firing and retreating British regulars; caught Tecumseh in his breast. And finally, we heard from an anonymous British soldier's diary that the Canadian militia, anxious over the anticipated approach of the Americans, accidently fired and against all odds, inadvertently took down Tecumseh. As incredible as it seems, if any of these accounts are true, than even Tecumseh's participation in the Battle of the Thames is in question.

Is there anything that we can absolutely conclude about Tecumseh at the Battle of the Thames? Yes, he was killed.

Unfortunately, no particular actions of Tecumseh in the battle can definitively be assigned to him. The reports are too many and too varied.

It's not likely, it's not popular, and it certainly does not make for a good ending to a mystery, but there is only one question left to be asked: Was Tecumseh killed by a stray bullet, either before or during, the Battle of the Thames?

It is possible.

Epilogue

*Born in a Shawnee village in what is now Ohio, Tecumseh became
in the 1790s co-leader with his brother, the Prophet, of a movement to restore
and preserve traditional Indian values. He believed a union
of all the western tribes to drive back white settlement to be
the one hope for Indian survival and spread this idea
the length of the frontier. Seeing the Americans as the immediate
threat, he allied himself with the British in 1812, assisted
in the capture of Detroit and was killed near here
at the Battle of the Thames on 5 October 1813,
while retreating with General Proctor
from Amherstburg.* [1]

Tecumseh was a renowned personality. Many of his contemporaries have said that he was a noble, charismatic, fair, and wise leader; the likes of which are rarely seen through the generations. The superlative adjectives to describe him are endless. He was taken from this earth too soon, but he died the way he would have wanted to, as a warrior defending his people and his principles. By whose hand he fell, will never be known.

The Indian confederation was as strong as it would ever become by the autumn of 1813, but it died with Tecumseh. The British continued to fight the Americans until a peace treaty was signed early in 1815, but in the interim, they never regained superiority in the *Northwest*. The Americans continued to expand westward across the continent, but made no further attempts to occupy what is today Canada.

The so-called glory of having been the one to have killed Tecumseh was not sought after because it was considered to have been an act of good over evil. Tecumseh rallied against all forms of wickedness including immorality, cruelty and cowardice. Tecumseh was a stellar human being, not a vile monster. The glory of having killed him

Photo courtesy of the Kentucky Historical Society.

British drum from the Battle of the Thames.
Inscription reads: Drum taken at the battle of the THAMES, and presented to the
42nd REGIMENT MILITIA having turned out more volunteers during the late War
than any other REGIMENT in K.–H. Harrison.

would have come from one having defeated a polished, crafty and brazen warrior–the finest in his class.

There are but few surviving physical remnants of this *Battle of the Thames*. A lone British drum has been salvaged and stored at the *Kentucky Historical Society*. The rifle of William Whitley is still on display at his home in Crab Orchard, Kentucky. The pistols used by Richard Johnson were last reported on display in 1886 in the Capitol Hotel of Frankfort. Kentucky. Later they were said to be in the possession of the *Polytechnic Society* in Louisville, Kentucky. But when that institution transformed into the *Louisville Free Public Library* at the turn of the century (and still operating today), no records of the pistols ever surfaced. The British medal, which some claim was worn by Tecumseh in the battle, was reported to have been given to the *United States Mint* in Philadelphia in the 1880's, but has since been unaccounted for.

Still other people have claimed to be in possession of various artifacts from the battle including Tecumseh's tomahawk, his pipe, and his belt or sash. None of these claims are verifiable.

The final resting place of Tecumseh is as much of a mystery as the one we just explored of how he was killed. It is discussed in depth

*Grave of
Richard M. Johnson
in the Frankfort Cemetery,
Frankfort Kentucky.*

*The literal
de-facing of Johnson
astride his horse as he
slays—Tecumseh?*

Photos courtesy of the author.

by many other authors.

William Whitley was buried in an unmarked grave at the Thames battle site.

David King is assumed to be buried somewhere in Henry county, Tennessee.

Only Richard Johnson, because of the service he gave to his country all his life, has a prominent grave in the *Frankfort Cemetery* of Kentucky. One of the four sides of his monument bears a relief sculpture depicting him shooting an Indian assumed to be Tecumseh. It has been defaced, literally, for some time—Johnson's face has been chipped off of the scene. Why or by whom this was done is unknown. The marks are worn and smooth, leading one to believe it happened some time ago.

There was political antagonism toward Johnson's claim over the years; perhaps it was a result of those sentiments. During the Civil War era there was also a cultural phenomenon of people wanting to capture *a piece of the time* and Union soldiers were in particular known to have chipped away similarly at the monument over Daniel Boone's grave, just a few yards away. In fact Boone's monument was so ravaged that it had to be replaced years later. Perhaps it was done at this time with a positive motive.

On one of the four sides of Johnson's monument is an inscription which in part reads, "Distinguished by his valor, a Colonel of a Kentucky Regiment in the Battle of the Thames." No mention of his having killed Tecumseh is made.

Chapter Notes

Chapter 1 – The Death of Tecumseh

1. John Richardson, *Richardson's War of 1812, With Notes and a Life of the Author*, (Toronto, Historical Publishing Co., 1902) p. 212.

Chapter 2 – The Life of Tecumseh

1. Words of Tecumseh, per Lee Sulzman, *Shawnee History* website: http://www.tolatsga.org/shaw.html, (Accessed April, 2010).
2. John Johnston, *Recollections of 60 Years on the Ohio Frontier*, (John Henry Patterson, 1915), p.12. (Reprinted from *Cist's Miscellany*, Cincinnati, 1842).
3. John Sugden, *Tecumseh – A Life*, (New York, Henry Holt and Co., 1997), pgs. 23, 92, 415.
4. John Sugden, Article – *Tracking Tecumseh's Descendents*, in *The Hoosier Genealogist*, Vol. 42, No. 4., (per McKenney and Hall, *Indian Tribes of North America*, 1:78).
5. Henry Howe, *Historical Collections of Ohio*, (Greene County, 1888) Vol. I. The term "squaw" is presumably used by Mr. Galloway because it was an accepted term the white men used to identify a female Indian. In actuality, as used by the Indians, the term is derogatory. Directed at a female Indian, "squaw" would carry the insinuation that such a woman was "morally loose". The Indians would have used the appellation "maiden" in the way Mr. Galloway certainly intended.
6. Sugden, *Tecumseh*, p. 8. (per James Worthington to Benjamin Drake, 13 February 1840, *Frontier War Papers*, 5U174.)
7. A. J. Conner, Draper 8YY21.
8. Letter – Harrison to Secretary of War, from Vincennes, August 6, 1810, in Logan Esarey, *Governor Messages and Letters*, (Indianapolis, Indiana Historical Commission, 1922), p. 456.
9. Samuel G. Drake, *Indian Biography*, (Boston, Josiah Drake, 1832), pgs. 333-6.
10. Ibid., pgs. 336-7. (per Schoolcraft)
11. Thomas L. McKenney, *History of the Indian Tribes of America*, (Philadelphia, D. Rice & Co., 1872), Vol. 1, p. 64.
12. Alfred Pirtle, *The Battle of Tippecanoe*, (The Filson Club, 1909, p.v.) per R. T. Durrett in the Introduction.
13. Stephen Ruddell, Reminiscences of Tecumseh's Youth, Wisconsin Historical Society, Document No. AJ-155 – C.
14. John Bertrand, Interviewed by Alex A. Halls, Letter to Draper, Feb. 9, 1886. Draper 6YY111.
15. Letter – Tecumseh Holmes to Draper, Draper 7YY66.
16. B. F. H. Witherell, *Reminiscences of the Northwest*, (Wisconsin Historical Collections, 1857), Vol. 3, pgs. 315-7.

17. Johnston, *Recollections*, p. 12.

18. Letter–Stephen Johnston to Draper, 1880, Draper 11YY3.

19. *The Canadian Antiquarian and Numismatic Journal*, (Montreal, July, 1878), Vol. VII, No. 1.

20. Drake, *Indian Biography*, p. 337-8.

21. Edna Kenton, *Simon Kenton His Life and Period 1755-1836*, (Salem, NH, Ayer Company, Publishers, inc., 1989), pgs. 270-1., (Original Printing 1930).

22. Article–*Narrative of Spoon Decorah*, Reuben Gold Thwaites, ed., *Collections of the State Historical Society of Wisconsin*, (Madison, Wisconsin Historical Society, 1887), Vol. 3, pgs. 448-60.

23. Julia L. Dumont, *Tecumseh and other stories of the Ohio River Valley*, (Bowling Green, OH, Sandra Parker, ed., Bowling Green State University Popular Press, 2000), p. 38.

24. John Richardson, Tecumseh: *A Poem in Four Cantos*, (London, Canada: Canadian Poetry Press, 1992) Canto 4: XL –XLI.

25. Caleb Atwater, *A History of the State of Ohio, Natural and Civil*, (Cincinnati, Stereotyped by Glezen & Shephard, 1838) p. 237.

26. Howe, *Historical Collections of Ohio*, Vol. 1.

Chapter 3 – Independence Challenged

1. *Columbian Centinel*, (Boston, Saturday, June 27, 1812).

2. E.D.M. (writer) in *Cincinnati Daily Gazette*, May 23, 1873.

3. Letter–Van Rensselaer to Governor Tompkins, August 31, 1812, in Henry Adams, *The War of 1812*, (New York, Cooper Square Press, 1999), p. 28.

4. United States vs. Macedonian, 25 October, 1813, Per Website: http://www.historyofwar.org, (Accessed April, 2010).

Chapter 4 – The Call to Kentucky

1. Robert B. McAfee, *Book and Journal of Robert B. McAfee's Mounted Company*, May 19, 1813, in *Register of the Kentucky Historical Society*, The McAfee Papers, (Frankfort, KY., The Kentucky Historical Society, 1928), Issue 26, April, 1928, pgs. 4-5.

2. Letters to Secretary of War, op. cit. Packet 309 J, 1813, Johnson to Jackson, May 12, 1813, in Leland Meyer, *The Life and Times of Colonel Richard M. Johnson of Kentucky*, (New York, AMS Press, 1967), p. 105.

3. Henry Adams, *The War of 1812*, (New York, Cooper Square Press, 1999), p. 165.

4. Ibid., p. 163.

5. Henry Adams, *History of the United States of America during the Administrations of James Madison*, (New York, Viking Press, 1986), p. 593.

6. Meyer, *The Life and Times of Col. R. M. Johnson of Kentucky*, p. 97.

7. Garret Glenn Clift, *Remember the Raisin!* (Frankfort, Kentucky, Kentucky Historical Society, 1961) p. 90. (Originally in *Niles Weekly Register*, III,

February 20, 1813, 397).

8. Elias Darnall, *A Journal Containing an Accurate and Interesting Account of the Hardships, Sufferings, Battles, Defeat and Captivity, of Those Heroic Kentucky Volunteers and Regulars Commanded by General Winchester...*, (Paris, Kentucky, Joel R. Lyle, 1970), pgs. 52-4.

9. Letters to Secretary of War (MSS.), Packet 38 J, 1813, Old Records Division, War Department, Johnson to Armstrong, received February 23, 1813, in Meyer, *The Life and Times of Col. R. M. Johnson of Kentucky*, p. 101.

10. Letter–Armstrong to Johnson, February 26. 1813, in Kentucky Reporter, April 3, 1813, in Meyer, *The Life and Times of Col. R. M. Johnson of Kentucky*, p. 101.

11. Israel Harrington, "Recollections of Israel Harrington", in *Sandusky Whig*, April 18, May 9, 1840.

Chapter 5 – North to the Lake

1. Marching Order from Col. R, M, Johnson at Camp St. Mary's, June 4, 1813; in *Book and Journal of Robert B. McAfee's Mounted Company*, June 4, 1813; in *Register of the Kentucky Historical Society*, The McAfee Papers, (Frank fort, KY., The Kentucky Historical Society, 1928), Issue 26, April, 1928, p. 8.

2. Letter–Johnson to Harrison, May 23, 1813, in *Harrison, Messages and Papers*, Vol ii, p.459; in Leland Meyer, *The Life and Times of Colonel Richard M. Johnson of Kentucky*, (New York, AMS Press, 1967), p. 111.

3. Ibid., p. 113, Letter–Johnson to Armstrong, June 4, 1813; (originally in *Letters to Secretary of War*, Old Records Division, War Department, Packet 214 J, 1813.

4. Alfred Lorrain, *The Helm, the Sword and the Cross*, (Cincinnati, Poe & Hitchcock, 1862), p. 111.

5. Ibid., pgs. 120-1.

6. Ibid., pgs. 124-5.

7. Methodist Episcopal Church, *The Ladies Repository*, (Cincinnati, J. F. Wright and L. Swormstedt, 1845), March, pgs. 75-81.

8. Speech of Tecumseh, *Niles Register*, V, 174, Amherst berg, Sept. 18, 1813, in Esarey, *Messages and Letters of William Henry Harrison*, (New York: Arno Press, 1975), p. 542.

9. Letter–Leslie Combs to Lyman Draper, March 3, 1869, Draper 6YY21.

10. Interview–Russ Hatter with Author, Hatter is Assistant Curator of the Capital City Museum, Frankfort, KY. as of 2010.

11. Nelson W. Evans and Emmons B. Stivers, *A History of Adams County*, (West Union, Ohio, E.B. Stivers, 1900), p. 34.

12. Alfred Brunson, *A Western Pioneer: or Incidents of the Life and Times of Rev. Alfred Brunson, A.M., D.D.*, (Cincinnati, Hitchcock and Walden / New York, Carlton and Lanahan, 1872), p. 107.

13. Ibid., pgs. 107-8.

14. Ibid., p. 110.

15. Terrence Kirby, *The Life and Times and Wonderful Achievements of the Adventurous and Renowned Captain Kirby, The Hero of the War of 1812*, (Cincinnati, 1865), p. 6.

16. Ibid., pgs. 6-7.

17. Letter–Shelby to Harrison, March 27, 1813, in Esarey, *Messages and Letters of William Henry Harrison*, (New York: Arno Press, 1975), p. 398.

18. Lucy Eliot Keeler, *93rd Anniversary of the Battle of Fort Stephenson*, (Columbus, Ohio, Ohio State Archaeological and Historical Society, 1907), p. 76.

19. Letter–Shelby to Harrison, August 2, 1813, in Esarey, *Messages and Letters of William Henry Harrison*, (New York: Arno Press, 1975), p. 508.

20. Ibid., p. 394, Letter–Shelby to Harrison, March 20, 1813.

21. Ibid., pgs. 519-20, Letter–Shelby to Harrison, August 8, 1813.

22. Kirby, *The Life and Times and Wonderful Achievements...*, pgs. 7-8.

23. Letter–John Arrowsmith to Lyman Draper, March 1860, Draper BB10-13.

24. Brunson, *A Western Pioneer...*, p. 112.

25. Ibid., p. 112-3.

26. Keeler, *93rd Anniversary of the Battle of Fort Stephenson*, p. 84.

27. Brunson, *A Western Pioneer...*, p. 115-6.

28. Message–Harrison to Croghan, July 29, 1813, in Esarey, *Messages and Letters of William Henry Harrison*, p. 503.

29. Message–Croghan to Harrison, July 30, 1813, in Esarey, *Messages and Letters of William Henry Harrison*, p. 503.

30. John Richardson, *Richardson's War of 1812*, (Toronto, Toronto Historical Publishing Co., 1902), pgs. 245-6.

31. "But this chief's son, in 1862, raised a great war in Minnesota." in Brunson, *A Western Pioneer*, p. 118-20.

32. J. B. Patterson, *Black Hawk's Autobiography*, (Rock Island, IL, American Publishing, 1912), p. 40.

33. Letter–Harrison to Secretary of War, August 4, 1813, in Esarey, *Messages and Letters of William Henry Harrison*, p. 512.

34. Brunson, *A Western Pioneer*, p. 120.

35. Kirby, *The Life and Times and Wonderful Achievements...*, p. 10.

36. Keeler, *93rd Anniversary of the Battle of Fort Stephenson*, p. 76.

37. Ibid., p. 77.

38. Ibid., p. 80.

39. McAfee, *Register of the Kentucky Historical Society*, p. 15.

40. Ibid., p. 16.

41. Ibid., p. 22.

Chapter 6 – By Land and By Sea

1. William S. Dudley, *War of 1812: A Documentary History*, (Washington, D.C., Naval Historical Center, 1992), p. 553.

2. Report on October 5, 1813, in *The War* Newspaper, (New York, S. Woodworth & Co., 1813), p. 2.

3. Letter–Harrison to Secretary of War, August 22, 1813, in Esarey, *Messages and Letters of William Henry Harrison*, (New York: Arno Press, 1975), p. 525.

4. Terrence Kirby, *The Life and Times and Wonderful Achievements of the Adventurous and Renowned Captain Kirby, the Hero of the War of 1812*, (Cincinnati, 1865), p. 10.

5. Alfred Brunson, *A Western Pioneer or Incidents of the Life and Times of Rev. Alfred Brunson, A.M., D.D.*, (Cincinnati, Hitchcock and Walden, New York, Carlton and Lanahan, 1872), p. 120.

6. Esarey, *Messages and Letters of William Henry Harrison*, p. 525.

7. Samuel R. Brown, *Views on Lake Erie*, (Troy, N.Y., Francis Adancourt, 1814), pgs. 4-5.

8. G. Auchinleck, *A History of the War between Great Britain and the United States During the Years 1812, 1813 & 1814*, (Toronto, Maclear and Co., 1855), (republished in Toronto by Pendragon House Limited, 1972), p. 209-10.

9. Brown, *Views on Lake Erie*, p. 5.–Lawrence, here referred to, is the noted Capt. James Lawrence who just three months earlier gave his life while commanding the USS *Chesapeake* in a fight against the British frigate *Shannon*.

10. Ibid., p. 7.

11. Ibid., p. 8.

12. William F. Coffin, 1812; *The War and Its Moral: A Canadian Chronicle*, (Montreal, John Lovell, 1864), p. 214.

13. Brown, *Views on Lake Erie*, p. 10.

14. Ibid., p. 10.

15. Ibid., pgs. 8-11.

16. John McDonald, *Biographical Sketches of Nathaniel Massie, General Duncan McArthur, Captain William Wells and General Simon Kenton*, (Cincinnati, Morgan & Son, 1838), p. 132.

17. Ibid., p. 133.

18. Ibid., p. 132.

19. Brown, *Views on Lake Erie*, p. 45.

20. Letter–Harrison to Shelby, in Esarey, *Messages and Letters*, p. 539.

21. Ibid., p. 134.

22. Brunson, *A Western Pioneer*, pgs. 129-30.

23. Letter–Lieutenant-Colonel Matthew Elliott to Colonel Wm. Claus, Oct. 24, 1813, in E.A. Cruikshank, *Campaigns of 1812-14*, (Niagara, Ontario, Niagara Historical Society, 1902), No. 9, pgs. 40-1.

24. Speech of Tecumseh–*Niles Register*, V, 174, in Esarey, *Messages and Letters of William Henry Harrison*, p. 540.

25. John Richardson, *Richardson's War of 1812*, (Toronto, Historical Publishing Co., 1902), pgs. 206-7.

26. Auchinleck, *A History of the War*, p. 215.

27. Aura P. Stewart, *Recollections of Aura P. Stewart, of St. Clair County, of Things Relating to the Early settlement of Michigan*, article in Pioneer Society of the State of Michigan, ed., *Pioneer Collections*, (Lansing, The Society, 1874-6), Vol. IV, p. 326-7.

28. Robert B. McAfee, *Book and Journal of Robert B. McAfee's Mounted Com pany*, September 13, 1813, in *Register of the Kentucky Historical Society*, The McAfee Papers, (Frankfort, KY., The Kentucky Historical Society, 1928), Issue 26, April, 1928, pgs. 116-7.

Chapter 7 – Into Canada

1. Daniel Cushing, in Harlow Lindley, *Fort Meigs and the War of 1812*, (Columbus, Ohio Historical Society, 1975), p. 64.

2. Alfred Brunson, *A Western Pioneer: or Incidents in the Life and Times of Rev. Alfred Brunson, A.M., D.D.*, (Cincinnati, Hitchcock and Walden / New York, Carlton and Lanahan, 1872), p. 131.

3. Ibid., pgs. 131-2.

4. Lieutenant-Colonel Eleazar D. Wood ; annotated and indexed by Robert B. Boehm and Randall L. Buchman, *Journal of the Campaign of 1812-1813 under Major-General Wm. H. Harrison*, (Defiance, OH., The Defiance College Press, 1975), p. 31.

5. Brunson, *A Western Pioneer*, pg. 133.

6. Robert B. McAfee, *Book and Journal of Robert B. McAfee's Mounted Company*, September 25, 1813, in *Register of the Kentucky Historical Society*, The McAfee Papers, (Frankfort, KY., The Kentucky Historical Society, 1928), Issue 26, April, 1928, pg. 119.

7. Samuel R. Brown, *History of the Late War*, 1815 in: John MacDonald, *Biographical Sketches of General Nathaniel Massie, General Duncan McArthur, Captain William Wells, and General Simon Kenton*, (Cincinnati, E. Morgan and Son, 1838), pgs. 137-8.

8. Alfred Lorrain, *The Helm, the Sword and the Cross*, (Cincinnati, Poe & Hitchcock, 1862), pgs. 149-50.

9. Brunson, *A Western Pioneer*, pgs. 133-4.

10. Letter–Harrison to Armstrong, September 27, 1813, in Esarey, *Messages and Letters of William Henry Harrison*, (New York: Arno Press, 1975), pgs. 550-1.

11. Ibid., Letter–Harrison to Meigs, September 27, 1813, p. 550.

12. Ibid., Letter–Harrison to Armstrong, September 27, 1813, p. 551.

13. Ibid., Letter–Harrison to Armstrong, September 30, 1813, p. 555.

14. Terrence Kirby, *The Life and Times and Wonderful Achievements of the Adventurous and Renowned Captain Kirby, The Hero of the War of 1812*, (Cincinnati, 1865), p. 13.

15. Lorrain, *The Helm, the Sword and the Cross*, pgs. 150-1.

16. Brunson, *A Western Pioneer*, p. 135.

17. Samuel R. Brown, *History of the Late War*, 1815, in John MacDonald, *Biographical Sketches*, p. 140.

18. Lorrain, *The Helm, the Sword and the Cross*, pgs. 152-3.
19. Samuel R. Brown, *History of the Late War*, 1815, in John MacDonald, *Biographical Sketches*, pgs. 140-1.
20. Robert B. McAfee, *Book and Journal of Robert B. McAfee's Mounted Company*, October 2, 1813, in *Register of the Kentucky Historical Society*, pg. 122.
21. Procter Report of October 23, 1813, in Henry Adams, *The War of 1812*, (New York, Cooper Square Press, 1999), pgs. 71-2.
22. Letter–Lieut.-Colonel Matthew Elliott to Colonel Wm. Claus, October 24, 1813, in Colonel E. Cruikshank, *Campaigns of 1812-14*, (Niagara, Niagara Historical Society, 1902), No. 9, p. 41.
23. Aura P. Stewart, *Recollections of Aura P. Stewart, of St. Clair County, of Things Relating to the Early Settlement of Michigan*, in Pioneer Collections, *Report of the Pioneer Society of the State of Michigan*, (Lansing, MI., Pioneer Society of the State of Michigan, 1900-8), p. 329.
24. Ibid.
25. Brunson, *A Western Pioneer*, p. 136.
26. Letter–Harrison to Armstrong, October 9, 1813, in Esarey, *Messages and Letters of William Henry Harrison*, p. 559.
27. Letter–James Johnson to Editor, Oct. 12, 1813, published in *Missouri Gazette*, Nov. 6, 1813.
28. Letter–Lieut.-Colonel Matthew Elliott to Colonel Wm. Claus, October 24, 1813, in Cruikshank, *Campaigns of 1812-14*, p. 41.
29. Letter–Harrison to Armstrong, October 9, 1813, in Esarey, *Messages and Letters of William Henry Harrison*, p. 559.
30. Aura P. Stewart, *Recollections*, in Pioneer Collections, *Report of the Pioneer Society*, p. 330.
31. James Bentley, Draper 17S179.
32. Ibid., 17S180.
33. Col. Bennett H. Young, *The Battle of the Thames*, (Louisville, KY., John P. Morton and Co.–Printers to the Filson Club, 1903), pgs. 118-9.
34. Esther Whitley Burch, *Speech to Logan-Whitley Chapter of DAR*, at Stanford, KY, January, 1943.
35. Benson J. Lossing, *The Pictorial Fieldbook of the War of 1812*, (New York, Harper & Brothers Publishers, 1869), pg. 550.
36. Robert B. McAfee, *Book and Journal of Robert B. McAfee's Mounted Company*, October 4, 1813, in *Register of the Kentucky Historical Society*, pg. 124.
37. Letter–Samuel Boone to Draper, Draper 22S266.
38. Letter–Major James S. Whitaker to Draper, Draper 18S141-2.
39. Robert B. McAfee, *Book and Journal of Robert B. McAfee's Mounted Company*, October 4, 1813, in *Register of the Kentucky Historical Society*, pg. 124.
40. Ibid., pg. 125.
41. Letter–Tecumseh Holmes to Draper, Draper 7YY66.

Chapter 8 – Battle Lines Are Drawn

1. Robert B. McAfee in *Book and Journal of Robert B. McAfee's Mounted Company*, October 5, 1813, in *Register of the Kentucky Historical Society*, The McAfee Papers, (Frankfort, KY., The Kentucky Historical Society, 1928), Issue 26, April, 1928, pg. 128.
2. Ibid., pg. 125.
3. Letter–Tecumseh Holmes to Draper, Draper 7YY66.
4. Letter–Captain James Davidson to Editor, *The Louisville Daily Journal*, October 22, 1859.
5. Letter–Lieut.-Colonel Matthew Elliott to Colonel Wm. Claus, October 24, 1813, in Colonel E. Cruikshank, *Campaigns of 1812-14*, (Niagara, Niagara Historical Society, 1902), No. 9, p. 41.
6. Col. Wm. Stanley Hatch, *A Chapter of the History of the War of 1812*, (Cincinnati, Miami Printing and Publishing Co., 1872), pgs. 121-2.
7. Letter–Lieutenant Richard Bullock to Major Richard Friend, Dec. 6, 1813, in Carl F. Klink, *Tecumseh, Fact and Fiction in Early Records*, (Englewood Cliffs, NJ, Prentice-Hall Inc., 1961), pgs. 191-2.
8. John Richardson, *Richardson's War of 1812*, originally published 1842, (Toronto, Historical Publishing Co., 1902), p. 208.
9. William Caldwell to Draper, Draper 17S221.
10. Letter–Lieutenant Richard Bullock to Major Richard Friend, Dec. 6, 1813, in Klink, *Tecumseh*, p. 192.
11. Ibid.
12. Richardson, *Richardson's War of 1812*, p. 209.
13. William Caldwell to Draper, Draper 17S221.
14. Ibid.
15. Richardson, *Richardson's War of 1812*, p. 212.
16. William F. Coffin, *1812; The War, and Its Moral: A Canadian Chronicle*, (Montreal, John Lovell, 1864), p. 228.
17. Letter–Maj. Gen. Procter to Maj. Gen. De Rottenburg, October 23, 1813, in *The Quarterly Bulletin of The Historical Society of Northwestern Ohio*, (Toledo, The Blade Printing & Paper Co., October, 1930), Vol. 2, No. 4.
18. Richardson, *Richardson's War of 1812*, pgs. 227-8.
19. Letter–Harrison to Armstrong, October 9, 1813, in Esarey, *Messages and Letters of William Henry Harrison*, (New York: Arno Press, 1975), pgs. 560-1.
20. Ibid., p. 561.
21. Col. James Johnson in *Missouri Gazette*, Nov. 6, 1813.
22. Letter–Harrison to Armstrong, October 9, 1813, in Esarey, *Messages*, pgs. 561-2.
23. Letter–Robert McAfee to Editor, *The Kentucky Gazette*, Jan. 6, 1817.
24. Samuel Brown, *History of the Late War*, (1815), in John McDonald, *Biographical Sketches of Gen. Nathaniel Massie, Gen. Duncan McArthur, Capt. William Wells and Gen. Simon Kenton*, (Cincinnati, E. Morgan and Son, 1838), pgs. 144-5.

25. Letter–Robert McAfee to Editor, *The Kentucky Gazette*, Jan. 6, 1817.

26. Alfred Brunson, *A Western Pioneer: or Incidents in the Life and Times of Rev. Alfred Brunson, A.M., D.D.*, (Cincinnati, Hitchcock and Walden / New York, Carlton and Lanahan, 1872), p. 139.

27. Benson J. Lossing, *The Pictorial Fieldbook of the War of 1812*, (New York, Harper & Brothers, Publishers, 1869), pgs. 551-2.

28. Letter–Dr. Samuel Theobold to Ben J. Lossing, Jan. 16, 1861, Draper 7YY33.

29. Letter–Harrison to Armstrong, October 9, 1813, in Esarey, *Messages*, p. 562.

30. Letter–Robert McAfee to Editor, *The Kentucky Gazette*, Jan. 6, 1817.

Chapter 9 – The Battle of the Thames

1. Harrison's Order to Col. James Johnson, in Letter of Robert B. McAfee to the Editor, *The Kentucky Gazette*, Jan. 6, 1817.

2. Robert McAfee, *History of the Late War*, (Original: Lexington, KY., 1816), (Bowling Green, OH., Bowling Green, Ohio Historical Publications Co., 1919), p. 422.

3. Samuel Brown, *History of the Late War*, (1815), in John McDonald, *Biographical Sketches of Gen. Nathaniel Massie, Gen. Duncan McArthur, Capt. William Wells & Gen. Simon Kenton*, (Cincinnati, E. Morgan & Son, 1838), pgs. 145-6.

4. Letter–James Johnson to Editor, Oct. 12, 1813, published in *Missouri Gazette*, Nov. 6, 1813.

5. Speech of Richard Johnson, Lafayette, KY, Oct. 17, 1840, in William Galloway, *Old Chillicothe*, (Xenia, OH, The Buckeye Press, 1934), p. 156.

6. Robert B. McAfee in *Book and Journal of Robert B. McAfee's Mounted Company*, September 25, 1813, in *Register of the Kentucky Historical Society*, The McAfee Papers, (Frankfort, KY., The Kentucky Historical Society, 1928), Issue 26, April, 1928, pgs. 127-8.

7. McAfee, *History of the Late War*, p. 425.

8. John Richardson, *Richardson's War of 1812*, (Toronto, Historical Publishing Co., 1902), p. 209.

9. Lyman Draper, *Biographical Field Notes, in The Historical Society of North western Ohio*, Oct. 1933, Bulletin No. 4, Vol. 5.

10. Letter–Captain Hall to Colonel Harvey in *Michigan Pioneer & Historical Collections, Campaign of 1813*, (Lansing, MI, The Society, 1890), Volume 15, p. 376.

11. Letter–Maj. Gen. Procter to Maj. Gen. De Rottenburg, October 23, 1813, in *The Quarterly Bulletin of The Historical Society of Northwestern Ohio*, (Toledo, The Blade Printing & Paper Co., October, 1930), Vol. 2, No. 4.

12. Speech of Richard Johnson, William Galloway, *Old Chillicothe*, (Xenia, OH., Buckeye Press, 19340, p. 157.

13. Letter–Samuel Theobold to Benjamin Lossing, Jan. 16, 1861, Draper 7YY33-7YY43.

Chapter 10 – Nothing but the Facts

1. Col. William Stanley Hatch, *A Chapter in the History of the War of 1812*, (Cincinnati, Miami Printing and Publishing Co., 1872), p. 156.
2. Robert B. McAfee in *Book and Journal of Robert B. McAfee's Mounted Company*, October 5, 1813, in *Register of the Kentucky Historical Society*, The McAfee Papers, (Frankfort, KY., The Kentucky Historical Society, 1928), Issue 26, April, 1928, p. 128.
3. Robert McAfee, *History of the Late War*, (Original: Lexington, KY., 1816), (Bowling Green, OH., Bowling Green, Ohio Historical Publications Co., 1919) pgs. 423-4.
4. Ibid.

Chapter 11 – History's Perspective

1. Quote from Richard Emmons poem, (Originally in *Argus of Western America*, August 4, 1824), in Leland W. Meyer, *The Life and Times of Co. Richard M. Johnson of KY*, (New York, Columbia University Press, 1932) p. 316. (Originally in *Argus of Western America*, August 4, 1824.)
2. *Kentucky Gazette*, October 19, 1813.
3. Ibid.
4. Letter–Maj. Gen. Procter to Maj. Gen. De Rottenburg, October 23, 1813, in *The Historical Society of Northwestern Ohio Quarterly Bulletin*, (Toledo, OH, The Blade Printing and Paper Co., October, 1930), Vol. 2., No. 4.
5. *Ohio Republican*, October 25, 1813.
6. *Kentucky Gazette*, October 26, 1813.
7. *Missouri Gazette*, November 6, 1813.
8. Letter–Lewis Cass to John Armstrong, October 28, 1813, in *Michigan Pioneer and Historical Collections*, Vol. 40, 1929, pg. 542.
9. *Missouri Gazette*, November 20, 1813.
10. Leland W. Meyer, *The Life and Times of Co. Richard M. Johnson of KY*, (New York, Columbia University Press, 1932) pgs. 315-6. (Quotes originally in *Argus of Western America*, August 4, 1824).
11. Julian Hawthorn, *History of the United States From 1492 to 1910*, (New York, P. F. Collier & Son, 1899), Vol. II, p. 724.
12. G. A. Aynge, *The Death of Tecumseceh; and Political Fragments on Various Subjects*, (Dartmouth, R. Cranford, 1821), Preface.
13. Political broadside from the 1840 U.S. presidential campaign.
14. B. Woodbury, *Battle of the Thames*, (Boston, Martin & Reals, 1848).

Chapter 12 – The Forlorn Hope Testifies

1. Letter–Samuel Theobold to Editor, *Kentucky Gazette*, December 9, 1816.
2. Ibid.
3. Letter–Samuel Theobold to Benson Lossing, 1861, Draper 7YY33-43.
4. Ibid.

5. Letter–Theobold, *Kentucky Gazette*, December 9, 1816.
6. Letter–Theobold, Draper 7YY33-43.
7. Ibid.
8. Letter–Harrison to Tipton, May 2, 1834, in Esarey, *Messages and Letters of William Henry Harrison*, (New York, Arno Press, 1975), p. 754.
9. Ibid., pgs. 749-53.
10. Ibid.
11. Ibid.
12. Ibid.
13. Ibid.
14. Letter–Abraham H. Edwards to John Wentworth, June 10, 1881, in John Wentworth, *Early Chicago: Fort Dearborn: An Address*, p. 58.
15. William Emmons, *Authentic Biography of Col. Richard M. Johnson of Kentucky*, (Boston, Published for the Proprietor, 1834), pgs. 37-8.
16. Benjamin Drake, *Life of Tecumseh and of his brother The Prophet with a Historical Sketch of the Shawanoe Indians*, (Cincinnati, Anderson, Gates and Wright, 1858), p. 69.
17. Letter–Charles Wickliffe to Editor, *Bardstown Gazette*, 1859.
18. James Coleman in *Kentucky Gazette*, January 6, 1817.
19. Article in *Washington Post*, December 16, 1900.
20. Drake, *Life of Tecumseh*, p. 69.
21. Draper 2YY57.
22. Letter–William Gaines to Draper, Draper 7YY71.
23. Lyman Draper, *How Tecumseh Was Killed*, in *The Historical Magazine*, May, 1864, Vol. VIII, No. 5, p. 183-4.
24. Mann Butler, *A History of the Commonwealth of Kentucky*, (Cincinnati, J. A. James and Co., 1836), pgs. 547-8.
25. *Kentucky Gazette*, December 9, 1816.
26. Ibid.
27. Statement by R. I. Spurr of *Events of the Battle of the Thames 1813*, October 2, 1895, Courtesy of The William Whitley State Historic Site.
28. Spurr, *Events*.

Chapter 13 – Two Key Testimonies

1. Letter–Captain James Davidson to Editor, *Louisville Daily Journal*, (Written October 27, 1859, Published November 3, 1859).
2. Robert B. McAfee, *Book and Journal of Robert B. McAfee's Mounted Company*, October 4, 1813, in *Register of the Kentucky Historical Society*, pg. 128.
3. Robert B. McAfee, *History of the Late War in the Western Country*, (Originally published in 1816), (Bowling Green, Ohio, Historical Publications Co., C. S. Van Tassel, 1919), p. 426.
4. Ibid.
5. Letter–Robert McAfee to Editor, *Kentucky Gazette*, January 6, 1817.

6. Ibid.
7. Article in *The Commentator*, December 6, 1831, (Hand-copied notes of C.S.Todd, April 21, 1836, Draper 7YY141).
8. Ibid.
9. *Who Killed Tecumseh?* Extract of article originally in *Louisville Daily Journal*, November 3, 1859, (*Historical Magazine*, July, 1866), Vol. X, No. 7, pgs. 205-6.
10. Letter–Samuel Theobold to Editor, *Kentucky Gazette*, December 9, 1816.
11. Letter–Leslie Combs to Draper, March 3, 1869, Draper 6YY21.
12. Draper 18S141-3.
13. Article in *The Commentator*, Draper 7YY141.
14. Letter–Captain James Davidson to Editor, *Louisville Daily Journal*, November 3, 1859.
15. Article in *The Commentator*, Draper 7YY141.
16. Letter–Captain James Davidson to Editor, *Louisville Daily Journal*, November 3, 1859.
17. Ibid.

Chapter 14 – I Knew Tecumseh When

1. *Who Killed Tecumseh?*, C.H.Jackson in *Cincinnati Daily Gazette*, May 29, 1873.
2. Letter–Charles Wickliffe to Editor, *Bardstown Gazette*, November 25, 1859. (In *Register of the Kentucky Historical Society*, 1962, Vol. 60).
3. Ibid.
4. Ibid.
5. Edna Kenton, *Simon Kenton His Life and Period*, (Originally published in Garden City, NY, The Country Life Press, 1930), (Salem, NH, Ayer Co. Publishers, Inc., 1989), p. 284.
6. Ibid.
7. Ibid., pgs. 284-5.
8. Ibid., p. 285.
9. Letter–Samuel Baker to Draper, 185_, Draper 5BB46.
10. Draper 8S46-7.
11. Draper 8YY21.
12. Ibid.
13. Letter–F.M.Finch to Draper, June 8, 1891, Draper 8YY18.
14. H.S.Knapp, *History of the Maumee Valley*, (Toledo, Ohio, Blade Mammoth Printing and Publishing House, 1872), pgs. 202-3.
15. May Stocking Knaggs, *Memoir of James Knaggs of Monroe*, in *Michigan Pioneer & Historical Collections*, Vol. 17, 1890, p. 223.
16. Talcott E. Wing, *History of Monroe County, Michigan*, (1881), in *Report of the Pioneer Society of the State of Michigan*, (Lansing, Wynkoop, Hallenbeck, Crawford Co., State Printers, 1906), p. 323.
17. Biographical Field Notes of Dr. Lyman C. Draper, in *The Historical Society*

of Northwestern Ohio, Bulletin No. 4, Vol. 5, October, 1933.
18. Ibid.
19. Ibid.
20. *Recollections of a Pioneer*, in Toledo Blade, June 11, 1872.
21. B.J.Griswold, *The Pictorial History of Fort Wayne, Indiana*, (Chicago, Robert O. Law Co., 1917) p. 222.
22. Letter–Tecumseh K. Holmes to Draper, April 20, 1882, Draper 7YY67.
23. Letter–Tecumseh K. Holmes to Draper, May 4, 1882, Draper 7YY129.
24. Article in *Chatham Weekly Planet*, September 6, 1883, in Guy St. Denis, *Tecumseh's Bones*, (Montreal, McGill-Queen's University Press, 2005), pgs. 48-9.
25. Letter–Ben Warfield to C.S.Todd, November 27, 1840, Draper 2YY199.
26. Draper 5S80.
27. Draper 5S85.
28. Letter–Samuel Boone to Draper, Draper 22S266.
29. Interview–Samuel Baker, *Cincinnati Daily Gazette*, May 29, 1873.
30. Ibid.
31. Interview–Samuel Baker, *Cincinnati Daily Gazette*, July 27, 1886.
32. Ibid.
33. Aura P. Stewart, *Recollections of Aura P. Stewart of St. Clair County, in History of Monroe County, Michigan*, in *Report of the Pioneer Society of the State of Michigan*, (Lansing, MI., Wynkoop, Hallenbeck, Crawford Co., State Printers, 1906), p. 331.
34. Ibid.
35. Statement of General George Sanderson of Lancaster, OH, April, 1870, in *Memoranda and Notes by the late Alfred T. Goodman* in *Western Reserve and Northern Ohio Historical Society*, Tract No. 36, January, 1877, pg. 2.

Chapter 15 – Shaubena At His Side

1. Originally in *Niles Register*, August 30, 1839, in Draper 7YY56.
2. John T. Kingston, *Death of Tecumseh*, in *Wisconsin Historical Collections*, Draper 7YY14.
3. Thomas L. McKenney, *Memoirs, Official and Personal*, (Lincoln, NE., University of Nebraska Press, 1973), pgs. 181-2.
4. Ibid., pgs. 182-3.
5. Letter–Perry A. Armstrong to Draper, December 23, 1881. Draper 9YY71.
6. Ibid.
7. N. Matson, *Memories of Shaubena*, (Chicago, Donnelley, Gassette & Loyd, Printers, 1880), pgs. 27-8.
8. N. Matson, *Sketch of Shaubena, Pottawattomie Chief*, in *Collections of the State Historical Society of Wisconsin*, (Madison, State Historical Society of Wisconsin, 1908), Vol. 7. Pgs. 418-9.
9. Lecture–John Wentworth, *Wentworth's Early Chicago*, Draper 7YY44.
10. *The Life and Death of Shabbona*, (originally in *Ottawa Free Trader*, July 23,

1859), in *Journal of the Illinois State Historical Society*, Vol 31, No. 3, September, 1938. p. 345.

11. Letter–Robert Anderson to Benjamin Drake, November 8, 1839, in *The Pennsylvania Magazine of History and Biography*, Vol. XLI, No. 2, 1917.

12. Albert G. Brackett, *History of the United States Cavalry*, (New York, Greenwood Press Publishers, 1968), p. 26. (originally published by Harper & Bros., 1865).

13. John Sugden, *Tecumseh's Last Stand*, (Norman, OK., University of Oklahoma Press, 1985), p. 162.

14. Letter–Forsyth to Edwards, March 31, 1816, in *Thomas Forsyth, Letter-book of Thomas Forsyth–1814-1818* in *State Historical Society of Wisconsin Collections*, (Madison, 1888), Vol. 11, pgs. 346-7.

15. Letter–Forsyth to Draper, Draper 8YY56.

16. Draper 22S99.

17. Draper 21S278.

18. Draper 7YY56.

19. Letter–D.K.Foster to Lyman Draper, December 9, 1884, Draper 7YY19.

20. Letter–D.K.Foster to Lyman Draper, December 30, 1884, Draper 7YY20.

21. Draper 23S185.

22. Letter–John E. Hunt to C.C.Trowbridge, March 13, 1876, Draper 5YY7.

23. Letter–W. Hickling to Lyman Draper, September 1, 1875, Draper 9YY109.

24. Letter–Gordon Hubbard to Lyman Draper, September 4, 1875, Draper 9YY104.

Chapter 16 – They Knew Him Best

1. Andrew J. Blackbird, *History of the Ottawa and Chippewa Indians of Michigan*, (Ypsilanti, MI., The Ypsilanti Job Printing House, 1887), p. 23.

2. Draper 8YY10.

3. Alfred Brunson, *A Western Pioneer*, (Cincinnati, Hitchcock and Walden, New York, Carlton and Lanahan, 1872), pgs. 140-1.

4. Ibid., p. 142.

5. Ibid., p. 143.

6. Ibid.

7. Draper 17S220.

8. Ibid.

9. Letter of Forsyth, Draper 8YY56.

10. Letter–Anonymous, April 17, 1874, Draper, 9YY27.

11. Draper 22S51.

12. Letter–G.C.Johnston to Draper, July 28, 1874, Draper 11YY2.

13. Letter–C.C.Trowbridge to Draper, March 14, 1874, Draper 5YY6.

14. A.H.Edwards correspondence to John Wentworth originally in *Early Chicago–Fort Dearborn–An Address*, p. 58, Draper 7YY10.

15. B.F.Witherell, *Reminiscences of the Northwest*, (State Historical Society of Wisconsin, 1857), Vol. 3, pgs. 310-11.

16. John Sugden, *Tecumseh's Last Stand*, (Norman, OK., University of Oklahoma Press, 1985), p. 100.

17. William B. Allen, *A History of Kentucky*, (Louisville, KY., Bradley & Gilbert, Publishers, 1872), p. 324.

18. *Louisville Times*, October 26, 1893.

19. Letter–Andrew Jamieson to Draper, March 13, 1882, Draper 7YY65.

20. Major John Richardson, *Tecumseh and Richardson The Story of a Trip to Walpole Island and Port Sarnia*, (Toronto, Ontario Book Co., 1924), pgs. 52-3.

21. Ibid., p. 53.

22. Peter Dooyentate Clarke, *Origin and Traditional History of the Wyandots*, (Toronto, Hunter, Rose & Co., 1870), p. 113.

23. Carl F. Klink and James J. Talman, *The Journal of Major John Norton 1816*, (Toronto, The Champlain Society, 1970), p. 343.

24. Blackbird, *History of the Ottawa and Chippewa Indians of Michigan*, p. 23.

25. Letter–John Askin to Louis Grignon, December, 1813, in *Lawe and Grignon Papers*, 1794-1821, in *State Historical Society of Wisconsin Report and Collections*, (Madison, State Historical Society of Wisconsin, 1888), Vol. 10, p. 99.

26. Col. William Stanley Hatch, *A Chapter of the History of the War of 1812*, (Cincinnati, Miami Printing and Publishing Co., 1872), pgs. 155-6.

27. Article from "W" titled *Black Hawk–Tecumseh*, in *Baltimore American*, October 31, 1838.

28. Letter–J.D. Butler to Draper in 1880s. Draper 7YY79.

29. Black Hawk, *Black Hawk an Autobiography*, originally published in 1833, (Champaign, IL., University of Illinois Press, 1990) p. 68.

30. Reuben Gold Thwaites, *The Story of the Black Hawk War*, (Madison, WI., State Historical Society of Wisconsin, 1892), p. 6.

31. Perry A. Armstrong, *The Sauks and the Black Hawk War*, (Springfield, IL., H.W. Rokker, Printer and Binder, 1887), pgs. 524-5.

32. Henry Schoolcraft, *Personal Memoirs of a Residence of Thirty Years with the Indian Tribes on the American Frontiers*, (Philadelphia, Lippincott, Grambo and Co., 1851), pg. 613.

33. Caleb Atwater, *History of the State of Ohio, Natural and Civil*, (Cincinnati, Glezen & Shepard, 1838), p. 236.

34. Caleb Atwater, *Remarks Made on a Tour to Prairie du Chien; thence to Washington City in 1829*, (Columbus, OH., Isaac N. Whiting, 1831), p. 119.

35. A.D.P. Van Buren, *Noonday, the Ottawa Chief, He was in the Battle of the Thames, and Sees Col. R, M. Johnson Shoot Tecumseh, Whom He Carries Off the Battlefield*, in *Michigan Pioneer Collections*, 1888, Vol. 10, pgs. 159-60.

36. William A. Galloway, *Old Chillicothe*, (Xenia, OH, The Buckeye Press, 1934), pgs. 152-3.

Chapter 17 – Colonel Johnson Says...

1. Reception and Speech of Col. R.M. Johnson at Springfield, IL, May 19, 1843,

in *Journal of the Illinois State Historical Society*, (Springfield, IL., Illinois State Historical Society, July, 1920), Vol. 13, No. 2, p. 205.

2. Article in *Frankfort Roundabout*, June 29, 1901.
3. Ibid.
4. Leland W. Meyer, *The Life and Times of Colonel Richard M. Johnson of Kentucky*, (New York, AMS Press, 1967), p. 126.
5. Lyman Draper in H.S.Knapp, *History of the Maumee Valley*, (Toledo, Blade Mammoth Printing and Publishing House, 1872), p. 203.
6. Johnson Speech at Lafayette, IN, October 17, 1840, in *Lexington Intelligencer*, November 27, 1840. Courtesy Filson Historical Society.
7. Speech of Johnson in Oswego, New York in 1843, Courtesy Filson Historical Society.
8. Reception of Col. R.M.Johnson at Springfield, May 19, 1843, in *Journal of the Illinois State Historical Society*, (Springfield, IL., Illinois State Historical Society, July 1920), Vol. 13, No. 2, pgs. 204-5.
9. Draper 7YY63.
10. Letter of John. T. Viley, Circa 1898, Courtesy Filson Historical Society.
11. Letter of R.B.Duncan, Draper 8YY27.
12. Benjamin B. Griswold, *The Death of Tecumseh*, in *The Century Magazine*, January, 1885, Vol. XXIX, No. 3, p. 477.
13. Letter–Alfred Brunson to Draper, May 8, 1882. Draper 7YY11.
14. Ibid.

Chapter 18 – More Evidence For and Against Johnson

1. Article originally in *Mobile Register*, in Joseph Sullivant, *A Geneology and Family Memorial*, (Columbus, OH, Ohio State Journal Book and Job Rooms, 1874), p. 316-7.
2. Samuel R. Brown, *Views on Lake Erie*, (Troy, NY., Francis Adancourt, 1814), pgs. 61-2.
3. Letter–Dr. John B. Richardson to The Filson Historical Society, Read at The Filson Club, April 1, 1901, Courtesy The Filson Historical Society.
4. Letter–Joseph Desha to Captain A, Mitchell, October 4, 1840, in *Register of the Kentucky Historical Society*, Issue 51, October, 1953, pgs. 300-1.
5. Letter–Scott Harrison to Draper, June 30, 1873, Draper 7YY74.
6. H.S.Knapp, *History of the Maumee Valley*, (Toledo, OH., Blade Mammoth Printing and Publishing House, 1872), p. 203.
7. Samuel G. Drake, *Indian Biography–Lives of 200 Indian Chiefs and a History of Their Wars*, (Josiah Drake, 1832), p. 338.
8. Letter–Marcia Harlan to Draper, June 30, 1884, Draper 7YY122.
9. Letter–Nancy Wright to Draper, March 4, 1879, Draper 6YY18.
10. Thomas S. Woodward, *Woodward's Reminiscences of the Creek, or Muscogee Indians*, (Montgomery, AL., Barrett & Wimbish, Book and General Job Printers, 1859), pgs. 84-5.
11. Mabel Nisbet McLaughlin, *The Endicotts of Indiana*, in *Indiana Magazine of*

History, Vol. 29, Issue 1, pgs. 30-1.

12. Letter–William Gaines to Draper, April 26, 1882, Draper 7YY71.
13. Letter–William Gaines to Draper, December 4, 1881, Draper 5YY47.
14. Letter–William Gaines to Draper, November 25, 1881, Draper 5YY45.
15. Sullivant, *A Geneology*, p. 315.
16. *Kentucky Gazette*, January 6, 1817.
17. Sullivant, *A Geneology*, pgs. 316-7.
18. Alfred M. Lorrain, *The Helm, The Sword, and The Cross*, (Cincinnati, Poe & Hitchcock, 1862), p. 151.

Chapter 19 – The Cases for Whitley, King and Others

1. Captain Tarrance Kirby's Letter to President Abraham Lincoln, September 5, 1864, in Maurice Helm Kirby, Senior, *The Kirby Family*, 1954, p. 89. Mentioned by Kirby to highlight his patriotism in his solicitation of President Lincoln to release his grandsons from a Union prison during the Civil War.
2. Draper 9CC61.
3. Speech of Esther Whitley Burch, January, 1943. Courtesy Kentucky Historical Society.
4. *Louisville Daily Journal*, October 25, 1859.
5. Letter–S.B. Nisbet to Editor, *Louisville Daily Journal*, November 22, 1859.
6. Letter–Ambrose Dudley to C.S.Todd, *Scioto Gazette*, September 24, 1840.
7. Letter of Ambrose Dudley, February 24, 1841, in Benjamin Drake, *Life of Tecumseh*, (Cincinnati, E. Morgan and Co., 1841) pgs. 215-6.
8. Tarrance Kirby, *The Life and Times and Wonderful Achievements of the Adventurous and Renowned Capt. Kirby*, (Cincinnati, Published for the Author, 1865), p. 16.
9. John C. Fredricksen, *Kentucky at the Thames, 1813: A Rediscovered Narrative by William Greathouse*, in *The Register of the Kentucky Historical Society*, Spring 1985, Vol. 83, No. 2, pgs. 102-4.
10. Benjamin Drake, *Life of Tecumseh and His Brother the Prophet with a Historical Sketch of the Shawanoe Indians*, (Cincinnati, E. Morgan and Co., 1850), p. 215.
11. War of 1812–Declaration of Soldier for Pension, by William R. Watts Sr., April 14, 1882, Courtesy William Whitley State Historic Site.
12. Draper 2SS236.
13. Entry–December 15, 1856 in *Passages from the English Notebooks of Nathaniel Hawthorne*, Vol. II.
14. Letter–Sallie Ann Higgins to H.C.Whitley, Date Unknown, in *A History of Kentucky*, (Author Unknown), p. 211. Courtesy William Whitley State Historic Site.
15. Speech of Esther Whitley-Burch, January, 1943. Courtesy Kentucky Historical Society.
16. Ibid.
17. Letter–William T. Sinclair to Draper, Draper 6YY116.

18. Letter–Captain James Davidson to Editor, *Louisville Daily Journal*, November 3, 1859.
19. Drake, *Life of Tecumseh*, pgs. 213-4.
20. Alfred Brunson, *Death of Tecumseh*, in *Wisconsin Historical Collections*, IV, 1857-1858, p. 373.
21. Early Recollections of John P. Hedges, in *The Indiana Quarterly Magazine of History*, (Indianapolis, The Indiana Historical Society, 1912-13), Vols. VIII-IX, pgs. 172-3.
22. *Who Killed Tecumseh?*, in *The Historical Magazine and Notes and Queries Concerning the Antiquities, History and Biography of America*, October, 1866, Vol. X, No. 10, p. 318.
23. Draper 18S228.
24. Draper 18S141.
25. Robert B. McAfee, *History of the Late War in the Western Country*, originally published 1816, republished C.S.Van Tassel, (Bowling Green, OH., Historical Publications Co., 1919), p. 424.
26. Beverly Stercula, *Biographical Sketch of Gen. David Thompson*, in *The Thompson Family Magazine*, Vol. 13, p. 1.
27. *Louisville Daily Journal*, December, 1859.
28. Lowell Harrison, *Nat Crain and the Battle of the Thames*, in *The Filson Club Historical Quarterly*, July, 1990, Vol. 64, No. 3, pgs. 381-2.
29. Draper 6YY18.
30. Thomas McGee, *A History of the Irish Settlers in North America*, (Boston, Patrick Donahoe, 1855), p. 103.
31. *The Bourbon News*, Paris, Kentucky, September 28, 1906.
32. *Louisville Daily Journal*, November 23, 1859.

Chapter 20 – And the Slayer Is...

1. Comment from audience at Reception & Speech of Col. R.M.Johnson in Springfield, IL, May 19, 1843, in *Journal of the Illinois State Historical Society*, (Springfield, IL., Illinois State Historical Society, July, 1920), Vol. 13. No. 2, p. 205.

Epilogue

1. Words on historical plaque posted near the Thames battlefield by the Historic Sites and Monuments Board of Canada.

Index

9 780615 415222